P9-DDN-018

"*The Gettysburg Gospel* is a magisterial work, a brilliant and moving story that will fascinate the general reader while setting a gold standard for scholarship that will make the book an instant classic."

—Doris Kearns Goodwin, author of *Team of Rivals: The Political Genius of Abraham Lincoln*

"An elegant and absorbing book . . . the first to place Lincoln's familiar words in the fully realized context of the town of Gettysburg and of the battlefield itself. This is, I think, a definitive book."

—David Herbert Donald, author of *Lincoln*

"Even readers who think they know all about the town, the battle, and Lincoln's great speech will feel a surge of discovery from this revelatory, ingenious study. After Boritt, the Gettysburg Address can never be read, heard, or interpreted the same way again."

—Harold Holzer, author of *Lincoln at Cooper Union*

"As a nation and as individuals we return again and again to Abraham Lincoln and his stunning Address—for a sense of unity, conscience and meaning. No one has parsed those magnificent sentences or that remarkable man as well as Gabor Boritt."

—Ken Burns, creator of the PBS epic *The Civil War*

"The key ingredient most often missing from historical texts is the sense of *story*, that which grabs us, holds us in place, carries us back to the past and allows us to enjoy being there. What is also missing from most historical texts is that special ingredient, which might, dare I say, *entertain* us. This book is an unexpected surprise, meaningful, entertaining, and full of fresh and untrampled imagery. Gabor Boritt has given us something that many historians simply fail to do—he has given us a terrific read."

—Jeff Shaara, author of *Gods and Generals*

"*The Gettysburg Gospel* is remarkable for its richly detailed contextualization of this famous old speech. Professor Boritt gives the Address a refreshingly original political emphasis."

—Mark E. Neely, Jr., McCabe-Greer Professor of History of the Civil War Era, Pennsylvania State University

"Gabor Boritt has mined a remarkable wealth of sources to reconstruct this arresting and previously untold story of the genesis and context of Lincoln's address at Gettysburg, its mixed reception at the time, and how it became a sanctified and emblematic text. Combining prodigious industry, vivid writing, and authoritative analysis, *The Gettysburg Gospel* makes a distinguished contribution to Lincoln studies."

—Richard Carwardine, author of *Lincoln: A Life of Purpose and Power* and Rhodes Professor of American History, Oxford University

"Take a well-known story, add rigorous scholarship by an historian with the soul of a poet, and a wonderful new understanding emerges. That is what Boritt has done in *The Gettysburg Gospel*."

—Tom Schwartz, Illinois State Historian

"Abraham Lincoln delivered his Gettysburg Address at a moment of enormous social, political, and military flux. *The Gettysburg Gospel* masterfully places readers within that turbulent context, affording them a wonderful opportunity to engage Lincoln, his words, and his audience on their own ground and in their own time."

—Gary W. Gallagher, author of *The Confederate War* and
Nau Professor of History, University of Virginia

"This innovative, unique, and moving account of the Gettysburg Address and its reputation over the past 143 years has many layers of meaning. We learn how it was received in Gettysburg in 1863 and how it has become not just America's but the world's foremost statement of freedom and democracy and the sacrifices required to achieve and defend them."

—James M. McPherson, author of *Battle Cry of Freedom: The Civil War Era*

"[Gabor Boritt] has the background and the authority to make *The Gettysburg Gospel* as interesting to Civil War experts as it will be to neophytes. . . . Accessible and interesting in exploring Lincoln's intent."

—Janet Maslin, *The New York Times*

"Engrossing. . . . A revealing history of that most famous piece of American oratory, the Gettysburg Address. . . . This elegant account will delight readers who enjoyed Garry Wills's *Lincoln at Gettysburg*."

—*Publishers Weekly* (starred review)

"Boritt's account has a freshness appealing in such an exhaustively examined subject."

—*Booklist*

"A fresh perspective on one of America's most famous speeches."

—*Library Journal*

"By placing Lincon's powerful words in their specific wartime context, and undermining many of the myths surrounding America's greatest speech, Boritt has allowed readers to gain fresh perspective on those 272 immortal words."

—Chuck Leddy, *The Philadelphia Inquirer*

"Enjoyable, closely argued."

—Justin Ewer, *The Washington Post Book World*

"Why has the Gettysburg Address had such reverberating effects in America and around the world? Readers can discover answers to these and other questions in the 204 pages of Boritt's text, and if not there, in the book's lengthy appendices, notes and bibliographical essay. In discovering them, they will see that Lincoln's Gettysburg Address is a living masterpiece and that Gabor Boritt does justice to Lincoln and his address."

—Myron A. Marty, *St. Louis Post-Dispatch*

"Definitive. . . . [Gabor Boritt] conducts an exegesis of the speech, but does not restrict himself to that subject. The book, in fact, doubles as a portrait of post-battle Gettysburg. . . . and [Boritt's] love for the place shines through."

—Greg Pierce, *The Washington Times*

Alexander Gardner took this albumen photo in his Washington studio eleven days before Lincoln's trip to Gettysburg. The above rendition, newly produced from the Gardner original, tries to bring out the smallest hidden elements from the photograph, thus providing the clearest image created in Lincoln's day or since. This is the first publication of this version of the "Gettysburg Lincoln." (Abraham Lincoln Book Shop, Inc., Chicago, IL.)

GABOR BORITT

THE GETTYSBURG GOSPEL

THE LINCOLN SPEECH THAT NOBODY KNOWS

SIMON & SCHUSTER PAPERBACKS

NEW YORK   LONDON   TORONTO   SYDNEY

SIMON & SCHUSTER PAPERBACKS
1230 Avenue of the Americas
New York, NY 10020

First Simon & Schuster trade paperback edition February 2008

SIMON & SCHUSTER PAPERBACKS and colophon are registered trademarks of
Simon & Schuster, Inc.

For information about special discounts for bulk purchases,
please contact Simon & Schuster Special Sales at
1-800-456-6798 or business@simonandschuster.com.

Designed by Dana Sloan

Manufactured in the United States of America

10   9   8   7   6   5   4   3   2

The Library of Congress has cataloged the hardcover edition as follows:
Boritt, G. S., 1940–
The Gettysburg gospel : the Lincoln speech that nobody knows / Gabor Boritt.
p.   cm.
1. Lincoln, Abraham, 1809–1865. Gettysburg address.   2. Lincoln, Abraham, 1809–1865.
3. Gettysburg (Pa.)—History—19th century.   I. Title.

E475.55.B68   2006
973.7'349—dc22   2006050578

ISBN-13: 978-0-7432-8820-0
ISBN-10:   0-7432-8820-3
ISBN-13: 978-0-7432-8821-7 (pbk)
ISBN-10:   0-7432-8821-1 (pbk)

CONTENTS

~ THE ~
GETTYSBURG
GOSPEL

PREFACE

The meaning of the Gettysburg Address has changed generation after generation. It has become one of the nation's most revered texts, even as historians and public figures have used it and puzzled over its meaning. Connotations given to it have twisted and turned. That Lincoln could not have meant all the things attributed to him over the years is clear. Nor could the various versions of how he created his great speech all be true.

Today, the image of the Gettysburg Address still swings between two extremes. At one end is a persistent tradition that goes back to 1863. It tells of a speech written on the train to Pennsylvania on a piece of wrapping paper retrieved from the floor. Then, at the National Cemetery, people received the speech in silence. It had failed utterly, and the president knew it.

Ward Hill Lamon, Lincoln's friend and biographer, and Marshal of the District of Columbia, gave the strongest voice to this tradition: a tale of genius and an uncomprehending public. Many believed what Lamon said. After all, he was at Gettysburg and served as the marshal of the dedication ceremonies. He had introduced the president before he spoke. If anyone knew, he did. The eldest son of the president, who had little use for Lamon, certainly credited him at one time: "My father's Gettysburg Address,"

1

Robert Lincoln wrote in 1885, "was jotted down in pencil, in part at least, on his way to the place."

The Alabama-born writer Mary Shipman Andrews gave the story its great currency. One day, her son Paul's history teacher, one Walter Burlingame, reminisced in class about his own youth. He told about hearing Edward Everett tell his father, diplomat Anson Burlingame, who also knew Lincoln, that the president "wrote his address on a piece of brown paper on the train going up to Gettysburg." Everett, too, had to have known. He gave the main oration at Gettysburg.

Young Paul Andrews went home and told his mother, who then wrote a captivating little book: *The Perfect Tribute*. An interesting provenance, this. Edward Everett tells Anson Burlingame something that is overheard by Walter Burlingame, who tells Paul Andrews, who tells Mary Shipman Andrews, who tells the world. Americans learned this history by heart. For long *The Perfect Tribute* reigned as the most popular book on the subject, indeed perhaps on any Lincoln subject. Though Andrews's name is now mostly forgotten, the ideas she popularized still sway no small part of the general public. She admitted, in private, to taking one liberty in telling the tale: she turned the reputed silence of the Gettysburg crowd into vast reverence, "the perfect tribute." The little book continues to go through endless editions; Project Gutenberg makes it freely available on the Web; and it has been filmed at least twice, in 1937 and 1991. That, then, is one end of the Gettysburg Address spectrum.

At the other end looms the learned analysis of an extraordinary man of letters, Garry Wills, *Lincoln at Gettysburg: The Words That Remade America*. If Andrews's speech was written in a few minutes on the train and received with silence at Gettysburg, Wills's was prepared with care and "stealthily . . . remade America." If the broad public, the millions who make the pilgrimage to Gettysburg year after year, still hold with Andrews, a good part of the reading public has moved to Wills and made his book a best seller, also the winner of the Pulitzer Prize. Admiring scholars have taken his ideas further.

It is not surprising that the fiction writer, the artist, Andrews, for whom a moment of inspiration is all-important, sees Lincoln creating his speech in a flash of insight; and the scholarly writer, Wills, sees Lincoln laboring long and with care. It takes a heroic effort for the students of Lincoln to separate themselves from their subjects. Most of us fail to a smaller or larger degree.

Between the two ends of the spectrum, the Gettysburg Address suffers no neglect from writers of history. Yet perhaps once they collected every scrap of the often confusing and contradictory information—and surely there will be more—it has been all too easy to get lost in the tangle. David C. Mearns, onetime chief of the Manuscript Division at the Library of Congress, a careful student of Lincoln, considered the many dubious recollections about the speech in an essay entitled "Unknown at this Address." He then recommended that historians "with cleared minds and jaundiced eyes, begin again from scratch." This work attempts exactly that. In the process it grew clear, to cite Mearns again, that some things were just "transparently truthful." Some were not. And so a new story emerged.

This book tries to clear away the range of meanings later generations laid upon the Gettysburg Address. Kent Gramm, author of wonderful prose poetry about the president, wrote that "if we Americans can't find Lincoln, we are lost." Gramm described the address as "a transaction between the dead and the living, between the past and the future, from which the speaker has disappeared." These words fit the study of the address itself. The chief purpose of the present work is to let twenty-first-century readers find the speaker, and his audience, as they were in 1863.

The story begins with a picture of Gettysburg after the battle, the site of the greatest man-made disaster in American history. This is where the president came to explain why a bloody war had to go on. These chapters give voice to the dissonance, confusion, and disruption of all that was normal for this town. A glance back at peacetime Gettysburg, in its moments of happiness, is included for contrast.

But the book attempts a little more. "Gospel" suggests spiritual rebirth. When Lincoln's words are best understood, they bring that potential to Americans, indeed to people everywhere. The novelist John Steinbeck recounted his visit with his son to the Lincoln Memorial, and the awed young man blurting out, "Oh! Lord! We had better be great." The final chapter considers how Lincoln's speech rose to be American Gospel, the Good News, for it was not that at birth. That, too, is quite a story.

Gettysburg, July 4, 1863. Dreadful silence. It rains. People crawl out of their cellars blinking in the gloomy light, trying to find their neighbors, food, news—life. Strange, awful odors overpower the air and seem to be growing, trying to imprison all in unbearable stench. Dead bodies are scattered over the streets, dead horses and mules. When the oppressive hush breaks, the clatter comes not from rifles or cannon fired to salute Independence Day, but in dead earnest by enemy armies still facing each other at the edge of the town. No toasts are offered today, no fireworks, no parades, no services in churches that are filling up with grievously wounded men. Gettysburg, July 4, 1863.

But Sally Myers, twenty-three, full of life, forges ahead. The sun comes out and in a free moment she'll write in her diary: "I never spent a happier Fourth. It seemed so bright. . . ." The Union had retaken the town. A soldier will later add: "The Glorious Fourth and we are still a Nation, and shall most likely continue to be for centuries to come." Professor Michael Jacobs comes out of his house on Middle Street, with his son Henry. So do others. A band marches down Baltimore Street, fife and drum breaking the noxious grip of stillness. People move toward the square.

Gabor Boritt
Farm by the Ford
Gettysburg

C H A P T E R   O N E

AFTER BATTLE

Gettysburg, July 4, 1863. Stench fills the air. Excrement from perhaps 180,000 men and more than 70,000 horses has been left behind in the area. There are thousands of flies, millions. Dead men barely covered in shallow graves. Seven thousand dead men? More likely close to 10,000. How many dead horses and mules? Three thousand, five? None buried. A nurse writes of carcasses "steaming in the sun." The smell of putrid animal flesh mingles with the odor of human decay. It extends into the spirit of the people. War had come to them. Then it had gone and left the horror behind.

Gettysburg is—was—a modern, progressive, small town, though with nearly 2,400 souls as the war started the census counted it as a city. The houses were brick, mostly, spacious fenced yards behind each, with a vegetable garden, perhaps chickens, a cow, a shed, and the privy. The town took pride in its College, the Lutheran Seminary, and all the benefits educational institutions bestowed. It had three weekly newspapers: one Democratic, the *Compiler*, and two Republican, the *Adams Sentinel* and the *Star & Banner*. They were all highly partisan, but then so were most newspapers throughout the United States. During elections the area tended to divide evenly between the two parties.

Politics provided one of the most important and at times all-absorbing cultural activities; religion provided the other. Gettysburg had eight churches with nine congregations, with Lutherans and Presbyterians predominating. It had a new rural burial ground on Cemetery Hill. The schools were public: Pennsylvania required public education and, as one would expect in a college town, Gettysburg had good schools, including two private ones for girls, and many private instructors. The town had gaslight and some paved sidewalks, but its streets were alternately dusty or muddy. The seat of government for Adams County, it had a beautiful new courthouse, built in 1859, close to the central square, "the Diamond," as the locals called it. It had new warehouses around a railroad station, also newly built in 1859, right after that modern mode of transportation had arrived in town.

Gettysburg was on the move, with lawyers, doctors, merchants, bankers, blacksmiths, and various craftsmen serving the surrounding countryside of small farmers. It had hotels, taverns, and the county prison. Carriage manufacturing thrived, with more than ten shops. There were tanneries: twenty-two people made shoes and boots. Indeed, half of the population worked as artisans, a quarter as professionals, a quarter as unskilled laborers. The ethnic stock was Scotch-Irish and German, but everyone else also seemed to be represented, including new immigrants, who made up nearly 7 percent of the town's population. Black people, mostly the poorest part of the community, numbered 190, about 8 percent of the population. There were professionals and craftsmen among them, and even for the poorest hope often lived—one third of the black people had escaped from slave states, and freedom meant everything.

Basil Biggs, for example, moved his family from Maryland to Gettysburg in 1858 so that his seven children would have educational opportunities, and rented a farm from one of the most prominent members of the community. Biggs farmed and worked as a veterinarian—he must have been very good with animals—and by the end of the war would own his own farm, right on Cemetery Ridge, including the copse of trees toward which Robert E. Lee had sent his doomed soldiers on July 3. Gettysburg was a modern town, a place of hope for many.

But soon the battle came and, for a time, making coffins would become an important occupation. So would ferrying bereaved visitors to one of the many makeshift hospitals or the battlefield and digging up the dead. Gettysburg had been transformed into a blighted land and needed to recover in body and soul.

*   *   *

July 4, 1863. The rebels are still on the outskirts, but the town is free. Blue-clad troops march in, their bands playing in an attempt to divert soldier and civilian from the horror. It is Independence Day, after all, and the armies are leaving. Life can begin again. But the wounded and dead remain—on the fields, in houses, in barns, and in hospital tents. Twenty-one thousand wounded, perhaps 10,000 dead. Disinfecting chloride of lime spread over the muddy streets turns them white for a while, and adds to the odors. Snow in July. The townspeople try "to extinguish, as far as possible, the sense of smelling," one woman writes. They try to control disease. They pour kerosene on the bodies of horses and mules, light the fire over them, let them go up in smoke. The smell of burning flesh dissipates after a while; the smell of rotting carcasses will stay around for months. If a carcass is too close to a building or a good tree, it cannot be burned. It must rot.

Many days are stiflingly hot. Even the nights. To keep the stench out, most people don't open their windows. It is hard to keep the stench from their spirits. Rumors fly: the civilians are dying, too. Sarah Broadhead, a wife, mother, and now nurse to the wounded of the battle, writes in a diary about her fears that "we shall be visited with pestilence." Yet among the town's population there is no increase of disease and death; a resilient people.

When strangers approach the town, "the odors of the battle-field" attack them long before they get there. But the visitors come—many to help, some to gawk, some to plunder, most looking for their lost loved ones from the armies. Masses of strangers. Where to put them all? On July 9, the *New York Times* reports "no accomodations or food here for visitors and last night many were compelled to roost in the barns, or upon the steps of dwellings." A man feels lucky when he gets a chair to sit through the night in front of a hotel; better than wandering till daybreak. On July 13, the Broadheads' house, in addition to a family of three, has three wounded soldiers and twenty visitors. The strangers "are filling every bed and covering the floors."

Some complain about the visitors. Too much "idle curiosity." Professor Michael Jacobs of the College, however, sees it differently. He wishes "the whole land had come." Seeing the bloodstained fields, the sacrifice of the mangled soldiers, and the newly dug graves would rekindle people's "patriotism and their gratitude to God for a most signal deliverance" at Gettysburg.

Many do come and stay in uncomfortable quarters, but their problems shrink in face of the immeasurable suffering of the wounded and the dying. Private George R. Frysinger arrives with an emergency militia unit sent to help maintain order. "We had a severe trial for young soldiers," he writes home to his father. His unit had limped into town on "blistered feet" and got placed in a church. The sacred structure reminded him of his home, which now felt "like a distant Jerusalem to the ancient Jews."

> So here we are quartered in a building, which it was little thought at the day of its dedication would ever be used to serve the purposes of war . . . I see the pews occupied by forms moving amid the din and clanging of arms, which the soldiers are brightening up for duty; and instead of singers on the gallery, boys writing letters to their friends far away. . . . Everything remains in the church seemingly just as the congregation left their last Sabbath's service. Hymn books are scattered through the pews, spittoons and footstools remain in the aisles, and the altar and pulpit carpeted with Brussels. Even the clock hangs suspended ticking the hours as they fly, and which, instead of meeting the minister's eye, now catches the eye of the sergeant of the guard as he says, "Fall in, second relief."

"Perhaps we will not deface it much," this church, Frysinger writes to his father, adding, "Gettysburg can not be called a town, but a large collection of hospitals."

Eliza Farnham, a volunteer nurse from Philadelphia, tells much the same story. "The whole town . . . is one vast hospital. . . . The road, for long distances, is in many places strewn with dead horses . . . the earth in the roads and fields is ploughed to a mire by the army wheels and horses . . . avenues of white tents. . . . But, good God! What those quiet-looking tents contained! What spectacles awaited us on the rolling hills around us! It is absolutely inconceivable. . . . Dead and dying, and wounded . . . torn to pieces in every way." Moans, shrieks, weeping, and prayer fill the houses, the barns, the tents, the fields and woods, the whole area. The land itself seems to wail. Nothing but suffering. Sights, sounds, smells unbearable. Horror. The piles of limbs dripping blood, the dying, the dead. Hell on earth.

The muddy streets with the German Reformed Church (see cupola) that served as a hospital. Photograph by C. J. Tyson, 1867. (Gettysburg National Military Park)

Newspapers that seem loath to report on the horrors admit that the "area is one vast hospital." Red and some green flags sprout everywhere identifying places housing the wounded. Nothing like this has ever happened in the United States. Looking back in September 1863, the U.S. Christian Commission would report "a scene of horror and desolation which humanity, in all the centuries of its history has seldom witnessed." The more measured tones of an army medical officer's report would still be blunt: "The period of ten days following the battle of Gettysburg was the occasion of the greatest amount of human suffering known in this nation since its birth. . . ." And the government was utterly unprepared for the greatest man-made disaster of American history.

Jonathan Letterman, the medical director of the Army of the Potomac, had developed a remarkable system of caring for the wounded, but it was crippled by the commanding generals, first by "Fighting Joe" Hooker who, chasing after Lee as he invaded Pennsylvania, did not wish to be encumbered by substantial amounts of medical supplies. This left "no system at all," as Letterman would write in an official report that tried to minimize the disaster. Then Hooker's successor, George Gordon Meade, timidly kept much of what remained out of the possible reach of the Confederates—and so also of his own army. This Letterman would liken to engaging in battle "without ammunition." Even as the fighting went on, the war-hardened nurse Ellen Orbison Harris of the Philadelphia Ladies' Aid Society understood what was happening: "An evident reluctance to forward hospital stores to Hanover or Gettysburg, where a conflict supposed to rage, betokens a want of confidence in the position or strength of our forces. Can it be that our soil is to be crimsoned with the blood of our bravest and best?" Crimsoned it was, and Dr. Letterman, who obeyed orders, would later write with anger: "Lost supplies can be replenished, but lives lost are gone forever." The U.S. Sanitary Commission (USSC), organized to provide civilian support for the military, sent two supply wagons to Gettysburg on July 4. One was captured, its personnel sent to prison in Richmond.

It would have been impossible to cope fully even without the bumbling of generals. The able Letterman himself went along when, with victory in hand, Meade followed the retreating Lee and, expecting another major battle, took with him most of the medical corps. "It was absolutely necessary that I should carry away the greater portion of my Surgeons and medical supplies," Meade would explain. Close to 21,000 wounded Union and Confederate soldiers remained behind in Gettysburg. "What! Take away surgeons here where a hundred are wanted?" exclaimed Andrew Cross, speaking for the U.S. Christian Commission, which focused on both the spiritual and physical needs of the men. "But so it is." Even the angry commissioners vastly understated the problem, reporting that "there was no more than one for ten" of the surgeons needed. In fact, out of the 106 medical officers left behind, perhaps 35 could actually operate. A distraught Ohio army doctor and ordained minister, Harry McAbee, who stayed back and had to care with three assistants for "a thousand badly wounded men," would resign with bitter words when the crisis passed: "[I]t is my deliberate opinion, that the failure to furnish sufficient number of medical officers . . . cost the country more good men than did the charge of any rebel brigade. . . ." The official medical report in the fall, however, would state that of the more than 14,000 Union wounded, "not one . . . was left on the field . . . on the morning of July 4." Yet Dr. Letterman was sufficiently aware of the disaster to order the improvement of the system of medical supplies and ambulances. As for Dr. McAbee, not long after he sent in his protest, an accident would take his life.

The Confederate army might have done even worse. Not only did it have to prepare for another possible battle and also keep medical personnel and ambulances in reserve for those who became ill on the retreat, it did not have sufficient transportation back to Virginia for movable casualties. Lee's medical director, Lafayette Guild, ordered left behind "abundant supplies for the wounded and the sick," but that could not be done. In the disaster that followed, the Confederate government and army would take even less note than did the Union side. Not much would be said about its helpless soldiers drowning by a flooding creek or left lying unattended for days.

One of the Gettysburg papers claimed that the rebels "left behind them six drunken, inefficient and worthless surgeons and 11,000 wounded." Another local paper bemoaned this "Inhumanity and Poltroonery." But the Sanitary Commission's report described the Confederate doctors as "intelligent and attentive" even as it accepted the army's explanation that impending battle required the removal of most of its surgeons. In short, no "neglect" was admitted, though Meade took with him more than four out of five of his doctors. Christian Commission delegates digging graves for the dead reported more boldly, but with masterful understatement, that the Army of the Potomac "did not leave a sufficient force to bury the dead, much less to afford necessary attendance upon the mangled and bleeding forms." Union and Confederate, "they lie *side by side*, many without even a straw under them, some with a rail or bottle under their head, half clothed, destitute and suffering; many carried fresh from the amputating table."

Washington was oblivious. President Lincoln had no idea about what was going on in Gettysburg. His wife Mary had suffered a terrible injury in an accident on the second day of the battle and seemed in danger: she had jumped out of a runaway carriage and received a head wound that grew infected. The private distress of the president was compounded by the inability of Meade to finish off Lee's army. While the rest of the country celebrated a victory at Gettysburg, Lincoln's eyes focused on the retreating Confederate army, hoping to see it annihilated. He thought that defeat of the fleeing Confederates might end the war.

The Secretary of War, Edwin Stanton, appeared equally oblivious. He, too, looked to the upcoming days of hoped-for battle. Subordinates who were supposed to handle medical problems didn't understand, either. When Nurse Harris of the Ladies' Aid Society went to the War Department on July 3 "to beg permission" to bring supplies to Gettysburg, "besought the privilege with tears," her pleas were flatly rebuffed. She went anyway. "The Lord will carry me there safely," and only regretted that she obeyed orders about provisions.

Nor did the Surgeon General, William A. Hammond, recognize the magnitude of the emergency in Gettysburg. At first he even refused the offer of civilian help. "How many volunteer surgeons may I send," Pennsylvania governor Andrew Curtin asked, and was told, none. "The Medical Director of the Army of the Potomac has plenty of surgical Aid." General Robert C. Schenck, in command in Baltimore, in turn complained that "Barns, houses and yards are full" of the wounded. "Pennsylvania is not taking care of them." Eliza Farnham's call for help was published in Philadelphia, but the press remained mostly silent about the horrors. "The army has left Gettysburg," Nurse Farnham wrote, "and we are not here an hour early for the suffering. Please send all that you can. . . ." On July 9, Nurse Harris wrote home about wounded men drowning in flash floods and thousands who were "still naked and starving. God pity us! God pity us!"

As disaster engulfed Gettysburg, the *Philadelphia Inquirer* boasted that "Our wounded left in Gettysburg are well cared for." But visitors saw, as a woman from Maine wrote, that "the newspaper accounts were very different from reality." Men didn't talk much about what was happening all around them. Men need to be strong, need to be men. If you are a wounded, dying soldier, in great pain, you try to suppress your cries. Die like a man. If you are a caretaker, you don't often write letters telling about the horror. If you write official reports, you stress the positive.

When civilian doctors finally started helping, the medical inspector of the army would find in late July that the hard work of the "citizen surgeons"—just like that of the army doctors—had been performed with "fidelity and ability." By October, however, with the emergency passed, Dr. Letterman's final report would blame many, except himself, and revert to the standard army line, citing the judgment of the head of the general hospital, which was organized by the end of July to take care of all the patients, that the civilian doctors were "of little use."

Reverend Henry Bellows, head of the Sanitary Commission, had to work with the government, and so he was charitable, writing to Hammond that the task at hand could not be done "by anything short of arch-angels in prescience and resources." There was some truth to that. To his own people, asking for help, he admitted that "no energy you can use . . . can equal the demand here." Telling the world how badly the system failed was not likely to encourage donations now or in the future.

Mrs. Farnham would stand no more than four days at the battlefield. Others left quickly, too. Most stayed. Those first days were the worst. A friend would later note how "the constant feeling of inability to give adequate relief" devastated Farnham. She wrote of "a man and his son lying besides him, each having lost a leg; other men with both legs gone. But the most horrible thing was to see these limbs lying, piled up like offal. . . ." She left Gettysburg, her friend would testify, "and never recovered. . . . For a long time after she could not sleep." She died six months later. Her friend objected indignantly to the death being ascribed to "consumption"; the cause: "but a simple loss of vitality."

Doctors worked day and night. "I never saw men work harder and complain less," an army medical inspector would report. Day and night. Decide who should be looked at first. Leave hopeless cases alone. Lift a body onto the makeshift operating table. Try to stop the soldier's thrashing and howling; administer anesthesia. Be careful about the right dosage. A nurse would write to her mother: "I saw a man die in ½ a minute from the effects of chloroform . . . it seemed almost like deliberate murder." Amputation followed amputation. There was no end to the wounded. Piles of limbs were stacked on the ground under one tree. Surgeons had to be held up while continuing to operate; they fainted from exhaustion. One doctor recorded in his diary getting up at 2 a.m. and working "incessantly" until midnight. "Anxiety is constant, the strain upon both physical and mental faculties, unceasing." Some went almost berserk. One witness spoke of the doctors' "roughness and brutality" that made the blood chill. "Language as profane as it was brutal."

After the rebels left, the stunned people of Gettysburg shared a sense of terrible isolation; there were no newspapers, the railroad and telegraph were cut, barricades still stood in the streets, the army blocked all roads in and out of town, and so many of the menfolk were gone. But the disaster around them brought out the best in most people. They got back on their feet and many devoted themselves to the suffering.

At first, the people of the town and the surrounding countryside, especially the women, bore a significant part of helping the wounded. Private homes were filled with the maimed. Churches, warehouses, barns, homes, the Seminary and College buildings, all came to house them. Robert G. Harper, the editor of the *Adams Sentinel*, quartered fifty in his large house on the Diamond, "nursed and attended almost exclusively by members of the family." Every bed was filled and suffering human beings covered every inch of the floors.

Harper's wife, Harriet Ann, got to work. She headed up the Ladies' Union Relief Society, which had toiled since 1861 to send the troops food, clothing, and medical supplies, whatever was needed—and sometimes what was not. Men helped, too, but as Fanny Buehler would remember: "Here was women's work, and they did it nobly." Having assigned such work to the women, the town would in turn provide grateful recognition. The Christian Commission report later went so far as to state that "the only hospitals at that time that were properly managed were those in which ladies were engaged. . . ."

The College building echoed with the groans of the wounded. These were Confederates only. After days of starving, some got a few dried apples. "Never did we see men enjoy a little thing more," came a report. Weeks earlier, President Henry Baugher had lost a number of his students to Governor Curtin's call for emergency troops. When the battle arrived, Baugher called off classes. The excitement was too much, and, in any case, as one of the students recalled long after, the Reverend Professor told them that they knew "nothing about the lesson anyhow." Old Dorm was hit several times during the battle, filled with wounded, and in place of a hundred students, six or seven times that number filled the rooms. The students' possessions were all piled into one room and guarded. But books became bloody pillows or served as a place for the dying to record their names and hometowns. During the battle, the professor's own home had held Union wounded, and hid an officer from repeated searches; it now held seventeen Confederate wounded. July was nearly over before they were removed. The school year would never be completed.

In the Baugher home, the professor's "estimable wife and kind hearted daughter" were singled out for praise, and all over Gettysburg the women worked hard to house and feed not only the wounded but also the caretakers who started coming into town to help. People thought that this was women's work, but what struggle it took to overcome the overwhelming feelings of horror. The initial exposure to the wounded shocked the most. Nurse Emily Souder spoke of her first day as "a day of horror, I might almost say, yet a day of blessing."

When Sally Myers was called to the Roman Catholic church-turned-hospital while the battle still raged, she wrote in her diary that she did not think she "could do such work, but I went." She found men lying on pews, the floor, everywhere, the church filled with the pitiful sounds of the suffering. She went up to the first soldier she saw:

> *What can I do for you?*
> *Nothing; I am going to die.*

Sally ran out of the church and cried. But then she went back in. The man, Sergeant Alexander Stewart, died four days later in her arms.

Sarah Broadhead also kept a diary and said the same: she had to do "what I never expected to do or thought I could." When she first saw the wounded at the Seminary, she "turned away and cried." In the dirt basement of the building that was supposed to teach love, Union soldiers lay in rain-soaked muck. No one seemed to pay attention to them. She went over to one soldier to ask about his wound, and he pointed to his leg. "Such a horrible sight I have never seen and I hope never to see again. His leg was all covered with worms." The days went on. "I am becoming more used to sights of misery." Some soldiers died. "It is sad; and even we, who have known him so short a time, will miss him."

Nurse Sophronia Bucklin watched a visiting wife "clasping to her bosom a little child of eighteen months," and sitting "for hours with bowed head" next to her gut-shot husband, "stupefied with morphine." A "humane" surgeon allowed the drug to ease, Bucklin wrote. The soldier looked up, a "wild glare of pain in his eyes. . . . 'Oh! Mary, are *you* here?' His groans were terrible to hear, and in mercy he was again given the opiate, and slept his life out. . . ."

The *Compiler* later reported on one wife looking for her husband's body, opening twenty graves in vain. "Her heart almost failed." Then, in the twenty-first grave, she found him. But in the hot, humid weather, people feared an epidemic. The newspaper wrote of potions that will "destroy the foulest smells." The Army of the Potomac's provost marshal, Brigadier General Marsena Patrick, whose job was to keep order, halted exhumations for August and September. Many presumably obeyed. But by then perhaps a thousand bodies had been removed.

Visiting Nurse Cornelia Hancock wrote her cousin that "there are no words in the English language to express the sufferings I witnessed. . . ." The country was "very beautiful, rolling," but contrasted to the "awful smell of putrefaction." In another letter, she told her sister: "I shall never feel horrified at any thing that may happen to me hereafter." At first, Hancock dealt with the horror one way: "I have lost my memory almost entirely." But, she added, "it is gradually returning."

Nurse Emily Souder eased her shock by writing letter after letter to family and friends: "The sights and sounds" were "beyond description"; the stench "ever-present."

> *The amputation-table is plainly in view . . . I never trust myself to look toward it . . . the groans the cries, the shrieks . . . I buried my head in the pillow to shut out the sounds which reached us, from a church quite near . . . the Union soldiers and the rebels lie side by side, friendly as brothers. . . . Monday, there was no bread . . . manna in the desert. . . . Almost every hour has its own experience to tell . . . from seven in the morning till seven in the evening . . . I am sorry to say that I gave out totally . . . a perpetual procession of coffins is constantly passing to and fro . . . it will be a place of pilgrimage for the nation.*

If this was "women's work," men helped, too; it was difficult not to with one's house filled with wounded and dying soldiers. Professor Jacobs would write early the following year about the men in Gettysburg who, like women, "would have fainted at the sight of blood, and would have started back at the groans of suffering," suddenly finding the strength needed to face the horror. Men, too, helped the helpless.

Writing letters to the soldiers' loved ones was one of the most horrendous tasks. Cornalia Hancock would break down doing this chore. Writing to wives, she explained to her cousin, "that I cannot do without crying which is not pleasant to either party." A surgeon said the same. He could "take a man's leg off," but when asked, " *'Can't you write to my wife and tell her how I died and tell her to kiss Mary,'* that I cannot do." Nurse Souder managed not to find time for the letters and wrote with regret that "many that were alive yesterday are gone to-day and several that we saw to-day, I fear we shall see no more forever."

In the midst of the horror, Robert Harper published a long letter from a Missouri minister and Gettysburg native, trying to give meaning to the bloodletting. The letter voiced thoughts growing all over the North. To those who called "for the direst punishment" on the enemy, "no . . . 'Father, forgive them, for they know not what they do.' " At the heart of the conflict: "*Slavery.*" "It is the mortal antagonist of Democratic Institutions. . . . The deadly war that is now waging, is, on the one hand, the price we are paying for past and present complicity with iniquity; on the other, it is the cost of a higher, purer, nobler national life and character, the realization of the grand idea enunciated in the Declaration of Independence." "God forbid" that the war should stop "short of this glorious end." Some months later, the people of Gettysburg would hear some of the same thoughts voiced, more beautifully, by the President of the United States; and then, in 1865, they would read them in his Second Inaugural Address.

Nurse Ellen Harris was one of the many nurses, clergymen, and eventually doctors who thronged to Gettysburg to help. With the government unable to cope, private individuals and organizations stepped in. The U.S. Sanitary Commission was first on the scene and played a central role in the rescue efforts. "Uncle Sam is very rich, but very slow," Nurse Hancock mused. "If it was not for the Sanitary, much suffering would ensue." The Sanitary Commission made so much of a difference that appalling Gettysburg summer.

During the later 1850s, Americans had heard the many tales of neglect in the Crimean War, and they wanted better for their own. As strong Mary Livermore, wife of a Chicago editor and an important leader of the USSC, would later say, women refused "to release their hold on the men of their households, even when the government had organized them into an army." At first regarded by some in the War Department as "well meaning but silly women," led by "weak enthusiasts," bumbling males, the Sanitary Commission came to play a large role in the war, helping the government to care for sick and wounded soldiers.

Established in the major cities and towns of the North by reformers— leading clergymen, businessmen, and civic leaders—the USSC aimed to improve society and brought men and women into close working relations. It organized thousands of relief groups and employed hundreds of paid agents. It combined charity with the desire to return the men to their units rapidly. It counseled control of individual attachments and each soldier's body. "The Sanitary" also served as an army watchdog for camps, hospitals, even kitchens, and demanded sensible waste disposal, clean drinking water, and proper drainage. It held fairs and raised millions of dollars, mostly for medical supplies but, when needed, for food as well. And these were badly needed in the July heat and stench of Gettysburg. Its workers, the "angels" of the battlefield, mostly middle- and upper-class women, created a nurturing world; and over it, Nurse Georgeanna Woolsey mused, "we women rather reigned." Below them were the many women from all walks of life, some black, who worked for pay doing the bulk of the chores—cleaning, cooking, laundry, and more. They would not write letters about their experiences in Gettysburg, would not write memoirs, or if they did, the future swallowed them.

The first wagons of the Sanitary Commission arrived on July 6. A day later, rail communication was restored by an ingenious former Gettysburg College professor, Herman Haupt—but with the temporary terminal a mile east of town. "Refrigerating cars"—cars which had been converted to moveable icehouses—brought "tons of ice, mutton, poultry, fish, vegetables, soft bread, eggs, butter," not only the necessities but luxuries, "delicate food." Provisions were badly needed. "Lee's army had taken everything," leaving the area "almost entirely destitute." One newspaper added: "This region is eat out." The USSC also sent clothing, furniture for the hospitals, and more. After the initial shortages, many of the wounded would receive better food than most of them ever had in their whole lives. As one medical director told the nurses: "clean avenues and clean tents would not cure a man. . . . There is nothing better, Feed them, I say feed them."

The men were in charge and at times the women chafed. They wanted the doctors out of the way. But relations between men and women worked, even as the women reached for ever larger roles.

Eventually, the army sent supplies, and coffins, too, but the private groups continued to play a major role. The Sanitary's coworker—and rival—the Christian Commission, pooled the efforts of the churches, and contributed food and other necessities. The Sanitary Commission's Reverend Bellows could not but commend "the enterprise, zeal and blessedness of the labors of this sister institution." In private, however, Sanitary Treasurer George Templeton Strong characterized Christian Commission members as "an ugly looking set. . . . Some were unctuous to behold, the others vinegary; a bad lot." They seemed to him "one of the many forms in which the shallowness, fussiness, and humbug of our popular religionism are constantly embodying themselves."

The excellent connection the Christian Commission now developed with the press seemed to bother its rival. "From this source we have realized considerable advantage," the organization noted. In fact, the USCC quickly brought much-needed material help to Gettysburg, even if its chief concern remained the spiritual needs of the men, to fight "the dark side." It conducted prayer meetings, and provided Bibles, hymnals, prayer books, temperance and religious tracts, books, and newspapers—religious or otherwise. Of "The good that has been done. . . . Eternity will disclose the account," its report would conclude. The commission's delegates believed that they were finding mostly receptive wounded, including "quite a number of true Christian men who gave evidence of their having been born again."

Believers indeed could find their last moments in the light. One delegate wrote that "it is impossible to describe the beam of glory" on the face of a "saved" dying man, "unearthly and beautiful beyond all." The soldier pointed to heaven "as though he would have contrasted here and THERE."

The townspeople felt that both commissions, Sanitary and Christian, were "doing a noble work here." "Whoever aids them," Sarah Broadhead wrote in her diary, was doing "the noblest work on earth, and will be amply rewarded even here, not to mention the hereafter." Adding to the efforts of these large relief organizations, the Catholic Daughters of Charity came from a convent in nearby Emmitsburg. In their medieval dress, the sisters brought hope and created doubt about anti-Catholic prejudices. Some of them worked at the Lutheran Seminary that now served as a hospital. "Blessed, pure, angelic women . . . noble-hearted and self sacrificing," the *Compiler* described them. The Patriot Daughters of Lancaster came, too. So did a Baltimore Fire Department, the Adams Express Company of that city, some state delegations, and numerous other groups and individuals. But Gettysburg was the greatest man-made disaster in American history, and the reality was that the town, the country, the North, at first had a very difficult time coping.

The Confederate soldiers fared the worst. Lee had left behind his most badly wounded men, and when help came to the battlefield, it went first to the soldiers of the Union. When Reverend Bellows arrived, he walked into a barn, "unwillingly neglected," filled with rebel wounded. He found "every foot" occupied by "wretched" men. "Those above in the barn might almost be said to be in heaven, as compared to those below in the stable, who might with equal truth be said to be in hell. For upon heaps of dung, reeking with rain and tormented with vermin, the wounds still undressed . . . lay fair and noble youth. . . ."

In emergency, medical or otherwise, the Union soldiers got help first. When the floods came in early July, "the mean little creek got mad and rose *seven* feet"; in a mad scramble, men waded into the waters, pulling out "several hundred wounded and dying men, the rain falling in torrents all the time. How I *did* work," wrote one hospital steward to his wife; "how the poor fellows did suffer." Later, the official report of the surgeon in charge would register in carefully chosen words that none of "our men were swept down the creek and drowned." Rebs were not mentioned. Men can only do what they can do.

A disgusted Union colonel fumed when Confederate wounded were ignored. "I fear I should be very hard on such fellows," who refused to help. Still, before long, the rebs, too, were collected, and given more or less equal care, if not equal moral support. Whatever horrors might await them as prisoners, the caregivers instinctively gave the Southern wounded their best. One young rebel officer had "a face innocent enough for one of our New England boys. I could not think of him as a rebel," wrote Nurse Woolsey; "he was too near to heaven for that." "We are rebels you know, ma'am," said another. "Do you always treat rebels so?" They generally did, "except in a few instances," one of the first historians of the battle, Professor Michael Jacobs, would write. In some cases, "the imprudent zeal of sympathizers transcended the bounds of propriety and decency." One visitor overheard rebel officers half complaining that the gentle treatment will *"perfectly subjugate us."* It will "bind us together."

A visitor from New Hampshire who came to retrieve a body marveled that among the wounded there seemed to be "no feeling of hatred or spite." He quoted the words of his dead soldier friend, borrowed from the Reverend Henry Ward Beecher: one should "pray for the soul of a rebel at whom he was aiming his unerring rifle." The long-ago message of St. Augustine lived. Helping the wounded rebs? "Gospel rules command us."

But people complained about the terrible extra burden put on them by the Confederates, who had just plundered the region and had left thousands of casualties behind. The women caring for them had to let off some steam.

Nurse Hancock felt relieved that "I have one tent of Johnies in my ward but I am not obliged to give them anything but whiskey." Nurse Broadhead was happy she could write in her diary, "[t]his day has been spent in caring for *our* men." And Nurse Souder noted: "I felt I could hardly wait upon the rebels. . . . I have seen as many rebels as I care to see for the rest of my life." Sometimes the rebs were dubbed "white trash."

People were conflicted about helping the enemy. The town had seen nearly five thousand prisoners herded through on their way to prison. Official policy was to make no distinctions toward the wounded. But revulsion for traitors, hatred for robbers and killers called for one thing; charity for another. The Christian Commission felt the need to provide a whole litany of reasons why its original purpose of aiding the soldiers of the Union had to be changed and extended to the rebels, too. A member of the Sanitary Commission also had to explain why supplies collected at home would be given to Confederates. They got equal treatment when it came to food, but clothes only went to "our own men, except now and then, when a shivering rebel needed it." With the Patriot Daughters of Lancaster, on the other hand, clothing went "first to the Union soldiers and then to the enemy."

One could sense among the medical workers "the disgust and horror felt for *rebels*, giving place to the kindest feeling for *wounded men*." Rebs would report that in hospital tents, "Confederate and Yankee are often promiscuously thrown together." At the Sanitary Commission's supply house in the center of Gettysburg, doctors waited for their turn to get supplies, regardless which side they belonged to. After a general hospital was established west of town, a cemetery went in next to it, and a man from Massachusetts would be buried next to another from Virginia. Indeed, one of the most remarkable faces of Gettysburg is the charity it showed to the enemy. If many died, others were nursed back to health. But then every so often news like this came to the people of the town: "Sixty or seventy rebel officers and men were sent off yesterday. . . . Their future destination we know not." In fact, a steady stream of the wounded, train after train after train, took the Confederates to prison hospitals along the eastern seaboard. Nor would charity go so far as to provide places for the Confederate dead when the National Cemetery was created.

Clergymen ministered equally to both sides, but that, too, could be a mixed blessing. If you were Catholic or Jewish, or perchance a non-believer, all too often you still got a Protestant minister. One reb with the unforgettable name of Decimus et Ultimus Barziza—the last of ten children—would long remember "sanctimonious" New England preachers coming into his room at the College, and "after sighing, and wheezing, and sucking their breath . . . condescendingly give a poor rebel a tract and a cracker." But a Christian Commission delegate found among the rebels "four professing Christians to one such Federal," though not all agreed. A visiting pastor recounted telling a soldier, "I was a Minister and came to point him to the Lamb of God who taketh away the sins of the world," and the dying man refused to let go of him. The scene was common: a soldier, Union or Confederate, crying, "Oh, Jesus! Jesus! Help me." A minister kneeling and praying, joined by women singing a hymn: " 'Alas, and did my Saviour bleed.' And the chorus: 'Oh, Lord, remember me.' "

Then there was the rebel lieutenant who wrote in his diary about a Sanitary Commission minister: Morning, day, and night he comes and prays "alike for friends and enemies." One day he bursts in with the glorious if erroneous news of Lee's defeat and capture. Rebels remind him who the minister is talking to, whereupon the hapless man exclaims: "Excuse me, boys, excuse me! Really I thought you were OUR boys."

Union and Confederate soldiers lying side by side—"quite friendly," as Nurse Emily Souder noted, "friendly as brothers," suffering together, treated equally—this made for reconciliation. The future looked brighter. But being together could also be "A cross to many." Though the attempt was made to avoid "political discussion," serious talk did occur, with less than happy results. Nurse Harris claimed that rebel officers "all admit" that the war was about slavery. To her astonishment, a Confederate chaplain, "an intelligent Christian man, justified the war, saying 'The preservation of slavery, one of God's wisest and most beneficial plans for Christianizing the African race, demanded and deserves all the blood and treasure given to its defence.' " "Is it not wonderful?" she exclaimed.

"Secesh ladies" from Baltimore were allowed to come and take special care of the Confederate wounded. In a few cases they smuggled in civilian clothing and helped soldiers to escape. So restrictions were put in place but not enforced with great care. After one of these young nurses, Effie Goldsborough, went back home to Baltimore, her sister would recall, "We did not know her at first. . . . She returned to us the most dilapidated young girl that tongue or pen could describe." Another woman would write of "shrieks, cries and groans . . . the amputating tables . . . those ghastly bleeding limbs. . . . Never will those scenes of suffering pass away." And she added: "Would that we could forget them! In our working hours they are constantly before us, and they haunt us yet in our dreams."

Gettysburg's gruesome work went on. But if it sometimes seemed unbearable, the work could be both liberating and fulfilling. Weak women grew strong; strong women grew stronger. Cornelia Hancock wrote to her sister: "There is all in getting to do what you *want* to do and I am doing that." She told her mother: "it seems to me as if all my past life was a mythe. . . . I feel like a new person eat onions, potatoes, cucumbers anything that comes up and walk as straight as a soldier feel life and vigor which you well know I never felt at home." The women thought their service equaled that of the soldiers. At summer's end, their great adventure also ended. Sophronia Bucklin would muse: "All were gone—my occupation was gone; the strain of months was suddenly let go, and I found how much the strength of my hands depended on keeping them steadily employed."

In well-to-do homes, black women servants helped with the huge burdens. They cooked, washed, and provided care and company. Exhausted physically and emotionally, all soldiered on, white and black. When at last most of the wounded were gone, or dead, then the women would have time to recover. One woman would remember decades later: "For weeks I wanted to do nothing but sleep."

As the care of the wounded continued to improve, the town tried to resume its normal life. But the shadow of the battle was not easy to escape. Nurse Woolsey reported that children played war games. "The streets of Gettysburg were filled with the battle. People thought and talked of nothing else." Some settled political scores. The Democratic proprietors of the Globe Inn were dragged before Provost Marshal Marsena Patrick accused of aiding the enemy. The editor of the Democratic paper, the *Compiler*, Henry Stahle, was arrested and sent to Fort McHenry. He was eventually released. His paper, according to the Republican *Sentinel*, had "long been regarded by unconditional Unionists as being of very doubtful loyalty." Charges were dismissed. Stahle expressed great indignation at these political machinations, but some of his opponents thought he should have been "hanged on the spot." The national press continued to talk about "Copperheads" in the area—Democrats deemed disloyal and tarred with the name of a poisonous snake. Partisanship thrived. Josephine Forney, a Gettysburg native who married a Virginian and lived in that state, noted in her diary that those who were "not true union people" here "have a heavy burden to bear." But toward the wounded, defeated rebels, the local people held much less bitterness or rancor than one might expect.

Caring stories about the Confederate dead appeared even in the Republican press. One report in the *Sentinel* described two locks of hair found on a dead soldier from Louisiana, with his wife's "beautiful handwriting . . . '*Our darlings!*' Tender mementoes . . . home and children." The other Republican paper, the *Star*, reported that Lydia Smith, a "colored woman," paid for "one horseload" of food and clothing and went among the stricken soldiers distributing her gifts. She ministered equally to Union and rebel wounded. Editor John McIlhenny marveled at the generosity toward "Gen. Lee's army of kidnappers and horse thieves who came here and fell wounded in their bold attempt to kidnap and carry off these free people of color." Charity runs deep.

There could have been more rancor and hatred. The issue of the *Sentinel* that reported the touching story about the locks of hair carried another report that referred to the Confederate prisoners as "dishonored wretches." The Gettysburg area had suffered grievously. A large part of the black population of the region escaped before the battle, a majority never to return, and some who stayed had been taken into slavery, mostly women and children. The men who left mistakenly assumed that women and children would be safe. But Southern chivalry did not extend to black people. War is ugly, and the hunt for black people, with little distinction between free and escaped slave, was war at its ugliest.

Sally Myers, seeing her town emptied of black folks, wrote in her diary: "I pity the poor creatures. . . . I am glad I am neither a man nor a darkie, though girls are not so much better off." She would later become a teacher of black children and be ostracized by some. One Virginia colonel, William S. Christian, wrote back to his wife: "We took a lot of negroes yesterday. I was offered my choice, but as I could not get them back home I would not take them. In fact humanity revolted at taking the poor devils away from their homes. They were so scared that I turned them all loose." Others were not turned loose, though some distance from Gettysburg indignant people attacked a wagon train and freed some thirty or forty women and children. The horror that overtook black folks matched the horror of the wounded, if not those of the dead. And a few white people were also taken prisoners; some would die in captivity.

And where were the black wounded? Thousands of support personnel came with the armies. Enslaved men on the Confederate side, mostly; freed men on the Union side. Confederate blacks sometimes escaped. Neither side put them in uniform yet, not at Gettysburg, though elsewhere black Union troops were growing into heroes. Here they were civilians: wagoners, cooks, artisans, laborers. During the battle they stayed mostly behind the lines, but some of them were wounded. The Confederates took most, except for those impossible to move. What happened to the rest? Who cared for them? Good God, where are they? Confederate or Union, nobody talked about them.

Gettysburg was damaged in many ways, but the countryside was devastated. Though prized horses were spirited away by the wary before the Confederates came, the enemy took much of the area's livestock—horses, cows, pigs, and fowl. One visitor noted in a field the remains of more than fifty oxen. Homes were vandalized, larders emptied, fences destroyed, fields trampled, orchards picked clean, and roads rutted when not made impassable by tens of thousands of feet and their impedimenta. Fields near the roads were so abused that plows sometime could not break open the ground. A little government compensation would come—slowly and often capriciously. Victims or their descendants would still seek recompense when the twentieth century dawned.

The widow Lydia Leister had the misfortune of owning a house and farm just behind the Union lines that General Meade took as his headquarters. The Confederate bombardment that heralded the great charge of the last day of battle overshot its mark, hitting the Reserves and Meade's headquarters. When Mrs. Leister returned to her property, she was overwhelmed. Two years later, she would still pour out her angry heart to a reporter. " 'She lost a heap.' The house was robbed of almost everything. 'I had seven pieces of meat yit, and them was all took. All I had when I got back was jest a little flour yit.' " That was only the start.

I owed a little on my land yit, and thought I'd put in two lots of wheat that year, and it was all trampled down, and I didn't get nothing from it. . . . The fences was all tore down, so that there wa'n't one standing, and the rails was burnt up. One shell came into the house and knocked a bedstead all to pieces for me. . . .

The porch was all knocked down. There was seventeen dead horses on my land. They burnt five of 'em around my best peach-tree and killed it; so I ha'n't no peaches this year. They broke down all my young apple-trees for me. The dead horses sp'iled my spring, so I had to have my well dug.

But the widow, with the help of her son, rebuilt the house and barn, and replanted the fields. She would even acquire more land, though the government paid her next to nothing in compensation. She was like the people of Gettysburg, resilient.

In town, one young woman, Ginny Wade, was shot to death in her home while making bread. People thought at first she had been killed "by our own sharpshooters." Several other civilians received slight wounds, including John Burns, sixty-nine years old, shoemaker and sometime constable, the civilian who went out to fight with the army. He became famous; his picture appeared on the cover of *Harper's Weekly*, the major newsmagazine of the time. Burns was pictured as "the only citizen of Gettysburg who shouldered his rifle and went out to do battle in the Union ranks against the enemies of his country. . . . Honor to his name!" In fact, the locals strenuously objected to Burns being described as the only man who fought back—during the war perhaps 3,000 men from the county went to war; some left only days before the battle in the emergency militia.

One group of local boys, Company K of the First Pennsylvania Reserves, were the town's special heroes: they had come home to fight with the Army of the Potomac. People said that the Reserves' great charge, on the second day of the fight, saved Little Round Top and decided the fate of the battle. The newspapers told their story: "To the hill, up the hill, and on to the top of the hill, the column passed its way." Death awaited many. On came the enemy. "In a moment more the day would have been lost." But their general, Samuel Crawford, "rode to the head of the troops, took the colors, and the Pennsylvanians rushed forward with a shout heard around the battlefield and beyond." They became "irresistible."

The town remembered that shout well. While it was still struggling to cope with the wounded and the dead left by the battle, Professor Jacobs wrote of this unforgettable moment in his history. He described how for two endless days the people of the town lived with "the almost deafening sounds of exploding cannon, of screaming and bursting shells, and of the continuous roar of musketry." Rebel shrieks permeated their homes, their cellars, their souls—"unearthly yells of the exultant and defiant enemy."

Then, around 6 p.m. of that second day of battle, a different cheer rocked the fields. Jacobs overheard rebel soldiers' worried voices: "Listen! *the Yankees are cheering.*" Was the battle turning? Hope was rekindled. Not until July 4 did the people find out that their boys had been the ones cheering—and the rest of the Pennsylvania Reserves. Their boys fought for "hearth and firesides. . . . Over the heads of their helpless wives and children" flew "murderous shells . . . they showed no fear of the rebel invaders." Their "single action saved the day."

But the company left to continue to fight the war, and its wounded stayed behind. At the hospitals, people talked of the "noble Pennsylvania Reserves" and their "war-cry," and the country talked of it, too. The Company K boys did not have to stay put in the hospitals and some went home, improving their chances. The newspapers listed their casualties: "Calvin Hamilton, leg amputated, ball struck his knee. Jas. Culbertson, of Emmitsburg, ball through his neck, may survive. Wm. Magrew, ball through arm and leg, flesh wounds. Wilson Nailor, ball through shoulder, not dangerous. Obediah Beard, piece of shell struck his back, not dangerous. David Woodring, ball glanced of his forehead, not dangerous. Jacob Arendt, ball glanced off his shoulder, not dangerous." It might have been worse.

Then, at the end of July, Will McGrew died. All three newspapers reported that the widow's son, "aged 26 years 8 months and 14 days," died of the wounds he had received in the charge. People who knew Jane McGrew, and her three younger children, also knew that her oldest son had been their chief support. To work the farm alone with children, with the one adult son in the army, put a very heavy burden on her, eased a little by the knowledge that families all over Adams County, indeed all over the entire country, faced similar troubles. But now the breadwinner was dead. After the battle, Mrs. McGrew had cared for Will on the farm. Then the end came. "An amiable youth, a faithful and patriotic soldier, may he rest in peace. Long live the Republic in defence of which he gave his life."

A poem appeared soon after Will McGrew's death, written by "one of his comrades."

> *Another name is added to*
> *The list we call "OUR LOST,"*
> *We're called again to mourn anew,*
> *What this Rebellion cost.*

The anonymous soldier-poet promised that McGrew would never be forgotten while his comrades traveled "life's rough steeps." He had offered up his blood to "vindicate our laws" when "the cause of freedom waned, when treason stalked about."

> *Our list of names is growing small*
> *And one by one we fall.*
> *We pray that God the cause will bless*
> *In which we offer all.*

Sincere, deep patriotism helped ease the burdens of Gettysburg. The town had much to mourn. But it buried the dead and took care of the wounded. Gettysburg went on with life.

If the town suffered, grew famous overnight, became a sacred place, it also received some very harsh criticism. The criticism came from numerous quarters and was laced with anti-Dutch—that is, anti-German—prejudice. Since the countryside tended to vote Democratic, Gettysburg was labeled "Copperhead." The visitor who spoke with the widow Leister, who lost so much, concluded that "this poor women's entire interest in the great battle was . . . centered in her own losses. That the country lost or gained she did not know nor care, never having thought of that side of the question." Even the charitable Christian Commission, which praised the women of Gettysburg, noted that "benevolent feeling" in the area was not "universal." One reporter complained about a man selling loaves of bread for fifty cents to the "hungry, faint and weary" wounded soldiers, while another charged a dollar. "The loaves may have been large," the sarcastic observer remarked. "I did not see them."

Farmers who at times lost their whole crop, their livelihood, tried to make a living. Surely others without such losses hoped to make something, too. One officer became so disgusted with the money grubbing that he wrote in his diary he would have rejoiced had Gettysburg been "leveled with the ground." Nurse Woolsey called local farmers "evil beasts" and excused her words by saying, "I only use Scripture language." She believed that all "acts of kindness and self-denial were almost entirely confined to women." Even a local paper was not above making fun of disloyal Dutch farmers caught in "Ein Pig Schwindle." Prejudice ran in many directions.

Much thievery also took place. The battlefield was littered with discarded weapons, cartridge boxes, blankets, coats, haversacks, shovels, saddles—all sorts of valuables. To one visitor, "the appearance of the field" was as if an army "had started up in the night, leaving everything but was fastened to their bodies." People came "in Swarms to Sweep and plunder," according to Provost Marshal Marsena Patrick. A New York reporter wrote that plunderers took away "any and everything they consider of pecuniary value." A minister watched "a young lad" cutting off buttons from dead soldiers' uniforms and heard him exclaim: *"Why, that man is still alive. See how he breathes."* Others even pulled bodies from shallow graves. A weapon is worth a great deal. Who cares who the dead man was? Who was it? Dead.

At one point, General Schenck issued an unenforceable order forbidding civilians to "visit the vicinity of the battle-ground." Thieves caught red-handed were obligated to augment the burial details or forced to do other unwelcome chores. Millions of dollars' worth of government property lay about, and though the thieves and robbers might be from anywhere, locals got plenty of the punishment. In the countryside the army went from house to house searching for stolen goods. Later, one man would recall so many farms being raided that the officer in charge found himself leading a wagon train of farmers returning their plunder. On the other hand, the outraged locals called the soldiers collecting army property the "forty thieves."

Gettysburg was raked over with harsh criticism, but from among the many complaints, one rankled above all else because it appeared in the *New York Times*. Though not yet the dominant paper of later days, it was copied in "a hundred other journals" all over the country, as the locals complained. Reporter Lorenzo Livingstone Crounse, who damned the German-dominated Eleventh Corps after the Battle of Chancellorsville, now went after the "Dutch" farmers for their "sordid meanness and unpatriotic spirit." Their cowardly menfolk "mostly ran away," and when they finally showed up, after danger passed, they came with exorbitant bills for damages. *Harper's Weekly* added insult to injury by printing a cartoon showing a stereotype "Dutchman" selling water to a soldier at "6 cents a glass."

The people of Gettysburg believed they had earned "a good and undying name" with their labors, and now their indignant papers kept up a steady barrage of defense against Crounse. "Ignorant, drunken, lying . . . slandering . . . defamation," the *Star* shouted. But the town gathered support from outsiders who testified to people's generosity. A "card of thanks," signed by surgeons working in one of the Presbyterian churches, singled out Gettysburg's "noble ladies with that self-sacrificing heroism." One of the signers was a Confederate doctor. The criticism of the town hurt and made people ever more determined to show great hospitality to visitors— now and in the future, too. Still, when Lorenzo Crounse reappeared in town in 1865, an excited mob gathered, threatening his "forcible ejection." Instead, a meeting at the courthouse allowed much angry steam to escape. Crounse would backtrack enough in the *New York Times* to admit that "on recovering from the paralysis of the battle," many in the town had devoted themselves to the care of the wounded. However, he also wrote about the "demagogues" who threatened to lynch him. The rival *New York Tribune* could not resist quipping that the folk in Gettysburg "expected to show that they were a liberal and hospitable people by lynching a writer who had stated the contrary."

If Gettysburg received some less than fair criticisms, if it poured its heart and muscle into the relief effort, Sarah Broadhead's assessment in her diary was also true: "the old story of the inability of a village of twenty-five hundred inhabitants, overrun and eaten out by two large armies, to accommodate from ten to twelve thousand visitors, is repeated almost hourly." What she did not understand was that the "visiting" wounded, alone, came to nearly 21,000 terribly needy souls. After battle, Gettysburg, as one soldier put it, had become "this vast charnel house."

CHAPTER TWO

REBIRTH

By late in July most of the remaining wounded were brought to a well-organized general hospital east of town, Camp Letterman. This was a new world. In the clean, efficient hospital of four to five hundred large tents, devoted nurses (mostly women) and male doctors and their many helpers took very good care of the patients—Union and Confederate. "A splendid Camp hospital," Nurse Hancock would write with the pride at the end of August. "The water is excellent here and there is order about everything." "A beautiful spot," noted another, and the Sanitary Commission helped make the hospital "a thing of wonder." A Vermont doctor, Henry Janes, headed up the operation. He was thirty-one. Most everyone was young.

The men longed for women. "You little know the pleasure a soldier feels in seeing a woman at camp," one wrote to Nurse Hancock. He had left the hospital and screwed up his courage to say this much. But the women knew. "It is wonderful how the eyes of these fellows will brighten at a friendly word from a woman," Nurse Emily Souder noted. Even a loving look seemed to do wonders. It did no harm that "there are many good looking women here," Cornelia Hancock told her niece. "Most people think I came into the army to get a husband." The army's superintendent of women nurses, Dorothea Dix's celebrated dictum that "all nurses are required to be plain-looking" could be circumvented. "The need was so great."

The men sang about their women. "When This Cruel War Is Over" would sell a million copies before the war ended, but proved to be so sad that some officers had discouraged its singing. They could not deny it to the wounded now.

> *Dearest Love, do you remember,*
> *when we last did meet,*
> *How you told me that you loved me,*
> *kneeling at my feet?*
> *Oh! How proud you stood before me,*
> *in your suit of blue,*
> *When you vow'd to me and country,*
> *ever to be true.*
> *Weeping, sad and lonely,*
> *hopes and fears how vain!*
> *When this cruel war is over,*
> *praying that we meet again.*

If the wounded men longed for women, many of the women of Gettysburg missed their men who had gone off to war—more than ever now with so many young soldiers all around them. At the end of July, Eliza Jane Miller, "Lile" to her husband, Sergeant Michael Murray Miller of Company K, wrote him, "You are gone such a *long long* time I have never wished so much to see you as the last week that passed. . . . O dear Murray it makes my heart leap when I think of your return, Charley often says he does wish papa would come home." Their five-year-old son bound them together as tightly as did their absence from each other.

The townspeople's lives got slowly better. Still, what happened to them, around them, filled their lives and their conversations. This would continue for decades: huddling in damp cellars while the world outside exploded, hiding Union soldiers, dodging Confederate patrols, defending home and hearth from marauders, escaping for dear life.

People looked for consolation in the churches, but as long as they were filled with soldiers, there could be no services. It was very hard on religious folks. People would long remember the time when nothing broke up the

Sergeant Michael Murray Miller. Detail from photo of Company K, 1st Pennsylvania Reserves, 1863. Photographer unknown. (Gettysburg National Military Park)

weeks, no church bells, no day of rest. President Baugher of the College held a service at Christ Lutheran Church on July 12, but it was abbreviated, and was intended for the wounded men quartered there. Some sang along—"sad pathos in the voices of these poor wounded men." But by the second half of July most of the churches were cleared and a Christian Commission member noted that Gettysburg's "holy Sabbath was an old fashioned Sunday." Most of the churches held services. During one, a wounded soldier passed from "the scenes of the earth to the spirit world."

Planning for the future began. The town was cleaning up, rebuilding, and many of its black people, probably those with property or jobs, returned. If the battle changed much in the town, the social structure did not change. Blacks still mostly served. They cooked for the wounded under the direction of white women. And they sang—"not under our direction," Georgie Woolsey quipped—"at the top of their voices all day, 'Oh darkies had you seen my Massa,' or 'When this *cruel* war is *over.*'" Black women washed mountains of soiled clothing. Black men rebuilt the railroad and received "very little care" in return. After the backbreaking work of the day, they held prayer services night after night. "Such an 'inferior race,' you know!" Woolsey noted sarcastically. Their hymns, their sad singing touched the white women who joined them. Sounds coming from the deep, the sounds of the earth. The women sewed gifts for the neglected men, touching them. The women also marveled at the "reverential affection" the laborers had for Lincoln, who after all was a politician and controversial president. Some worshipped him, and in their supplications, "whatever else" they asked for," they prayed that he should have "strength and comfort and blessing."

By September, Gettysburg was getting close to normal. The Christian Commission reported "a scene . . . greatly changed." So much help came that "we felt for once in our lives that there was a spring in the hearts of the people which had never before been well tried . . . people had to be bidden not to send any more." The Sanitary Commission noted much the same. Supplies overflowed. "It was a grand sight to see this exhibition of the tender care of the people for the people's braves." The College opened for its fall term, as did the Seminary. The public schools opened, too, and private teachers offered instruction in piano, guitar, the Spanish language, and more. The General Hospital's patients had been steadily distributed around the North. Fewer than 1,200 patients were left as fall came, with only 34 remaining in town. Lile Miller continued to nurse wounded soldiers and also continued to chafe at the difficulties caused by their presence. Yet when they left—and they left in a steady stream—"it is very dull here . . . and no news whatever."

Yet those who remained still caused problems for the town. "A person is just like a slave," Lile wrote her husband, Murray; "you cannot go or come as you please, you must have a pass for this place and that one, and this is for a soldier, and that is also I cannot give it I was ordered to give it to none but soldiers, indeed we all feel sick and tired of asking for any thing and have come to the conclusion to do with things until the soldiers are gone, perhaps we can get what we want at reasonable prices."

In September, the "noble, God-approved Christian Commission," the Sanitary Commission, and "the Ladies of Gettysburg" jointly put on a "grand entertainment" for the recovering men. Nurse Hancock had left by then, "the hosp. got so full of women," too full for her, and a soldier wrote to her that she "would hardly know the camp the tents are ornamented. . . ." Patriotic designs and evergreens crowned the hospital streets. A great ban-

quet was served, a band played, and the men got "delicacies and substan-
tials" galore.

The party was for the soldiers of both armies, though the Union boys
went first to avoid what took place at an earlier feast when the rebs elbowed
aside the Northerners and grabbed the best foods. A great banquet. Soldiers Blue and Gray hobbled to the well-laden tables: "Gala day . . . cheerful
look." The bitter war was still on, but here feelings of reconciliation filled
the air. Blessed peace seemed not so far away—"When this *cruel* war is *over*."
But the celebration had its ominous aspect, too. After a "bright and balmy
day . . . the crowning pleasure," one woman reported, came with a show,
"an entertainment of *negro* minstrels,—the performers being all *white* soldiers in the hospital." A minstrel show was much fun for the men, but its
songs lampooned black folks. Northerners or Southerners, racial attitudes
seemed not that different. The reconciliation that filled the air had a chill-
ing aspect, too.

The party spilled into the town. A "fantastically dressed company of
cavalry" performed. Foot races "in bags and out of bags," gander pulling,
greased pole climbing, and "every other amusement" gladdened the day. If
evening brought quiet to the hospital, the town kept hopping. Enjoying the
night, a young woman lost her "Crimson Crape Shawl" and advertised for
it. Gettysburg was getting back to the usual.

Politics came alive with the fall elections energizing the people. Lincoln's long letter to an Illinois meeting defending Emancipation and the
use of black troops got much attention from the local press. There can be no
"appeal from the ballot to the bullet," the president's campaign document
explained. And when victory came "there will be some black men who can
remember that, with silent tongue, and clenched teeth, and steady eye, and
well-poised bayonet, they have helped mankind on to this great consummation; while, I fear, that there will be some white ones unable to forget that,
with malignant heart, and deceitful speech, they have striven to hinder it."
"Forcible and Characteristic" the *Star* headlined on its front page. "Confiscation and negro emancipation policy" keep the war going, the Democratic
Compiler rejoined. A few weeks later, the *Star* went further: "President
Lincoln's letter goes into every household like a welcome guest.—The
hardest prejudices give way before its sincerity, and the most bigoted partisan dare not deny its truth."

Lincoln's suspension of the writ of habeas corpus and his call for

300,000 additional men for the army received similarly impassioned partisan attention. But the proposal to establish the Soldier's National Cemetery and save the battlefields united the people and crowned the town's recovery, infusing Gettysburg with fresh spirit. The town understood immediately that it had "become historic," and quickly local lawyer David McConaughy proposed erecting a monument to the soldiers at the local burial place. He was the president of Evergreen Cemetery, which, he noted, also happened to be "the center and apex of the battle-field." It did indeed see crucial action in the battle. Back in 1862, McConaughy had already proposed setting aside a section of Evergreen for soldiers from Gettysburg.

Now he also suggested saving important parts of the "battlefield itself, with its natural and artificial defences, preserved and perpetuated in exact form and condition they presented during the battle. . . . There could be no more fitting and expressive memorial of the heroic valor and signal triumphs of our army." Some of the leading members of the community immediately got behind the idea.

Governor Andrew Curtin had come to Gettysburg quickly after the battle and was appalled by what he found: "The heart sickened at the sights that presented themselves at every step . . . remains of our brave . . . partially covered with earth . . . left wholly unburied." "Other sights" were "too shocking" to describe in official documents. Opened graves left open, bones scattered, bodies dug out and mutilated by dogs, hogs, or wild animals. Skulls "kicked around like footballs." "And this, too, on Pennsylvania soil!" The governor wanted action and chose a young local lawyer, David Wills, as his agent. Wills went at the task with great energy.

McConaughy wanted Evergreen to be the resting place for the honored dead, but Wills proposed instead a separate National Cemetery. Wills won. Public appeals ensued: an officer of the Christian Commission wrote of the need for the cemetery "to avoid the disgrace which would be upon us as a nation." The idea "suggested itself," the official report would later say, but people continued to wrangle over credit. Some think that a New Yorker, former army surgeon Theodore Dimon, had the idea first. Surely many others talked about it. How to deal with the war dead had been on the national consciousness since 1861. The solution emerged out of the clearing air of Gettysburg, a "happy inspiration of patriotism."

Wills was an Adams County native whose mother died when he was four years old. He was raised by a single father, graduated from the Gettysburg

College, and worked for a year in Alabama before returning North to study law under Thaddeus Stevens. At the start of 1854, Wills began his practice in Gettysburg and rose rapidly. Elected superintendent of the county's schools, a director of the Bank of Gettysburg and of the local railroad company, a manager of the county's Fire Insurance Company, also of the Gas Company that brought modern light to the town, in five years Wills bought one of the finest homes, three stories high, on the Diamond. By then he was married to Jennie Smyser, and in time they would have seven children.

Governor Curtin had a good eye, and when he picked the dynamic Wills as his agent, he got all that he had hoped for. The young lawyer bought land—on some of it an apple orchard had to be dug up root and branch. He made friends (and enemies) and obtained the support of the governors of the states which had "soldier-dead on the battle field." He, and others too, also started to think about the dedication of the new cemetery.

To design the burying grounds, Wills hired "the celebrated rural architect" William Saunders. He was "at the head of his profession in this country," Henry Stahle declared in the *Compiler*, the country's leading

Attorney David Wills, Lincoln's and Everett's host in Gettysburg. Photographer unknown. (Adams County Historical Society)

"landscape gardener and horticulturalist." The Scottish immigrant had created the first rural cemetery in the country, Mount Auburn in Massachusetts. In Gettysburg, Saunders would shape a sacred space on a triangular field that "overlooks the whole battlefield."

By mid-October, the people of Gettysburg knew that they would have a grand consecration ritual of the new cemetery, "an immense concourse of people, probably fifty thousand." The great orator Edward Everett was picked to deliver the dedication speech, and President Lincoln "will also be present and participate in the ceremonies." A very large number of other dignitaries were scheduled to come, as well as bands and the military. Gettysburg would produce "one of the most imposing and interesting occasions ever witnessed in the United States." David Wills, and his governor, had high ambitions.

Governor Curtin most likely procured Lincoln's acceptance, though no one could be certain whether a crisis might interfere. Whatever the governor told Wills, the young lawyer told everyone that the president was coming. He did not even bother—or find time—to get off the formal invitation to the White House until the start of November. Then his invitation made clear that he understood soldiers: they were men willing to die but they were not willing to be forgotten. As late as November 16, Governor Curtin wrote to the editor of the Philadelphia *North American*, Morton McMichael, that "although not definitely settled when I left Washington I have no doubt the President will go." The governor had been at the White House two days earlier.

Originally, October 23 was to be the day of dedication, but Everett could not accept. "It is doubtful whether, during the whole month of October, I shall have a day at my command," he told Wills. The venerable orator would not say that he was recovering from serious illness, but did explain that the work would "demand as full a narrative" of the battle as time would permit, and also a "discussion of the political character of the great struggle." Everett did not wish to speak at a cemetery without its honored dead. Burials were to start in November, and Everett knew that his words would be "more effective uttered over their remains." Unlike Wills, the seasoned orator understood the importance of surroundings. He would be glad to come to Gettysburg, but November 19 was the earliest he could do so. That became the date.

Wills had invited another New Englander, Henry Wadsworth Longfellow, to write and deliver a poem for the dedication. "An ode or dirge by the distinguished poet Longfellow is to be sung," the newspapers announced. The poet was interested in the occasion and had a son in uniform. But he had also complained about "an unusual pressure of those numberless nothings, which like the remora, impede us as we sail the sea of life." Not much later he would decline former Maine governor Israel Washburn's invitation to provide a "Hymn or Ode to be sung or read" on the first anniversary of the Emancipation Proclamation. He declined the Gettysburg invitation, too, as did William Cullen Bryant, John Greenleaf Whittier, and the less known George Henry Boker. Poets are sensitive souls and muses often fail to speak upon demand. Wills appears to have failed with all. Finally, he had an unknown public functionary step into the breach.

The Everett-inspired postponement of the dedication worked well enough. The digging up of bodies had been stopped by the military for August and September, and Wills himself thought that "proper respect for the health of this community" suggested it should not start again until cold weather came. The fear of pestilence still infused Gettysburg. Now there would be at least some graves in the National Cemetery by the time the big day arrived. "The affair will be a magnificent one," editor Harper predicted in September.

The papers also reported on William Saunders's arrival and his laying out of the grounds. He created a semicircular shape for the graves, arranged by states, and reserved the two ends for the unknowns, with a separate space for the U.S. Regulars, who belonged to the entire nation. Saunders would have preferred intermingling the bodies, but the states insisted on individual placement. At least no distinction was to be made between soldier and officer. Saunders also reserved space for a monument to the dead in the center of the semicircle. The "National sepulchre," as Andrew Curtin wrote, would be magnificent. "Such was the origin," the report to Pennsylvania would explain, "of this final resting place for the remains of our departed heroes, who nobly laid down their lives a sacrifice on their country's altar, for the sake of Universal Freedom and the preservation of the Union."

Governor Curtin corresponded with the executives of the states whose soldiers died in the battle. All were invited. Telegrams were exchanged; officials were eager to come. Governor F. J. Pierpont of the new state of West Virginia wrote: "I will be with you at one o'clock on the seventeenth inst."

Gettysburg Nov. 2ᵈ 1863

To His Excellency,
    A. Lincoln,
        President of the United States,
            Sir,
                The several States
having soldiers in the Army of the
Potomac, who were killed at the
Battle of Gettysburg, or have since
died at the various hospitals which
were established in the vicinity,
have procured grounds on a
prominent part of the Battle Field
for a Cemetery, and are having
the dead removed to them
and properly buried.

27781

David Wills invites Lincoln. (Library of Congress)

be the same, their remains
will not be uncared for.

We hope you will be able
to be present to perform this
last solemn act to the Soldiers
dead on this Battle Field.

I am with great
Respect, Your Excellency's
Obedient Servant,

David Wills
Agent.

A.G. Curtin Gov. of Penna
and acting for all the States

Some governors could not accept, their legislatures being in session. Delaware had an election. Minnesota's Edward Salomon telegraphed: "the draft is now in progress." And Wisconsin's Alexander Ramsey: "I leave on the next boat & If I can get through in time will be with you."

Gettysburg was back on its feet. The town's spirits soared. The same community passion that brought the railroad, that built the beautiful new station, the warehouses, the courthouse, now focused on the coming dedication of the National Cemetery. The November days passed and Wills outlined in detail for Curtin—and the public—what would take place on the 19th. The words "immense concourse of people" kept reappearing. The newspapers brimmed with excitement: "Largest preparations . . . extra locomotives . . . fine display of military . . . Rev. Dr. Stockton . . . Mr. Everett . . . President Lincoln . . . Odd Fellows . . . Governors . . . Heads of Departments. . . ." The leading citizens formed an "energetic" committee. Homes were to be opened to the masses of strangers "and thus maintain the reputation of the town for generous hospitality." A modest uniform price was suggested for room and board. "A magnificent flag" on a pole over 100 feet tall went into the Diamond—"all honor to the ladies."

Pilgrims started arriving early. The town was in a frenzy, "fast filling up with visitors." Wind knocked down a giant flagpole on Little Round Top, and it was replaced. A large platform for the dignitaries went up at the cemetery, with a flagpole in front of it. "Juvenile poles" and patriotic buntings sprouted all over town. A great graphic *Panorama of the War* depicting the Civil War battles from their start in South Carolina to the present moment arrived for exhibition. General Meade's letter to Wills regretted that "army duties" prevented him from attending, but expressed "deep and grateful feelings . . . for the tender care" of the "heroic dead."

Politics remained ever present. A Copperhead hotel keeper in neighboring Littlestown refused accommodation to a soldier on his way to the ceremonies. "Outrageous Treatment," blared a headline in the *Star*. The report explained that the soldier was traveling "to attend the raising and burying his two sons, both of whom were killed in the battle of Gettysburg. In addition to this he had *three brothers* killed in the same battle, and he was himself wounded in the arm and the breast." Sensationalism was alive and well in town.

The Reverend Professor Baugher lectured on the battle, no doubt more soberly. Others gave patriotic talks, too. The "Stirring Speech" given by

Illinois governor Richard Yates at Cooper Union in New York was reported in detail:

> *When free schools and the true aristocracy of this land—free labor—is established, we shall again have a true Union and a glorious country. But there will be no peace until slavery is destroyed . . . Mr. Lincoln could not move faster than God and providence permitted. When he telegraphed to President Lincoln his fiery dispatch for confiscation and emancipation, Old Abe telegraphed back: "Dick, hold still and see the salvation of God." [Tremendous cheering] There has been great complaint that we have interfered with men's rights, but when a traitor is convicted and hung, he is only getting his rights. They only have the right to be hung on this earth, the divine right to be damned forever after. [Cheers.]*

Gettysburg was getting ready for "an event such as has never been witnessed before in this country," the *Star* proclaimed.

As great new energy invigorated the community, it was paid out, in no small part, by the people who reburied the dead. On October 27, the work of exhuming the bodies had resumed. Find a grave on the battlefield. Dig it up. You don't know what you are going to find. On the first day's battlefield mostly unidentified skeletons. All body matters had rotted away, or were eaten up. The Confederates had taken the field on that first day and had no time to bury enemy soldiers. For nearly a week the Rebs held the ground. Soaring heat and drenching rains beat on the dead bodies, and began to decompose them. Then the Union army retook the land and soldiers buried soldiers, getting rid of the stinking bodies quickly. There was not much time to find out who they were. The burial squads covered the dead with dirt and followed after the army that followed Lee.

Now the bodies are dug up. Dig the dirt. What you'll find in most spots will depend on the soil. Heavy clay and marshy land preserved bodies; sandy soil leaves nothing but bones. Some of the bodies are partially decomposed. You lift them up and they come apart. Flies, they seem like millions, are hovering around. Everywhere. A nightmare. The stench is unbearable. But the work must go on. Some of the dead are almost wholly preserved. They almost look alive. Like some of the dead horses.

Many men were buried in trenches: two, four, fifteen bodies to a trench. In some, 150 soldiers lay, maybe more. There were also individual graves "with no mark whatever to show who sleeps there," a visitor noted. Some had "a stick with the initials scratched on it." Many other graves were marked, or had been, once. A rough board, a name scrawled on in pencil; sometimes the name of the unit marked. But by the time the reburials started, the sun had often bleached the names off and the rains had washed them faint on the rough planks.

Who is this dead man? Many graves were never marked. Men barely buried. By now some graves are level with the ground. First, summer overgrew them with new life, and then, after autumn came, covered them with wilted weeds or dead leaves. Were there any humans here ever?

Massachusetts sent its own contingent to do the work and hired locals to help. New York sent men, too, at least to repaint headboards before all writing disappeared. But the task overwhelmed them. Individuals came "by thousands," opening graves, looking for loved ones, closing them poorly when finding a stranger. Undertakers did a booming business. Many worked carelessly. They left graves open, bones and hair scattered. Grisly fields became grislier.

Black men dug up the bodies under the leadership of Basil Biggs. Eight to ten men working in a gang from early morning to late at night. If you worked hard, you made money. The pay was good—for black men. Thirty-four bids were made to rebury the Union dead, from $8 to $1.59 per body. A local white man, F. U. Biesecker, put in the lowest bid and got the job. He hired Biggs. Or perhaps Biesecker did the bidding for Biggs because a "colored" man would have a hard time getting a contract.

If the dead were "well buried," the job was harder. Each body must be examined, rebel or Union. If the enemy, you leave him there. Cover him up with dirt and be done. They would stay there for years. Some forever. Farmers would plow over them, bones come up and be thrown away. And, gravedigger, you wasted your time because you don't get paid for Confederates. Still, you must open every grave you find, unless plainly marked as enemy.

A white drayman and photographer, Samuel Weaver, superintended the exhumations. He kept records of every name found, recorded every item recovered. No grave could be opened unless he was present. Some believed one could never be too careful with black gravediggers—though in fairness some, like Biggs, grew to be much respected. Black or white, errors crept

Confederate Graves. July 1863. Photograph by Timothy O'Sullivan. (Library of Congress)

in: some men were misidentified and buried in the wrong graves. Rebs slipped into the National Cemetery, too.

When you open a grave, you first look to see if the uniform is blue or gray. But often you can't tell what you have found. So you search the dead for identifying documents and valuables. Poking into the decomposing clothing of decomposing bodies is an awful job. Weaver does it with an iron hook. He must also examine every bit of clothing, "everything about the body to find the name," as he'll report. "Relics" can help a great deal. Men can be identified by "pocket diaries, by letters, by names in Bible, or Testament, by photographs, names in pocketbooks, descriptive list, express receipts, medals, names on some part of clothing, or on belt, or cartridge-box, &c., &c."

Rebels "stole" blue pantaloons, and they might have been buried in them. But they would never go into battle with a blue coat. That was a sure way to be killed by your own. So that also helped separate friend from foe. Rebels wore cotton; patriots wool. Rebel shoes were differently made, but shoes sometimes got mixed up. If all else failed, the cotton of the rebels' undershirts gave them away. Traitors found; traitors stayed in the ground.

Some fields where rebels fell had the "appearance of a vast bone yard," one soldier wrote. Yet, bit by bit, the Republican *Sentinel* reported, there was "considerable feeling in and around Gettysburg" in favor of setting apart land for the Confederate dead. The ground should not be close to "our own National Cemetery . . . but let it be done, for the sake of common humanity. The hostility of the dead has ceased; and let them be in a spot where a father, a mother, a sister or brother, can visit their last resting place, 'when this cruel war is over.' " Southerners should pay for the work, editor Robert Harper suggested. But the Confederacy had other problems to deal with. The dead remained where they were.

When news of "the exposed condition rebel dead" reached Governor Curtin, he ordered the graves and burial trenches covered before the ceremonies started on the 19th. Some discussion took place about establishing a Confederate Cemetery, spearheaded by the brother of New York's Democratic governor and presidential hopeful Horatio Seymour. Then there was the good doctor John W. C. O'Neal, Virginia-born, and so with loyalties suspect, though a graduate of the local College. He came from Baltimore to Gettysburg months earlier to start a medical practice. As he made his rounds, he recorded the names and locations of many Confederate dead. Samuel Weaver, too, kept Confederate records. He was sometimes assisted by his son, Rufus Benjamin Weaver, another graduate of the College, who would become a professor of anatomy in Philadelphia's Hahnemann Medical School. The relatives and friends who years later managed to recover the bodies of their loved ones in gray would have O'Neal and the Weavers to thank. "May the Lord bless you is the prayer of many Southern hearts," one mother wrote in 1866. But as for the National Cemetery, much of the North seemed well satisfied that "none but loyal soldiers of the Union lie here."

When the working squad dug up remains, it put them into coffins. Weaver recorded the name, company, regiment on the coffin, and gave it a number. He did the same in a book. When a headboard was found, it was nailed to the coffin. Then Biggs sent one of his men with a two-horse team to haul nine coffins at a time to the cemetery. A white boy, Leander Warren, thirteen, plenty old enough to work, hauled six with his father's one-horse wagon. On a good day of "close hauling," when the disinterred bodies didn't have too far to go to the cemetery, the men could handle sixty bodies a day.

But many of the dead must come a long way. Some would be brought from as far as Hanover, fifteen miles off. Another Weaver son, photographer Peter, even took a picture there.

Sometimes, relatives stood by when the bodies were dug up. The photo taken would show a woman and a child, among others. What would come out of the earth: A skeleton? Bones with flesh hanging on? Or someone who seemed to have just died yesterday? A hand or other body part might be missing. A sweetheart might faint, or a mother. Sometimes relatives would take the loved one away home. But, as Nurse Souder told many, "The Cemetery at Gettysburg is the most honorable burying-place a soldier can have." She predicted that, "Like Mount Vernon, it will be a place of pilgrimage for the nation."

When the coffins arrived at the cemetery, teams of men did the burials under the direction of surveyor James S. Townsend. This was not as repugnant a job as pulling up the decomposing dead. This was a good job, so white men did it. At least one of them was a rebel deserter. "Quite a boy," Lile told her husband Murray, he is "boarding with us . . . digging and burying at the Nathunal Cemetery." Dig the hole four feet deep. Put the coffin in. Cover it with the earth from the grave you dig next. On and on, hundreds, thousands, all buried according to the Saunders plan. Weaver and Townsend kept separate lists, and each evening Wills compared them.

Between October 1863 and the following March, with a break between because of the winter's frozen ground, the gravediggers moved 3,354 bodies. Handling its own dead, Massachusetts would add 158 more. But nearly twice the number of graves had to be opened "in searching for the remains of our fallen heroes." Samuel Weaver "firmly believed" that not a "single mistake" was made "taking the body of a rebel for a Union soldier." Indeed, astoundingly, very few mistakes were made.

Weaver carefully packed valuables, making countless bundles, just as the Christian Commission did for those who died at the hospitals. In some places, Gettysburg mementoes went on exhibit. But the treasures, "valueless to others," often reached family and friends. When names and addresses were known, the packages were mailed immediately to the survivors. "Words would fail to describe the grateful relief that this work has brought to many a sorrowing households," David Wills noted. "They would know for certain what happened to their loved ones and that they got properly buried in the SOLDIERS' NATIONAL CEMETERY."

The list of articles that could not be mailed to friends and relatives was printed: 287 bundles. "Maine: Unknown, 20th Regiment, Testament, and letter signed Anna Grove." "Connecticut: William Cannell, letters, $8 rebel money, diary, &c." "New York: Theodore Bogart, Company I, 120th Regiment, medal, breastpin, pencil." "Solomon Lesser, $30 in gold, $6 in greenbacks, and certificates of deposit for $300 in German Savings Bank, New York." The bounty for signing up was often $300. An immigrant who had no family might carry all his worldly goods on his person. "Pennsylvania: James Kelley, Company K, 69th Regiment, ambrotype, sixty cents, comb, medal." "New Jersey: J. F. 7th Regiment, knife, fork, and spoon." "Ohio: B. F. Pontious, Company D, 29th Regiment, letter, ring, diary, book and glass." "Michigan: James F. Bedel, Company F. 7th Regiment, muster roll list, and certificate of back pay from April to July, diary, &c." "Unknown, supposed New York, ambrotype of mother and two daughters." Nine hundred and seventy-nine nameless soldiers were buried in the plot reserved for the "Unknown."

This was the place for which on November 18, 1863, the President of the United States set out. Here he would have to explain to the people why the bloodletting must go on.

CHAPTER THREE

LINCOLN COMES TO GETTYSBURG

Provost Marshal-General of the United States James B. Fry, assigned as the president's personal escort, arrived at the White House on time. The carriage and driver had been waiting, the horses ready, but there was no president. At last the tall man came out of the big house and General Fry urged him on, politely, as one would the president. Trains had to run on schedule, the military man explained; no time could be lost. But Lincoln only smiled at Fry and told him a story from back in Illinois: A man was going to the gallows and saw the curious eager throngs hurrying past him. "Boys, you needn't be in such hurry to get ahead," he called out to them, *"there won't be any fun until I get there."* This was not the yarn of a man eager to go to a funeral.

That Lincoln was expected to attend the Gettysburg ceremonies, he and the townspeople had known since mid-October, some weeks before the official invitation arrived at the White House. Even as he got on the train heading to Gettysburg, it would be reported that he could not go. The presidency created endless exigencies, but the secretary of state could serve as Lincoln's stand-in. Wills, who had already invited Secretary of State William Seward, wrote again, inviting him to do the honors—if needed. The second letter went out on November 14 because Wills still did not know if Lincoln would come. John G. Nicolay, the first secretary in Lincoln's White House, would later remember that only two days before the ceremonies could the overburdened president actually decide to go. Most likely he did not get to start on the remarks he would have to make at the new National Cemetery until the evening before he left for Gettysburg: Tuesday, November 17. And then he probably got interrupted in midsentence. His text remained unfinished when it came time to leave.

Once Lincoln had made his decision, he urged cabinet members to go, too. He talked with the designer of the cemetery, William Saunders, and with others as well. When the railroad's directors, knowing how busy he was, proposed to take him to Gettysburg and back on the same day, Lincoln demurred. "I do not like this arrangement. I do not wish to so go that by the slightest accident we fail entirely, and, at the best, the whole to be a mere breathless running of the gauntlet."

So now he left a day before the ceremonies, on the 18th, but without his wife, who was expected to accompany him. For once their travel promised to be luxurious. Mary would have liked that. But their ten-year-old son Tad was ill. The newspapers would call it "scarlatina," and not only would Mrs. Lincoln not go, she wanted her husband to stay, too. He left anyway, but could not help but share his anxiety about the boy with others. Both he and Mary had been affected deeply by Willie's death the year before and both remained in mourning. But Gettysburg called.

General Fry and the president rode to Union Station, built in 1851. In earlier days Lincoln had liked to ride the rails, but the presidency had left him with little time to travel. Now they got on board around noon. The Baltimore & Ohio had arranged a "special train of four elegant cars" for this trip—some newspapermen saw only three—and special indeed they were. The train would not have to make regular stops and would have the right of way. The cars got decked out with wreaths of jasmine and evergreen and, of course, the American flag. Inside, the president's car was sumptuousness itself.

In the early days of railroading, hardship was taken for granted, a world created for men. The rails and males were twins—labor, technology, business, powerful engines, brave engineers. When women also took to the iron horse, slowly the comforts of home crept in. By the 1850s, railroads had reached sufficient prosperity and sophistication to provide private cars for privileged guests. The B&O's president, John W. Garrett, had a luxurious director's car built for his use. He lent it to the president, and others who had traveled on it described its wonders in detail.

The car had an entrance, a hall, a bedroom, a sitting room, and at the front an outside balcony with railings—all well furnished. A young Englishwoman who had the opportunity to travel on it gushed over the "beautiful car, forty feet long by eight wide." Though she had high expectations—Mr. Garrett talked of the director's car—what she found boggled the mind: "The sofas are covered with a pretty green Brussels carpet (small pattern) quilted like a mattress with green buttons, chairs covered with corded woolen stuff. . . . Bed-room berths much higher and wider than in a ship. . . ." Venetian blinds, looking glasses, twenty-two windows, lamps that would be lit if in a dark tunnel, a writing table "covered with green baize stretched tightly over it . . . a large blotting-book, ink, and pens, three or four daily newspapers. . . . Garrett knew how to travel in comfort.

Progressive communities of the time wanted the railroad; many wanted it to come right into the center of town. Gettysburg was like that. As early as 1836, construction had begun with state help procured by Representative Thaddeus Stevens. The "Tapeworm railroad," as the locals called it for following such a roundabout trail, headed west toward the Potomac River and the Baltimore & Ohio line—one of the first major railroads in the country. Then the Panic of 1837 struck, the economy crashed, and by 1838 the project died. Miles of empty roadbeds testified to broken dreams. In 1863, the long-unfinished ditch heading west from town became a terrible killing ground.

Following the Panic, construction of the railroad would not resume until February 1856. Young David Wills, who later would be instrumental in establishing the National Cemetery, was secretary to the directors of the new Gettysburg railroad company.

Construction began on a depot for travelers two blocks north of the Diamond. Warehouses started to go up around the station and all along the route. A new lifeline for Gettysburg. On December 16, 1858, the railroad opened. The festivities started. People had been descending on the town for days. Nothing like this had ever been seen here before. Some came from as far away as Philadelphia. The local papers estimated 8,000 to 10,000 people were present. Each time another train arrived with visitors, the boom of

Gettysburg, 1867. Tyson Brothers. William Frassanito, Early Photography at Gettysburg *(Gettysburg: Thomas, 1995).*

cannon greeted them, and when they departed, the cannon would boom out its farewell.

Though at first the country's railroad station architecture followed simple local forms, it did not take long before imaginations soared. Gettysburg built an Italianate villa, two stories high, with a cupola on the top. In time it got a "bell of fair size and excellent tone." Bracketed cornices under the eaves, flat roof. Nothing like it in all of these parts, people thought. Beautiful. "An ornament to the town and honor to the Railroad Company."

Gettysburg believed itself special, but Italianate villas like this proliferated and came to be known as the "railroad style." By the end of the Civil War, the people of the town could read the condescending news that the style borrowed from London clubs was "appropriate" for rural areas because it improved "the taste of the community." The depot quickly grew into a community center. The trains brought people, merchandise, mail, and news. It was a big thing to travel: saying good-bye and welcoming the new arrivals a heartfelt ritual. People watched who came and who went.

The road prospered rapidly, and with it the town. The company ordered a new engine for the large sum of $8,500—four times what it cost to build the depot. "The Engine is to weigh from forty-eight to forty-nine thousand pounds." It took people's breath away. The name of the engine was: *Gettysburg*. Each time a train departed, the large brass bell in the depot's cupola rang to alert the passengers and sing out good-bye.

Then the war came. The railroad continued in service. At one moment war business promised great prosperity, at another bankruptcy. Soldiers left for the front and came back, sometimes in coffins. In the winter of 1861–62, the upper floor of the depot served as the rehearsal hall for a military band. When the battle came to town, the station, like most every building, became a hospital. With victory won and rail service restored, supplies came to the depot, the wounded departed for hospital or home, the coffins left, visitors arrived and departed. Life returned to normal wartime traffic.

The special cars of the B&O with the president's party first headed out of Washington for Baltimore. Newspapers listed the names of the famous who rode with Lincoln—including some who did not. Later, all too many would claim to have been there, like the future railroad magnate Andrew Carnegie, who was supposed to have remembered handing Lincoln pencil and paper to write the speech he was to give. Carnegie at the time was miles away.

William H. Johnson certainly accompanied Lincoln, and he may have been the only black person on the train to Gettysburg. He was the president's valet. The United States, like some other places that adopted railroad transportation, had to figure out how to handle race relations in this new situation—just as it did the relations between men and women. Some hoped, and others feared, that the old order would be subverted. The people of Gettysburg were familiar with the question of whether blacks should travel on the same train with whites, and even the Republican paper would use vulgar racial epithets in such a context.

A British visitor, Lord Wharncliffe, harshly observed that in Northern railways and hotels black people were "never looked upon as men and brothers, but rather as dogs." Reverend Henry Ward Beecher replied to the accusation in a speech that admitted Northern prejudice but pointed to the "moral revolution" taking place in the country during the Civil War.

Lincoln himself illustrated the "moral revolution." He had brought Johnson, a young, dark-skinned man, when he came from Illinois. Lincoln and Johnson had traveled together to Washington in early 1861, and newspaperman Henry Villard commented on the black man's "untiring vigilance," describing him as "the most useful member of the party." Lincoln wanted Johnson at the White House, but the staff there would not accept an outsider. As the president tried to find a job for Johnson, he explained that "the difference of color between him & the other servants is the cause of our separation." The White House staff was light-skinned. America had created some strange race relations.

"Valet" and "servant" may not describe well the developing relationship between the two men. Lincoln had the knack of making everyone feel his equal. He characterized Johnson as "honest, faithful, sober, industrious, and handy." At another time he wrote: "I have confidence as to his integrity and faithfulness." Still, he referred to him at first in the parlance of the time as "a colored boy." By the time Lincoln issued his Preliminary Emancipation Proclamation in September 1862, he could speak of Johnson as "a worthy man." Johnson was a year older (we don't know his exact age) and the president, too, was growing in other ways.

Johnson was not shy about asking for the repeated help of his mentor and sometimes could end up with a note the president often wrote for others, too: "I would be glad for him to be obliged, if he can be consistently with the public service." After Lincoln talked with Treasury Secretary Salmon P. Chase, and made clear that "if you can find him the place shall really be obliged," Johnson landed a job at the Treasury Department, which allowed him to return to the White House to help Lincoln, shaving him, serving as a messenger; and if black memory in Washington is to be trusted, the president "depended upon him for protection"—in short, a bodyguard and friend. Lincoln took along Johnson, for example, when he went to Antietam to visit General McClellan in the fall of 1862. He wanted to gauge the general's hostility to Emancipation and his readiness to fight—and that of the Army of the Potomac. And now Johnson would accompany Lincoln to Gettysburg. A curt note went to the Treasury on the morning of the 18th: "William goes with me."

Lincoln's secretaries, John Nicolay and John Hay, who had also come with him from Illinois, rode on the train. They were the two young men closest to the president. Both adored their boss and both knew how to wield a pen. Their anonymously published reports provided him useful service. They were ready to write about Gettysburg, too.

The French minister to Washington, Henri Mercier, his Italian counterpart, Joseph Bertinatti, and their staffs, were on the train. The Secretary of State had his own reasons for wanting the diplomats to be part of a friendly outing. Confederate sympathizer Napoleon III of France certainly needed neutralizing. Canada's William McDougall was invited. The only female in the group may well have been Charlotte Wise, the daughter of Edward Everett, who traveled with her husband, Captain Henry A. Wise of the U.S. Navy. The disabled soldiers of the Invalid Corps, in a separate car, provided the ceremonial military escort—in addition to General Fry. The men also served as a constant reminder that a war was going on. To provide music, the Marine Corps Band came too.

Significantly, there were three cabinet members on board; two of whom was closely allied with Lincoln: Secretary of State Seward and Postmaster General Montgomery Blair; as well as the somewhat politically distant John P. Usher of Interior. Treasury Secretary Chase refused to go, so another Lincoln ally, Secretary of War Edwin Stanton, stayed put, too, to mind the store. He sent a son instead. Other politicians came or got on board later, including the rising young star of Pennsylvania Republicans, chairman of the Republican State Committee, Wayne MacVeagh. The Keystone State was important. MacVeagh may have been invited personally by the president to conduct business on the trip.

Chase was working to take away the president's job next year, an election year. It would not do to play a supporting role in a major public event that had significant political implications. And certainly he had to get his annual report ready. Lincoln had tried to force Chase to go, making clear that he took for granted his attendance: "My Dear Sir: I expected to see you here at Cabinet meeting, and to say something about going to Gettysburg. There will be a train to take and return us. The time for starting is not yet fixed, but when it shall be, I will notify you." But Chase pleaded "imperative public duties"—and refused. The confident U.S. Treasurer Francis Spinner snickered at the group that went: "There's a d___d good Scripture for that . . . *Let the dead bury the dead.*"

So there would be no show of cabinet unity in Gettysburg. And indeed, with their own annual reports due, not to mention their sections of the president's Annual Message, which would be published in December, cabinet members labored hard at the time. Lincoln had "strongly urged" Navy Secretary Gideon Welles to go, who noted in his diary that work on the annual report "compelled" him to decline. The press reported that Lincoln, too, was working on his message before going to Gettysburg, and indeed, upon returning, though ill, would meet with his cabinet to review the document. Attorney General Edward Bates wrote cryptically in his diary: "I could not go," without giving an explanation.

The presidential race of the coming year loomed. Young Hay, ever attentive to Lincoln's thinking, wrote in his diary about the subject constantly during the Gettysburg period. Lincoln himself noted in his inimitable way to a congressman friend: "A second term would be a great honor and a great labor, which together, perhaps I would not decline, if tendered."

The wedding of Kate Chase, the daughter of the Secretary of the Treasury, and Senator William Sprague of Rhode Island, was the big social event of the season, held a week before the Gettysburg ceremonies. Lincoln attended, not merely out of politeness. The reception allowed him to be face-to-face with some of the most important politicians in the country. A lot of them from all over the North would converge on Gettysburg now. Pennsylvania and Ohio, crucial to the 1864 election, would have the largest delegations, with New York, also in the balance, close behind. The first two states would also hold early October elections the following year, before the rest of the states voted, serving as bellwethers and providing inordinate influence over the final outcome.

Lincoln knew that he would be staying in the home of David Wills, together with the newly reelected governor of Pennsylvania, Andrew Curtin. There would be others at the house; meals, conversation, and a chance to make friends. Lincoln understood the crucial role of personal contacts in politics. He had traveled the circuit in Illinois more than other lawyers, and he rose much higher than any other in the state's political hierarchy. He was very good with people. He took their measure, let them take his, and forged connections that lasted. Lincoln went to Gettysburg with a trusted group of followers. The presidential campaign was on.

But even before Lincoln got there, his trip came under attack. The Democratic press did not know that the presidential party was traveling in a luxury car, but its military escort was obvious. The Invalid Corps that went with him became a threatening bodyguard. The *Cincinnati Enquirer* asked, "Why? . . . No other President ever traveled so escorted." It commented on "the incongruity of a plain Republican President, thus assuming the state and manners of a King."

Lincoln knew that among the people who rode the rails with his party the reporters formed a most important contingent. They had been selected because of their loyalty. The *Chicago Tribune*, on the day it reported the Gettysburg proceedings, would print a list of twenty-three journalists, "the manufacturers" of the news from Washington, while admitting that there were many others "less intimately connected." Indeed, the list was very incomplete. The newspaper people played so potentially critical a role in making the Gettysburg trip a success that places had been reserved for them on the speaker's platform. Yes, they were supposed to be close enough to hear well, but there they would sit with the speakers, cabinet members, and governors. The Republican press would so dominate at Gettysburg that one of the reporters recalled that while waiting for the president to arrive at the cemetery, newsmen threatened to manhandle one of their number "who did not admire Lincoln" and made himself obnoxious by acting disrespectfully and smoking a cigar.

Lincoln had cultivated newspapermen since his early days in politics. To lead a democracy in a civil war, he had to chart a new road: the newspapers played a central role in this, helping him and thwarting him. With the invention of the telegraph and the creation of the Associated Press in New York, news became a flash of lightning. Every part of the country received the same information at the same time, multiplying the impact untold times. The AP cooperated with Reuters, so that even Europe might come under the same sway, if a bit later. Lincoln understood this power and used it. It may be true, as some claimed, that the president desired no personal praise, but he also knew, as he said in 1858, that "Public sentiment is everything."

The press served as his main channel to that public sentiment. After the Republican losses in the 1862 elections, the president put no small part of the blame on his own party's press, which had been "vilifying and disparaging the administration." Then he went further, adding that "the ill-success of the war had much to do" with the newspapers. But earlier, too, he had been ready to write about "those villainous reporters."

To take the pulse of the country, and also to exert a positive influence on it, he held his *"public opinion-baths."* He opened up the White House, and even his summer retreat, the Soldiers' Home, to visitors of all stripes, newspapermen among them. "I do not often decline seeing people who call upon me," he noted a week before leaving for Gettysburg. He ventured out among the people in the capital city, and on rare occasions beyond it. These personal contacts supplemented the many politicians he corresponded with, including a number of influential newsmen. In addition, he looked at some of the masses of incoming mail from around the North. But a chief means of his listening was the press as digested by his assistants, and it was through the press that he could shape how the words he would speak at Gettysburg would be received.

The last president to be reelected was Andrew Jackson, in 1832. For Lincoln to be reelected, people had to endure the hardships of war and still maintain the will to fight on. For the country to be saved, the war had to go on. And the bereaved—the whole country was bereaved—needed consolation of the highest order. As Wills had written the president when asking that he "set apart [the cemetery] grounds to their Sacred use by a few appropriate remarks":

> *It will be a source of great gratification to the many widows and orphans that have been made almost friendless by the Great Battle here . . . it will kindle anew in the breasts of the Comrades of these brave dead . . . a confidence that they who sleep in death on the Battle Field are not forgotten . . . their remains will not be uncared for.*

People had to understand what the war was about. Some had urged Lincoln to speak out. He had done so repeatedly, most recently in a letter to a public meeting in Illinois that the Gettysburg press, too, reported, and which lauded black soldiers, who "with silent tongue, and clenched teeth, and steady eye, and well-poised bayonet" aided the war effort and so "helped mankind on to this great consummation." Lincoln met head-on the issue of Emancipation. Taking part in the Gettysburg memorial ceremony would provide a moment to be less partisan, to appear to rise above politics. Was that possible for a president running for reelection, even if unofficially? He would speak from the heart. It could be an important moment— if the press would help.

Americans indeed read newspapers. Traveling in the United States during the Civil War, a visiting Oxford professor of history, Goldwin Smith, marveled that farmers "are great readers of newspapers, and eager attendees of political meetings." Close to one third of all the papers of the globe were printed in the United States—about 4,000. By the end of the war, 700 periodicals covered the country. The industrial revolution that had created the railroads also remade the technology of publishing, with circulations soaring and costs plummeting. The railroads distributed weekly editions well beyond their place of publication. The big-city papers could afford to have their own correspondents, and their reports were also copied in countless small towns.

In Illinois, Lincoln had read the newspapers, wrote for them (often anonymously), courted editors, even owned a German-language paper to ensure a Republican voice. Though the independent commercial press grew as the war approached, most newspapers remained unabashedly partisan. If the railroads tied together the economy, the editors did the same for political parties. Lincoln courted them vigorously, and they not only served as his eyes and ears in many places but also smoothed his way—or hindered it.

Once in the White House, reading the papers became a luxury, but Lincoln brought two journalists from Illinois to be his personal helpers. John Nicolay was first secretary, John Hay second in command. To assist them, Lincoln added a third journalist, William O. Stoddard, who was charged with creating a digest of important comments in the press, but remembered giving up on the task in "despair" because he could not get the president's attention. The secretaries reported to the president and also continued to write in the press—anonymously, but serving "the Tycoon," as Hay referred to the boss. Hay, in particular, in addition to enjoying the life of a young man, would not only serve as Lincoln's eyes and ears in Gettysburg, together with Nicolay, cabinet members, and other confidants, but would also appear to do yeoman's duty as a reporter.

Lincoln's steady quest for information, which kept him in touch with journalists, in part arose from his need to crosscheck the information he received from the army and elements of his administration. Journalists could serve as independent sources of information. And he was very generous to many newspapermen.

Trying to lead the country, the president became the master of the patronage, like no other before him. The list of his beneficiaries among news-paper people is long, and the aid and comfort Lincoln received in return often matched the gifts he gave. Notwithstanding the establishment of the Government Printing Office, he bestowed printing contracts, and also ad-vertising, government jobs, military commissions, and good words when needed.

Perhaps no newsman received more favors from Lincoln than onetime Democrat John W. Forney, whose *Philadelphia Press* had helped the Repub-licans capture Pennsylvania in 1860, and who during the war became Lincoln's most important ally in the medium. Though the time of the "offi-cial" government newspaper had passed, Forney would be looked on as the "administration organ." Lincoln needed Forney. He believed that "No man, whether he be private citizen or President of the United States, can success-fully carry on a controversy with a great newspaper, and escape destruc-tion, unless he owns a newspaper equally great with a circulation in the same neighborhood." These words were put into Lincoln's mouth long after they had been uttered, but his actions demonstrated that they accu-rately reflected his thinking.

Forney was routinely described as "Lincoln's dog," and the newsman did not fail to inform the president of this. The president, in turn, helped him unstintingly. Forney got the lucrative job of secretary of the Senate, his son a commission with the Marines, his brother-in-law a route agency with the Post Office Department, and his cousin a sinecure in the Interior De-partment. Even Forney's employees fared well, and his several papers, of course, also received profitable government printing contracts. In return, he started a pro-administration weekly in Washington, the *Sunday Morning Chronicle*, this at Lincoln's urging and with the government's financial sup-port through advertising and the printing of official notices. The paper grew into the *Daily Morning Chronicle*, with 30,000 copies distributed among the soldiers of the Army of the Potomac. Now Forney, too, was rid-ing on the president's train, heading to Gettysburg. There he would get roaring drunk and make a violently pro-Lincoln speech.

The presidential train with its cargo of important people sped toward Bal-timore. Harvested fields, scattered houses, and towns flew by. The lieu-tenant leading the Marine Band later remembered handing a copy of the

New York Herald to the president, and seeing him laugh about the nonsense it carried in the guise of military news. But it was a treat for him actually to read the paper. Hay would later report Lincoln's oft-repeated comment about newspaper news: "I know more about that than any of them." In addition to the exceptional articles his secretaries called to his attention, he regularly read only the Washington papers' telegraphic dispatches. As Nicolay wrote to the editors of the friendly *Chicago Tribune*: "the President rarely looks at any papers, simply for want of leisure to do so." The hour and ten minutes it took to ride from Washington to Baltimore, aside from the politics conducted, gave Lincoln the gift of some leisure time.

Then the train arrived at Camden Station in Baltimore, on "a most delicious day," noted the diarist John P. Kennedy, who would play a large role in Lincoln's drafting of what posterity would take to be the definitive version of the Gettysburg Address. Another observer thought, or so he would later say, that Secretary Seward looked "uneasy." The last time Lincoln had been in the city, en route to his inauguration, he was hustled through in the middle of the night incognito because of reported plans to assassinate him. Seward had played his part in the imbroglio. Ambassador Mercier reported to Paris on the incident and also wrote that Mr. and Mrs. Lincoln "seemed like a real family of western farmers." Now Lincoln was traveling in broad daylight, and in a large company that included the friendly newspaper reporters, but also men of the Invalid Corps.

Only a small crowd welcomed the presidential party at Camden Station. He had not been "expected so soon," one paper offered as the explanation. But the two hundred or so who were there cheered, and Lincoln came to the train's balcony, "modestly," and bowed several times in acknowledgment. General Robert C. Schenck and staff got on board, a significant presence because the wounded veteran had gone back to Ohio to run for the congressional seat of arch peace advocate—some thought arch traitor—Clement Vallandigham. Schenck won. Now newspapers reported military "abuses of election" in Maryland, under Schenck.

B&O president John Garrett also came to welcome Lincoln, as did the railroad's "Master of Transportation," who had arranged the trip. Horses were hitched to the cars so they could be pulled through the city to Bolton Station, the point of departure for Hanover Junction and then Gettysburg. The fancy, decorated cars received a good bit of gawking from onlookers along the way. But "no demonstration worthy of notice" waited at the other end. Since even the director's car had no facilities for cooking, at the station a baggage car with food was coupled to the train. Then it sped on its way.

Lunchtime: Lincoln led the party to the baggage car, where a big table waited. He sat down at the head. Only during the last few years had the railroads started to serve meals and these left something to be desired. After one dining experience, a reporter mused: "We should require to be very hungry before we should desire to see another one." Good thing Lincoln wasn't a fussy eater. The French and Italian ministers, Count Mercier and Chevalier Bertinatti, left no comments about the fare on the rail—or indeed any other aspect of the adventure.

They left no impressions about the president's tabletalk, either. People mostly remembered the jokes their host dished out. When the train went through a deep cut, darkening the car and increasing the noise of the engine, Lincoln told the story of the non-religious man stuck in a terrible thunderstorm. The man turned to heaven and said to the Lord, "If it is all the same to you, give a little more light and a little less noise." After the meal, the bantering continued while business got conducted, too. Here and there the train stopped and Lincoln bowed to people or said a few words. At one stop a little girl gave him flowers and lisped, "Flowrth for the President!" He replied, as a politician-turned-soldier present would recall, "You're a sweet little rose-bud yourself." The very tall adult wished the girl a life of "beauty and goodness."

The charming episode impressed some, but what Hay noted in his diary was how the young MacVeagh "pitched into the Tycoon" about politics and patronage in Missouri, where radical and conservative Republican factions battled. The Pennsylvanian had "some matters" to discuss, as he would recall, and took a sharp radical line. Hay thought the young politician spoke "recklessly" but, realizing that he had gone too far, retreated. All the same, after a good bit of drinking that evening, MacVeagh would boast, as Hay's diary noted, that Lincoln had to be given the "truth." "The President got a good deal of that from time to time and needed it." Still later that night, MacVeagh would make up for it all by giving "a most touching and beautiful speech," which would be remembered decades later as "rattling good." In the night MacVeagh's companion was a "silent" young man, equally remembered years later, "silent then as now, but to become the cause of speech to a considerable extent. . . ."

*   *   *

Politics played a central part in Lincoln's going on this trip, but so did the largest issue before him and the country: the meaning of the war. Wills's invitation specifically requested that the president comfort "the many widows and orphans" and also honor the dead soldiers and thereby inspire their comrades to fight on. One traveler would remember the president speaking on the train with a father who had lost his only son at Gettysburg. Perhaps so. But Lincoln did not need to speak with a grieving father to know, as he would soon say, that the war had gone on so long that "it can almost be said that the 'heavens are hung in black.' " Death had been his intimate companion since childhood: a mother dead when he was nine, a sister after that, then a sweetheart, then a son, Eddie. But the war multiplied deaths a thousandfold, and it also remained near him as friends died as did another son, Willie, in 1862. American society as whole showed a deep interest in death; but for Lincoln it was his special companion, and he might have sung, as Walt Whitman would:

> The knowledge of death as walking one side of me,
> And the thought of death close-walking the other side of me.
> And I in the middle. . . .

Lincoln had participated in the funerals of his mother, two of his sons, friends, and the children of his friends, and public figures, too. He was present for the three hour service for his young friend from Illinois in 1861, Col. Elmer Ellsworth, shot dead in cold blood, perhaps the first combat casualty of the war. Afterwards he wrote to Ellsworth's parents: "May God give you that consolation which is beyond all earthly power." Now he must do for the whole country what was perhaps beyond "all earthly power."

At one point on the trip, Lincoln excused himself and went into the private part of the director's car. Later, some would be certain that he wrote either part or all of his speech while the train left Hanover Junction for Gettysburg. But no handwriting survives that would indicate being penned on a rolling, swaying train. He probably had half-finished remarks with him, starting with the promise of the Declaration of Independence, and his thoughts must have wandered again and again to what he was to say. Back in July, victory in battle around Independence Day brought Jefferson's words to mind and he told a serenading crowd, "this is a glorious theme, and the occasion for a speech." But he was not then "prepared to make one worthy of the theme and worthy of the occasion." Now, little time was left to prepare.

As the president's locomotive headed toward its destination, a special "Governors' train" coming from Harrisburg tried to meet up with it at Hanover Junction, but failed. Andrew Curtin of Pennsylvania, the host, certainly traveled on the "Governors' train," as did, probably, the chief executives of Indiana and West Virginia; a former governor, governor, and governor-elect of Ohio; and the former Secretary of War and powerful Pennsylvania politician Simon Cameron. A number of generals also rode on this train, including Abner Doubleday, George Stoneman, and the Hungarian-born Julius Stahel, who would in old age remember having been on Lincoln's train. It is possible that New York's Democratic governor, Horatio Seymour, another likely candidate for the upcoming presidential election, was a passenger. On this train, too, the business of politics mixed with simple good fellowship.

The "Governors' train" seemed to take forever getting to Gettysburg. It would have been "painfully tedious," one reporter grumbled, were it not for the "good cheer" and the hard liquor provided by the military, and the performance of a singing group, which was also on its way to the National Cemetery. Philadelphia's Birgfeld's Band, often anglicized to "Birgfield," also played to while away the time. The train may have been "special," but its engine broke down. Not until eleven at night did it arrive, five hours late, and then even the most distinguished visitors learned that lodgings could not be found in the small, overburdened town.

If the "Governors' train" had its problems, ordinary folks had more, yet they kept coming all the same. A Philadelphia paper had reported as early as October that Gettysburg expected "fifty thousand strangers from all part of the loyal States." "Upwards of one hundred cars will leave Calvert Station this morning," a Baltimore paper noted on the day the president and the governors traveled. "Crowds have gone from here," John P. Kennedy noted in his diary. Special trains also were leaving from both Harrisburg and Philadelphia. For days now, at least since Monday, November 16, the trains had been taking unending crowds to Gettysburg. "Interminable trains," groused a Philadelphia reporter, and by the 18th, "standing room could not be obtained in any of the cars." Only a "single thread of railroad" went into the town, complained the reporter from Cincinnati. From Hanover Junction, where the Northern Central made its connection, "this little branch of twenty-six miles, with meager rolling stock and poor management . . . was expected to convey the immense masses of people." The Gettysburg Railroad, which had made the town so very proud, was getting its comeuppance on the rails and in the press.

Problems also included thievery or worse. Trains broke down, made unscheduled stops, travelers milled about, and the newspapers started shouting about "the most systematic robbery of purses by pickpockets we ever heard of . . . thousands of dollars stolen. . . ." The "unprecedented success of the pick-pockets" led to the press angrily demanding an "explanation."

One reporter traveled the distance with the crowd packed into freight cars, the sole "passenger car proper . . . given up to the ladies." Nurse Emily Souder, returning to Gettysburg on a train for the ceremonies, wryly noted that "in the march of improvement, so manifest in various directions, the distance between Hanover Junction and Gettysburg seems to have been left quite out." People on the trains had neither light nor fire. Luckily, the rains had stopped on this November 18, "the weather moderated, and the moon shining, a succession of mitigating circumstances on which the railroad managers had no right to calculate at this season, and for which the passengers had no occasion to thank them."

American expectations had come a long way since the first trains moved at ten miles an hour while soot filled the passengers' lungs. Now people looked for the comforts of home combined with rapid travel, perhaps as much as twenty-five miles an hour. Instead, on the way to Gettysburg, the pilgrims got open freight cars and snail-pace movement. The angry Cincinnati newsman summed up: "It is but just to say that there are no railroads in the United States that comprise so many discomforts, delays, vexations, and privations to the passengers, or which exhibit so mean and illiberal spirit as the Northern Central and its legitimate offspring, the Gettysburg Branch."

Many of the passengers were relatives of the dead: "fathers, mothers, brothers and sisters, who had come from distant parts to look at and weep over the remains of their fallen kindred, or to gather up the honored relics and bear them back to the burial grounds of their native homes." Heart-wrenching tales followed each other. "I have a son who fell in the first day's fight, and I have come to take back his body, for his mother's heart is breaking and she will not be satisfied till he is brought home to her," said a man from Massachusetts. Another lamented: "My brother was killed in the charge of the Pennsylvania Reserves on the enemy when they were driven from Little Round top. But we don't know where his remains are." This soldier's home would be the new National Cemetery. "And so the mournful story" went, from one to another, "from lip to lip, each being a fresh revelation of affection wounded and bleeding." This reporter for the *Cincinnati Daily Commercial* also noted that the tears were mixed "with proud recollections that the dead had fallen in strife so noble and upon a field so glorious."

Many of the newspaper reports of the ceremonies would later stress the tragic yet uplifting atmosphere, and speak of people who came to mourn and pay their respects to the heroic dead, to listen to Everett, Lincoln, and the others. Yet from the start it became clear that many had come to have a good time. On the train to Gettysburg, young men "who were anxious to obtain seats near a party of young ladies," as Nurse Souder reported indignantly, spread the rumor that the strange smell in the car came from an amputated limb. Seats were vacated and the young men quickly took them. "It was subsequently discovered that the unpleasant odor, which seemed to give a coloring to the truth to the report, proceeded from a box of Dutch cheese."

Some on the trains where the going turned out rough found humor in their troubles. With others, one newspaper would report, "grumbling became almost mutiny." On still another train that broke down, a new engine was brought in and had to be rested every five miles. Misery led to tall-tale telling. "About every ten miles we ran back three 'to see how far we had got,' or if there was any way to keep from getting further," this reporter went. In the end, "darkness, delay, sleepiness and hunger and all other irritating influences were fairly broke down, and we became good humored from sheer force accumulated distress." That was until the travelers arrived at Gettysburg and could find no place to stay for the night.

The president's train, however, enjoyed a trouble-free ride, making its sole "lengthy" halt of eight minutes at Hanover. There, a crowd of hundreds waited, for people had been told that the president would be stopping at the junction. "Long before the hour," the local Republican paper noted, "we could see men, women, and children going hurriedly toward the depot all anxious to get a 'good look' at the President." Or, as the Democratic paper reported, the people "congregated to see the 'elephant.' " Lincoln appeared to have been less well prepared, but the crowds outside gave "cheer after cheer," making it obvious they expected to see him. He hesitated until the local preacher's voice boomed out: *Father Abraham, come out, your children want to see you!* Lincoln may have muttered something about people expecting him *"to make some remarks,"* got up, and walked out to the platform at the rear of the car. People noticed that his tall frame required that he take his hat off as he came through the door. But he would have taken off his hat anyhow. A speech he did not have, but he was used to the entertaining give-and-take with crowds. Now he provided one of his "brief, quaint," bantering speeches, and reporters took it all down.

> *Well, you have seen me, and, according to general experience, you have seen less than you expected to see.*

People laughed, and he went on.

> *You had the Rebels here last summer, hadn't you?*
> *Yes.*
> *Well, did you fight them any?*

Lincoln was still joking, but people fell silent. The "long, tall form of the president leaned from the car as he waited for the reply." None came. Fighting was no jocular matter for folk who had worried about their houses being burnt, their property stolen, who experienced the massive death and destruction around them. The day before the great battle began a few miles away, a cavalry engagement had left nineteen Union dead at Hanover. The people buried most of the men in the Reformed Church cemetery and held solemn funeral services.

No wonder an embarrassed silence greeted Lincoln now. Would any of the people here remember these words of a president, often accused of flippancy, when the dead from the church were moved to the National Cemetery the following February? The silence must have been painful.

Did Lincoln understand? The awkward moment was broken when women came forward with flowers. A young boy gave Lincoln an apple from his own yard, and would never forget. Then the time was up. People had waited for some while to see the president, but the visit turned out to be very short. "The whistle screamed, the brakes loosened, the assemblage gave one long, hearty cheer, and the car rattled up the Gettysburg Road."

The afternoon wore on. Dusk came but the moon was bright. The end of the trip approached as the train sped past a "beautiful valley, studded with substantial homesteads." Each farm, one traveler would report, was "adorned with the characteristic old German barn." A land worth fighting for. Then suddenly a hospital camp appeared. The travelers knew where they were. Crowds increased; people were everywhere, "riding, driving, promenading, loitering, or standing thickly packed."

The train came into the station, where coffins waited. So did a welcoming throng. Earlier in the day, "the last car-load of mutilated men" had left. The members of the press who had arrived before were "all on hand." The crowds had been there by the depot for days now, "on the *qui vive* for the expected dignitaries," as one reporter noted. Some got tired of waiting and left, like Nurse Souder's group, but others took their places. "Passage had almost to be forced" by new arrivals, and when the celebrated failed to show, people would be disappointed.

They were not disappointed now. The president had come. Old Edward Everett, the principal speaker, stood there to welcome him—and also to greet his daughter, Charlotte, to whom Lincoln paid special attention on the trip. Her husband, the naval captain, was the cousin of the famed former Virginia governor Henry A. Wise, now serving as a brigadier general in the Army of Northern Virginia. Henry Wise missed the Battle of Gettysburg because Lee left his brigade behind to guard Richmond. Both sides knew what "brothers' war" meant. How would Lincoln deal with that?

David Wills came to the station, as did Ward Hill Lamon, Lincoln's friend, Marshal of the District of Columbia and of the dedication ceremonies. Joe Hooker's second in command, General Darius Couch, came. As Lincoln shook the general's hand, the president might have thought it lucky that he had not sent his ugly letter after the battle questioning where Couch, commander of the Pennsylvania home-guard unit, had been. Well, he was here now, and, as Everett would record in his diary: "the president extricated from the good natured pressure, with some difficulty. . . ." The "immense crowd" backed off, and together with a company of the Invalid Corps, the dignitaries escorted Lincoln to the Wills House.

They march the short distance south toward the Diamond. The Marine Band plays. A newspaperman notes the "shimmering moonlight."

CHAPTER FOUR

CAROUSING CROWDS

Much preparation preceded Lincoln's arrival at the Gettysburg Station on Wednesday evening, November 18. David Wills had been working for two months, creating what he hoped would be an unforgettable consecration for the cemetery. The rest of Gettysburg worked, too. Josephine Forney Roedel, who now lived in Virginia, complained, "I have seen only a few of my friends, all are engrossed. . . ." All around her she saw "the greatest preparation for the consecration of a National Cemetery in G." A little star-struck, like others, she added, "never in my life will I have the same opportunity of seeing so many of the great men of the nation again." Pride, fear, and hope for profit intermingled as people expected huge crowds. "Our old town is roused up to action," a Baltimore Street resident wrote. Meetings were organized, committees created, "churches, public schools, town halls, all the private dwellings, barns, etc." planned to be opened as sleeping quarters for the thousands of expected visitors. When the great day came, some of the "most humble families" would be amazed to discover that their guests were "Senators, Congressmen, and the great men of the nation."

News of the upcoming event stirred the men of Company K at far-off Kellys Ford in Virginia. "I suppose there will be a great time there on the

19th especially to see Old Abe," Murray Miller wrote his wife Lile. He added that if people could see him as he appeared in reviews, with "60 (sixty) lb" on his back, "there would not So many want to See him." But on the 19th, Miller would be thinking of home. "O how I wish I was there, although to tell you the truth if I had my choice I would Sooner Be there when every thing was quiet, for I think I would have more Satisfaction." Still, he wished that all would go well in Gettysburg.

Jockeying to host distinguished guests could not but cause some hard feeling in the community. Young Wills reserved for himself the president, the governor of Pennsylvania, and Everett. His neighbor, *Sentinel* editor Robert Harper, got the Secretary of State and diplomats. The Democratic governor of New York and leading presidential contender, Horatio Seymour, went to a leading Democrat of the town. There were plenty of greats to go around, though some would be disappointed. Expected guests might fail to show up. One household was told to anticipate the Vice President of the United States, the governor of Maine, and the Secretary of the Navy. None of them made it. Quickly, the empty spaces filled. For this particular hostess, wife of a prominent banker, the brother of General John Reynolds, the highest-ranked casualty of the battle, had to do.

To serve as the marshal of the dedication ceremonies Wills had invited Ward Hill Lamon, Marshal of the District of Columbia, Lincoln's friend from Illinois and sometime bodyguard—a fortunate choice. Lamon considered Lincoln's protection a most important duty, but doing so in Gettysburg with tens of thousands of people milling about would be an impossible chore, either for the military or the marshals. A local sergeant, Hugh Paxton Bigham, later claimed to have had the assignment, as did another, Sergeant James A. Rebert, and the military and the marshals were there to help. But safety was not regarded a major issue by most people; certainly not by the president.

Lamon's chief responsibility was the parade and the ceremony. He proposed that the marshals, coming from the different states, dress uniformly. He suggested to Governor Curtin that "Flags be hoisted at half mast on all public buildings throughout the United States on the 19th inst." The governor so ordered for Pennsylvania. Other states, in turn, ordered flags to be flown conspicuously. Lamon asked Benjamin French of New Hampshire, the good-natured Commissioner of Public Buildings in Washington, to be

Lincoln's friend Ward Hill Lamon, Chief Marshal of the Cere-
monies. Photographer unknown. (Bradley R. Hoch)

his second. "This will be a task," French noted in his diary; but "Patriotism"
called the sixty-three-year-old. "If alive & well I shall be there. . . ."

On November 13, French and Lamon took the train to Gettysburg via
Baltimore, and found themselves traveling in the company of "hundreds of
secession prisoners." They got rooms in the Eagle Hotel and quickly went
to Wills's house to discuss the events of the 19th. Things went smoothly.
When their host told them that Longfellow, Bryant, Whittier, and George
Henry Boker had all turned down the request to write a poem for the occasion, Benjamin French's "muse volunteered." He stayed up at night to com-
pose "some rhymes for the celebration. . . . Perhaps it will be used, perhaps
not. I did my best." He left the following morning.

Then, on the 17th, French returned for the big event—but the upper-
class gentleman had been impractical enough to make no reservation to

stay. The hotels were full. He ended up as the guest of fellow Mason Robert Harper, who lived next to David Wills on the Diamond.

For nearly four days, French had a grand visit at the Harpers' and made quick friends with the sixty-four-year-old editor, who "moves about with the elasticity of a boy." Like French, Harper had a young second wife, who gave him two children to add to the ten by his first wife. Wrote French, "The whole family is remarkably hospitable and pleasant."

Mrs. Harriet Ann Harper regaled her guests for hours with stories of the battle—as did most every other eyewitness for the visitors streaming into town. Like so many other Gettysburg men, her husband had disappeared when the Confederates came, and she stayed in her house, which became a hospital. Two bullets entered it, one hitting a crib next to a wounded officer, the other whizzing past the lady of the house. A shell that had landed in the garden now sat on her parlor table—minus the charge.

As many as fifty wounded had stayed in the Harpers' house at one time, occupying it wall-to-wall with bleeding and dying men. But that gruesome subject, the disaster that overtook Gettysburg after the battle, had to be politely skirted though Andrew Cross, of the Christian Commission, also at Harper's, had been one of the honest critics. If anyone high in the government ever got a real glimpse of Gettysburg's after-battle tragedy, they said not a word about it.

The day after he arrived in town for this second time, Benjamin French toured the battlefield. So did increasing throngs. "The hills [are] alive," a reporter from the West wrote. But work had to be done to prepare for dedication day; French, Lamon, and Wills had to review for a last time the plans for the 19th. The military contingent would lead the marchers, followed by "the dignitaries" and marshals on horseback, and then the civilians. With the Marine Band at the head, and other bands sprinkled in the line of march, they would take the route of less than a mile to the cemetery, where the distinguished guests would sit on a 12- by 20-foot platform. Assigning seats was a delicate matter, as was providing a tent for the orator of the day, Edward Everett, whose kidney problems demanded such privacy.

The town was filling up, but at first the surroundings of the old Camp Letterman hospital were tranquil. Only a few of the staff still remained. Nurse Sophronia Bucklin walked the grounds; she could at last allow herself to feel tired. In the area where the hospital tents had stood, the ground was trampled, "marking where the corpses had lain after the death agony passed, and where the wounded had groaned in pain. Tears filled my eyes. . . . So many of them I had seen depart to the silent land; so many I had learned to respect *and* my thoughts followed them. . . ." Then the crowds descended, and the white tents reappeared in the old Camp to house soldiers who came to participate in the ceremonies. People kept coming; after all, they had been told that "extensive arrangements . . . have been made by the citizens of Gettysburg to accommodate those wishing to stay overnight."

By the time the president arrived on the evening of the 18th, the place was roaring. "The tranquility of the little town," Nurse Souder reported, was "completely broken up." Lincoln marched to David Wills's house and went upstairs to his room to have some time alone. Whether he rested or worked on his remarks for the next day no one knows.

After a while, he came down to the parlor and joined a large group for dinner. The president could not but be disappointed about the misadventure of the "Governors' train" that caused some of the most important politicians of the country to miss this evening. Well, there would be time later. Now, curious eyes sized up the President of the United States. He was used to it. At six feet four, he stood eight or nine inches taller than the average man. Rumors surrounded the supposedly uncouth Westerner, and a year later Everett would still see the need to assure a dinner gathering in Boston that Lincoln's "appearance, manners, and conversation" had been "gentlemanly."

The local worthies mingled at dinner with the greats of the land. The Wills House, too, had seen the battle, a subject that no doubt came up during dinner. The Provost Marshal, Marsena Patrick, had made his headquarters here and for a while the Sanitary Commission used the house, too. Of course, it had also served as a hospital. The president had another *"public opinion-bath,"* hearing what people thought, especially about politics. In crucial Pennsylvania, which had barely squeaked into the Republican column in October, every vote would count in the forthcoming presidential election. And though the press never quite got hold of who met with Lincoln at the Wills House—as one correspondent remembered, "Lincoln became invisible to us"—many important people would speak with him before his trip was finished. Thanks to the magic of the railroad, during the extended week between the Chase-Sprague wedding in Washington and the Gettysburg dedication, Lincoln put himself before many of the leading politicians of the day. It was an unusual feat for the time.

The boisterous crowds milling in the square and beyond repeatedly interrupted the dinner. Twice during the evening the president received the serenade of a military band, once that of a singing group. Loud voices called for "the President," "Old Abe," "Father Abraham," and "the Next President." Again Lincoln had to speak. Later, the Democratic *Compiler* would report that he "said he had no speech to make, and therefore made none." The *Sentinel* would not print his words either, though it characterized them as "pure and honest" as the man. The *Star*, as well as many other papers across the country, provided the president's speech that acknowledged a serenade:

> *I appear before you, fellow-citizens merely to thank you for this compliment. The inference is a very fair one that you would hear me for a little while, at least, were I to commence a speech.*

The inference was fair indeed; the president knew what the crowd wanted and he obliged them—a little.

> *I do not appear before you for the purpose* [of speechifying] *. . . and for several substantial reasons. The most substantial ot these is that I have no speech to make.*

The crowd laughed. People expected the president to be funny; they liked what they were getting.

> *It is somewhat important in my position that one should not say any foolish things if he can help it . . .*

"If you can help it," a voice rang out. The delighted crowd laughed again heartily.

> *. . . and to help it is to say nothing at all. Believing that that is my precise position this evening, I must beg you from saying "one word."*

In 118 or so words, Lincoln acquitted himself: his first Gettysburg address. The following day, he would speak in a different vein and would not need many more than twice the number of words to say his piece. This night the crowds got the bantering, vintage Westerner, funny and humble. They applauded long when he finished. Thursday, the 19th, would be another day.

Young Hay wrote in his diary: "The President appeared at the door said his half dozen words meaning nothing & went in." Lincoln knew better. He had shown the people that he was one of them. That was not unimportant. That his opponents would fault him, "the great American humorist," he also knew. And if he had even more serious purpose in coming to Gettysburg, he understood that the throngs came in no small measure to enjoy themselves. Nor would all of them make sharp distinctions. Local butcher Harvey Sweeney heard Lincoln that evening and on the next day, too, and in a letter to his brother ten days later would lump it all together as "noble speeches": "the greatest of the great men," whose words "endeared him to the hearts of the people and added thousands of friends to him. . . ."

When Lincoln went back indoors after his speech, he could hear people whooping, singing, carrying on, and going next door to serenade the next dignitary. In the Harpers' house, the Secretary of State was the most honored guest. Seward had been the president's stand-in until a few days ago. On the train, had the two men talked about what they would say? They were heading into a festive town and Seward knew that he would be asked to speak, too. He had his backup speech ready.

The two were close. Back in 1860 they had been rivals for the Republican nomination for the presidency, and even after Seward joined the Lincoln cabinet, they had to work out their relationship. But this they did, forming a remarkable political partnership until many believed that they were too close. The fact that they much enjoyed each other's company did no harm, either.

If Lincoln still had not finished his remarks for the next day, he knew that his few words of consecration would be above partisan politics. He had to speak to all Northerners, all who would give him a hearing. Many would not do that, he knew, but that could not be helped. Lincoln would try. He would speak in the broadest terms and try to give meaning to the great Civil War—for all Americans.

Seward, too, wanted to focus on the meaning of the war—Lincoln and he agreed on that—but he would be specific. He would not invoke Jeffer-

Lincoln's friend, Secretary of State William H. Seward. Matthew Brady studio, circa 1861. (Library of Congress)

son's "all men are created equal," he would speak directly about slavery. When the serenaders came and a few musical pieces were heard, he stepped out of the house, ready.

"I am now sixty years old," Seward began, but explained that never before had he spoken so close to Maryland—a slave state.

"This is Pennsylvania," someone yelled, perhaps not hearing, perhaps drunk.

"Pennsylvania," Seward repeated, and went on. For forty of those sixty years he had predicted that unless slavery was removed, it would open "a grave yard that was to be filled with brothers." Slavery caused the present "dreadful strife," but now, with Emancipation, he thanked God, "this strife is going to end with the removal of that evil. . . ."

The crowd shouted "good."

With slavery gone, the country would unite forever, "vouchsafed to us by Heaven,—the richest, broadest, the most beautiful, the most magnificent . . . that has ever been given to any part of the human race. . . . Then we shall feel that we are not enemies, but that we are friends. . . ." Then, "we shall mourn" for the Southern dead "with the same heartfelt grief with which we mourn over his brother," our loyal dead.

Seward was reaching his crescendo:

When we part to-morrow night, let us remember that we owe it to our country and to mankind that this war shall have for its conclusion the establishing the principle of democratic government . . . the freest, the best, the wisest, and happiest in the world. . . .

That government would be "immortal."

Cheers.

Fellow-citizens, good night.

Hay complained in his diary that Seward "spoke so indistinctly that I did not hear a word of what he was saying." They both may have had too much to drink. Democratic papers would later suggest, euphemistically, that Seward was having "a lively time." But so was the crowd that applauded repeatedly. Nurse Souder at least would write to her cousin that she found a place close to the speaker and "heard his remarks quite distinctly." And one of John Forney's reporters, John Russell Young, would remember that Seward "threw his sentences like clanging oracles into the night. . . . What a voice for the Ghost of 'Hamlet.' " Young, too, was having a good time, and when Seward finished, Young looked "mournfully" at the scanty notes he had taken. But as it turned out, Seward had given his text to the Associated Press to make sure it was broadcast far and wide. Clearly, he had more time than the president who had no speech to give to the press. Skeptical reporters, Young explained, kept accosting Hay asking for Lincoln's speech, and the secretary kept repeating that he had no speech to give nor had he any idea what would be in it. None knew that if people listened with care to what Seward said, they could get an idea of what Lincoln would say in his own way. The Secretary of State had delivered the speech that, most likely, he would have given at the National Cemetery, had the president been unable to come.

The *New York Tribune* reporter found Seward's speech too long, and groaned that the secretary used the personal pronoun "I" ten times. (The next day, Everett would use it twenty-six times; Lincoln none.) But in the days to come newspapers across the country would reprint the speech from the AP, often headlining it and giving it equal treatment with Lincoln's words at the cemetery. Many of the editors sensed that the two speeches complemented each other. The *Chicago Tribune* would explain that the president "means that this nation shall 'have a new birth of freedom.' Mr. Seward is still more emphatic. He denounces slavery. . . ." Not surprising, the notion got around that Seward may have written Lincoln's speech, and the English historian Goldwin Smith would have to make strenuous efforts to stop the rumors that "correspondents of the English press" spread overseas. On the day of the cemetery's dedication, or the next day (or so it would be recalled much later), someone asked Seward whether he had helped write the president's speech. The secretary demurred; only Abraham Lincoln could have written those words. But the Secretary of State thought well enough of his own effort to make sure it would be published with the proceedings of the dedication day.

Speechifying continued to liven the night, though no one else appears to have spoken as seriously as Seward. Little was recorded of what another cabinet member, Montgomery Blair, said, and for a while a local hero, Edward McPherson, the former captain of Company K and then congressman for the district, was ignored even by the local papers. In the end the *Sentinel* would comment that he spoke "in his happiest manner" to loud cheers. "There was so much to hear, and so much to record, that a very large amount has to remain unsung," Robert Harper noted, and John McIlhenny of the *Star* chimed in, "We regret that our paper is not as large as a barn-door."

Governor Seymour of New York also spoke, supporting the war—together with the Constitution, which, for those who understood, translated into opposing the "unconstitutional" Emancipation and other policies Democrats objected to. As a presidential aspirant, he tried to stay above partisan fray even as he got his message across. None recorded his "most eloquent" words which, the Democratic *Compiler* explained, were "those of a statesman, not a groveling political partisan." Much later it would be recalled that Seymour did not get a serenade, but a loyal lieutenant procured a band that "played exquisitely a number of their sweetest and most appropriate airs." The governor in turn then rose "into the empyrean of the inspired orator." Politics served as a lifeblood of public entertainment in this era before movies, radio, and television, and the Web.

Seymour's presence was significant since, with much justification, many Democrats objected to what they assumed would be mostly political proceedings in Gettysburg, a start to the president's reelection campaign. Indeed, the Republican *Sentinel*, for example, might write in one column about who the "Next President" would be, and in another right next to it, report on the preparations for the "great occasion" at the National Cemetery. The same issue of the paper told of the great flagpole on Round Top breaking in a windstorm and being quickly replaced, and also a tale of Copperheads, Peace Democrats, breaking a liberty pole in another county. Discovered at midnight, Union men "divided into squads," dragged the Copperheads into the woods, forced them to cut down a pole, haul it into town, erect it, and cheer the flag. Then "they were permitted to go to bed."

It worked the other way around, too. Even after Lincoln gave his address at the cemetery the next day, a Philadelphia Democratic paper would jeer that he "came to laugh and joke and electioneer" on hallowed ground. The same was true across the land. Politics could not be separated from the celebrations and it could all turn into naked partisanship. If the Republicans found the consecration eve's speechmaking "able, appropriate and patriotic," the local Democratic paper saw "low political tirades."

One of the speeches of the night came from Forney, who could be always relied upon and could be an excellent speaker. A few weeks earlier, leading New York politicians had beseeched him to visit and campaign for the Republican ticket there—"we urgently solicit you to come and speak for us . . . you can do us great good." But tonight, Forney was drunk. Nicolay and Hay were also drunk enough to suggest that Forney make a speech. That required finding a band to serenade him and so "request" a performance.

Getting a band in Gettysburg that night was easy enough, but meanwhile Hay began to get second thoughts as the drunken Forney "growled" and promised, "if I speak, I will speak my mind"—or so the bemused Hay recorded in his diary, once he sobered up. The band came, but Forney was not so far gone as to forget to make sure that "recorders" were in attendance. When assured of the presence of correspondents, Forney wanted to know whether they were "congenial." The coverage, after all, depended on the political slant of the newspapers.

Then he appeared to wild cheers and, in Hay's words, proceeded to "blackguarding the crowd" for insufficient gratitude to the president, "that great, wonderful mysterious inexplicable man. . . . Do you know what you owe to that Great man? You owe your country—you owe your name as

American citizens." On this night, not only the "Arch traitor Jeff Davis" received his due but also that "most corrupt organization that ever existed—the proslavery Dem. Party." Forney also babbled about how he had been actually "for Lincoln in his heart in 1860" and pretended to support Stephen Douglas only to divide the Democrats. Before he began to speak, "somebody commended prudence," but the drunk Forney replied, "I am always prudent."

Politics were alive in Gettysburg. Later, John Nicolay, who like other revelers that night neglected some part of his duties to serve as the ear of the president, remarked that one of the chief issues of the moment was "whether the President would or would not succeed himself by a renomination and reelection in the coming campaign of 1864." Thirty years later, Nicolay could not explicitly include Lincoln's speech among the evenings many political comments, though he noted that politics "rarely failed to color every word of a public speaker."

Meanwhile, if upstairs in his room in David Wills's house Lincoln wanted quiet to write out what he would say the next day, he would not have it. The noise outside penetrated everything. Perhaps around 11 p.m. he walked round the corner to visit Seward. They spent a good bit of time together; to French it seemed "about an hour." What they may have talked about in private, no one knows. Politics, maybe, or the war, or young Tad, sick back in Washington. But they were both here on business, and Seward had helped Lincoln write his Inaugural Address back in 1861, and helped at other times, too. Most likely, if Lincoln had not read Seward's speech earlier, he did so now, and the two talked about the words the chief would utter the next day.

To get back to his quarters, Lincoln had to step out of the Harpers' house into the square, and there the crowds thronged. Harper announced the President of the United States, who was greeted by "speech, speech." The "urgent calls" had to be denied. *I can't speak to-night gentlemen. I will see you all to-morrow. Good night.* Great cheering followed him as he headed over to Wills.

Did Lincoln work on his remarks after he returned to his room? Indeed, when did he write his speech? We do not know. Contradictory reminiscences, most of them recorded decades later, leave the careful student in doubt. Lincoln made two copies of his speech before adding more for charity afterwards. What appears to be the first of these has two parts, and appears to have faint traces of having been folded in three. When, we do not know. The first page is on White House stationery, written in ink, and ends in midsentence: "It is rather for us, the living, to stand here." The second page, in pencil on lined paper, completes the speech; but Lincoln had to cross out three words on the previous page to make a match. James Speed, who did not know any of this, and who became Lincoln's Attorney General about a year after the trip to Gettysburg, wrote in 1879 that Lincoln had told him that "The day before he left Washington he found time to write about half the speech. He took what he had written with him to Gettysburg, then he was put in the upper room of a house, and he asked to be left alone for a time. He then prepared the speech, but concluded it so shortly before it was to be delivered he had not time to memorize it." Speed's independent testimony neatly fits the layout of the Wills House, as well as physical evidence of the "first draft" that trumps speculation about the two pages having come from two separate versions of the speech. James's brother, Joshua Speed, in turn commented a few years later on Lincoln's "wonderful facility" to overcome interruptions and readily take up again "writing an important document . . . where he left off."

Earlier, on the evening of November 17, the day before Lincoln left for Gettysburg, William Saunders, the architect of the National Cemetery, visited the White House by invitation of the president. Saunders came in the evening to explain the plan for the cemetery. Much later, telling his story, Saunders would remember Lincoln's sincere interest in the cemetery, his approval of the equal placement of the dead, and his knowledge of Gettysburg topography. And if Speed had it right, the Saunders visit might have been a moment of inspiration, combined with a little free time in the evening, that led Lincoln to put pen to paper and begin his remarks.

Seward, Nicolay, or perhaps William Johnson may have seen Lincoln's speech before he delivered it. Nicolay recalled the expected from a first secretary—having recovered from the night's revelry, he was with Lincoln on the morning of the 19th when Lincoln wrote out the copy to be read at the cemetery. A number of others claimed, also much after the fact, to have glimpsed the speech—not impossible, but of little consequence.

Several men remembered having seen it beforehand in Washington, a more important assertion, and two deserve consideration because serious scholars had credited them. Newspaperman Noah Brooks made the first confused, even impossible claim. He insisted that he went with Lincoln to

Alexander Gardner's photographic studio on November 1 with a copy of Everett's speech. But Lincoln actually went on the 8th and Hay wrote about the trip in his diary. Some of the best pictures ever taken of Lincoln were done then, the secretary noted, including what would be later dubbed the "Gettysburg Lincoln" (the frontispiece of this book). Hay mentioned who went, "the Presdt," "Nico," himself, and a Mrs. Ames. And he added triumphantly that Nicolay and himself got "immortalized . . . by having ourselves done in group with the Presdt." Perhaps Brooks wished he had been there, too.

The physical impossibility of what he kept recalling, which was supposed to prove his closeness to the martyred president, is painful. Brooks maintained that Everett's speech appeared in a photograph taken at the time; but on November 14, a Saturday, Everett wrote in his diary that he did not receive proofs of his speech from the *Boston Daily Advertiser* until 5 p.m. that day. So if Lincoln had a copy before he went to Gettysburg, it had to have been later than November 14. Brooks also quoted Lincoln quipping about the Everett speech: "Solid men of Boston, make no long orations," and telling him that his own Gettysburg speech was "written, 'but not finished,' " and that it would be "short, short, short." In another version, Lincoln tells Brooks: "I have written it over two or three times, and I shall have to give it another lick before I am satisfied."

All of this has been very attractive to historians and laypeople alike, but Brooks also misremembered the physical layout of Everett's address, as well as the name of the paper that printed it. That over the years Lincoln had prepared notes and drafts for important communications does not mean that he had time to do so for his Gettysburg speech. Annoyed by the uncritical parroting of generations, David C. Mearns of the Library of Congress called the recollections "Brooks' fantasy." That may be a little strong, but Brooks's reminiscence does not appear to be much more trustworthy than his substantially earlier loving statement: "I am glad to say that I have a firm belief in Mr. Lincoln's saving knowledge of Christ; he talked always of Christ, his cross, his atonement." As historian Wayne Temple had written, "Lincoln mostly spoke of God and to God."

Brooks illustrates well the problem identified in the introduction to this book, that students of Lincoln have a difficult time separating themselves from their subject. If Brooks's memory stretched the truth, it is possible to imagine him visiting the White House in the morning of the 18th, though no record survives, and Lincoln showing the newspaperman the finished part of his remarks. By then even Everett's speech might have arrived, too, though the orator's diary, which recorded so many details, fails to mention his sending it to the president.

The second aspirant for the early sighting of the Gettysburg Address, Ward Hill Lamon, made such a claim for the first time in 1887: "Just before the dedication of the National Cemetery at Gettysburg, Mr. Lincoln told me he would be expected to make a speech on the occasion—that he was extremely busy and had no time to prepare. . . ." Lincoln then supposedly read to his friend "a memorandum of what he intended to say," which turned out to be much the same as what he did say. In the posthumously printed version of his memoir, prepared by Lamon's daughter, this took place "a day or two" before the dedication. The marshal was still in Washington on the morning of November 17, and if the president had something drafted by then, he could have shown it. However, Lamon's frequent unreliability should make scholars hesitant about giving him much credit, especially over Speed. Certainly the notion that Lamon learned "just before the dedication" that the president was expected to speak is ludicrous, since Lamon, as marshal, was in charge of the program and knew that if Lincoln was able to go, he would speak. The Stanford professor and great Lincoln scholar Don E. Fehrenbacher gives this recollection his worst grade, "probably not authentic."

Did Lincoln work on his remarks after he returned to his room on the night of November 18? He probably did, but we may never be certain. Did he take out the first page that he brought from Washington and, with a pencil, complete on another sheet his 239 words? Speaking much later, David Wills seemed sure that Lincoln completed his speech that evening. Before the president went over to see Seward, he had called on his host to inquire about the proceedings of the coming day, "what was expected of him." Others, too, remembered that Lincoln had with him that evening what they assumed was his speech. Wills's memory was good enough even to remember the name of his guest's "colored servant, William." This was long after almost everyone else—except the black community of Washington—had forgotten William Johnson. The young man was called to Lincoln's room. Was he there when the president completed his speech, when Lincoln wrote the words "a new birth of freedom"?

It had to be well after midnight before the president tried to go to sleep

The Wills House, the home of five or six people, accommodated thirty-eight on the night of November 19, 1863. Shown in the 1880s in this picture, the house looked much the same in 1863. Photographer William H. Tipton. (Bradley R. Hoch)

with the hubbub unabated outside. The Wills House itself was dreadfully crowded and pregnant Mrs. Wills had her hands full. Her husband had extended his generosity to all too many people. Everett would record in his diary a total of thirty-eight lodgers. Only he and the president had their own beds, and the latter almost lost his in the course of the evening. Quite late, Governor Curtin showed up—the man to whom Wills owed his prominence of that moment—only to find that all but two of the beds in the house had two or more occupants. Where was the governor to sleep? Wills looked around and followed protocol. The president must have his own bed. So he asked Everett to share his. Everett, sixty-nine, had suffered a stroke earlier and had a bladder problem. He protested vigorously and Curtin relented, leaving the house to find quarters elsewhere.

But Everett, with the long day and a two-hour performance looming, found it hard to get to sleep. "I did not get to bed until ½ past 11," he complained in his diary. "The fear of having the Executive of Penna, tumbled in upon me kept me awake until one." His daughter, Charlotte, fared worse. With two other ladies sharing her bed, it broke, and as Everett dryly noted, "she betook herself to the floor."

The venerable old giant must have had a hard time falling asleep also because of the noisy crowds outside. "They sang, halloed, and cheered," Benjamin French noted, and he himself did not get to sleep until somewhere between one and two in the morning. The town of 2,500 people had perhaps 15,000 guests, most of whom had no decent accommodations. Private homes and public buildings bulged with guests. A Baltimore correspondent wandered into a church. The wounded were gone, but what congregation was this, "sleepers, whose loud breathing and nasal accompaniments made a most inharmonious lullaby"? Some stayed in railroad cars or carriages, some ended up sleeping outdoors, and some stayed up all night. "There was so many people that there was no comfort," one Ohio woman wrote back to her husband.

A visitor might feel favored to sleep indoors on a floor or get a chair to sit on all night. That was the fate of William Saunders, as he would long remember, "celebrated landscape gardener" though he was—as the *Washington Chronicle* described him on its front page—designer of the National Cemetery, who would sit in the front row on the platform at the ceremonies the next day. A chair for him for this night's sleep. A Philadelphia "lady" wrote of "five in a bed" without explaining how that was done, of seventeen on the floor in a single room and "the floor . . . literally black with blood stains that could not be moved with scrubbing." Others felt lucky to have "boards laid upon trussels, in the kitchen of a 'hospitable' Gettysburger."

But some were not eager to get to bed. People crowded the town square, the streets, the taverns, their voices filling the night. A reporter wondered whether it was "the want of sleeping quarters" or an "irrepressible enthusiasm" that kept people celebrating. But he noted that "bands of people walked the street through the night." The morning hours still found "Bonnie Blue Flag" and "The Star-Spangled Banner" echoing "up and down the would be silent streets and lanes."

People would not forget this night. Reporter John Russell Young wrote that the place "was in chaos over the new invasion, and a corner in a tavern was a crowning mercy," while "serenading parties were bewildering the night with music." The fortunate had rooms to stay in for the night, John Nicolay added. "Restless tramping" occupied "the less fortunate."

Earlier in the day, a flag-raising ceremony around the long pole in the center of the Diamond whipped up the crowds and a New York military band gave an hour-long concert. By the evening, three different bands vied for the crowd's favor. The Maryland Musical Association, popularly known as the Baltimore Glee Club, sang "Our Army Is Marching On." Then they had the crowd join in "We Are Coming, Father Abraham, Three Hundred Thousand Strong."

In Washington and en route to Gettysburg, the song had been repeated again and again for Lincoln. Written by an abolitionist Quaker, James Sloan Gibbons, after the 1862 presidential call for 300,000 new volunteers, the tune was only a year old, but everyone in the North seemed to know the words.

> *We are coming, Father Abraham, three hundred thousand more,*
> *From Mississippi's winding stream and from New England's*
> > *shore;*
> *We leave our plows and workshops, our wives and children dear,*
> *With hearts too full of utterance, with but a silent tear;*
> *We dare not look behind us, but steadfastly before,*
> *We are coming, Father Abraham, three hundred thousand more.*

The song was long, with a long refrain:

> *We are coming, coming our union to restore*
> *We are coming, Father Abraham, with three hundred thousand*
> > *more . . .*

In the Gettysburg Diamond, the people sang on and on. Did Lincoln wonder about so many knowing all the words to the long song?

> *You have called us and we're coming, by Richmond's bloody tide,*
> *To lay us down for Freedom's sake, our brothers' bones beside;*
> *Or from foul treason's savage grip to wrench the murd'rous blade,*
> *And in the face of foreign foes its fragments to parade;*
> *Six hundred thousand loyal men and true have gone before,*
> *We are coming, Father Abraham, three hundred thousand more.*

Union, freedom, treason, foreign foes, murderous blades. Whiskey, loud voices, patriotism, and bloodlust. The night air of Gettysburg thickened with emotion. At one point when a crowd got ugly, a high-ranking military officer averted trouble by promising to lead people to still another speech. There were many quiet mourners, too, people who came from afar to say good-bye to a loved one in a fresh grave of the Soldiers' Cemetery. Some came to look for the missing. They all needed to be comforted. Many were professing Christians and could not but be insulted by what was going on. But the quiet folk did not get to sway this night of "brilliant moonlight." That is how it has been time immemorial: mourning the dead combined with rowdy celebration allowed people to feel a sense of community, doing something important, belonging together.

People celebrated. They gawked at the famous, shook hands, cheered. In Harrisburg, "on the way to Gettysburg," an Indiana man reported, "Governors and celebrities are as thickly scattered on the street as if they had been rained down like frogs." Vendors hawking a variety of things added to the carnival atmosphere. But this was Gettysburg, so "little stands on every street" sold "grape-shot, solid balls, and shell of all shapes." The Provost Marshal's threat to arrest those who sold relics was long forgotten. By 1865, the *New York Herald* would complain about "the Money Changers in the Temple."

Lincoln's two young secretaries, Hay and Nicolay, went to the College, mingled with the students, "got a chafing dish of oysters then some supper," and caroused on. The crowds wandered from tavern to tavern in torch- and gaslit streets, drinking whiskey and ale, singing songs, playing music, and listening to speeches. Like others, Hay "drank a little whiskey," so his diary recorded, "and drank more whiskey." John Forney, who "had been drinking a good deal during the day," Hay thought got "to feel a little ugly and dangerous." "Hay, we'll take a drink." One of Forney's reporters would later describe Hay as "Handsome as a peach, the countenance of extreme youth."

Forney's papers reported enthusiastically on the doings in Gettysburg, the *Washington Chronicle* in particular providing a long, evocative report, signed "J.H." Of course, nothing about drinking, wild crowds, and the like would appear in the article. Or perhaps J.H. wrote about some things candidly, but the editors cleaned up his report. A little more than three months earlier, Hay, who may well have been the author, complained to Nicolay, "I'm getting apathetic & write blackguardly articles for the *Chronicle* from which West extracts dirt & fun & published the dreary remains." J.H.'s reports from Gettysburg would be anything but dreary, but what appeared later in print would differ substantially from what lay hidden in Hay's diary.

One of the local papers made it a special point to report that "not a drunken man was seen and there was not a single street brawl among the vast assemblage of probably 30,000 people." Some out of town wrote of as many as 150,000 people being present. Josephine Forney Roedel, too, wrote that "scarcely one drunken man was to be seen." Another letter from Gettysburg made a special point of noting that "when large masses of our men congregate together, no matter to what purpose, there is quarreling, cursing, drunkenness," but here all this was absent. "Every face betokened the mournfulness of the occasion." The town had got some bad press after the battle and there would be some mixed reports this time, too, so defending it was important. But clearly friendly correspondents focused on the orderliness of the next day's ceremonies—"there was no drunkenness, no excess"—and said nothing about the subject of the evening before.

The *New York World*, on the other hand, reporting on the evening, complained of the "many who came to Gettysburg simply to have a good time, and to them it did not much matter whether the occasion was a funeral or a marriage. . . . This little village has been rocked" by a second invasion. The *Daily Courier* of Buffalo reported on "The National 'Wake' at Gettysburg . . . a relic of barbarism," a huge, joyous celebration, full of laughter, and regretted the reticence of the wire services on the subject. No doubt in addition to the visitors, many of the locals took advantage of the happy night, and if the Seminary students abstained, it is not likely that all that many College students did.

Patriotism on dress parade mingled with drunken vulgarity that night. A people under the horrendous pressure of war let out some steam. Of course, they also came for an important, solemn occasion. But that would be tomorrow. The revelry went on into the early morning hours. Nicolay sang about "Three Thieves." Almost certainly Gettysburg had many more that night. Pickpockets worked the crowds, as they would the next day, and according to "Reditus," one of the newspeople present, had "unprecedented success."

Perhaps the most frequent tune of the evening that the president, and everyone else, heard over and over again came from the Methodist hymn that Julia Ward Howe turned into the "Battle Hymn of the Republic." But the revelers used the more popular version:

John Brown's body lies a-moldering in the grave
John Brown's body lies a-moldering in the grave . . .

Back in 1859, Lincoln had denounced Brown's violence. Four years had changed much for him and for the country. In the less than sleepfull night now he had to think about the graves he would help consecrate the next day.

The president knew that he was the most famous person present for the big event and that his words would be reproduced in the press all over the North. He also knew that he would be a supporting actor, not the main performer. He was there "to help to deepen the impressiveness of the scene," as one Washington paper explained.

Mrs. Lincoln telegraphs Mr. Lincoln. (Gettysburg National Military Park)

Was he still working on his remarks when he arose in the morning? Most likely. His host, David Wills, would later write that the president composed the entire speech in his house. Similarly, Nicolay would be absolutely certain twenty-some years later that when he went to Lincoln in the morning, he was writing his speech. As the end of one century came and a new one started, the myths would grow and grow. By the end of the twentieth century, many would believe that Lincoln's 272 words "remade America."

Sometime during the evening of the 18th a telegram came from Mary Todd Lincoln: "The Dr. has just left. We hope dear Taddie is slightly better. Will send you a telegram in the morning." When Lincoln went to bed, boisterous masses still prowled the town.

> *John Brown's body lies a-moldering in the grave . . .*
> *He's gone to be a soldier in the army of the Lord . . .*
> *They will hang Jeff Davis to a sour apple tree . . .*

John Brown, John Brown, John Brown. . . .

CHAPTER FIVE

THE GETTYSBURG GOSPEL

The bugle call from Cemetery Hill awoke Gettysburg. The misty hills echoed the "matin notes" and the town got ready to consecrate the home of its dead. The cavalry climbed the hill to guard the land and soldiers fanned out around the cemetery to maintain order among the masses of humanity that crowded every road streaming toward the now sacred place. Cannons boomed their salute. A glorious sun spread its warmth. The great day had come.

The ceremonies would not start until late in the morning, and people wandered the battlefields in ever-growing numbers. Hands and skulls no longer protruded from the soil, but the rubble of war seemed everywhere. The beauty of the land overwhelmed many, but so did the graves and the places where the graves had been, the flat boards that marked the dead, the countless unknowns, the skeletons of horses, hides, "ragged and muddy knapsacks, canteens, cups, haversacks, threadbare stockings trodden in the mud, old shoes, pistols, holsters, bayonet sheaths, and here and there fragments of gray and blue jackets."

The fields had been losing their Union dead, taken one by one to the National Cemetery or back home. "Their mute disappearance is eloquent and sacred," *Star* editor John McIlhenny mused, "or have they a shape in the mists and woods, a voice on the boundary of silence, in the mystic airs that sweep over the battle field like a secret whispered by the dying into the ears of the living?" The rebels stayed in their shallow graves, condemned "in wretched bedfellowship." The sun came up higher, then disappeared, and the sky grew overcast and threatening.

The president and Secretary of State toured the fields. Lincoln's original travel plans included as much as two hours for seeing the battlefield, and this indeed was a part of the reason why he came to Gettysburg. Since the start of the war he had followed many important battles, but this one he followed with almost desperate intensity and formed very strong opinions about. Lincoln had to see the grounds. Because the dedication would be on Cemetery Hill, with its great vista, the Seminary Ridge area was his destination now. What went on in his carriage ride no one knows. If the commander in chief thought that he understood the ground well from July reports, reality turned out to be different. Back in the Diamond, a newspaperman overheard him say that he had "expected to see more woods."

Having seen something of the field of battle, Lincoln returned to his room at Wills's house and, if we can trust John Nicolay's recollection, wrote out the remarks he would make at the cemetery. He liked to take his time crafting his writing. But assembling some two hundred seventy or so words over two or three days—most likely a thirty-six-hour period— during which the words were constantly in his mind would not have been that hasty. His remarks were based on long years of accumulated learning and wisdom. Lincoln knew that he could give awful off-the-cuff speeches, but he could also rise to the occasion and work over his text before publication. His finest poetry so far had come in the emotion-laden moment when he said good-bye to his Illinois hometown to begin his presidency:

My friends—No one, not in my situation, can appreciate my feeling of sadness at this parting. To this place, and the kindness of these people, I owe every thing. Here I have lived a quarter of a century, and have passed from a young to an old man. Here my children have been born, and one is buried. I now leave, not knowing when, or whether ever, I may return, with a task before me greater than that which rested upon Washington. Without the assistance of that Divine Being, who ever attended him, I cannot succeed. With that assistance I cannot fail. Trusting in Him, who can go with me, and remain with you and be every where for good, let us confidently hope that all will yet be well. To His care commending you, as I hope in your prayers you will commend, me, I bid you an affectionate farewell.

In one piercing moment he looked at the past, the present, and the future. Back in February 1861, Lincoln had begun to write down his Farewell Address on the moving train taking him away from Springfield, but turned the task over to Nicolay, and then himself finished the final words. Most likely, he dictated to Nicolay, though they may have used a stenographic copy or Hay's notes, and Lincoln worked the text until it satisfied him.

The president would do much the same when serenaded after his re-election in November 1864, less than a year after Gettysburg. He would speak to the celebrating crowd with wisdom:

It has long been a grave question whether any government, not too strong for the liberties of its people, can be strong enough to maintain its own existence, in great emergencies.

Proving that it could be done made the election "a necessity."

We can not have free government without elections; and if the rebellion could force us to forego, or postpone a national election, it might fairly claim to have already conquered and ruined us. . . . It [the election] has demonstrated that a people's government can sustain a national election, in the midst of a great civil war. Until now it has not been known to the world that this was a possibility. It shows also how sound and how strong we still are.

Three days later, Hay noted in his diary Lincoln's comment about his reply to the serenades: "Not very graceful, but I am growing old enough not to care much for the manner of doing things." Hay, however, wrote out Lincoln's off-the-cuff speech, from which the president in turn prepared what he would read to the next group of celebrants.

Lincoln could indeed rise to the occasion. Now, on this November morning in Gettysburg, he would have the chance to write out his remarks before he spoke. It is possible that he had Everett's speech with him, and indeed in a few places the two men's words would overlap strikingly. Yet if he did, it is unlikely that the president had time to read the long oration. As

Nicolay had later testified, the Tycoon used the time available before the parade to work on his own speech.

This second draft very likely served as the reading copy, though we cannot be certain. It has no traces of folding, but one can put two sheets into a breast pocket without causing folds in the paper. The lined paper used matches the second page of the first draft that Lincoln may well have written on the night before, the page that completes the page one on White House stationery. Many years later, when John Hay, who ended up with the draft, was asked whether Lincoln held this copy as he spoke, he replied honestly: "Don't Know." The theory that the second draft was written after Lincoln returned to Washington runs aground on the absence of two crucial words from the second draft: "under God." Lincoln added these as he spoke, and if some would wrongly question the sincerity of his religious feelings, few would deny that he was a great politician. No such president would remove those crucial words from the speech after so many of his religious constituents heard it and read it in the newspapers. Such transgression would have been a scandal. Though we can not be certain when Lincoln made his minor corrections to this second draft, it is quite close to what the Associated Press would report and much of the North would read—though misprints would abound.

If Lincoln had time on his hands, he may have also practiced reading out his speech. Liberty Hollinger, then a young girl, would remember many years later how she watched the assembling parade from a house on the Diamond and noticed Lincoln coming to the window twice, looking over the crowds and holding a paper in his hands. Liberty also thought that she saw "inexpressible sadness" on his face, contrasting sharply with the excitement of the masses below.

The people in the square indeed seemed ready. But before Lincoln could move out into the teeming throng, reporters managed to work their way into the house; perhaps others did, too. The president was ready to talk. "The best course for the journals of the country to pursue, if they wished to sustain the Government," he explained, "was to stand by the officers of the army." Instead of criticizing military blunders, the people should be urged to provide "all the aid in their power."

Then Lincoln stepped out into the square, to find himself mobbed by the adoring crowd. The people greeted him with three "hearty cheers." Three more came for the "next President of the United States." This would not be lost on the Democrats in the crowd—or those who would later read reports in the press. Josephine Roedel was astounded: "Such homage I never saw or imagined could be shown to any one person as the people bestow on Lincoln. The very mention of his name brings forth shouts of applause. No doubt he will be the next President, even his enemies acknowledge him to be an honest man."

After a while the marshals, dressed in their finery, had "mercy upon his oft-wrung arm" and pushed back the throng. But the people's enthusiasm could not be controlled as they went at it once more with three cheers for "honest Old Abe," outdoing what went before. The parade had assembled. The Marine Band stood at the head, then the Second U.S. Cavalry, followed by Generals Darius Couch and Julius Stahel, with staffs, more cavalry, and artillery. Next, on horseback, came the president and cabinet members, escorted by the marshals and Generals Abner Doubleday, John Gibbon, and Horatio Wright; these were followed by state commissioners, members of the Sanitary Commission, fraternal lodge members, the delegation from Baltimore, another band, College and Seminary students and faculty members, and finally private citizens. Everett rode in a carriage, accompanied by the Reverend Thomas A. Stockton, chaplain of the House of Representatives, who would give the invocation, President Henry Baugher of the College, and Mrs. Wills. One reporter noted that flags, "plentiful" but not in "over-abundance," festooned the town, but along the route, another added, "every window and door" displayed Old Glory. The marchers, too, carried flags and banners. In the Diamond and on many of the houses, flags waved at half-staff. Guns from Cemetery Hill boomed their mourning. Joyful celebration vied with a more subdued religious feeling that began at last to take hold.

The procession started to move slowly, as in a funeral, with dirges wailing their sad accompaniment. From a far part of the line another dirge might answer "in fine confusion." Although many of the people who attended the ceremony did not march, it would take a long time to reach the cemetery, three quarters of a mile away.

"Like Saul of old he towered a head taller than any man," marveled one resident on the line of march. He saw a modest but dignified man, head uncovered, cheerful; but "an observant eye" could not miss "the dreadful responsibility" weighing on him. Here he was in his black suit, white gauntlets, carrying a hat with a mourning band on it in memory of his dead son, Willie. People bowed to the president along the route, and thought it an "honor." They also cheered him, breaking the funeral mode. "Hurrah for Old Abe"; "We Are Coming, Father Abraham"; and a solitary voice: "God save the President." The line of march stretched on and on. Gettysburg had never seen anything like it; many thought that the country had not, a magnificent mass rolling toward immortality. The *New York Times* was less impressed because so many people went first to the battlefield, or hurried to the cemetery to get a good spot for the ceremonies.

"It was a clear autumn day," Nurse Emily Souder would write her cousin. At the cemetery, "the last leaves of summer were fluttering down under the newly broken soil and over the dense crowd of thousands." But not everyone in Gettysburg celebrated the great event. The *Compiler* editor, Henry Stahle, had been arrested after the battle and his paper would reflect some hard feelings about that. An Indianapolis reporter, and so many others, perhaps hearing how decisively Governor Curtin had lost Adams County in the fall elections, commented ironically on all the local enthusiasm and flags, "as if the county were not a stronghold of rebel sympathizers." Nor was Sally Myers very sure about all the excitement. She went to see the procession, saw Lincoln and the other dignitaries, but "had little time to look at them." She went home to work rather than go on to the cemetery.

The crowd there was way too large, anyhow. It looked on the president with mixed curiosity and reverence as he climbed onto the platform. He shook hands and chatted with governors and other dignitaries while all waited for the orator of the day to come out of the tent provided for him. The bands played somber music until Marshal Lamon stepped forth to read messages from missing dignitaries: General Winfield Scott, who was too old to come; General Meade, who stayed with his army still facing Lee; and Secretary Chase, whose "imperative public duties" made it "impossible" to be present. When it grew clear that some would be too far from the platform to see or hear well, they "charged indiscriminately" upon those already close to the dignitaries. Even after the ceremonies began, some moments of disorder interfered. People tried the impossible: fit two where there was space but for one.

Band music interrupted and then brought to silence the jostling, chattering crowd. A committee of governors escorted to the stand the orator of the day, together with the famed Methodist preacher and chaplain Thomas Stockton.

The chaplain stood up, head bowed, the paper with his prayer in his hands. People's heads were already uncovered. "Oh God, our Father, for the sake of Thy Son, our Saviour, inspire us with Thy Spirit . . ." The sudden silence seemed overpowering. "Father of Moses, and the God of all comfort . . ." The moving invocation lasted perhaps eight minutes. The chaplain recounted the history of the campaign—the work of God. How proudly the victorious enemy came "to cast the chain of slavery around the form of freedom. . . . One more victory and all was theirs." The fear so many had experienced back in early July was true: If Gettysburg was lost, the war was lost.

But led by God, our heroes, too, came, and triumphed. The many who died "for us and mankind" left so many bereaved: "comfort them." "As the trees are not dead, though their foliage is gone, so our heroes are not dead, though their forms have fallen. . . . Liberty, Religion, and God." The heavy clouds that come later in the morning and persisted into the time of the procession broke and the sun began to shine. Those grieving for lost sons, husbands, fathers, sweethearts, friends—those grieving for lost countrymen—were comforted. "Our Father, who art in Heaven, Hallowed be Thy name." As Reverend Stockton finished with the Lord's Prayer, "almost the entire multitude" joined "spontaneously."

A Chicago reporter noted that the old chaplain looked as if, having communed with the Gettysburg dead, he had "just risen from the tomb to invoke the God of nations and liberty." "Never was a man" so fit for a task. People listened breathlessly. By the end, many were crying; Lincoln and Everett both wiped tears from their faces. People insulted by the carousing of the previous night were mollified. This was what they had come for. One of the carousers, however, young Hay, recorded in his diary: "Mr. Stockton made a prayer which thought it was an oration." It was four times longer than Lincoln's remarks would be. But the Reverend Stockton's words would be reported in major papers almost as often as the president's and noted in headlines.

The Marine Band started up. The majority of the talented group, led by Francis Scala, had an Italian heritage. One of the band members, Antonio Sousa, had a nine-year-old boy named John Philip. The band played "the grand old hymn," "Old Hundred," perhaps the most popular religious song of the time. Many, probably most, in the crowd knew the words. Many must have mouthed them, America's *Te Deum*:

Praise God from Whom all blessings flow,
Praise Him all creatures here below
Praise Him above, ye heav'nly host;
Praise Father, Son, and Holy Ghost.

The time for the main event of the day had arrived. There sat the venerable Everett, imposing with his white hair, the greatest orator of the land. He had been a New England minister, professor, and later president of Harvard College, with a doctorate from Göttingen, the great German university. He'd also served as a congressman, governor of Massachusetts, minister to Great Britain, senator, and Secretary of State. His orations about Lexington, Concord, Bunker Hill, the great shrines of American liberty, made him famous nationally, the heir of Daniel Webster.

Much later, John Russell Young wrote of obtaining what seemed like an audience, not an interview, with Everett at Gettysburg. "The antique, courtly ways, fine, keen eyes, a voice with a singular charm, old-fashioned tones of pronunciation, perhaps only old-fashioned to our uncouth ears; the soft white hair, sunny, silken, clinging, and that caressed handkerchief. . . . He was the embodiment of a noble and stainless fame." To the reporter's "young revering eyes," Everett, sixty-nine years old, seemed to step out "from a sacred past."

In the 1850s he had added to his laurels by giving a speech about "The Character of George Washington." He traveled from Maine to Mississippi, spoke to 129 paying audiences, and donated his royalties, nearly $70,000, to save the embarrassingly dilapidated home and grave of Washington. The Father of the Country served Americans as a great symbol; Everett's work to save Mount Vernon also symbolically tried to save a Union that seemed to be falling apart. He generally delivered his orations to immense and enthusiastic audiences. On one occasion in New York City, when he was to speak at the Academy of Music, which could seat 7,000, the throngs left outside rioted, ran past the doorkeepers, filling the aisles and even the stage. Years later, the famed author Richard Henry Dana, Jr., in his eulogy for Everett, would say that the Washington speech had been heard by more people than any other "since the beginning of time."

In 1860, Everett ran against Lincoln on the Constitutional Union Party's Bell-Everett ticket. Their only stated goal was to save the Union and the Constitution. Everett had strong antislavery views, but kept them quiet; peace and union trumped all. He made many very angry at him because of this. Many Republicans came to despise him and some of the reactions to his address at Gettysburg would show that hatred could last long.

Yet the war began with a goal of restoring the "Union as it was"—that is, with slavery intact. The Massachusetts giant did not think much of Lincoln at first: "He is evidently a person of very inferior cast of character, wholly unequal to the crisis." Still, Everett supported the Union and started on a new speaking tour on the causes of the war, blaming it on slavery. Not everyone loved him, but his old fire continued to burn bright. After hearing him speak in Brooklyn, the great preacher Henry Ward Beecher came up to him excitedly, saying that Everett's oration made him want to enlist. "Something of a compliment," Everett wrote to his son, coming "from a person so completely *blasé*;—and altogether and the *'nil admisere'* school."

Lincoln courted Everett. In 1862, hoping to send him as an emissary to Europe, he wrote a letter of introduction for him saying that "I am quite conscious that he could better introduce me than I him," and assuring Everett that the president valued him as much as a cabinet member. Everett would not go. Nor did he like the idea of the Emancipation Proclamation, firmly antislavery though he was, because it would not actually free slaves and would endanger the loyalty of the border states. Lincoln issued that Proclamation on January 1, 1863. Sitting now next to Everett on the Gettysburg platform, did the president wonder what the orator would say? Would he speak about the Constitution and its guarantee of state sovereignty? Would he speak in favor of the "Union as it was"? Would he, even implicitly, disavow Emancipation? Would he project the optimism the country needed?

Lincoln knew what the people needed. However disappointed he may have been about what he saw as the incomplete outcome of the Battle of Gettysburg because Lee's army had escaped, Independence Day, 1863, seemed like a miracle to so much of the North. Gettysburg and Vicksburg: a Living God had shown His mercy to America. The turning point of the war had come; victory and peace were in sight. But then, as the war went on and the end still seemed just out of reach, the memory of that Fourth of July could not be allowed to fade. Its treasure had to be kept alive to give strength to the people to continue to shoulder the burden of war. "The power of hope," Lincoln knew, was all-important. But Everett had not spoken optimistically about the war.

If the president worried about Everett's speech, he did not show it. Nor did he need to. The orator gave his usual storied performance for two hours. People expected a long address; they came from near and far and looked forward to a memorable event, one free of charge. A two-hour oration was about right.

Everett knew he was the greatest orator of the land. He knew that great expectations awaited him. Even Forney's paper made clear that the president would be the extra, that Everett was the star, that his oration "will probably be the finest production of his life. What a wonderful man is Edward Everett!" The orator knew, too, what should be said. He would recount the "terrible and glorious" history of the battle; explain its meaning; not really touch the horrors; include religion, women, and black people; and look with hope to the future. Even as he modestly explained that, given the time limitations, he could not do "anything like full justice to the all-important events," he would give perhaps the most significant address of a grand lifetime.

Everett researched the subject with care and got much help from the staff of General Meade. He also asked General-in-Chief Henry Halleck, for information not openly available, "if the public service will permit . . . facts . . . of interesting character." He repeatedly discussed the battle with John B. Bachelder, who showed him the "beautiful and minute" drawings he had made of the site that would be engraved into a map. He checked Lee's official report in the *Richmond Enquirer*, a "well-written article, purporting to be an account of the three days' battle," and compared it to what Meade's staff sent, finding it "equally striking & painful to see the different manner in which the very same incidents are related" by the two. Of course he chose to credit the Northern account, though, as it later grew clear, he could not examine Meade's official report with care until after the trip to Gettysburg because it was only then made public. Everett even looked abroad to consult an article from *Blackwood's Magazine.* In his speech he would also mention "the astonishingly minute, accurate, and graphic accounts" of many brave reporters. When his Gettysburg Address was published as a pamphlet, Everett would send it to all who had helped him.

Professor Jacobs would earn special thanks in Everett's speech; the two had corresponded, and with Everett in town, the Gettysburg professor "kindly dismissed his class" so they could tour the battlefield. A black driver had guided their carriage. He was a "contraband," a man who escaped from

Professor Michael Jacobs of the College, the author of a history of the battle, helped Everett with his speech. Photograph by Tyson Brothers, 1862. (Gettysburg College)

slavery to freedom. The tour showed rebel dead between the Round Tops covered only with rocks, for there was no dirt to throw over them.

The scholar from Harvard wanted to be one of the first definitive historians of the battle, though researching Gettysburg convinced him more than ever "how uncertain accounts of great battles must be." But he wanted, too, to be more than a historian. An old man now, who would die in not much more than a year, he reached for supreme oratorical heights. His grand speechmaking tours before the war, like so many other efforts, had failed to keep the Union safe. Now he had the incomparable opportunity to help save it yet by holding up in glory the great Battle of Gettysburg that had been fought for America's democratic ideals. As a young man, Everett had tramped the fields of Greece's ancient glory. In a long lifetime he taught America the greatness of the example of Greece. Now he would use his learning to do for his countrymen what the ancients did for Athens.

The newspaper reporters—there was at least one woman among them—could give themselves over to enjoying Everett's performance. They had his speech already. They knew it would begin with words about Athens. Everett, in turn, knew that his address would be reproduced, or summed up with telling quotations, across the North. In large city newspapers and small country ones hundreds of thousands of Americans would read his words, often aloud to their families. For Everett, the great moment had arrived.

Two chief authoritative versions of his speech exist. One is handwritten, with corrections in Everett's hand; the other is the official printed copy that he shepherded to publication. He would donate the handwritten copy to the New York Metropolitan Fair in the spring of 1864, the gift including across each handwritten page the corresponding page of the printed official version. A map of the battlefield, a diagram of the cemetery, and handsome prints of Governor Curtin and numerous generals would also grace the manuscript. Everett even procured a copy of Lincoln's speech for the same charitable purpose. In a "Note" that accompanied the manuscript, he would explain that the text differed from the official printed version because the manuscript had been completed before General Meade's report of the battle came out. Everett then made his corrections and by early January 1864 had the address at the printer. Other differences between the manuscript and official versions, though many are minor, abound (see Appendix A).

The handwritten copy then appears to be the text that he took to Gettysburg and that is quoted here. Still, what exactly Everett said, we do not know. In addition to Everett's corrections, the manuscript contains numerous passages in brackets, perhaps marking parts to be left out of the oral delivery. Since he had sent the text of his oration to the press some time before he began his trip to Pennsylvania, reporters evidently took no notes; and as his "Note" indicated, "about one third was omitted in the delivery on account of length."

Before him now at the cemetery the thousands of men, women, and children all wanted to see but certainly hear. They heard more or less, mostly depending on where they stood. "Every word . . . must have been heard by them all" was the identical opinion of the *Star* in Gettysburg and the *New York World* and *New York Times*. On the other hand, the reporter from Indianapolis ventured that "very few" heard, "though full 20,000 came for nothing else." Those who did not hear presumably wandered off to see

the battlefield. The *Washington Chronicle* guessed that some stayed "just enjoying the scene."

As Everett began, the reporters must have perked up.

> *Standing beneath this serene sky, overlooking these broad fields now repos-*
> *ing from the labors of the waning year, the mighty Alleghenies dimly towering*
> *before us, the graves of our brethren beneath our feet, it is with hesitation that I*
> *raise my poor voice to break the eloquent silence of God and Nature.*

This was not how the address was supposed to start. The orator who
carefully wrote and revised his speech, who polished it to perfection and
memorized it word for word, allowed Gettysburg, or this very moment, to
overcome him. Poetry and humility gushed out of him.

But as he began, disorder broke out in one area as people jostled to get a
better spot. The marshals on horseback, could not get there because the
crowds proved too dense. But Everett's magic quickly captured people so
that they quieted and thereafter stood in "breathless attention." Tightly
packed as they were, breathing must indeed have been difficult for some.

Nurse Souder politely noted in a letter to her cousin that "the crowd
was excessive." "There was no place allotted to the ladies"—though plans
had been made for that. Nurse Bucklin spoke more forcefully: people
"seemed packed like fishes in a barrel. . . . We stood, almost suffocated."
The personnel from Camp Letterman hospital came together. The ceremonies "had to *us* a deeper interest than to many," Anna Holstein, who had
run the kitchen with an iron hand, would later write; "many of the quiet
sleepers, by whom we were surrounded, we had known, and waited upon
until care no longer was needed." Only the hospital director, Dr. Henry
Janes, had a place on the platform. He deserved the place more than most,
but there were few women up there.

Everett spoke in a clear voice that carried far. He knew that until now
Americans considered Gettysburg their Waterloo, recalling the most famous battle of modern times in which Wellington and his allies defeated
Napoleon. Everett now spoke of Marathon, reaching deep into time and
myth to the Athenian defeat of Persia that saved democracy. "As it depended
upon the event of that day whether Greece should live, a glory and a light
to all coming time, or should expire like the meteor of a moment. . . ." At
Marathon, the Greeks "rolled back the tide of Persian invasion . . . the dark

banner of Asiatic despotism, and slavery. . . ." Their fallen "martyr-heroes" received honors no other Athenian did: "They alone of all her sons were entombed upon the spot which they have forever rendered famous." All in the audience, and later the readers of the speech, understood: this was their country, the new Athens, that Everett spoke of.

Classical history had grown into common knowledge for Americans long before the Civil War. If the Revolutionary generation still looked to Rome as its model, the nineteenth century cited the example of democratic and learned Athens. America would become a second Athens. This idea that captured the country grew most visible in architecture. The "Greek Revival" style dominated city, village, and farm. When the College in Gettysburg built its main "edifice" in the 1830s, or when the Lincolns enlarged their house in Illinois in the 1850s, "Greek Revival" came as a matter of course.

Christianity and the ancient pagan Greeks might have made for an uneasy mix, but the Europeans of the Renaissance (as the Muslims before them) made the symbiosis work. Americans took the combination to great heights. The religious might lament the paganism of the ancient Greeks, but many loved their writings and regarded their deportment and democratic government as models. Everett illustrated these sentiments well.

Now, at the cemetery, with classical setting drawn, Everett turned to the present moment and the present place. The rebellion that raked the United States had been planned for decades and the goal of capturing the city of Washington loomed long. The rebels had wanted it from the start of the war. The campaign that led to Gettysburg aimed at capturing the capital, and other major cities, but the able General Joseph Hooker frustrated it. When the maneuvering for Washington turned into an invasion—perhaps against General Robert E. Lee's wishes—the rebels got pushed west to Shepherdstown and Williamsport.

The orator seemed to show some respect for Lee but only contempt for the famed Confederate horseman, J. E. B. Stuart, whose cavalry was "severely handled" by Alfred Pleasanton. Stuart's cavalry was cut off from Lee for a "fortnight" and became useless. Still, following a brigade of raiders, the entire enemy army—some 105,000 men—crossed into Pennsylvania. All knew "that a great battle must soon be fought."

As Everett started on his military history, the audience must have been transfixed. After major battles, newspaper circulations soared perhaps five times above normal. The war was alive to the people. But if most in the audience would not be able to judge how accurate a history they heard, they did want to hear of the glorious victory. Some had strong opinions about what took place on the battlefield and would voice them before long. As Everett spoke, he pointed to different parts of the field.

George Meade took over the army, with great skill, and took after Lee. From Gettysburg, people saw the mountains "lighted up at night by the camp fires of the enemy's advance, and the country swarmed with his foraging parties." Then "the momentous day, a day to be forever to be remembered in the annals of the country, arrived."

Everett divided his history of the battle into four parts, each day receiving about equal time, the "Aftermath" more. The First Day saw the Union cavalry under General John Buford "warmly engaged," but General John Reynolds arrived, got into the fray, and at the head of his troops fell mortally wounded. Then Abner Doubleday took command of the First Corps, and the newly arrived O. O. Howard of the entire field. Numerous generals were mentioned on both sides: the heroes of the North, and the losers and the champions of the enemy, not least among them Jubal Early, whose arrival turned the fortunes of the first day against the Union army. But the well-prepared Howard, who had sent a large number of men to occupy Cemetery Hill, withdrew them in good order, even if the Eleventh Corps and part of the First, as it tried to retreat "through Washington and Baltimore Streets," got caught and took heavy losses.

Sent by Meade to take command, Winfield Scott Hancock arrived, and together with Howard fortified Cemetery Hill. Soon the men repulsed a feeble attack on their right. Nightfall saw Union reinforcements arriving. "Success to our arms, followed by a reverse, but ending in the occupation of this all-important position," summed up the day.

Everett did not neglect the local people; spoke to them as "you," who saw the dead and wounded, the prisoners, "the wanton burning" of a home, and the enemy taking their town. "You passed the anxious hours of the night in feverous expectation." By the end of the speech he would speak of "friends, fellow-citizens of Gettysburg." Everett added the name of the town to his manuscript as an afterthought and later, for the official version, removed "the wanton burning." Visiting Gettysburg helped to clarify his story.

The Second Day:

*The full moon shone down that night on a strangely unearthly scene. The si-
lence of the grave-yard broken by the heavy tramp of armed men; by the neigh of
the war-horse; the harsh rattle of the wheels of artillery hurrying to their stations; and all the roll of the drum, and all the indescribable tumult of preparation.*

Troops continued to arrive; General Meade, too, who decided to stay and
fight.

As the two armies positioned themselves on opposite ridges a mile to a
mile and a half apart, rebel lines extended beyond the wings of the Union
lines. Everett used broad gestures as he pointed to positions on the field. He
spoke beautifully. The Army of the Potomac, "probably" outnumbered by
more than ten thousand, had half of its men exhausted by the previous
day's fight, half by the forced marches to Gettysburg. On this second day,
"nothing but a miracle could have saved the army from great destruction."
But the miracle came in "the providential inaction of the Rebel army." If
Everett's numbers did not exactly add up, few seemed to know or care.

Fighting resumed in late afternoon with rebel brigades attacking, one
after another, from right to left, on to the center. Daniel Sickles, having
moved forward to better his position, brought on "the critical moment" of
the day. The furious attacks of James Longstreet and A. P. Hill's troops,
however, were stopped by Union reinforcements. "By sunset the enemy was
driven back in confusion."

"Important service" of the Pennsylvania Reserves between the Round
Tops deserved special notice: "One company was from this town and neighborhood." When the time came to print the address for posterity, "Important service" became "The most important service." Talking with the
people of Gettysburg left its mark here and there. Only a minor rebel success marred this second day on the weakened Union right, where Ewell got
a "foothold." The address went into some detail, but the mourning relatives
of the dead surely wanted, if anything, more; they wanted the deeds of their
heroes remembered.

The Third Day began with Union forces reinforcing the right wing, redeeming the losses of the previous night. After the "cheering commencement" came a long pause. At last, "the awful silence, more terrible than the
wildest tumult of battle was broken." Two hours of "a cannonade of unsurpassed violence" followed from 250 guns. Then came the "last grand as-

sault" across the plain, men moving forward "with equal spirit and steadiness." The best of the Confederate army, including George G. E. Pickett's elite division, charged and failed—" 'a determined and gallant struggle,' " in the words of General Lee. From among the participants in "the prodigious slaughter" at the center, special notice went to the Second Corps, Abner Doubleday's division, and George Stannard's brigade. Everett mentioned the names of numerous generals that most of the listeners were familiar with from news reports. The wounded on the Union side included Hancock and John Gibbon; on the rebel side, Lew Armistead, mortally; James Kemper, J. J. Isaac Pettigrew, and Isaac Trimble. Richard Garnett was killed.

And so in summation: the Confederates brought superior numbers led by their ablest commanders; had the initiative in "choosing time and place"; and carried along "the prestige of former victories over the army of the Potomac." The Union had the stronger position. Its victory, "under Providence," had to be ascribed to patriotism and to "the consciousness that they were fighting in a righteous cause."

On the Fourth Day, heavy rains came. Having lost some 37,000 men, Lee withdrew rapidly—"sad celebration of the 4th of July for an Army of Americans." The battle had resembled Waterloo and if, like the Duke of Wellington, Meade had received major reinforcements, "the rout of the Rebels would have been as complete as that of Napoleon." As it was, with Lee protected by the easily defensible mountain passes, the Confederates reached Williamsport safely "and took up a strong position . . . on the heights of Marsh run." Meade got there on the 12th and with the Potomac swollen by rains, a battle loomed. But when he advanced on the 14th, Lee was gone, having left behind a third of his army, including 7,450 wounded. These men received "the Christian care of the victors . . . Heaven forbid, however, that I should claim any merit for behaving with common humanity."

It was useless to minimize the rebel disaster, as some tried. None could gainsay the magnitude of what took place at Gettysburg, the tremendous casualties on both sides. The names of the generals killed and wounded made a somber list; so did the numbers of soldiers and officers killed, wounded, and missing. They made clear that "not one of the great conflicts of modern times has cost victors and vanquished so great a sacrifice." As Wellington had said, "next to a defeat, the saddest thing was a victory."

On the horrors of the battle, no witness "can bear to dwell." The drop of balm that made the aftermath more bearable came from "the brethren and sisters" who arrived as soon as the fighting ended, bringing relief to the suffering. Christian hearts came to "moisten the parched tongue, to bind the ghastly wound, to sooth the parting agonies alike of friend and foe, to catch the last whispered message of love from dying lips." Everett had been given Georgy Woolsey's account of her three weeks of nursing after the battle, and wrote in his diary: "Nothing can exceed the energy and perseverance of these 'Sisters of Charity.' " Now, having spent several days in Gettysburg, was he at least a little aware of the disaster that befell the battle's wounded?

Women, he declared, deserved the highest admiration for taking over duties at home and for ministering to the casualties. In the Sanitary and Christian Commissions, they "rendered services as such millions could not buy." Christ's words came to mind: " 'Inasmuch as ye did it unto one of the least of these, my brethren, ye did it unto me.' " Many decades had gone by since Everett's ordination as a Unitarian minister and, as people will do, he mixed up some of the words he quoted from the Book of Matthew. Many in the audience knew their Bible well—Lincoln did—but none showed that anything was amiss. Back home, Everett would find the accurate text and put it into the official version of the address. Nor did any who might have found some irony in hearing on a battlefield these words from the Gospels comment on the matter. As for the many women in the audience, they surely took special notice of these kind sentiments about them. Lincoln did, too. So would the press. Yet, as men spoke of the "angel" women, did any wonder whether such admiration also had a downside?

With the history of the battle and the longer part of the address done, Everett moved on to the relationship of the rebellion to the Constitution. Speaking to a devout people, he introduced the subject via religion. "The litanies of every church in Christendom" implored deliverance from "sedition, privy conspiracy and rebellion." Rising up against tyranny was acceptable, but rising to extend and perpetuate "injustice and wrong" was not. It was an awful crime. It was like the rebellion of the " 'Infernal Serpent' " against God.

Everett marshaled classical learning, too, interspersed with Latin phrases, to support philosophically his argument against rebellion. He contrasted " 'the *Conditores Imperiorum*, founders of States and Commonwealth,' " who nobly united people, with *"Eversores Imperiorum,"* the selfish destroyers of states. If some eyes glazed over before such learning, others were surely impressed by the mighty scholarship. If, as the two hours stretched by, some people fidgeted, whispered, wandered off among the graves and over the fields, most listened respectfully and with interest.

Everett went on to put forth a wonderfully original argument against the constitutional right to secession. He was nearing seventy, not far from the end of his days, but his mind remained sharp and innovative. To maintain that the Constitution made the Union perpetual, he was able to rely on a literal, strict reading of text—something neither Lincoln nor the secessionists had been able to do, however much they might have wanted to. The Constitution, after all, seemed silent on the question. In the Cooper Union speech of 1860, Lincoln had mostly appealed to the original intent of the founders; in the First Inaugural Address, he relied on history and theory. John C. Calhoun, and his disciples, in turn had theorized that the federal government was an agency of the states and therefore the states could leave the Union if they wished.

Everett proclaimed this "simple nonsense." His counterargument was simple, too, but strong: the states, all their officeholders, took an oath to the Constitution that empowered the U.S. government; the government did not take an oath to the states. Which was the agent of which, then? One can just see the lawyer Lincoln straining with all his power, absorbing with pleasure every word. Everett may have rendered the history of the battle with less than full accuracy—truth was elusive—but here he produced something new, something needed. If the brackets he put around parts of his manuscript were meant to identify places where the oration might be cut, he did not follow the markings as he spoke from memory. He bracketed his constitutional arguments—heavy going for many, no doubt—but the next day the president would write to the orator to say that "The point made against the theory of the general government being only an agency" of the states is "new to me, and, as I think, is one of the best arguments for national supremacy."

Everett next moved on to politics and world history. The country had read much about the possibility of negotiating a truce with the Confederacy, but he knew that the president stood firm against stopping the war. So did Everett now. As for permitting independence to the rebels, he affirmed that it would amount to "hideous national suicide." In many parts of the South, "the great majority of the people are loyal to the Union"; not one of the states would have seceded had there been a ballot "without fear or favor." There must have been some among the listeners who wondered whether this was true. Giving in to the rebels who refused "to quarter colored troops," the orator went on, now would return black people to bondage, "thousands of whom are periling their lives in the ranks of our armies." It would mean surrendering loyal men, "white or black," to the worst terror. Indeed, terror served as the enemy's "chief instrument." Everett was repeating some of Lincoln's arguments.

The future looked bright. However much "the Rebels and those who sympathize with them" claimed that reconciliation was impossible—it would come. Civil wars were fought with "peculiar bitterness," but America might boast that this war was different.

I do not believe there is, in all history, the record of a civil war of such gigantic dimension where so little has been done in the spirit of vindictiveness as in this war, by the Government and commanders of the United States.

This held true in spite of the rebel government's abuses. Two of the examples of such abuse touched local nerves especially because the Gettysburg area experienced both: "selling into slavery free colored men from the North who fall into their hands" and the mistreatment of prisoners.

History showed that even after the bitterest wars, people only want to "bind up and heal all those wounds." ("To bind up the nation's wounds," Lincoln would say in his Second Inaugural Address.) So it had been in England after the Wars of the Roses and the Puritan Revolution; in Germany after religious and dynastic wars; in Italy, where "Dante was able to fill his imaginary hell with the real demons of Italian history"; and in France, where century after century of wars led to the Jacobins and the guillotine but, in the end, to peace. So America would surely find reconciliation. So much bound the people together; what divided them was "imaginary, factitious and transient. The heart of the people, North and South," Everett confidently announced, *"is for the Union."*

Lincoln must have nodded as Everett spoke about reconciliation, for it gave scholarly historical foundations to what Lincoln himself had said a year earlier: "Our strife pertains to ourselves—to the passing generations of men; and it can, without convulsion, be hushed forever with the passing of one generation." Everett considered his discussion of reconciliation to be original, and the most important part of his address. The opportunity to point out to the country, and Europe too, that "a civil war, does not prevent the restoration of harmony when the war is over," served as one of the reasons for him to come to Gettysburg. Even before receiving the invitation, he was thinking about the idea. Weeks after delivering his address, he thought wishfully about a lecture tour focusing on this subject; but his health would not permit it. Sitting on the platform behind the speaker, John Forney, now sober, thought that Everett "looked like a prophet of old" as he spoke of reconciliation and every heart added "Amen."

Then the conclusion came. The great moments of American history had been surpassed at Gettysburg, Everett proclaimed. Striking words from the orator made famous by his speeches about Lexington, Concord, Bunker Hill, and Washington. A new height had been reached. The blood of the brave men who fell on this land made the Union more precious than ever.

> *Seminary Ridge, the Peach-Orchard, Cemetery, Culp, and Wolf Hill, Round Top, Little Round Top, humble names, henceforward dear and famous—no lapse of time, no distance of space, shall cause you to be forgotten.*

Everett spoke to "you," the land around him, and surely pointed, and then returned for a moment to ancient Greece:

> *"The whole earth," said Pericles, as he stood over his fellow-citizens, who had fallen in the first year of the Peloponnesian War, "the whole earth is the sepulchre of illustrious men." All time, he might have added, is the millennium of their glory.*

So it would be for this sacred land here:

> *wheresoever throughout the civilized world the accounts of this great warfare are read, and down to the latest period of recorded time, in the glorious annals of our common country, there will be no brighter page than that which relates THE BATTLES OF GETTYSBURG.*

"Down to the latest period of recorded time." Surely many in the audience thought, so it would be. Lincoln knew those words; they echoed *Mac-*

beth, his favorite play. The United States at last had its life-saving battle. If the president valued that battle less highly, saw it as not all that it might have been, he also knew that Everett's view would help the nation live "down to the latest period of recorded time." As the speech ended, the president jumped up to shake the orator's hand with "great fervor." "I am more than gratified, I am grateful to you."

Everett had been placed in a physically awkward position as he spoke, with the dignitaries of the platform behind him and the people before him. The *New York World* remarked that he "was obliged either to turn his back upon the audience or the President." Everett compromised, turning sometimes to his audience, sometimes to the president. Lincoln had listened intently and twice interrupted when the orator mixed up the names of Generals Lee and Meade. The others on the platform, too, watched with undivided attention.

Now it was almost Lincoln's turn to say his few words. Two hours, however moving and enjoyable, was a long time. With the main event of the day done, people stretched their limbs, moved about, talked loudly, relaxed. They also knew that the president would speak soon.

Before that came another musical interlude, the Ode or "Consecration Chant" composed by Benjamin French. Set to music by Wilson G. Horner, the head of the Maryland Musical Association, his singers would perform it now. French had published poems before, but here he stepped into the place of major voices of the time. His nerves had to be taut; this was the great test before thousands.

Then the choir chanted his words: *This holy ground . . . Let tears abound . . . a thousand years shall pass away, a nation still shall mourn this clay— The soil is blest.* In a few minutes the choir finished; the applause was thunderous.

At the beginning of the day's program the audience seemed reluctant to applaud; indeed, the proceedings seemed in many ways like a church service. After all, consecrating a burial ground has been a solemn occasion since time immemorial. When Lincoln arrived, he had been greeted with "perfect silence" and people uncovering their heads. When Everett was introduced, someone called out for three cheers for the orator, only to be greeted with silence. The reporter who signed his name "J.H." called the man "Mr. Idiot," someone who did not understand the occasion. After Everett finished, once again deeply respectful quiet greeted him. French's ode changed the mood completely. Great applause greeted the glee club's performance and the lighter mood would continue for the rest of the day, broken momentarily only by the final dirge and benediction.

When the crowd quieted, Marshal Lamon belted out, "Ladies and Gentleman, the President of the United States," and there he was, already standing. Everett had spoken from memory. Lincoln had on reading glasses and held his speech in his hands. The applause subsided. We will never know the exact words he used, but the minor variations that would come down to posterity did not change the substance of what he said—not for the people at the cemetery or for the host who would read his words in the newspapers:

> *Four score and seven years ago our fathers brought forth upon this continent a new nation, conceived in Liberty, and dedicated to the proposition that all men are created equal.*

The crowd applauded. He had been invited to make a few "remarks" that would console "the many widows and orphans" and also "kindle anew in the breasts of the Comrades of these brave dead" a confidence that their dead "are not forgotten." Now he was trying to do that, and more. Some had urged on him the need to tell the people why they had to go on with this horrifying war, and his rarely erring sense told him that the need was there. Here he was giving the first prepared speech since his inauguration day, more than two and a half years earlier.

Back in July of 1863 his instinctive reaction to the greatest of battles was to look back into history, to 1776, and to Jefferson's words. Facing the horrendous casualties, "the success" and "the want of success," he looked for the meaning of America with impromptu awkward words. "How long ago is it?—eighty odd years—since on the Fourth of July for the first time in the history of the world a nation by its representatives, assembled and declared as a self-evident truth that 'all men are created equal.' "

As he found those words, his mind wandered back to another crucial moment of his life, the carefully crafted speech that he gave at Peoria, Illinois, in 1854, marking the start of his antislavery crusade. "Near eighty years ago we began by declaring that all men are created equal," he said then. Even before the speech at Peoria, his eulogy for Henry Clay, his "beau idéal" of a politician, began: "On the fourth of July, 1776 . . ."

The words of the Declaration of Independence had stayed on Lincoln's lips from the 1850s into his presidency. After he decided to go to Gettysburg, his thoughts returned to those lines. If he could not find time to put words on paper almost until he had to speak them, the thoughts he now expressed had churned in him for a long time. Even over the short run, as Nicolay would explain, "he probably followed his usual habit in such matters, using great deliberation in arranging his thoughts, and moulding his phrases mentally, waiting to reduce them to writing after they had taken satisfactory form." His whole life prepared him for Gettysburg. Ideas, phrases, rattled around in his head, and the pressure of the occasion brought them forth.

July 4, 1776, had been much on the mind of Americans at least since the 1820s. Abolitionists appealed to the words in the Declaration of Independence and called for the end of slavery. The many moderates also exalted the words, giving them a different meaning. Perhaps for most Americans, "created equal" meant by the middle third of the century the God-given right to rise in life: equality of opportunity. But every Fourth of July resounded with words from '76. Lincoln's friend James C. Conkling, to whom the president had sent his August 1863 public letter defending Emancipation and the use of black troops, began a July speech in 1857: "Four score years have elapsed since that memorable Declaration of Independence. . . ." Conkling, like countless others, easily mixed religious and classical references. July 4 was a day "as in Judea" when "its ancient tribes annually repaired to their magnificent temple . . . as in Rome. . . ."

Everett concluded his July 4, 1860, oration by declaring that "The question decided eighty-four years ago in Philadelphia *was* the greatest question ever decided in America; and the event has shown that greater, perhaps, never was nor ever will be decided among men. . . . The great Declaration, with its life-giving principles" had covered the continent, "crossed the land and the sea, and circled the globe." Like so many of the best American minds, Everett, too, thought in universal terms. "If it is the will of Providence that the lands which now sit in darkness shall see the day," the world will be "regenerated" and even "the ancient and mysterious regions of the East, the cradle of mankind," old Mesopotamia, "shall receive back in these later days from the West the rich repayment of the early debt of civilization." "Constitutional freedom" would reign everywhere.

As Everett listened now, he may have understood Lincoln's words in such terms. Like Everett, Lincoln believed that the Civil War would save or destroy America, and with it constitutional democracy. But what Lincoln meant now by "democracy" went far.

He certainly meant to include immigrants or children of immigrants, who made up perhaps a quarter of the Union army. Lincoln hoped that the promise of the Declaration would embrace them, make them feel part of the American birthright. "They have a right to claim it as though they were blood of the blood, and flesh of the flesh of the men who wrote that Declaration," he had said at the start of his debates with Douglas in 1858, "and so they are."

But quoting the Declaration of Independence in November 1863 cut much deeper: it defended the Emancipation Proclamation that had drastically changed the character of the war. It presented a strong message about liberty, without speaking of slavery outright and so alienating many. If Lincoln did not mention by name the great "evil," he knew that others would be explicit on the subject, as he had been on so many other occasions. Seward had already spoken the night before, and when he would receive congratulations on his words, Lincoln was immediately tied in: "God had exalted him for the very purpose" of freeing the slaves. Everett, too, had mentioned emancipation, and so would later in the day another serious speaker, at the Presbyterian Church on Baltimore Street, with Lincoln present. But by speaking in broad philosophical terms, the president now reached beyond Seward and the others. The promise of the Declaration was to be attained as quickly and as far as the country would permit. "All men are created equal" left room for him to write less than four months later to the governor of Louisiana that at least some black people there should have the right to vote. "They would probably help, in some trying time to come, to keep the jewel of liberty within the family of freedom."

That Lincoln's whole being had been tied up with freedom, however many contradictions one may point to, is also clear. He believed that if history would remember him, it would be for his Emancipation Proclamation. As an ambitious young man, he had announced that "towering genius" could reach great renown in America by either "emancipating slaves, or enslaving freemen." Soon after issuing the Proclamation, he invited the painter Edward Dalton Marchant, recommended by John Forney, to work in the White House for four months, during which Marchant created the presidential portrait with the broken chain [see insert]. He even ordered the painter's son to come from the army and help his father with the work. The painting was to go to Independence Hall in Philadelphia to keep company with the heroes of '76.

The president also invited another painter, Francis Carpenter, who would work at the White House for half a year. He recorded Lincoln saying that Emancipation was the "great event of the 19th century." However accurate the words attributed to Lincoln, Carpenter painted the moment in the cabinet when the president announced that event. The huge oil painting, *The First Reading of the Emancipation Proclamation*, shows Lincoln with the document in his hand. When Lincoln's oldest friend, Joshua Speed, came to visit—so the trustworthy Speed recorded in 1866—they reminisced, and Lincoln recalled his youthful fear that his moment of life would be gone without a trace. Well, Lincoln had issued the Emancipation Proclamation. Now he would be remembered for doing something for "his fellow man." This was "what he desired to live for."

Emancipation painters working at the White House, a confession to his oldest friend, and so much more, all make clear what Lincoln hoped for from history. But the Chief Mourner at Gettysburg wanted to avoid controversial words; a funeral was not a place to pronounce policy. Here he had to unite the people as best he could. And so he would rise for a moment above the squabbling of politics that he could be so good at. He would let his entire speech soar beyond the reach of the mundane world. He would not mention by name slavery, or Gettysburg, or the Confederacy, Lee's army or Meade's.

Yet being above politics itself was political. It allowed Lincoln not only the lofty presidential look, but also the ambiguity on the one hand to appeal to people desiring a quick radical route to equality, and on the other to keep in the fold those who did not care about the issue of slavery or were actively hostile to the idea of Emancipation. He knew that without a broad patriotic coalition the war would be lost, and with it the Union and Emancipation. Most of those who supported freedom for the enslaved would understand the meaning of "all men are created equal." Indeed, they could give it as broad a meaning as they wished. They would fully understand that "liberty," in which the United States was "conceived," applied to some; "freedom" that needed a "new birth," applied to all. As for angry opponents, Lincoln knew that they would lose no time in denouncing him for mixing the "negro" into the war and so desecrating the graves of Gettysburg.

But Lincoln needed the masses in the middle. Equating his use of Jefferson's words with the rights of black people was only one possible interpretation. Many did not understand the president's words in those terms. Equality could carry civil, economic, social, or racial connotations. To middle-of-the-road folk, the liberty he spoke about could be the white man's liberty. To think that way, they had to sidestep the full meaning of the Emancipation Proclamation; but people are always good at fuzzy thinking. They also had to bypass Lincoln's tendency, at his best, to think in terms of all humanity, to speak in universal terms.

Looking back to the Revolutionary War reminded people that the birth of America had cost great sacrifices. More specific, in appealing to Jefferson, Lincoln was certain that he appealed to the meaning the founders gave to the Declaration—though most scholars see this as historically inaccurate. Indeed, he did to Jefferson's words what future generations would do to his at Gettysburg. But in 1863 the meaning of the Declaration of Independence was much debated. And so how people understood Lincoln's words depended on what was in their heads. Lincoln understood that.

Now we are engaged in a great civil war, testing whether that nation or any nation so conceived and so dedicated can long endure.

Lincoln's opening sentence led here with the phrase "dedicated to the proposition," the word "proposition" coming from his study of Euclid's geometry, something that had to be proven. He had said some of this from the start of the war. In his July 4, 1861, war message to Congress, he explained that "our popular government has often been called an experiment," and it remained to be seen whether it would succeed over the long run. The Civil War was the test. But the implication at Gettysburg went further; it went from opposing the appeal from the "ballot to the bullet" to specifying that the rebel bullets aimed at the equality of all.

Yet, however much Emancipation cast its shadow over Lincoln's words, they reached beyond the American problem of slavery to the global problem of liberal democracy. Born in the optimism of the Enlightenment, democratic republicanism failed to triumph in Europe, much less anywhere else. Speaking to his countrymen, Lincoln's thoughts encompassed the world. The United States was, as he said in 1862, "the last best, hope of earth." Would the vision of progress that most Americans shared fail?

The United States had a universal mission, but the focus now had to be on home. Here on a piece of *a great battle-field*, Lincoln was helping to re-member *those who here gave their lives that that nation might live*. In the back of the minds of many in the crowd, Daniel Webster's unforgettable words must have hovered: "Liberty and Union." *The brave men living and dead, who struggled here*, Lincoln went on, already consecrated this land *far above our poor power to add or detract*.

People applauded again, and the reporters struggled to take down the words. Not all of them would get the exact same expressions. Now some heard Lincoln say "poor" before "power"; others missed it. Though many of the reporters had a place on the platform, many others were scattered in the crowd. While some heard people responding repeatedly "Good, good," oth-ers did not, or did not note audience reaction at all. What was applause to some was "great applause" or "immense applause" to others. Sitting in dif-ferent places with different vantage points, carrying various expectations and beliefs, the journalists, like Americans who would later read aloud to their families the Gettysburg reports, heard differing words and meanings.

> *The world will little note nor long remember what we say here, but it can never forget what they did here.*

No false humility in this. Everett had given his fine oration, touching hymns had been performed, Lincoln was saying a few words, and the news-papers would report them all. But he justly judged that the sacrifice of the soldiers should be and would be acclaimed. If he himself would be remem-bered, it would be for Emancipation. Nor was he considering Americans alone, but "The world."

As he spoke, a captain in the crowd with an empty sleeve buried his face in his good arm, shaking and sobbing aloud. Then he raised his eyes high and exclaimed in a low, solemn voice: "God Almighty bless Abraham Lin-coln!" The reporter, noting the faces around the soldier, thought that peo-ple responded silently with "Amen." And all the while the crowd applauded Lincoln again.

People had been roused. The next sentence, too, got applause:

> *It is for us, the living, rather to be dedicated here to the unfinished work that they have thus far so nobly carried on.*

Some of the best reporters would take down "refinished work," though this made no sense. Or perhaps the reporters did fine; the telegraph operators or typesetters fouled things up. The president had a voice that carried, but even those close to the platform could not take down everything accurately.

The great task remained before the country. All knew this meant carrying the war to victory; in the minds of some what victory would bring may have flashed for a moment. *We here highly resolve that the dead shall not have died in vain*— the crowd again interrupted with applause as Lincoln conjured up an image and words that had been hidden inside of so many since their childhood. "Their fall was not in vain," said the very popular Parson Weems's George Washington when he visited the graves of his soldiers. The applause quieted so Lincoln could finish:

> *that the nation shall, under God, have a new birth of freedom; and that government of the people, by the people, for the people, shall not perish from the earth.*

Silence—has the president finished?—then long, continued applause. Had Lincoln pronounced the universal "that government" as he spoke, departing from the written text of his second draft's "that this government," which referred only to the United States? He was a nationalist and could speak of Americans as an "almost chosen people." In his "first draft," he used the universal; but as he wrote out his "second draft," he changed to the particular, to *the* one nation on the earth devoted to building equality in a democracy. Surely that's what many wanted to hear, and surely that is how some heard what Lincoln said.

But if he spoke from the "second draft," the likely possibility, he made two significant changes at the cemetery. Not only did he add "under God," but also turned his final sentence into a universal declaration. Nor would he vary from that as he prepared later versions of his speech. In like spirit, though newspaper reports sometimes capitalized both "Nation" and "Liberty" in his first sentence, he capitalized only "Liberty." Was Lincoln speaking to humankind?

Firm as Lincoln's voice was, it carried no touch of stridency or self-righteousness. Nor did he make any overt reference to Christianity. Though his official invitation asked that his "remarks" help set aside the ground for their "sacred use," it is not likely that Lincoln was familiar with the Christian rite of sanctifying a piece of the earth for the burial of the dead. He had been to funerals, even spoke at one as a young man, but now gave no indication of being aware of the religious aspect of the occasion, or perhaps if aware, considered it improper to participate. The evening before the ceremonies certainly provided no edification in this regard. Only after imbibing the atmosphere at the cemetery, the uncovered heads, prayer, and hymns, did he add, in the moment's inspiration, "under God." One can almost hear him coming in his speech to "that the nation shall," pausing for a second, then adding a little awkwardly "under God, have a new birth of freedom." Later he would revise the word order to make the sentence read better.

And yet, whatever expectations he may have taken to Gettysburg, however reluctant he was to make a personal profession of Christianity, much of what Lincoln said carried the rhythms of the Bible. This was the music of the ancient Hebrew and Greek turned into King James's English. This was the language he was raised on. "Four score and seven years ago." Psalm 90: "The days of our years are three score years and ten," one of the best-known sentences of the Book. "Brought forth" is not only the biblical way to announce a birth, including that of Mary's "first born son," but the phrase that describes the Israelites being "brought forth" from slavery in Egypt.

Birth, sacrificial death, rebirth. A born-again nation. At a less than conscious level, Lincoln weaved together the biblical story and the American story: "Fathers." "Conceive." "Perish." "Consecrate." "Hallow." "Devotion." The devout in the cemetery heard Lincoln speak an intimately familiar beloved language. His words pointing to rebirth went even deeper than the Christian message, if that was possible, reaching the primeval longing for a new birth that humankind has yearned for and celebrated with every spring since time immemorial.

Lincoln's words came from the heart. The bloodbath of the war, and the loss of his own second child, Willie, in 1862, had slowly changed his religious outlook. The secular fatalist of old began to turn into a religious fatalist. He jotted down for himself perhaps in 1862: "The will of God prevails." Something of the Calvinism of his parents that he had rejected, even ridiculed, in his youth, started to reclaim him. He added "under God" to his remarks at Gettysburg. In his Second Inaugural Address in 1865, he would explain his course: "With malice toward none; with charity for all; with firmness in the right, as God gives us to see the right. . . ." And God helped Lincoln "to see the right" of abolishing slavery and leading the country toward black citizenship.

If God loomed ever larger in Lincoln's thought as the war went on, if his words at Gettysburg spoke deeply to the devout, they spoke also to more secular people, for in some part he remained one of them. He would not join a church, could not embrace the Christian concept of sin and re-demption, kept mostly silent about Jesus, and showed no inclination to build a personal relationship with God. The secularists could understand his Gettysburg speech largely on their own terms. Lincoln spoke from the heart to them, too.

A lesser person might have foundered on such bifurcation. Christians might have rejected him for not being sufficiently committed; the secular-minded for being too religious. Instead, the majorities embraced him as one of their own. His words at Gettysburg show how he did it. "Inauguration" is how Marshal Lamon described the ceremonies in the printed "Pro-gramme." In his own copy, Everett crossed out the word and replaced it with the religious "Consecration." As for Lincoln, "dedicate, consecrate"; he stayed in the middle, and so reached out to all—as many as he could reach.

His success depended in no small part on the beauty of his language. But with all the fresh graves around, the beautiful words would not hide the fact that the war had to go on. It had to go on indefinitely until victory came.

The rationalism of the Enlightenment combined with Protestant con-science. Lincoln's nine sentences had been welcomed by opening applause, interrupted by applause five times, and followed by applause. His perhaps two-and-a half-minute speech grew into something like three minutes. The people loved him. Lincoln had both voiced the beliefs of mainstream Amer-ica and urged America on toward a "new birth." He reflected the oratory of the ancient Greeks, especially Pericles, whose speeches appeared in the McGuffey Readers that educated children. His conclusion echoed not only Weems's *Life of Washington*, but words memorized by generations of chil-dren from their readers—some of the best known words of American his-tory, and of Lincoln's youth, the conclusion of Webster's 1830 reply to South Carolina's Robert Hayne in the Senate, denying that the U.S. govern-ment was a "creature" of the states. It was "the people's government," Webster had said, "made for the people, made by the people, and answerable to the people." In the Bible, Lincoln had read many a time in the Book of Proverbs: "Where *there is* no vision, the people perish." He was providing a vision "for us, the living," not the dead.

Not that people listening to his words analyzed their meaning. There was now no time for that; for most people no inclination, either. They took in its poetry, understood its overall tone and message. To give a very short speech, especially after Everett's long oration delivered from memory, could have been a major error. Yet that many would not recall whether he had a sheet of paper before him suggests he got away with it. In any case, his audience did not mainly come from the people present, important though they were, but from the North as a whole, perhaps even beyond. The chief goal was to bind the nation together; to create a ritual that tied the past to the present and pointed to the future. Wire services carried the whole ceremony around the North, wherever the telegraph went, immersing "the people" in one fastening ritual, creating community. This was new, but Lincoln was good at understanding the new.

From the platform, the dignitaries and the reporters could look right over the area of the town where most black people lived. But few of these townspeople appear to have come to the consecration, few enough that the papers would not comment on their presence. William Johnson came, surely, but Lincoln must have noticed the absence of blacks. Gettysburg was so different from Washington, especially now, with the capital's population swelling with people who had escaped from slavery. There when he would give his Second Inaugural Address perhaps half of his audience would be black. Did any come here? The College folk did arrive in strength, and their much-beloved black caretaker, John Hopkins, may have joined, perhaps some members of his family as well, and heard "a new birth of freedom." Hopkins's son, John Edward, would join the United States Colored Troops about two months after Lincoln's visit, and rise to become a sergeant.

At the end of Lincoln's remarks, three cheers followed the "long continued applause"; some papers would report "wild and lengthened excitement," and three more cheers for the governors present. The Massachusetts delegation, while praising Everett, would report that "perhaps nothing in the whole proceedings made so deep an impression," as Lincoln's speech. Was he happy with what he said? He did not say. Later recollections carry little credibility. What of his listeners? They applauded repeatedly, if we believe the AP and some other reports, but few said anything afterwards. The newspapers would be the place where at least one segment of the population, the scribblers, could say what they thought. Lincoln would have the chance to look at the papers later, if he could find the time.

The afternoon moved toward a religious conclusion. Many felt that they stood on a sacred spot and "one of the most beautiful on earth." The natural loveliness of the place had been raised to glory first by deeds and now by words. A Gettysburg choir, made up of twice as many women as men, accompanied by a band from Philadelphia, sang a mournful dirge written for the occasion. *O! it is great for our Country to die . . . Glory awaits us for aye . . . Warrior youth on his bier . . . Wet by a mother's warm tears . . . We shall look forth from our heaven, pleased the sweet music to hear.* They sang of manhood at its best as they understood. No greater gift could a man give than to lay down his life—for his country. So many people believed that. They heard the biblical voice. This was again a church service; no applause followed. The singers came mostly from the local church choirs, and the *Sentinel*, like other papers, would praise the "exquisite performance" of the dirge.

The Reverend Baugher, the College president, got up to give a brief benediction. He prayed as people expected: *Oh Thou King of kings and Lord of lords, God of the Nations of the Earth . . . grant us Thy blessings . . . May this great nation be delivered from treason. . . .* Lamon announced that there would be an afternoon program at the Presbyterian Church that stood part way on the street between the cemetery and the Diamond. The ceremonies were done. An artillery salute followed, eight rounds, then music, and the marshals started to shepherd the dignitaries and others into the marching column led by the Marine Band.

Throughout the day, a group of forty to fifty veterans stood up front. They had been "wounden in the battle hear," as a woman wrote back home; "it was enough to make the hardest heart melt." Many of the men shed tears as they listened to the proceedings. Many banners spotted the crowd, but that of the veterans' caught most eyes. On one side it showed an urn and the words: "Honor to our brave comrades"; and on the other side: "In memory of those who fell at Gettysburg, July 1st, 2nd, and 3d, 1863." Descending from the platform, Lincoln went over to the soldiers, saying that "The men upon their crutches were orators; their very appearance spoke louder than tongues." That's what he had said, more eloquently, in his speech. And then

"To the right of the President sits the Rev. Dr. Baugher, of the Gettysburg College, who is to pronounce the benediction—a semi bald head, a hooked Roman nose, clear blue eye, and a decidedly clerical face. He would pass anywhere for a theological professor, a man of firm will, but kindly," Cincinnati Daily Commercial, *November 24, 1863. Photographer Tyson Brothers [?]. (Gettysburg College)*

he was gone. If he understood that "something unspeakably satisfactory" had just taken place, he did not say. He was already ill, and would stay ill for weeks.

Along the route back to town, women in the windows, men in the doorways, cheered and waved. People wore their finest: little girls in white; boys with shoes shined but dusty; adults in somber colors. As the president passed, people uncovered their heads and cheered. They cheered Governor Curtin, too. A long crowd headed back to the Diamond.

The Letterman hospital group ran into a former patient.

"Is it Crolius?" Nurse Souder asked.

It was. William E. Crolius, Company A, 72nd Pennsylvania Infantry, Baxter's Fire Zouaves. Souder probably knew none of this minutiae; she remembered a soldier with "a frank, manly face," who had lost his right arm in the battle and had been sent to a Philadelphia hospital. When Souder last heard of him, he was "very low. I did not suppose he was in the land of the living." Life had its blessings.

Not everyone marched back. Many had loved ones lying in the ground. They "lingered until the shades of the evening approached, seemingly loath to leave the ground consecrated by the blood of those heroes who fought, died, and found a grave there." Others returned to town; the Diamond teemed with people, and the bands spelled each other until sunset, playing appropriate tunes. Speechifying continued, too, but now a very different feeling obtained from the night before. Solemn—thoughtful. Drayman and photographer William Weaver, who had supervised digging up all those bodies that had been taken to the cemetery, wrote to his brother that "the order of the day was so excellent everything was done in peace and harmony, I dident see one drunken man all day or evening." This was truly a different day.

The dignitaries had a quick dinner at David Wills's house, followed by a reception, with crowds trooping through to shake hands with the president and also with the Pennsylvania governor. Nurse Souder's group, too, went, "paying our respect." She wrote to her cousin that "it is worth the trip to Gettysburg to see our flag floating over Round Top, so grandly and beautifully." The governor's orders to bring it to half-mast had been forgotten there, and in other places, too.

Lincoln shook hands for close to an hour. He enjoyed meeting the people, and many of them would long remember. The Reverend H. N. Pohlman of Albany, New York, had already met him as part of a Lutheran delegation in 1862, at the White House, where he told the story of the only clergyman daring to pray for the president in Confederate-held Nashville. He was a Lutheran pastor, who preached in German. "The rebels couldn't understand German but the Lord could." Now, when Reverend Pohlman came, or so it would be remembered, Lincoln greeted him with "the Lord understands German."

If there were smiles in the reception line, to many, the president looked quite tired. He had gone to bed late, got up early, and had a hard day already. The *Sentinel* sympathized: the chief magistrate for "more than an hour was the victim of 'hand shaking' that must have tested his good nature." What none seemed to know, perhaps not even Lincoln, that he was becoming quite ill. Variola, a mild form of smallpox that was devastating Washington, had got to him, too.

Handshake after handshake, face-to-face. That is how variolas are mostly transmitted: through the breath of the sick person that others inhale, or through coughing. Infectious droplets sometimes can travel a little distance and affect people farther away. Less frequently, direct contact with a lesion can do the same. How advanced was the president's illness? Did he infect other people?

Handshaking done, Lincoln soon asked for John Burns, the old constable who had grown into something of a national hero. Perhaps the president wanted to see the kind of man he had failed to get at the Hanover stop on his way to Gettysburg, someone who fought for home. But Lincoln also knew the value of mixing with the people, making himself the equal of ordinary citizens. Robert Harper soon wrote: "In this touching incident, perhaps, more than any other, Gettysburg was truly dedicated." Arm-in-arm, Lincoln and Burns went over to the Presbyterian Church, accompanied by Seward and the Marine Band. Did Burns, did anyone tell the greats how the church had been filled with Union and Confederate wounded after the battle? Now there would be speechmaking. The Ohio delegation had organized the meeting and the main oration came from Colonel Charles Anderson, the newly elected Republican lieutenant governor of the state. The wounded veteran, brother of the hero of Fort Sumter, gave still one more history of the battle, spoke of "the cause," treason, despotism, "Peace and Freedom." He defended Emancipation, but added that the freed people would not come North, indeed, would attract Northern blacks back south. The United States was "God's best hope on earth."

Others made speeches in other places. "It seemed difficult to settle down to quietness," nurse Souder mused. New York's Governor Seymour reviewed troops from his state, spoke highly of them, expressed the pride he felt seeing "the manly and sturdy columns," and presented new silk standards with "firm confidence" that they would be carried with honor "through every field of triumph, of toil, and of danger. . . ." The Democratic press, others, too, would sometimes headline Seymour's speech and give equal space to it with Lincoln. But many Democrats did not like an even modestly pro-war utterance. A German paper in Milwaukee that would not report Lincoln's remarks commented curtly that Seymour's speech "apparently surprised many of his friends and left them astonished." Another, in Ohio, claimed that "angry cries" greeted him. Of course, the opposing party's reaction was destined to be negative, too. The *Tazewell County Republican* in Illinois wrote ironically how wonderful it was that Gettysburg "stimulated Seymour's patriotism." Both views echoed widely expressed sentiments.

John Russell Young would much later describe Seymour as "open, bland, courteous, expectant, might have been some peer of the realm," but also out of place at this Republican rally—"you can imagine the feeling with which a company of Roundheads would welcome a prince of the Cavaliers." But the president liked Seymour coming to Gettysburg. He would be an easier opponent in the 1864 election than General McClellan. Lincoln would be remembered telling a lifelong Democrat, also present, that he was "glad" to see the governor well received here. Some of Seymour's honor guard sounded less happy. The same soldiers who had earlier escorted the president and received his commendation now formed the New York governor's guard. By this time, however, the men had had enough. "I don't think he would have been so ready with his Praise," one of the soldiers wrote of his governor, "could he have heard the men curse, for being Kept standing in Line for ½ a Day and no Dinner."

The festivities wound down. As evening came, Lincoln said his thank-you's, went to the railroad station once again with the Marine Band, and then was gone. An utterly exhausted Everett traveled in the same car. The train moved slowly at first. The wheels squeaked as they gained traction. The engine gathered strength, gained speed, moved faster, and then the train was gone. The throngs around the station must have wondered when their chance to leave would come.

The passengers could see Gettysburg receding. First the moving masses rushed by, then the houses, the hospital ground tents, and the lush valley. Ride through the countryside, toward Hanover, then switch toward Baltimore. Easy conversations. A sense of satisfaction, duty well done. Banter, politics. Pennsylvania Republican State Committee chair Wayne MacVeagh was again on the train, again talking politics. But the president, as people would remember, who had already looked "sallow, sunken-eyed, thin, careworn" on the way to Gettysburg, now had "a grievous headache," had to lie down, and Johnson bathed his forehead in cold water.

Reporters were again invited, but sometimes the best intentions come to naught. The editor of the *Indianapolis Daily Journal* arrived, but "in the jam around the train, while waiting for Mr. Lincoln," his pocket got picked. He would report that, belonging to a meagerly paid profession, he only lost a small amount, and hoped that the thief "felt twice as bad when he found so little in the pocket book as I did when I found nothing in my pocket." Once he got on the train, it turned out to be overcrowded, filthy, and very slow. "The power of the President, 'tyrannical' as the Copperheads say it is . . . could not make the North Central Pennsylvania railroad a rapid or easy means of moving 'to and fro on the earth.' "

At Hanover Junction, the presidential train was moved to a sidetrack to wait for a westbound train to pass. Lincoln got up and the Ohio politicians, also on the train, gathered around him. These were the incoming Republican officials of the state, Congressmen-elect Charles Anderson and Robert Schenck, and Governor-elect John Brough. Ohio was a pivotal state, home to Salmon P. Chase, another would-be Republican president. It was also the home of the "arch-traitor" Vallandigham, freshly defeated but still dangerous. The railroad car is an intimate space, well suited to conducting political business even as it moves from place to place. Ohio loomed very large in the politics of Lincoln's first presidential nomination; that's why he made a speaking tour there in 1859. Ohio was still very important. But now the president is not well. There are people out there on the platform, crowding to see "Honest Old Abe." But he does not go out to greet them. He has given all he has. Lincoln's train finally leaves.

They were lucky. The Governors' special train that left Gettysburg an hour after the president had to stay at Hanover Junction until the next morning. "Some wretched junction," one would comment, and a reporter added: "The amount of blasphemy manufactured was considerable, and contrasted harshly with the solemn event of the day." However, Lincoln had left behind a great deal of goodwill, his popularity among the people had been made amply clear, and the stranded politicians cursed only the railroad.

Others were trying to leave Gettysburg, too. The great day held so many memories, hymns, cheering, echoes of the words of the president, Everett, Reverend Stockton, French, and more. One message stood out:

Gettysburg was the great battle of the war. Stockton's prayer had been un-ambiguous: "One more victory" for the enemy back then in July, "and all was theirs." Everett had been equally clear: the battle determined whether the nation "should live, a glory and a light to all coming time, or should ex-pire like the meteor of a moment." The president said something like that, too, using the word "perish," but he did not make Gettysburg the central event of the war, though probably most understood him that way. The hymns and the ritual all supported the message, and a good part of the North would echo it. After the battle, the feeling quickly blossomed that something all-important had taken place at Gettysburg. The dedication of the Soldiers' National Cemetery carved that sentiment into history.

Only days after the consecration, a Western reporter wrote that there had been many commemorations of the war, but never before had the na-tion showed its "gushing gratitude toward the brave fallen of the rank and file. . . . This is as it should be. Here was fought the great battle of the war." Those who came in November would never forget "this beautiful and for all time to come, renowned city of the brave dead, who with their lives saved this country. . . ." The Gospel of Gettysburg was born. American memory was being created.

CHAPTER SIX

ECHOES

S ergeant Michael Miller had wanted to be at home in Gettysburg to be with his wife—and to witness the cemetery dedication that he called the "Big time," the "great time." He could not come, and now the celebration was just about over. At home, Sally Myers watched with weary eyes and noted in her diary on November 20: "the town is all excitement—persons from abroad are as anxious to get away as they were to get here." The night before, all the trains were held until Lincoln left. The railroads had already received bitter complaints about bringing people to town—"the worst conceived, arranged and executed expedition of the war, not excepting the Peninsula campaign," wrote the Indianapolis correspondent. "If getting away from Gettysburg is half as hard . . ."

It was. On the evening of the 19th, the hundreds waiting at the station for Lincoln to leave grew to thousands. "Six mortal, long, wearying, slowly-dragging hours" people had to linger, complained the normally friendly *Washington Chronicle.* Then it quickly added: "our excellent President was not a party to the shameful mismanagement."

That last word kept reappearing. The town just could not handle all the visitors. Some had come prepared, like an important delegation from Baltimore, which brought a sleeping railroad car that could accommodate forty-eight in which they hoped to "enjoy a good night's rest." Others, too, had been told to bring along "a sufficient quantity of edibles to last them while away. It is not known that any provision has been made at Gettysburg to feed the vast multitude. . . ." A Philadelphia paper summed up matters this way: "The grand Gettysburg solemnity is now over with all its inspiring features and its wretched mismanagement."

Certainly, those who had to wander the cold night before the big day, or others who had to sleep out in the fields, had reason to complain. Some feared a second night like that because, as an Ohio paper wrote, "it was almost impossible to get out of town." But overall, people went away from Gettysburg glowing, and across the North the Republican press brought forth a stunning reaction to the great commemoration. Even the Democratic side generally felt obliged to provide extensive reports, though "Copperhead" papers especially also inserted barbs wherever possible. The wide coverage of the dedication ceremonies was crowned by the massive attention given to Edward Everett, particularly in big-city papers.

His full address usually appeared by itself on the front page of Republican newspapers—the page most noticeable and usually prepared ahead of publication—with some spilling inside. Breaking news went on page two or further back. The oration frequently appeared separately from the often long accounts of the dedication that would also pay much attention to Everett. When no space could be found for the full oration, readers tended to get ample selections or at least summaries. Even some Democratic papers printed the full speech, or provided sections of it, or a précis. Proof sheets had been distributed all over the North, as Everett wrote, "to prevent its being mutilated & travestied by the Reporters." This was not the exact speech that he ended up giving and, hard on himself, he not only noted in his diary that "I omitted a good deal of what I had written," but reproached himself for memorizing poorly some parts. He had to condense because of time constraints, and "several thoughts" also came to him "at the moment, as happens generally."

The Republican papers printed overwhelmingly favorable editorial comments. That Everett had run against Lincoln in the 1860 election, that he was long a personification of sectional compromise, that his speech could be seen as the return of the prodigal, all helped the celebration of the orator—though there were some who would not forgive. Forney's *Washington Daily Chronicle*, which went out to the Army of the Potomac in huge

The First Separate Printing of Everett and Lincoln, November 1863. (Abraham Lincoln Presidential Library)

numbers, seemed awestruck by what had taken place at Gettysburg, an occasion that "had no parallel in modern times." It declared Everett's "magnificent oration" to be "vivid as though written with a sunbeam." The praise seems to have stuck in the craw of a correspondent of Democratic presidential aspirant George B. McClellan, who nearly a year later denounced Everett's "Gettysburgh affair" that had "no sunbeam warmth." By then, Everett would support Lincoln in the 1864 campaign, over the objection of many of his old friends and associates.

But back in November 1863, the *Chronicle* would not restrain its praise of an oration that "glows with such vitality that no one can leave the read-

ing uncompleted who once commences it." Having published the entire
speech, it repeated some parts in its commentary. The *Chronicle* then went
on to publish the address as a separate brochure, with other items from the
ceremonies appended, including Lincoln's speech—perhaps making up for
the failure to publish the president's words in the regular paper. Much of
the Republican-inclined press sang the same hymn. The *Chicago Tribune*,
for example, wrote that the speech of the most famous orator of the land
was "unsurpassed by any previous effort in his life." Everett received perhaps twice as many editorials as Lincoln did.

The bulk of the Democratic press tended either to refrain from commenting on Everett or attacked him. If the orator thought history proved
that reconciliation was possible after a civil war, the *Chicago Times* saw "Hatred as a Bar to Reunion." Southern newspapers said the same, but with
ridicule added to the brief coverage, including Lincoln's remarks. The *New
York World* fully reported the "grandeur" and the "importance" of the Gettysburg celebration, admitted that Lincoln's words were "calculated to
arouse deep feeling," and commended Everett's "clear and perfectly modu-
lated voice." However, it also spent much space refuting his argument
against the right of secession. Some looked on him as a fallen man who
abandoned his principles of compromise to become a Lincoln man. The unkindest cut came from the *Brooklyn Daily Eagle* which, having condemned
the oration as partisan, noted that "A son of a certain Edward Everett of
Massachusetts was recently drafted into the service of the United States;
his father paid for him the price of exemption." It then went on to express
"doubt" that this Everett was the orator.

Partisan criticism was to be expected and ignored, though Everett could
not help but refer repeatedly in his diary to the "villainous assaults" and "a
most brutal attack" upon his address—"Outrageous." Even some of the Republican press, including *Harper's Weekly*, commented on the lack of heart in
the oration, matching Democratic complaints. Not until after the death of
the Massachusetts statesman would the magazine relent and, in a long history of the battle, speak of Everett's "elaborate and eloquent oration." But
now to one reporter Everett seemed like a "Greek sculpture—beautiful but
cold as ice." The irony could not have escaped the orator, who had prepared
for Gettysburg by reading Pericles' funeral oration in Thucydides. In his
diary, Everett had written that the Greek statesman "does not appear to me

to rise above plain good sense, which is certainly a good thing. But as for 'its going home to all the hearts' . . . I must humbly dissent." Now he found even some friends grousing with the same complaint about him.

The largest part of his address dealt with the history of the battle, and many who praised the speech singled out "Mr. Everett as a Historian of the War." The *Chronicle* admired his "manifest longing to do justice" to all sides and predicted that the work would place him "among the classics not only of this age, but of all other ages." Boston echoed by comparing his history to "the most brilliant pages of Macaulay or Prescott," but predicted only that Everett's would be "the best history of the campaign" for "this genera-tion." Milwaukee praised the broad grasp that went far beyond the battle, and spoke of "imperishable history"—words that appeared in other parts of the country, too.

If many liked the oration because of the history in it, others objected for the same reason, or objected to interpretation. Everett appears to have re-ceived critical comments immediately—Gettysburg was already full of ex-perts. On the very day of his oration he apologized to the history professor of the College, Martin Luther Stoever, for "inadequacy & possible errors." The professor assured him, however, that the history "was not only correct, but executed with skill & tact."

Before long, Everett got a taste of how passionate people felt about the subject. Not unexpected, the *New York Herald* complained of his "inac-curate account" citing the paeans to Hooker and Meade, "when as every-one knows Gettysburg was a soldiers' battle." It was the opening salvo of an unending debate. And William Cullen Bryant's Republican *New York Evening Post*, which should have been friendly, got upset with the mis-identification of a division from the Empire State and roared: "The ghosts" of the division "will haunt him forever!" A letter from an army officer appeared in another "friendly paper" and denounced his "unjust & inexcus-able . . . misstatements."

"Truly disgusting," Everett noted in his diary. Complaints about his history bothered him sufficiently to impel him to write to his host, David Wills, requesting support. As if knowing what was on the orator's mind, on the very day of Everett's letter, Wills wrote him expressing his "peculiar satisfaction" with those very parts of the address. Everett also continued his correspondence with Professor Jacobs, on whose history he relied and whose reliability had been attacked in the *New York Times*. He recorded in his diary that an officer from Meade's staff told him "my account of the battle of Gettysburg was very correct, & that Genl. Meade so regarded it." General Hooker, in turn, called to his attention two "slight" civilian's errors, and added that the "account was the most accurate ever written of the battle."

When Everett prepared his final text for publication, he kept, as would be expected of him, the disclaimer that the history was "inadequately recounted," but he only owned up to making use of newly accessible information and correcting "one or two slight errors of the first draught." Actually he went through his manuscript with a fine-tooth comb, counting punctuation and all, making hundreds of corrections (see Appendix A). But Everett felt good about his work and, in any case, for him its "most valuable" part was the historical analysis of other civil wars, which proved that reconciliation was indeed possible. Conciliation was the essence of the man. Of course he knew that this aspect of his address would be bitterly contested by both the Confederates and Northern opponents of the war.

The "official" version of the dedication that Everett shepherded through to publication at Wills's request was delayed first by Seward's wish to be included, which stopped printing in progress, and then by "a series of accidents," and so the orator apparently had his "Gettysburg Address" printed alone first. He also interceded at the Boston City Hall to make sure that his address would be included in the report of the Massachussetts delegation that went to Gettysburg. At least eight expanded editions appeared within six months of the cemetery dedication. Of course, Everett received the prime billing in all, but Lincoln was included for good measure—though not always. So were the other participants of the "Gettysburg Solemnities" (to cite the earliest title), as well as correspondence dealing with the event, much of it Everett's, and also Seward's speech from the night before. Seymour was left out.

The pamphlet crossed the Atlantic, though in early January 1864 Everett still had to write to Minister Charles Francis Adams in London that he had nothing yet to send of his "Gettysburg Address." In February, Everett was apparently sending the address, as well as two earlier ones, to a professor in Berlin writing the history of the United States. In April, he received from Adams the Glasgow edition, with various misprints. A complimentary note entitled "The End of the Civil War in America" introduced the publication. Nothing was mentioned of Lincoln's remarks. In May,

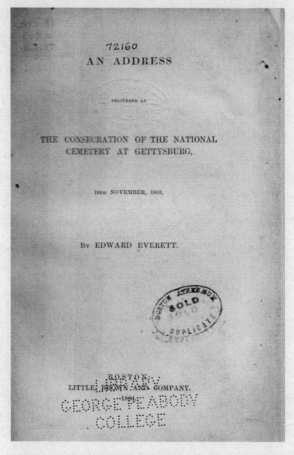

72160

AN ADDRESS

DELIVERED AT

THE CONSECRATION OF THE NATIONAL
CEMETERY AT GETTYSBURG,

19TH NOVEMBER, 1863,

BY EDWARD EVERETT.

BOSTON:
LITTLE, BROWN AND COMPANY.

*Everett's Gettysburg Address printed without Lincoln's Speech.
(Boston, Little, Brown, 1864). (Boritt Collection)*

Everett's diary recorded the possibility of a Greek translation of "a part of my Gettysburg Address." In July, he thanked the Secretary of State for sending him a German translation that came through diplomatic channels. Not many had doubts about who was the author of the Gettysburg Address.

In Virginia, Sergeant Miller and the rest of Company K followed avidly the great event at home. Lile had found no time to write, so he complained again: "I have looked for a letter till I am tired and Still each evening when the mail comes it is the Same time no letter for Miller." But he read the *Washington Daily Chronicle*'s full account, and "also the Speech of Mr. Everett which I think was elegant." Soon the other papers came, too, and

ADDRESS

OF

HON. EDWARD EVERETT,

AT THE

CONSECRATION OF THE NATIONAL CEMETERY AT
GETTYSBURG, 19TH NOVEMBER, 1863,

WITH THE

DEDICATORY SPEECH OF PRESIDENT LINCOLN,

AND THE

OTHER EXERCISES OF THE OCCASION;

ACCOMPANIED BY

AN ACCOUNT OF THE ORIGIN OF THE UNDERTAKING AND OF THE ARRANGE-
MENT OF THE CEMETERY GROUNDS, AND BY A MAP OF THE
BATTLE-FIELD AND A PLAN OF THE
CEMETERY.

PUBLISHED FOR THE BENEFIT OF THE CEMETERY MONUMENT FUND.

BOSTON:
LITTLE, BROWN AND COMPANY.
1864.

The Official Publication: Address of Hon. Edward Everett. . . .
(Boston, Little, Brown, 1864). (Boritt Collection)

the men read them all. "What a different Spectacle must that day have Presented," Miller mused, than "the 1st, 2nd, & 3rd of July, But as Remembrance of Such Scenes are Painful I will Say no more hoping I may never Behold any more Such Sights."

The sergeant said nothing of Lincoln. Nor did most other soldiers—anywhere. Indeed, he received much less editorial attention than Everett, though the brevity of the president's remarks ensured their wide publication. Smaller papers printed all 270-some words much more often than Everett's many thousands. The famed Massachusetts orator was the main speaker; focus on him made sense. His oration arrived days early at many newspapers; Lincoln's not until late on the day of dedication, leaving little time for editors to comment. Still, the virtual editorial silence about Lincoln's words came in spite of his popularity at the end of 1863, the understanding that he would be the Republican candidate for reelection, the very partisan nature of the press, and his assiduous cultivation of reporters.

Some simply disliked how Lincoln wrote. The *Hartford Courant* printed "copious extracts" from Everett, printed two versions of Seward's speech, ignored the president's without comment, but when discussing the December 1863 Annual Message, added: "Mr. Lincoln is not distinguished for elegance or perspicuity of style." To many ears, the Gettysburg remarks may have appeared as poetry, to be enjoyed or ignored; not analyzed, not something of great significance. His more obvious policy statements such as the Annual Message or the Amnesty Proclamation, which was soon to arrive—those one could get teeth into.

The coverage of the *New York Times* illustrates the response of the major Republican papers. Its editor, Henry Raymond, was not only a firm friend of the administration, but would also serve as chairman of the Republican National Committee, as a Lincoln campaign biographer, and, after the assassination, as his full-fledged biographer. The front page of the *Times* the day after the ceremonies reported in bold letters on Gettysburg under the heading **THE HEROES OF JULY.** In smaller letters came the words "A Solemn and Imposing Event." Below that, "Dedication of the National Cemetery at Gettysburgh"; and below that in somewhat larger letters: "IMMENSE NUMBERS OF VISITORS." Further down, this: "Oration by Hon. Edward Everett—Speeches of President Lincoln, Mr. Seward, and Governor Seymour." The headings concluded with larger letters: THE PROGRAMME SUCCESSFULLY CARRIED OUT. The place of honor, the right side of the front page, the *Times* devoted to Henry Ward Beecher's report on a visit to England; this was a New York paper, after all. His headline: A GREAT SPEECH.

"President Lincoln was there, too," reported the *Steubenville Weekly Herald* in Ohio; and he made, with others, "a brief speech, well to the purpose." In Gettysburg the *Sentinel* did more, prefacing the speech with "The President then delivered the following dedicatory remarks." When the Republican press commented more forcefully, it most commonly used the adjective "appropriate," with something like "eloquent" occasionally tagged on. Forney's *Philadelphia Press* went further: "brief but immortal speech." Another of his papers went much further, even if it printed only half of

THE HEROES OF JULY..

A Solemn and Imposing Event.

Dedication of the National Cemetery at Gettysburgh,

IMMENSE NUMBERS OF VISITORS.

Oration by Hon. Edward Everett—Speeches of President Lincoln, Mr. Seward and Governor Seymour.

THE PROGRAMME SUCCESSFULLY CARRIED OUT.

GREAT BRITAIN AND AMERICA.

Welcome to Rev. Henry Ward Beecher.

Demonstration at the Brooklyn Academy of Music.

A GREAT SPEECH:

His Impressions of British Feeling Toward America.

A speech of the Reverend Beecher received superlatives within an inch of the president's Gettysburg remarks, which were reproduced with errors and no comment. (Boritt Collection)

Lincoln's speech, writing of Sinai and "the ruler of the nation," who "never stood higher, or grander, and more prophetic." In Ohio, an editor perhaps hoping for a patronage job, wrote of a "calm but earnest utterance . . . brief but beautiful" that "stirred the deepest fountains of feeling and emotion in the hearts of the vast throng." Still others sent Lincoln their praise.

Perhaps the more honest and enthusiastic evaluations came from New England. The *Providence Journal*, having run the AP report that included Lincoln's speech, in addition to printing all of Everett's, and spending a good bit of time analyzing the long oration, concluded, "not less felicitous was President Lincoln. We know not where to look for a more admirable speech." "Those few thrilling words" carried the "charm and power of the very highest eloquence." The *Daily Republican* of Springfield, Massachusetts, which had long idolized Lincoln, now awarded him "the rhetorical honors" of the day, calling his speech "a perfect gem; deep in feeling, compact in thought and expression, and tasteful and elegant in every word and comma." The editors had got used to the "homely and imperfect phrase of his productions" and the "unexpectedness" of the words at Gettysburg bowled them over: "A model speech." Like some other papers, the *Wabash Express*, in Indiana, repeated the praise, but did not print the speech.

Harper's Weekly noted that "the few words of the President were from the heart"; they could not be read "without kindling emotion." The editors even cited a passage: "The world will little note nor long remember what we say here, but it can never forget what they did here." The magazine concluded that this was "as simple and felicitous a word as was ever spoken." Though the editors could not find space for more of the president's speech, their admiration for it was genuine. Indeed, perhaps because the magazine's weaker cousin and rival, *Frank Leslie's Illustrated News*, had reproduced all of the cemetery remarks—if in a rather muddled version—a week later, *Harper's* returned to the subject and compared Lincoln's words to those of Pericles.

Although the *Boston Evening Transcript* thought Lincoln's words "rough and loose," it also spoke of them as "jewels," and in general almost no direct criticism came from Republican papers. But comments of any sort came rarely, and their paucity in the Republican press suggested that most editors, in a hurry to get their papers out, understood the president's remarks at Gettysburg to be routine. Most knew that 270-some words did not a great speech make. In some cases, silence could also mask hostility: a desire to see Lincoln replaced as the party's standard-bearer in 1864, or little enthusiasm for "a new birth of freedom."

Lincoln had plenty of friendly journalists in Gettysburg. Many years later, John Russell Young would still ponder the harassment of a Democratic scribbler. Had reporters been less loyal, they might have written about the untold luxuries of Lincoln's train: how while soldiers marched and died, the people's president traveled in the lap of luxury. Not a peep showed up in the press about such subjects. The War Department had decided in that November to order a special train for the president, and when it was built, such scandal erupted that Lincoln refused to set foot on it. In April 1865, it would carry his body home to Illinois. Now, however friendly the group of correspondents whose business was writing came to Gettysburg, few found much good to say about Lincoln's remarks. Editors back home did the same. They printed the text. For most friendly papers, that was enough. When Lincoln received praise, it would largely come from people far away.

Most of the Democratic papers tried to hide, or entirely ignore, the president's speech, which they regarded as the start of his presidential campaign. Nor was this view wrongheaded. "Lincoln spoke, with an eye to a future platform and to re-election," the diarist Adam Gurowski commented in a matter-of-fact way. The same issue of a Baltimore paper that reported on the Gettysburg ceremonies took note of nominations from various quarters of both Lincoln and General McClellan and concluded that "both candidates are now fairly in the field." In Ohio, the *Fremont Journal* copied Pennsylvania's *Carlisle American*: next to the report of the Gettysburg ceremonies stood the endorsement of Lincoln for reelection. The *Toledo Blade* did the same, but at great length. On the day the president rode the rails to Gettysburg, the *Wabash Express* in Indiana spoke bluntly: MR. LINCOLN FOR THE NEXT PRESIDENT.

In Gettysburg, the Democratic *Compiler* truncated Lincoln's remarks, did not mention applause, and kept a tight lip. In New Jersey, the *Hudson County Democrat* would not directly notice the Gettysburg speech, but made clear that the country needed not "a new birth of freedom, or a 'new Union' " but a " 'new President.' " In Illinois, the *Freeport Bulletin* described the appearance of the National Cemetery, printed Seymour's speech, derided Everett's, and ignored Lincoln's. It also reported that black soldiers were worthless, and when the president's Annual Message came out, attacked it repeatedly at length, having wondered earlier whether he was "insane."

Democratic papers often gave the lead to Horatio Seymour, barely noting that "Other Addresses were made on the occasion." They commented on Lincoln's words negatively more often than did Republican papers positively. They tended to focus on the speech's beginning with the Declaration of Independence and its ending with "a new birth of freedom." What Lincoln made general they condemned in specifics by explaining that he had talked about the "negro."

None handled this better than the *Chicago Times*—one of the most influential Democratic voices in the Midwest, Stephen Douglas's old organ. The paper that had been suppressed by the military earlier in the year now asked how Lincoln "dared" to mock the Gettysburg dead by misstating "the cause for which they died, and libel the statesmen who founded the government." The soldiers had died for their country, and the founding fathers had "too much self-respect" to think of blacks as equals. In short, honest Abe "most foully" lied at Gettysburg. But the *Chicago Times* would match this performance with similarly bitter and much lengthier attention to the "atrocious features" of Lincoln's Annual Message and his December 1864 Amnesty Proclamation.

In Ohio, the "Copperhead" *Crisis* did not think much of the president's "mawkish harangue" and snorted: "*of* the people, *by* the people, and *for* the people"—state rights was where power belonged, not to "Despotism." Detroit's *Free Press*, like the *Indiana State Sentinel*, citing *The World*, saw fit to report only the first sentence of Lincoln's speech so that it could object to "obstetrical analogies" while affirming that the Constitution "does not say one word about equal rights."

Echoes of such voices could be heard from Democrats in reputedly abolitionist New England. That blacks were as good as whites was a "miserable falsehood," noted one editor by way of commenting on Lincoln's appeal to Jefferson's truth. "If it was to establish negro equality that our soldiers lost their lives, Mr. Lincoln should have said so before."

How the president's words were reported would impact how they were received. People often read papers out loud, and what they heard, if they read his remarks, varied widely. The reporter of the *Boston Advertiser* noted that the speech "suffered somewhat at the hands of telegraphers." Operators indeed made errors, decoding could be garbled, was again transmitted and further garbled, typesetters made horrendous mistakes, and so on. Editors added their skills, or lack of them and had their ways with the text, even when friendly. In Lincoln's home state, the citizens of Centralia could read in the Republican *Sentinel* that the Gettysburg "ceremonies were the most solemn and impressive ever witnessed on this continent," that Everett held "the vast audience spell-bound," and that Lincoln made a few "remarks," to wit: "Ninety years ago our fathers formed a Government consecrated to freedom." Clearly, biblical phraseology did not speak equally to all.

"Ninety years ago" also appeared in the *Hardin County Republican* and the German-language *Pittsburgher Volksblatt*. The *Chicago Times* started with "Four score and ten years ago." In Cincinnati, the *Daily Gazette*, like so many other newspapers, printed: "Four score and seven years ago our fathers established upon this continent a Government subscribed in liberty and dedicated to the fundamental principle that all mankind are created free and equal by a good God." That very language turned up in Lincoln's hometown in the newspaper that had been closest to him in his prairie years, the *Illinois State Journal.* "Our Father," as in the Lord's Prayer, seemed good enough for the *Rochester Daily Union Advertiser*. Of course when "Our Father" brought forth a "new nation," the meaning changed substantially.

"Now, we are engaged in the greatest civil war," the *Detroit Free Press* continued, "testing whether that nation or any nation so consecrated and so dedicated can stand for many years." "Can longer remain," said the *Chicago Tribune*. "The dead will little heed. Let us long remember what we have," the *Sacramento Daily Union* went on, and reported "immense applause." The *Steubenville Weekly Herald* quoted: "Let us long remember what we say here." "The world will little note and nothing remember of what we see here," was the version in the *Philadelphia Inquirer* and *Frank Leslie's Illustrated News* and, like so many others, both added: "We imbibe increased devotion." Perhaps what was imbibed the night before dedication day affected these transmissions. "We owe this offering to our dead" seemed to appear everywhere. The *New York Times* and the *New York Tribune* reported, as did so many others, dedication "to the refinished work." "Refinished" as in a piece of furniture? A not uncommon conclusion came in friendly outlets like the *Cincinnati Daily Gazette*: "Here let us resolve that what they have done shall not have been done in vain; that the nation shall, under God, have a new birth offered; that the Government of the people, founded by the people, shall not perish." The *Cincinnati Daily Commercial*, on the other hand, reported that "the freedom of man, may not perish from off the earth," whereas the *Sterling Republican* concluded: "That the Government the people founded, by the people shall not perish." None of this was Lincoln's poetry, nor was all of it fully intelligible, but the newspapers offered what they could or would.

Sometimes editors provided more modest modifications and followed what they took to be the intention of the speaker. For example, the *Christian Recorder*, the voice of black Philadelphia, after reporting the president's words as "we owe this offering to our dead. We imbibe increased devotion," made sure that none misunderstood the message. It changed the last part of "a government of the people, by the people, for the people," into "for *all* the people." That made matters quite clear. The *Recorder* also quoted the Reverend Thomas Stockton's prayer; but perhaps more noticeable than either was the request by a church association for help for the "destitute" refugees coming into the city of Washington.

Then there were the ethnic papers, whose editors often struggled to make new life in America and the English language understandable to their immigrant readers. The only sizable group of non-English-speaking newcomers used German, and translators could be immediately tripped up by Lincoln's first sentence with the verb "conceived." Did the president say that Americans "thought up" something new? If so, what to do with the phrase "in Liberty"? Was the nation "thought up in Liberty"? Or did Lincoln speak in terms of a woman conceiving a baby? The German papers thought best to avoid pregnancy altogether (*schwanger werden*) and write of a nation "dictated by Liberty" (*von der Freiheit diktiert*), "dedicated to Liberty" (*der Freiheit geweihte Nation*), or to opt for the religious connotation of "hallowed by Liberty" (*von der Freiheit geheiligte Nation*).

"All men are created equal" caused trouble, too—linguistic as well as ideological. Pennsylvania's *Pittsburgher Volksblatt* translated Jefferson's words conservatively to mean equality before the law, while the *Freiheits Freund und Courier* of the same city used the straightforward German with its broader sense that could include social equality. Both were Republican, as was the most influential German paper in the middle part of the country, the *Westliche Post* in St. Louis. It went with the more conservative wording, and its translation was also limited by the inaccurate English transcription it used to begin with. While "Liberty" was given more secular or more religious connotations, "a new birth of freedom" could entirely disappear. Other vital words of Lincoln's speech also suggested similarly and crucially varying meanings in German, testifying to the old Italian adage: "*Trauduttore, traditore*—Translator, traitor." In any case, it would have taken an extraordinary poet-translator to do justice to Lincoln's words.

Though the *Westliche Post*, supporting the president's party, printed his speech, it did not wish to see him reelected, for he was only "an honest citizen of ordinary talent." Its chief rival in the West, the *Illinois Staats-Zeitung* of Lincoln's home state, wrote that "the speech of the honorable Edward Everett, the festive dirge of the choir, and the dedication talk of President Lincoln will be added to the annals of the war." But it printed none of them. Neither did the most important German paper in the East, the fiercely Democratic *New Yorker Staats-Zeitung*, though it reported that at the Gettysburg ceremonies the congressional chaplain gave a "long prayer" and the president a "short speech." As for Everett's "big" speech, the paper provided excerpts on its front page.

The latest from the battlefields of course trumped other news, and there came a good bit this November, especially about General Ulysses S. Grant, who turned defeat into victory at Chattanooga. The triumphant charge up Lookout Mountain in the "battle above the clouds" came only days after the Gettysburg dedication. Even when reporting on the latter, most small papers, and some metropolitan ones, saw news that touched them directly as more important. The *Maine Farmer* paid more attention to an eight-foot woman supposedly roaming the woods than what took place in faraway Gettysburg. And if the same state's *Daily Sentinel and Times* saw fit to print a version of the president's remarks, the story about two local soldiers who had disappeared in the battle surely appeared more crucial. In New Castle, Indiana, the dedication of the new United Brethren Church received more space than the dedication of the National Cemetery at Gettysburg.

Lincoln understood what the press could do to one's words. He might have agreed with Everett's note in his diary: reporters "under pretence of giving what 'Mr. E. said,' put down a great many things which he did not say, omit a great many which he did, often rendering the whole in a dialect of their own." Lincoln liked to take great care with the writing that he wanted to get out to the country. That he did not get to his Gettysburg remarks so as to preempt their being "mutilated & travestied," to quote again Everett's words, may suggest not only how busy the president was but that perhaps he went to Gettysburg, in large part, to nurture the mourners there, and his own soul.

Lincoln knew he would be assaulted. Those who felt constrained from going after his words directly substituted Seward as their whipping boy. In Gettysburg, the *Compiler* attacked Seward's speech repeatedly. In one issue that copied the *Age*, Philadelphia's Democratic voice, editor Stahle wondered that the patriots who died for their country did not rise to "wrathful life" at "the demon" Seward, who claimed that the war was for "a cause that the majority . . . hated and despised." In nearby Harrisburg, the Democratic organ complained that the Gettysburg ceremonies were "gotten up" more for party purposes than for "the glory of the nation and the honor of the dead," that abolitionism had been exalted there, and that Lincoln made "silly remarks." Considering that its editors, too, had been arrested during the previous year, this was mild. The local Republican paper, however, did not consider that as a mitigating factor and replied unflinchingly: "To approach the grave of a Union soldier, and not approve of abolitionism, would be equal to approaching a shrine of religion and not praying to the only true and living God." The *New York Tribune*'s reply to such Democratic attacks was equally straightforward. It praised the change from "Slavery to Liberty" through the Emancipation Proclamation, and then quoted Lincoln's "new birth of Freedom" and "under God."

The unkindest attack on Lincoln came from those in the Confederacy, and some in the North, who would take note only of his performance on the night before the ceremonies, placed that little ditty into the cemetery, and concluded that while people mourned, "Lincoln acted the clown." Such a "dignified address," sneered the *Richmond Dispatch*, reprinting all of that night's banter. Echoed a Cincinnati voice: "disgrace upon the nation." The Philadelphia *Age* cried "shame." "With the groans of the wounded still resounding in the air—corpses of the slain unburied—the bereaved still clad in the emblems of mourning, and their tears still flowing—these men meet to laugh and joke and electioneer." Others, too, commented on the "vulgar jargon" Lincoln threw up "over the graves of his countrymen." "His excellency appeared to be under the impression that the occasion was a political one," commented one editor, focusing on the words from that carousing night; he also saw no problem in printing Lincoln's speech at the cemetery and dismissing it as "few formal remarks . . . written out for him by another." The Dutch ambassador did not go so far; but he, too, only commented on the banter of the night as one of Lincoln's "pasquinades," a miserable parody by the American president. *The Times* in London reported in like spirit, though it also printed a truncated version of the cemetery speech.

People would later have it that Lincoln was let down by his performance and that Everett and Seward spoke their own disappointment to each other on the platform. With so many present, it seems unlikely that people could whisper negatives about the president. Yet it is also true that Lincoln was feeling low; he would soon take to bed with variola. Everett certainly did not mention the president's remarks in his diary. However, the next day, Everett sent thanks to him for his kindness to Charlotte, Everett's daughter, adding his "great admiration" for the "eloquent simplicity & appropriateness" of Lincoln's thoughts. "I should be glad, if I could flatter myself that I came as near to the central idea of the occasion, in two hours, as you did in two minutes." He also mentioned that both his son and daughter agreed with his sentiments. Everett was the perfect gentleman. In his diary, he noted only that he "wrote a few lines to the President thanking him for special attention to Charlie."

Lincoln replied on the same day in his usual humble manner: "I am pleased to know that in your judgment, the little I did say was not entirely a failure." He was indeed pleased. He returned Everett's compliment, describing the oration as "eminently satisfactory." The president identified two especially appealing sections next to each other in Everett's speech: the constitutional discussion, "one of the best arguments for national supremacy," and the "tribute to our noble women for their angel-ministering to the suffering soldiers." This surpassed anything said on the subject by others. Perhaps the president sent such a message to put to rest any discomfort the orator may have had about his speech lacking heart; or perhaps Lincoln did learn, after all, something about the aftermath of the battle.

But he said nothing about the lion's part of Everett's address: the history of the battle. If the disappointment of last July no longer burned in him, with the Army of the Potomac still failing to engage Lee at that very time, Lincoln could not underscore the acclaim Everett bestowed on Hooker and Meade.

Hay noted in his diary that the Tycoon and Everett had exchanged "mutual congratulations & civilities about the Gettysburg business." Earlier, he commented: "Mr. Everett spoke as he always does perfectly—and the President in a firm free way, with more grace than is his wont said his half dozen lines [Hay crossed out "words"] of consecration and the music wailed and we went home through the crowded and cheering streets. And all the particulars are in the daily papers. . . . We came home the night of the 19th." Though one "J.H." wrote felicitously about the Gettysburg doings, it would take Hay decades, as it would the country, to decide that what the president said there was truly significant.

The silence of the soldiers about Lincoln's speech may have been the most hurtful. To some at the cemetery it seemed as though the president had spoken deliberately to the group of fifty or so wounded veterans of the battle to whom he went directly once the ceremonies finished. But Frank Haskell, who with General John Gibbon represented the Army of the Potomac, and the Iron Brigade, wrote to his brother a day later, "We had little interest in the ceremonies." Did they see only a horde of civilians, who had never witnessed battle, prancing and pontificating over the bodies of the brave? Haskell and his commander, who had been wounded in the battle, toured the fields, then listened to the early part of Everett's oration, then tramped some more and, as Gibbon much later claimed, returned in time for Lincoln's "touching address."

A main reason for the creation of the National Cemetery and for the dedication service, according to David Wills, came from the desire to "kindle anew in the breasts of the Comrades of these brave dead . . . a confidence that they who sleep in death on the Battle Field are not forgotten . . . their remains will not be uncared for." Frank Haskell, however, wrote almost angrily about the cemetery: "without this collection of their bones, the places of their graves would soon be unknown, and the plow would have obliterated them. But what so appropriate for the soldier's rest as the spot where he died nobly fighting the enemies of the country,—when perhaps the shout of victory went up with his spirit to Heaven . . . what if the mound had been leveled with the plow . . . would be a holy spot . . . for a thousand years." Haskell went on to object bitterly to the bones of the brave being collected "like the bones of so many of horses," put into a box, and all this done for money. "It may be all right, but I do not see it."

Was Haskell speaking for many others, too? Could he have been responding to Everett's speech, which began with the history of ancient Greece and told of the heroes of the Battle of Marathon who "alone of all her sons were entombed upon the spot which they had forever rendered famous"? Everett's point was that the same honor was now being given to the heroes of Gettysburg on Cemetery Hill. Haskell, however, complained, almost perversely, that the dead were now buried "on a spot where there was no fighting—where none of them fell." Was the fighting for Cemetery Hill to be forgotten?

Haskell remained silent about the commander in chief's Gettysburg remarks at the time, as did nearly all men in uniform; but a rare exception came from a camp newspaper in far-away Utah Territory. "President Lincoln is not a polished speaker, neither does he wield a polished pen," the *Union Vedette* declared. It repeated words from Boston, labeling his speech "rough and loose," yet also "full of jewels. The ideas of duty are almost stammered out," but they are "noble. . . . One sentence should shine in letters of gold throughout the land . . . 'It is for us, the living, rather to be dedicated here to the unfinished work that they had thus so far nobly carried on.' "

If Lincoln understood the soldiers' indifferent response, he left no evidence. He certainly never saw Frank Haskell's comments. But the weak Republican press response to the Gettysburg remarks must have been disappointing—though, once again, if he spoke of it, the words do not survive. For the first time he had taken the trouble of going away from Washington to give a prepared speech. And what happened? So many of his messages, even off-the-cuff remarks, received more comment than did his words at Gettysburg. Did the newspaper reaction represent well the feelings of the country?

As the press responded, or failed to respond, to his Gettysburg remarks, Lincoln put forth some of their ideas elsewhere. The Presidential Proclamation of Thanksgiving in 1863 gave thanks on behalf of the nation for a "large increase of freedom." Similarly, those who heard an expansive vision of equality and liberty in Lincoln's Gettysburg speech saw it reinforced in the more carefully constructed Annual Message. It appeared in the press in early December to prolific commentary. Unlike his Gettysburg remarks, which the major papers generally buried in the cemetery proceedings, the Annual Message stood alone on its own. It spoke not of a "new birth of freedom" but of the "new reckoning." Not that Lincoln was unrealistic about race relations. Had he not told Frederick Douglass, to his face, about the ugly necessity to move ahead deliberately, lest "all the hatred which is poured on the head of the Negro race would be visited upon his administration"? Douglass repeated those words for the public. Lincoln's Annual Message noted, too, that at first "hope, and fear, and doubt contended in uncertain conflict" about the "new aspect" that Emancipation and black soldiers "gave the future." But like Lincoln, Douglass also announced that "the mission of this war is National regeneration." Was Douglass repeating Lincoln, or was it the reverse? The president's Annual Message certainly made clear what the war now meant. He concluded his address with the ringing declaration that "the world must stand indebted" to the Union soldiers "for the home of freedom disenthralled, regenerated, enlarged, and perpetuated."

The press reaction to the Annual Message and the Amnesty Proclamation, which would spell out in December 1864 the terms for the return of Confederates to the national fold, followed the earlier pattern, but there was so very much more of it. The Republican *Berkshire County Eagle* of Massachusetts commended the Annual Message "to the careful study of our readers, who, we are sure, will find it distinguished by that practical sense and honest intentions which distinguished all the President's acts." The Raleigh, North Carolina, *Weekly Standard* saw that Lincoln "has chosen the proper means of making our *whole country free."* On the other hand, the *Coshocton Democrat* of Ohio mused that "no one can rise from its perusal without conjecturing that Lincoln has negro blood in his veins. Surely no other sort of a man could so humble the white race to benefit the negro. Under this programme, the old Government and Union may be considered gone forever, and Peace indefinitely postponed."

Lincoln's messages provoked wide and loud reactions and would remain points of contention through the election year of 1864. But his Gettysburg remarks were not entirely forgotten. In February 1864, he was asked twice for copies to help raise money for charitable purposes. The fact that the document was brief made it easier to anticipate success. Everett made the first appeal, together with Julia K. Fish, the wife of Hamilton Fish. "The manuscript of my Gettysburg Address," Everett wrote in his diary, would be beautifully bound together, "in full green morocco, gilt edges," and would include a map of the battlefield, the cemetery plan, "photographic likenesses" of Meade and various corps commanders, "and the manuscript of President Lincoln's remarks."

Lincoln indeed had agreed to help the Metropolitan Fair in New York and sent to Everett "my remarks," to use his own term. He probably used but did not copy either the "official" or the AP version of his speech; and he made two significant changes from his "second draft" that replicated, in his own hand, what he actually said at Gettysburg. In the long last sentence, he not only included "under God" and moved it to a more felicitous place, but also changed the focus from the United States alone to the universal "government of the people, by the people, for the people." He changed some other words, too, inserted commas, tried to improve cadence—in short, worked on the manuscript, seeing importance in it. [Appendix B has all versions.]

Presumably to help try to sell the document, cards of Lincoln's "eloquent remarks" were printed for the fair. As it turned out, the document did not sell, at least no evidence survives. Yet in advertising the availability of the manuscript, a Boston paper wrote that this was "frequently pronounced the most felicitous of the President's occasional speeches."

The second request for a copy of the speech came from the famed historian George Bancroft. The president's handwriting was to be lithographed for a volume of facsimiles to benefit the Baltimore Sanitary Fair. As Lincoln wrote out a copy, perhaps he took the time to read the words aloud to him-

Lincoln sends a copy of his speech to historian George Bancroft. (Cornell University)

self. He made his few changes with care, bringing back the memory of more leisurely times when he was not surrounded by a bloodbath. He improved punctuation and changed the function word "upon" into "on" in the second version. ("Four score and seven years ago our fathers brought forth, on [upon] this continent, a new nation, conceived in Liberty, and dedicated to the proposition that all men are created equal.") "Herewith is the copy of the manuscript which you did me the honor to request," went the laconic note accompanying the text.

The manuscript the president sent to Bancroft had no title, lacked a signature, had almost no margins, and was written on pages one and three of a folded sheet. The editor of the volume then complained that the manuscript could not be used for the purposes of printing and Lincoln made still another copy. He again changed punctuation and left out "here" from a middle part: "that cause for which they [here] gave the last full measure of devotion. . . ." Some might say that the little changes made improvements, that a great speaker-poet was at work; some might say that he was just careless. But for the first time he entitled his words "Address delivered at the dedication of the Cemetery at Gettysburg," signed his full name, and added the date: "November 19, 1863." The "remarks" were growing in stature before his eyes.

Bancroft kept the first copy. Alexander Bliss—Bancroft's stepson and another member of the Baltimore Sanitary Fair Committee—who prepared an autograph anthology for which he handled the second copy, kept that. Instead of being sold at the time, each stayed in the possession of their respective families well into the twentieth century. If the "Address . . . at Gettysburg" found no worthy buyers in 1864, an eagle resting on a globe, made from the hair of "President Lincoln and member of his Cabinet," did, and so did his "shocking bad hat."

A facsimile of the manuscript appeared in the very fine literary anthology also issued to raise funds for the Baltimore Sanitary Fair. *Autograph Leaves of Our Country's Authors*, edited by John P. Kennedy, contained the lithographed reproduction of handwritten manuscripts from Audubon, Bryant, Cooper, Emerson, Hawthorne, Holmes, Washington Irving, Lowell, Longfellow, Melville, Poe, Stowe, and Thoreau—among others. The shortest pieces were less than a page, the longest, seven pages, by the historian William H. Prescott and the poets William Cullen Bryant and Henry Wadsworth Longfellow. The literary elite came to the aid of the country's soldiers. If they did not contribute their best work, and if their handwriting was sometimes illegible, that made Lincoln's beautiful words, written in a beautiful hand, look all the more remarkable. Lincoln's two pages and few lines appeared second in the book, after Francis Scott Key's "Star-Spangled Banner."

The president could not have been in better literary company—unless Walt Whitman had been included. Lincoln also had much forgettable company in the book; did he wonder whether he would have been included were he not the president? Much more than the generally well hidden newspaper reports of November 1863, lost in the lengthy reports on the Gettysburg ceremonies, the *Autograph Leaves*, aided by the pamphlets of Everett's address that also included Lincoln, most likely allowed such luminaries as Emerson, Sumner, and Harriet Beecher Stowe to make highly complimentary comments after Lincoln's assassination about his cemetery speech. And the *Autograph Leaves* traveled abroad, too.

The two Gettysburg manuscripts were not the only ones Lincoln contributed to charity. A copy of his 1863 Thanksgiving Proclamation was also sent to New York for the Metropolitan Fair. For Philadelphia's June 1864 Great Central Sanitary Fair, which Lincoln attended in person, forty-eight copies of the "authorized" edition of the Emancipation Proclamation were printed, each signed by him as well as by Seward and Secretary Nicolay. Earlier, the original manuscript of the Proclamation had obtained the largest single sum at the Northwestern Sanitary Fair in Chicago: $3,000. Lincoln acknowledged wanting to keep that paper, but made the gift anyhow. The sale provoked other requests for manuscripts. Dollar signs danced in charitable eyes, but the funds went to a worthy cause. Lincoln may have known almost nothing about the after-battle disaster of Gettysburg, but all understood that the Sanitary Commission's wartime work, which the fairs supported, was beyond price.

In December 1863, Ohio senators John Sherman and Benjamin Wade had asked for the Presidential Proclamation of Amnesty and Reconstruction that had been issued on December 8. This time, the Great Western Sanitary Fair in Cincinnati was to benefit. The original having been defaced, Lincoln offered, in Sherman's words, "to copy it himself, retaining all the marks, erasures, notes, and additions. He said that if a great deal of additional labor by him would relieve the suffering of a single soldier, he would cheerfully perform it." The text was more than four times the length of the Gettysburg remarks.

The folks out west thought that the original manuscript, with Lincoln's corrections, would "make it much more valuable as an historical curiosity." It evidently did not occur to them to ask for the Gettysburg speech, though Ohio had soldiers specially furloughed to attend the dedication. The state had also sent a special train and three governors, past and present, leading Lincoln to ask, after being introduced, "how many more Governors has Ohio?" The special program that the state hosted on the 19th in the Presbyterian Church also received much publicity. But then, even if many in Cincinnati may have thought the president's Gettysburg remarks admirable, the Amnesty Proclamation had much more immediate interest, especially on the border of a slave state. Politics, after all, was politics. Indeed, the Cincinnati "Autograph Committee" collected and sold the handwriting of various celebrities from P. T. Barnum to President James Buchanan. Prices ranged from $5 to $15, with Lafayette fetching $35. The Amnesty Proclamation brought in $150.

Of course, not only the president's manuscripts were solicited for sale at charitable functions. It would have been too much of an imposition to ask Everett to copy his oration, but he did donate the copy of one part of "my Gettysburg address" to the Brooklyn Sanitary Fair. The full manuscript he gave to the New York Sanitary Fair. The printed versions he sent to a large number of people. On February 2, 1864, alone, his diary records his sending it to three Gettysburg professors, two cabinet members, and one general.

None of this is to say that Lincoln did not know that the words he spoke at the National Cemetery would be reported across the land and were therefore important. But when did he begin to have an inkling about the legend of Gettysburg that was being born even as he spoke? Everett understood more from the start, at least hoped for more, calling the battle (as Stockton and so many others did) "the" turning point of the war, where the nation was saved. But even after hearing both Stockton and Everett, Lincoln could not speak at Gettysburg of "the" great battle of the war, only "a great battle-field of the war." This was consistent with his letter earlier in the year to his friend Conkling, to be read out at an Illinois public meeting, which he surely considered much more crucial than the cemetery remarks, and which, as elections approached, eloquently defended the war and black freedom: "Among free men, there can be no successful appeal from the ballot to the bullet . . . a just God, in his own good time, will give us the rightful result." Only the careful listener, or reader, would have noticed that the president's letter lumped together the battles of "Antietam, Murfreesboro, Gettysburg"—having earlier alluded to the action at Vicksburg and Port Hudson that cleared the Mississippi River.

Lincoln's reluctance to anoint Gettysburg came in part from the need to emphasize the "unfinished work," which did not allow for declaring that the great battle, the turning point, had come. The politician had to be also careful about diminishing the valor on other battlefields by other soldiers. Even his impromptu remarks after the battle would name no names, "lest I might do wrong to those I might forget." But most fundamentally, Lincoln's disappointment in the outcome of the battle never quite died. As the North had celebrated in July the life-saving victory, the president addressed General Meade, though in the end only himself, since he never sent the letter: "I had been oppressed ever nearly since the battles at Gettysburg ... I do not believe you appreciate the magnitude of the misfortune involved in Lee's escape. He was within your easy grasp, and to have closed upon him would, in connection with our other late successes, have ended the war."

However that was, many in the North saw Lee's invasion in apocalyptic terms, and when victory came it seemed like deliverance to them, including to Stockton and Everett. Lincoln saw the invasion as a great and, in no small part, a lost opportunity. He was grateful for the Union victory, but for him Gettysburg was "a great battle-field of the war." Everett and the Northern people thought differently.

So again, when did Lincoln begin to have an inkling about the legend of Gettysburg aborning, or the part his own words were playing in it? Perhaps the adulation showered on the ceremonies, the reverence bestowed on Everett, the two separate requests he received for copies of his speech, helped begin to clear the air for him. James Speed, Lincoln's Attorney General, also remembered the president telling him that "he had never received a compliment he prized more highly" than the one received from Everett. Lincoln's son Robert recalled a similar reaction, his father even reading the Everett note to him shortly after returning from Gettysburg. Judge Advocate General Joseph Holt had much the same recollection. Lincoln was no braggart, but the man who wrote poetry in his younger days now seemed to need reassurance. By the spring of 1865, when Senator Charles Sumner showed him a letter from the Duchess of Argyll about the situation in America, the president copied a part of it in his own hand. The last sentence said that "the speech at the Gettysburg Cemetery must live." As far as Everett was concerned, it is possible that Hay was right to dismiss the exchange between the Orator and the Tycoon as "mutual congratulations & civilities about the Gettysburg business;" but he was wrong about his boss.

So Lincoln took satisfaction in knowing that some discerned a treasure in his rapidly written "remarks." But it is certain that he considered the Emancipation Proclamation his most important document, and the First Inaugural Address, which tried to prevent war, and the Second Inaugural, which hoped to help make a lasting peace, his crucial speeches. When he invited artists to work for long periods of time in the White House, they painted "the Emancipator." The market for popular art, not a bad measure of public interest in the second half of the nineteenth century, would second that judgment. As he was sanctified after his assassination, lithographs and engravings of the Emancipator, the family man, the dying hero or the heaven-ascending one, flooded the North. Gettysburg? That was a battle where the nation had been saved. That is what Everett had made crystal clear.

Thanks to Everett's efforts, the president's words would continue to appear in print in 1864—tagged on to Everett most of the time. The *American Literary Gazette* praised Lincoln's speech as being "something like Mr. Everett's writing, only with more force and decision. . . ." One of the campaign biographies, out of Boston, reproduced the speech, as well as others, admiring it as "brief, appropriate, touching, and beautiful. . . . His generous nature clasped the lifeless forms of those who saved their country nobly sacrificing themselves; and he would recognize the obligations of the living to the martyred dead." Additional early printings would occur each time Pennsylvania updated its report about the National Cemetery, though Lincoln's address could quite disappear among the minutes of meetings, letters, speeches, and what not. It certainly would not be highlighted on the title page of these books—as was, for example, Major General O. O. Howard's address delivered when the cornerstone of the soldiers' monument was laid at the Gettysburg Cemetery on July 4, 1865. Wills's report to the Pennsylvania legislature about the cemetery would quote Everett, not Lincoln.

Though the program of the 1865 dedication included only one item from the 1863 ceremonies, Benjamin French's Ode, Howard, the newly appointed head of the Freedmen's Bureau, proclaimed that Gettysburg's "dead did not die in vain, and the nation has *experienced already the new birth of freedom.*" The general repeated in full the martyred president's "few remarkable words"—after he spoke reverently of Everett's address that "has long ago become historical. . . . These grounds have already been consecrated," Howard noted, "and are doubly sacred from the memory of our brethren who lie here, and from the association with those remarkable men, Mr. EVERETT and Mr. LINCOLN. . . ."

At the 1865 cornerstone laying, many items were buried for future ages to find, among them copies of the Declaration of Independence, the Constitution, Washington's Farewell Address, and a lot more of much less consequence. Since a "Copy of the proceedings at the consecration of the 'Soldiers' National Cemetery'" was also buried, Lincoln's speech should have been there too, hidden. Among individual items honoring Lincoln were a silver medal, his annual messages, his Second Inaugural Address, and the Emancipation Proclamation.

During the Civil War, the U.S. government routinely published various presidential proclamations. Republican propaganda groups, the numerous "Loyal Publication Societies," printed an assortment of Lincoln statements and the Union League Clubs, formed to support the administration, conducted massive publication programs. People could obtain the Emancipation Proclamation; Lincoln's comments about slavery; various printings of the letter to Erastus Corning and the letter about Clement Vallandigham and "arbitrary arrests"; also a missive to Missouri radicals. Even the letter he sent to British workingmen expressing international solidarity found its way into a separate publication. During the 1864 presidential campaign, *Harper's Weekly*, perhaps atoning for having failed to publish the Gettysburg remarks, described the address as "the most perfect piece of American eloquence." But excepting the card printed for the failed attempt to sell the Everett-Lincoln manuscript in New York, and a printing for an Arlington Cemetery funeral service in 1868, not until the end of the 1880s does an elaborate listing of Lincoln-related publications include the Gettysburg Address.

Still, some with exceptionally good ears, like the Duchess of Argyll, began to see greatness in Lincoln's 272 words. That at least some people were talking about the speech seriously can be seen from the use of the word "creed" in an attack on Lincoln by the acerbic Polish refugee Adam Gurowski:

> *Shifter, shuffler, beast—an ass! Creed at Gettysburg?*
> *Bah! His eye on platform,*
> *Re-election.*

Oxford professor Goldwin Smith published a perceptive article about the American president in *Macmillan's Magazine* in February 1865, which inspired the duchess. It labeled Lincoln "the greatest orator of the United States," printed the text of the Gettysburg speech, and exclaimed, "it may be doubted whether any king in Europe would have expressed himself more royally than the peasant's son." In late March of 1865, Charles Francis Adams, Jr., twenty-nine, bowled over by the Second Inaugural Address, exclaimed to his father, the U.S. minister in London: "That rail-splitting lawyer is one of the wonders of the day. Once in Gettysburg and now again on a greater occasion he has shown a capacity for rising to the demands of the hour."

By then, the war's end was in sight; Lincoln, the victorious chief, began to look great. Before long, one could hear of the speech in Europe. In 1866, Ernest Duvergier de Hauranne described it as the height of "modern eloquence . . . he achieves grandiose simplicity, the austere and patriotic breath of antiquity; but one feels at the same time the emotion of a human and Christian soul facing the horrors of the civil war." And surely from France the word went to other places on the Continent.

The assassination made a difference, or at least gave people the opportunity to voice their views about the "nation's martyr." Some noticed beauty in Lincoln's Gettysburg words. Billy Herndon, Lincoln's old law partner, went about interviewing people and corresponding with many about Lincoln. In one of the hundreds of interviews and letters to him, the Harvard-educated lawyer Daniel Webster Wilder in 1866 mentioned the president's "greatest speech." In 1867, a Gettysburg hospital nurse and cook, Anna Holstein, published recollections of her work, and described the president's speech as "memorable." She said she was glad that her group had stood close enough to the platform that she "heard distinctly every word." A Christian Commission publication praised the speech. Joshua Speed labeled it the only speech that was "artistic complete," and also thought that "when the gems of American literature come to be selected," more would be chosen from Lincoln than from any other author. His brother, James, would recall similar reactions from others. Francis Lieber, who savored the English language perhaps the way only an immigrant can, suggested within days of the assassination that the finest monument to the American martyr would be the publication of his own words. The three-hundred-page book that quickly followed included the "speech" at Gettysburg and called it "world-renowned."

Ralph Waldo Emerson, who gave a funeral oration for Lincoln, declared that the "brief speech at Gettysburg will not easily be surpassed by words on any recorded occasion." Among other places this sentiment was heard in Utah, where the soldiers' paper, the *Union Vedette*, noted it had been "discovered" that the late president "was wonderfully eloquent." The paper made up for its earlier mixed judgment by printing his speech at last.

Isaac Arnold, in a book about his friend and the "Overthrow of Slavery," maintained that "for appropriateness, comprehension, grasp of thought, brevity, beauty, the sublime sentiment and expression, has scarcely its equal in English or American literature." Harriet Beecher Stowe perceptively identified Lincoln's three most beautiful utterances: his Farewell to Springfield, his Gettysburg Address, and the Second Inaugural. "Perhaps [in] no language, ancient or modern, are any number of words found more touching and eloquent than his speech on November 19, 1863." Stowe added for good measure: "He wrote it in a few moments, while on the way to the celebration." That her son had been seriously wounded at Gettysburg surely had something to do with her comments. James Russell Lowell in his "Ode" recited at the Harvard Commemoration wrote of the "new birth of our new soil, the first American." Most prophetical, Senator Sumner quoted the final words of Lincoln's address and called it "a monumental act," second only to the Emancipation Proclamation. As intellectuals are wont to do, for they prize ideas, Sumner explained: "the battle itself was less important than the speech." To the extent praise came to Lincoln's speech, it came not from those who heard him at Gettysburg, but mostly from people far away.

There must have been others who spoke in a positive vein, but these strong voices were unusual even in the year of Lincoln's assassination. The many sermons preached upon his death, with few exceptions, did not note his Gettysburg words, unless to declare that his visit there converted him to Christianity. Some might see the most revealing allusion coming from Philadelphia's Reverend J. G. Butler: "Nations, as well as individuals, may have their second birth—*must be born again*—before they are prepared for a pure, vigorous, and useful manhood. Our nation *has* been born again, amid the terrible carnage of the battlefield. . . ." Yet at Lincoln's funeral, the Methodist bishop Matthew Simpson quoted five different Lincoln speeches, his 1862 letter to Horace Greeley, and also words attributed to the "Great Martyr," the emancipator of a race—but not the Gettysburg remarks. A sermon preached and published in Gettysburg itself did not mention the speech, though it quoted his Farewell to his hometown, mentioned the Second Inaugural, and praised the "Great Liberator."

George Bancroft may have requested the copies of the Gettysburg speech hoping to raise money for soldiers, but his funeral oration took no notice of it. Instead, he said much about Union and Emancipation. Did Bancroft ask for those remarks because they were "short and sweet like the old woman's dance"—to borrow the words the young Lincoln is supposed to have uttered about a speech he made on his political principles?

Poetical tributes, too, poured out of the country upon Lincoln's assassination but with few exceptions did not mention the Gettysburg speech. The countless obituaries were no different. If the abolitionist William Lloyd Garrison's *Liberator* reprinted the text and quoted the praise of Oxford don Goldwyn Smith, the eulogy delivered by W. E. Guthrie to the American Literary Union did not conjure up Gettysburg. For more than two decades after 1863, Lincoln turned out to be the prophet who said, "The world will little note, nor long remember what we say here, but it can never forget what they did here." The fame of the battle grew and grew; Lincoln's remarks helped that growth, but beyond that mostly stayed in the background. In Gettysburg, the anniversaries would come and go, and almost nothing would be said about the long-ago speech of the Civil War president. Much the same appears to have been true in other parts of the country, too.

If Lincoln's words did continue to live as part of the larger Gettysburg story, it was because the 1863 commemorations as a whole, led by Edward Everett, played a significant part in making people see the battle as the decisive moment of the Civil War, the bloodiest days of the war that inexorably led to Appomattox. Other factors, too, would contribute to such vision. Among these were the numerous states that were represented both in the battle and at the cemetery; a central geographical location that many could visit; Gettysburg's own boosterism; the Eastern newspapers, which dominated the press; and the Westerners who could go along because, as the *Chicago Tribune* explained, "Bunker Hill speaks for New England, but Gettysburg speaks for the whole North. . . . Aye, and for the South, for are not her sons there also?" Indeed, before long, white Southerners created the Lost Cause mythology that, among other things, made the Gettysburg defeat central to the outcome of the war, the battle where the incomparable and blameless General Lee had been let down by his lieutenants. But Lincoln's words at first had a small role in all this.

Because he did not share the vision of Gettysburg's central significance, it was ironic that the president's words, too, however modestly, would support that perception simply by being associated with the battle. But it would take decades before it became important that he gave the Gettysburg, and not the Antietam or Chancellorsville Address. A generation had to pass before his "few appropriate remarks" grew into *the* Gettysburg Address. Out of the sacred space the sacred text would grow. Late in the century, Americans would rediscover Lincoln's remarks in their own right, call them by the name we still know, begin to turn the text into a revered document, and find the meaning of their country there. In the twenty-first century, Americans are still saying this is who we are.

Back in November 1863 in Lincoln's home state, far from Gettysburg, the *Chicago Tribune*, having reported 50,000 in attendance, summed up matters: "More than any other single event will this glorious dedication nerve the heroism, and deepen the resolution of the living. . . . More than anything else will this day's work contribute to the nationality of the great Republic."

The legend of Gettysburg was beginning to spread across the land. As people left the place of the nation's epic "deliverance," each took along a piece of the great festival, like a piece of the true cross. *"An altar will rise . . .* worthy of the future of the nation," Robert Harper wrote in the *Sentinel*. "Gettysburg [will] be forever a shrine of pilgrimage. . . . The memory of the day . . . will never leave them."

Benjamin French left Gettysburg on November 20. Once back in Washington, he recorded in his diary how deeply honored he felt to have his Ode sung before the president's remarks. In Gettysburg, the *Sentinel* would print French's lines twice, in consecutive issues:

> *A thousand years shall pass away—*
> *A Nation still shall mourn this clay.*
> *Which now is blest.*

Hundreds of thousands, perhaps millions around the country, would read his BEAUTIFUL POEM, as one newspaper defined it in big letters. Typeset with indented margins, readers' eyes focused on it immediately. Sometimes the Ode got equal headlines with Everett, and larger ones than Lincoln. If the president's words served to open the *Autograph Leaves of Our Country's Authors* in 1864, right after "The Star-Spangled Banner," French's Ode would serve to conclude it, occupying the next-to-last spot, before "Home Sweet Home."

French deeply respected the president and wrote that

> *Abraham Lincoln is the idol of the American people at this moment. Any-one who saw & heard as I did, the hurricane of applause that met his every movement in Gettysburg would know that he lived in every heart. It was no cold, faint shadow of a kind reception—it was a tumultuous outpouring of ex-ultation, from true and loving hearts, at the sight of the man who everyone knew to be honest and true and sincere in every act of his life, and every pulsa-tion of his heart. It was the spontaneous outburst of heartfelt confidence in their own* President.

French, too, exulted. Like thousand of others, he had lived an unforget-table day. And without intending to make invidious comparisons, the com-ments in his diary ranked clearly the different speakers. He mentioned only three. Everett gave an oration that "could not be surpassed by mortal man." Stockton "made one of the most impressive and eloquent prayers I ever heard." And Lincoln, "in a few brief, but most appropriate words, dedicated the cemetery."

French seemed not to want to leave Gettysburg. He toured the battlefield, and photographer Alexan-der Gardner caught him at the widow Leister's house, General Meade's old headquarters, and posed him on the porch on November 20, 1863. (National Archives)

CHAPTER SEVEN

GLORIA

French stayed an extra day in Gettybsurg after the ceremonies were over. He seemed to dislike to leave the place. He toured the battlefield once more. He went in a group with his horse, a "hard going" and "headstrong" beast, but had a very fine guide, John B. Bachelder, who was "preparing a map" and had studied the terrain thoroughly. The local papers carried advertisements for Bachelder's work, to be published soon, with ever more generals and professors of the College testifying to its accuracy. Bachelder described the ground for his visitors from various vantage points, clearly and in an "interesting manner." The group saw the spot where General John Reynolds died; went back to Cemetery Hill, where the third day's charge took place; and more. At "the clump of trees," many of the largest specimens "were cut off from 6 to 10 feet above the ground by shot and shell."

French wandered off by himself to find Meade's headquarters, perforated by "shot and shell." A *New York Times* reporter, walking close by, counted the carcasses of ten dead horses within "a stone's throw of the whitewashed hut" and blamed the "negligence, or laziness or stupidity of the people of Gettysburgh" that invited pestilence. French noted two dead horses right next to the house—"very offensive"—but took the trouble to talk to the son of the widow who lived there. A three-months' soldier back from service, the young man told of burning fifteen horses that had been killed close to the house, but the two were so close that he had to leave them lest he burn down the house. He had also repaired much damage, but plenty remained. His mother, the widow Leister, was not there to start on her litany: " 'She lost a heap.' The house was robbed of almost everything. . . ." Before French could leave, Alexander Gardner, the Washington "photographist" working around the battlefield, asked him to pose on "the piazza, or porch" of the house, and he did so in the company of two little children. As late as the 1880s, the body of an unknown soldier would be dug up on the property and reburied at the National Cemetery.

Back in town, French heard of a terrible new calamity. "In less than 10 minutes after I passed," he noted in his diary, "a man and a boy who were engaged in *unloading* a shell, were blown up by its exploding—the boy killed instantly & the man losing both arms. . . ." The local papers gave more exact details a few days later. A Philadelphia father had come to collect the remains of his soldier son, and also to witness the ceremonies. He took off the cap of a shell and was hitting it on a stone to loosen the powder and take out the balls when it exploded. Both his hands were so badly mangled they had to be amputated. A fragment struck an orphan boy standing by, cutting him almost in two. He died in a few minutes.

The horrifying story was not uncommon for Gettysburg. Most of the weapons and other valuables of war left on the battlefield had been collected, but the millions of bullets were free for the taking. Gathering them up could make money for people, and taking shells apart could be much fun—also deadly. Taking a hammer to a shell to unload it was inviting to both children and adults. When a mishap occurred, someone was maimed or killed, newspapers made much of it. Now on November 20, with so many reporters still stuck in town, the story of the new accident ran all over the country.

Reading it in the "Washington Cronicle," Sergeant Miller, in far away Virginia, got it into his head that the dead boy was his son. The men of Company K had heard of the accidents that had been taking place; the father of one boy who was killed had belonged to the unit until he had to be discharged for disability. Learning of still another death, Miller wrote an almost angry letter to his wife Lile: "Why in the name of common sense don't they let those things alone." No soldier would think of unloading a shell; only veteran artillerymen could do the job. "If I were in father's place I would take the hide off any of the boys that would touch them." The sergeant wanted his wife to be very careful about Charley. Even picking up and throwing down a shell on its cap could make it explode.

When no news came from home, Miller grew frantic about his son. Then at last a letter arrived from Lile: all was well. Relief, sweet relief—but how he yearned to go home. He sat down to write to his wife: "If only these Six months were Past that I could get there for good But I must wait and may god assist us to Bear it Patiently. . . . Heaven Bless and Protect you, a kiss for Dear Little Charley yours most truly M. M. Miller." He posted it off. The next day was Thanksgiving.

The holiday came a week after the consecration of the cemetery in Gettysburg. Americans celebrated Thanksgiving for the first time as a national day, so proclaimed by the president. Newspapers around the North had published the Proclamation when Lincoln issued it early in October and as the holiday arrived in November, often republished it. Set to music as "The President's Hymn" by a prominent Episcopalian minister, William A. Muehlenberg, on Thanksgiving Day it was sung in homes, churches, army camps, onboard navy ships, and at various gatherings, even abroad at American diplomatic posts. The Proclamation and the Hymn were probably the most reproduced Lincoln documents of the war. In Ballston, Vermont, the *Journal* offered one hundred copies for two dollars.

Almost as much as Lincoln's dedicatory words at the National Cemetery, the National Thanksgiving sprang from the Battle of Gettysburg. That victory, together with Vicksburg, gave the president confidence to create a national holiday. The editor of one of the most influential publications of the nineteenth century, Sarah Josepha Hale's *Godey's Lady's Book*, the magazine for women that reached well over a million readers a year by 1860, had championed such a holiday for long. The Civil War made her calls ever more urgent. She wanted *"our annual Thanksgiving made into a national and fixed Union festival,"* as she wrote the president in September 1863—her words underlined and with important words capitalized. The holiday was to become "permanently an American custom and institution." Hale suggested that to create this "Union Thanksgiving," the chief executive must approach every state. But Lincoln bypassed the states, going straight to the people.

"The year that is drawing towards its close, has been filled with the

Harper's Weekly, *December 5, 1863, devoted its centerfold to the first national Thanksgiving celebration.* (HARPWEEK)

blessings of fruitful fields and healthful skies" the president's call, countersigned by Secretary of State Seward, began.

Needful diversions of wealth and of strength from the fields of peaceful industry to the national defence, have not arrested the plough, the shuttle or the ship; the axe has enlarged the borders of our settlements, and the mines, as well of iron and coal as of the precious metals, have yielded even more abundantly than heretofore. Population has steadily increased, notwithstanding the waste that has been made in the camp, the siege and the battle-field; and the country, rejoicing in the consciousness of augmented strength and vigor, is permitted to expect continuance of years with large increase of freedom. No human counsel hath devised nor hath any mortal hand worked out these great things. They are the gracious gifts of the Most High God, who, while dealing with us in anger for our sins, hath nevertheless remembered mercy.

In Gettysburg the *Sentinel*, which carried no comment on Lincoln's speech at the cemetery, called it "a very beautiful document" and tied to it the "immortal deeds upon the heights" of the battlefield—together with the triumph of the moment at the Battle of Chattanooga. The wider press tended to treat the Thanksgiving Proclamation as it did Lincoln's Gettysburg speech: here was another poem/prayer. Once again the president did not bring forth a policy that readily called for defense or attack, though both came. The Proclamation could be admired or disliked, politicized or not. But in the end the establishing of a national holiday brought to Lincoln's words much more editorial comment and wider publication than did the Gettysburg remarks. Indeed, compared to the President's Proclamation and Hymn, his remarks at Gettysburg shrank to modest significance. On the very day Lincoln spoke at the cemetery, newspapers around the country that would ignore those words printed his Proclamation, or his Hymn, or both. In the midst of a bloody war they exuded tranquility. They promised "peace beyond all understanding."

In light of the later fame of the Gettysburg Address, the ultimate irony came from the fact that not Lincoln, but Secretary of State William Seward wrote the Thanksgiving Proclamation. But the public never found this out, and before too many years passed not only forgot the Proclamation but also Lincoln's decisive role in establishing the beloved national holiday.

The Lincolns' Thanksgiving Day was a quiet one. The president was ill. But Gettysburg had left its marks on him—even his dreams. Some weeks later in the midst of his night's sleep he found himself among a throng of plain folk and heard the comment: "He is a very common-looking man." Lincoln replied quickly: "Common-looking people are the best in the world: that is the reason the Lord makes so many of them."

His wife noticed a change in her husband. She knew that he was "not a technical Christian . . . had no hope & no faith in the usual acceptation of those words: he never joined a church"—but had seen her husband affected when Willie died in 1862. Then, "about the time he went to Gettysburg,"

The country's leading picture magazine knew what was important to the American People. (HARPWEEK)

Mary told Billy Herndon in 1866, her husband felt "religious More than Ever." Others must have noticed a change, too, because before long the legends began. In time the faithful would grow certain that at Gettysburg Lincoln became what Mary called "a technical Christian."

On his first day back in the White House, the president certainly spent time on pardons. "Major General Schenck," he wrote to the officer who had been on his train to Gettysburg. "It is my wish that neither Maynadier, nor Gordon, be executed without my further order. Please act upon this." Both were Confederates.

> *Major General Meade, Army of the Potomac. If there is a man by the name of King under sentence to be shot, please suspend the execution till further order, and send record.*

Major Gen. Meade, Army of the Potomac. An intelligent woman [in]
deep distress, called this morning, saying her husband, a Lieutenant in the A.P.
was to be shot next Monday for desertion; and putting a letter in my hand, upon
which I relied for particulars, she left without mentioning a name, or other
particular by which to identify the case. On opening the letter I found it equally
vague, having nothing to identify by, except her own signature, which seems to
be "Mrs. Anna S. King" I could not again find her. If you have a case which you
shall think [sic] is probably the one intended, please apply my despatch of this
morning to it.

But variola, the mild form of smallpox, overtook him. He was ill, and his
son Tad was still ill also. Lincoln stayed sick for the next three weeks and
more. Some days he felt better than on others; some days he felt more compelled to work than others, regardless of how he felt. News of his contagious
illness reached Gettysburg, as did his quip, "I have something now to *give* to
everybody." He insisted on reviewing his Annual Message with his cabinet,
but at one point his doctor forbade him to see visitors, another cabinet meeting had to be canceled, and the newspapers put out bulletins about the state
of his health. Republican papers wished him speedy recovery; Democratic
ones often made snide remarks. The *Richmond Dispatch* was sorry to hear
the news, "not on account of Lincoln, but of the varioloid. . . . Why don't he
get the smallpox?" Then, on November 28, the press reported that both he
and his son were "much better." Mrs. Lincoln even took a trip to New York;
she must have needed relief from the pressure, but her husband was still
weak. On December 4, he telegraphed her, "All going well," and sent the
same daily report thereafter, though his full recovery took another ten days.

During this period, Lincoln completed his Annual Message to Congress and issued his Amnesty Proclamation—both to an avalanche of
praise and condemnation. Lincoln thanked the Chicago jeweler who donated the watch Lincoln received as the largest donor to the Chicago Sanitary Fair, having made a gift of the manuscript of his final Emancipation
Proclamation. And at one point an unusual house guest arrived: his wife's
favorite half sister, Emilie Todd Helm. The president thought it best to
keep the matter quiet, though few things could be kept quiet in Washington. And what did Mrs. Helm, this widow of a Confederate general and the
commander in chief of the Union armies, talk about? We know only that
they hugged often.

Lincoln and his son both recovered, most likely they had partial immunity to smallpox. William Johnson, Lincoln's faithful friend and helper, did not, and when he fell ill, he had to be hospitalized. He had probably nursed Lincoln not only on the trip back from Gettysburg but in the White House, too. Now he had the smallpox and it was the president's turn to take care of him.

A *Chicago Tribune* reporter found Lincoln dealing with Johnson's pay from the Treasury Department. "This, sir, is something out of my usual line; but the President of the United States has a multiplicity of duties not specified in the Constitution or Acts of Congress. This is one of them." Even when feeling miserable, Lincoln tried to interject a light touch. He explained to whom the money belonged, and since Johnson could not claim his pay in person, added: "I have been at considerable trouble to overcome the difficulty and get it for him, and have at length succeeded in cutting red tape, as you newspaper men say." While chatting with the reporter, Lincoln counted greenbacks and put them in envelopes, labeling them, "according" to Johnson's wishes. Lincoln was a good man. He was also a smart politician. Perhaps the story might get into the papers. It might even get into a campaign biography. This was 1864, the election year.

Then Johnson died. An epidemic had been ravaging Washington, but how he got ill we will never know. Lincoln wondered. Johnson was "very bad with the small pox," the president had told the reporter. "He did not catch it from me, however; at least I think not." The story of how he took care of "a poor negro" appeared in one of his 1864 biographies, and continued in the editions after Lincoln, too, had died; but the author took the possibly "incriminating" part out. In the cold January of 1864, Lincoln had Johnson buried at Arlington Cemetery, and personally paid for the burial. His headstone identifies Johnson with a single word: "Citizen."

Gettysburg continued to bury its dead, too, after the November ceremonies were over. Then winter came, the ground froze, and further burials had to be put off until spring. But the town had changed forever. The memory of the battle gave it great distinction and in time that would grow into the lifeline of its economy. The Soldiers' Cemetery would be part of that memory, too.

The dedication was barely finished when David Wills announced the forthcoming publication of the proceedings of the great day: speeches, prayers, songs, together with some of the history that led up to them, and the map of the grounds. The profits would go to help erect a monument to the memory of "the brave soldiers whose remains are deposited in this hallowed ground."

It never occurred to Wills, or anyone else, to put up a statue to commemorate Lincoln's brief remarks. The battlefield—the good news of the war where the nation had been saved—attracted an ever larger number of pilgrims, but Lincoln's words rarely received notice. At the dedication of the Cemetery's Soldiers' Monument, which took place in 1869, the orator of the occasion, Senator Oliver O. Morton of Indiana, the wartime governor who had heard Lincoln's words in '63, quoted some of them, and quoted Everett as well. But his message focused on Emancipation and the Fifteenth Amendment to the Constitution, newly approved by Congress. As he put it: "The perfect reign of liberty is at hand." Bayard Taylor, the poet for the ceremony, placed the "Gettysburg Oration" into the "Nation's Litany" and was the first to adopt some of its words to his own use. So, on rare occasions, a smattering of recollection appeared. What was true of Gettysburg was true of the country as a whole. Having been reminded of the address by Morton, the *New York Times* commented that neither this new orator, nor Everett earlier, lived up to Lincoln's "supreme gem of eloquence." That was much more praise than the paper awarded the speech back in 1863.

Still, a segment of the last sentence of Lincoln speech was carved in stone quite quickly, when the first, small soldiers' monument went into the cemetery in 1867. The survivors of the 1st Minnesota, which suffered 80 percent casualties in the battle, placed an urn on a granite base. The front of the stone quotes Everett's words from the dedication: "All time is the millennium of their glory." The back quotes Lincoln: "These dead shall not have died in vain." "Their fall was not in vain," George Washington had said when visiting the graves of his soldiers—as so many had learned from the hugely popular Parson Weems. November 19, 1863, was not forgotten. Words that echoed Washington resonated.

Lincoln biographers of the postwar period always included the speech, sometimes commenting on its value, as with other Lincoln texts, sometimes keeping silent. For example, *New York Times* editor Henry J. Raymond's many editions of Lincoln's *Life* included the text of the "remarks" without comment. He did the same with the Thanksgiving Proclamation. Phoebe A. Hanaford's biography also included the Gettysburg text and explained that it reflected the president's "deep appreciation" of the soldiers' sacrifice and "the tenderness of his spirit." However, she was also sure that no document could be found "more chaste and beautiful in style" than the Thanksgiving Proclamation. David Brainerd Williamson's anonymously published cut-and-paste job used the very same words. The most popular of the biographers, J. G. Holland, who as editor of the *Springfield Republican* may well have written the most positive comments about Lincoln's speech back in 1863, provided the text, noted that it compared favorably with Everett, said it was, in short, "very effective, and betrayed a degree of literary ability quite unexpected to those who had read only his formal state papers." The Thanksgiving Proclamation received more heartfelt praise from Holland, though the text was only excerpted, and that from the one issued in July 1863. Of course, the Emancipation Proclamation received substantial treatment in all the biographies.

By 1870, so much had been placed before the public about the martyred president that a 275-page *Memorial Lincoln Bibliography* could be published, listing "books, eulogies, sermons, portraits, engravings, medals," monuments, and ephemera. A lengthy introduction by C. H. Hart summed up Lincoln's life and noted the Gettysburg speech, too, as "brief and appropriate." The bibliography, however, did not mention the speech. The three illustrations for the book included a Lincoln portrait, the plaster cast of his hand, and the "Original Emancipation Proclamation."

Early historians of the Civil War reflected the same inattention. Edward McPherson's oft-printed *Political History of the United States in the Great Rebellion* devoted a chapter to Lincoln's writing with the text of eight letters and speeches, but not the Gettysburg remarks. Peculiarly, Congressman McPherson, by then clerk of the House, Gettysburg-born and raised, included Lincoln's off-the-cuff response to a serenade right after the battle, but not what he said at the cemetery. McPherson had participated in the dedication in '63.

Newsman John Forney, "Lincoln's dog," did better than McPherson, but not much. He too had been present in Gettysburg in '63, of course, and published his memoirs ten years later. His chapter on Lincoln in *Anecdotes of Public Men* devoted a good bit of space to the president's use of the English language. He included part of the Gettysburg Address among those "things that will survive for many generations"—together with fifteen other sterling examples of Lincoln's use of language.

Horace Greeley's very popular three-volume book, *The American Conflict: A History of the Great Rebellion*, published from 1864 to 1867, featured an engraving of Lincoln as its frontispiece, had a full chapter on the Battle of Gettysburg, but mentioned nothing about the address. Greeley had plenty of conflicts with Lincoln during the war and still held some ill feelings, but earlier, Thomas P. Kettell's 1865 *History of the Great Rebellion* had done about the same. Nor did R. G. Horton's *A Youth's History of the Civil War in the United States* of 1867 have anything to say on the subject. In 1870, however, John William Draper's three-volume *History of the American Civil War* included the speech without comment, but with the information that the president did not know he was to speak: "It is intimated to me that this assemblage expects me to say something on the occasion. We are met here on a great battle-field of the war. . . ." By 1874, in Benson J. Lossing's three-volume *The Pictorial Field Book of the Civil War*, at last a favorable comment appeared: "Edward Everett delivered an oration, and President Lincoln a brief but remarkable and touching dedicatory address." Lossing included the full text in a footnote. This historian had immediately elevated the first days of July 1863 to preeminence—"The battle was the pivotal one of the war"—but like others, failed to see greatness in Lincoln's speech. Immigrants who learned their history of the Great Rebellion in German read of Edward Everett in Gettysburg, but not of the president. Needless to say, the history books devoted substantial space to the Emancipation Proclamation. In the immediate postwar years of Lincoln's apotheosis, his fame was firmly tied to the Proclamation.

Public monuments of the time tell the same story. Washington's National Lincoln Monument Association showed the adulation and the unrealistic ambition the president's martyrdom inspired when it adopted a grandiose design by Clark Mills. Mills had done the president's second and final life mask just two months before his assassination, and the president had walked many times by Mills's equestrian statue of Andrew Jackson in Lafayette Park. For the proposed monument, Congress offered a site next to the Capitol. It was to include generals on horseback, statesmen, and other civilian leaders, soldiers, nurses, freed slaves, and more; Justice, Liberty, and Equality would rise; and above the huge number of figures, Lincoln at his desk would be signing the Emancipation Proclamation.

In the end, nothing came of the Washington project; but in Illinois the National Lincoln Monument Association succeeded. In 1868 in Springfield, it exhibited thirty-seven designs submitted by thirty-one artists. They generally made Lincoln the Emancipator their common subject. Larkin G. Meade's winning entry showed Lincoln extending his hand with a scroll in it. No one needed an explanation about what the scroll represented.

As Lincoln's reputation grew, community after community erected monuments to honor him in public places. Henry Kirke Brown's *Abraham Lincoln Declaring Emancipation* appeared in Brooklyn in 1869. Randolph Rogers's *Lincoln*, holding the document in one hand and a quill in the other, came to Philadelphia in 1871. In Vinnie Ream's 1871 marble for the Rotunda of the Capitol, Lincoln bows his head, his eyes look down sorrowfully, and his hand clasps the Emancipation Proclamation.

In 1876, Washington's Freedman's Monument by Thomas Ball, purchased with money collected by and from black people—though with a congressional appropriation for its base and pedestal—followed the same theme. The inspiration for the sculpture came at the moment of Lincoln's assassination, from Charlotte Scott, who contributed the first wages she had earned as a freed woman. President Grant unveiled the monument in Lincoln Park; Frederick Douglass consecrated it with a remarkable address. The bronze Lincoln stands twelve feet high on a ten-foot pedestal. He holds the Proclamation in one hand, while he extends the other over a slave whose body (at least in the model, historians believe) was that of the sculptor, and whose head was that of the last person recaptured under the Fugitive Slave Act. The free man rises from his knees, his face to the future.

The United States—the Republican North, in any case—had made a commitment to providing a kind of equality to the freed black people, and needed the Great Martyr Emancipator for succor. The commitment faded as the years passed; but so long as it lived, Lincoln's Proclamation lived, too, in the culture as a whole. It is also likely that the Emancipator appealed to some who had no desire to further civil rights and saw in the image the proof that the work was done.

In any case, Lincoln's Gettysburg words were mostly forgotten. Lincoln might have been surprised by the adulation he received, but not by the fact that the world would "little note, nor long remember" what he said at Gettysburg. Knowing, as he did by 1864, that some thought well of his cemetery address may have been a balm after much initial indifference. He must have enjoyed the opportunity to revise the speech with care. But Lincoln understood that if history would remember him, it would be for his Emancipation Proclamation. The painters Edward Marchant and Francis Carpenter were far from the only ones to create Emancipation art in the Lincoln White House. David Gilmour Blythe, Alonzo Chappel, and lesser lights painted the subject, too, and printmakers made images widely available. Engravers and lithographers even reproduced the text of the Proclamation, or part of the text, with various motifs decorating the designs, which almost always featured Lincoln. He appeared in so many prints and was put above the mantel in so many Northern homes that printmakers could make a living from such work. Creating images of the Emancipator became an industry. If there ever was a boring and legalistic document, its words unfit for inspiring anything but a bill of lading, the Emancipation Proclamation was that. Yet it appeared everywhere. If ever there was a speech that lent itself to glorious representation in popular prints, the Gettysburg Address was that. But there was no such work in the nineteenth century. His Farewell to Springfield, yes; but not the words at Gettysburg.

The first whiff of change came in the presidential election year of 1876 that led to the end of Reconstruction. It also marked the centennial of American Independence. "Four score and seven years" had stretched to a hundred, and a New England artist, Albion H. Bicknell, started a large painting entitled *Lincoln at Gettysburg*. It is not surprising that the idea for the work came out of abolitionist New England. Certainly the most appreciative words, the first recognition in the United States of the brilliant light of Lincoln's address, came mostly from there. A few rare newspapers in 1863, and then soon after Adams, Emerson, Sumner, and Stowe, who also saw genius in Lincoln's words, all hailed from New England. There the memory of Lincoln's address never faded and even showed up in a schoolbook for speakers.

Bicknell painted the moment when Everett finished speaking and the president rose. In 1878, the *New York Times* reported that the "enormous canvas" was "under way," and the following year Bicknell issued a pamphlet seeking subscribers for "a fine steel-plate engraving" to be completed in two years. He started on a smaller version of his painting to facilitate the reproduction and promised that "No pains will be spared to make it the leading American engraving of an American subject by an American painter."

The enterprise failed. Bicknell's work was not great art, but such a fault had not stopped the public from making Carpenter's somewhat better *First Reading of the Emancipation Proclamation* the best-selling print of the postwar years. *Lincoln at Gettysburg* was never made because it lacked subscriptions. (Or, if it was made, there were so few prints that none appear to have survived.) If the time for the Gettysburg Address had not yet come, Bicknell's attempt measured the changing winds. Not that the neglect of Lincoln's words should be exaggerated. In 1875, the *New York Times* called the speech "memorable" and cited the end of its last sentence, and in the same year, John Bartlett, another New Englander, included the sentence in his *Familiar Quotations.* The forward-looking *Nation,* noting this, prophesied that the Gettysburg speech "promises to be the most classic and most enduring [of] American orations." The magazine compared two versions; and the *Congregationalist,* continuing the theme, wrote of "authenticity of scripture," in observing the speech. Perhaps for the first time the feel of holiness hovered in the air, even if unexpressed.

If the rise of the Gettysburg Address to sacred heights still lay in the future, the allure of the Emancipation Proclamation was fading: Reconstruction had come to an end. Over the nineteenth century, as democracy advanced and grew into a central part of American lives, people felt the need to give it spiritual dimension and so make it stronger. Scholars sometimes call this a civil religion—a secular faith that carries some of the characteristics of religious faith, with superhuman beings, sacred documents, in time temples and, some would say, a priesthood. Both secular and religious people objected, but devotion continued. Lincoln called the founding fathers "a fortress of strength," "pillars of the temple of liberty," and the Declaration of Independence the rock of his "ancient faith."

In the post–Civil War era, after the massive death toll, people elevated the greatest of their dead to sainthood and made his Emancipation Proclamation into a hallowed document. But a living faith evolves, combining the "ancient faith" with present needs. At Gettysburg, Lincoln himself helped give new life and new meaning to Jefferson's Declaration. And as Reconstruction ended and the nation changed, the image the country worshipped also changed.

In 1883, Augustus Saint-Gaudens won the commission to create a gigantic bronze for Chicago's Lincoln Park and, at last, Lincoln had his great sculptor. Unveiled in 1887, the monument did not include even an allusion to the Emancipation Proclamation. This was only the second sculpture to follow such a path, and the first important one among the twenty memorials created between 1866 and 1887. Later, Saint-Gaudens would create the Robert Gould Shaw Memorial for the Boston Common, with its respectful images of black soldiers. He was no negrophobe. But the Lincoln image was shifting.

The Gettysburg Address was starting to move to the fore. In the immediate postwar years, soldiers' and sailors' monuments generally made reference to Emancipation. In 1882, the Buffalo monument still did so but, for the first time, it also quoted the last sentence of Lincoln's speech. In Gettysburg itself, the flood of rising monuments was about to begin, but the address would remain absent until the new century. However, by 1877 a Pennsylvania Railroad Company pamphlet, looking for tourists, considered it good business to call the Soldiers' National Cemetery where Lincoln gave "his immortal speech" the "greatest attraction of the town." A year later, President Rutherford Hayes referred to "immortal words," and an account of the battle in the local paper closed by quoting the final sentence of the speech. Five years later, at last, the full address appeared in the *Star & Sentinel*, two decades after its two predecessor papers had first printed it.

As the fame of Lincoln's words grew, an argument erupted in the press on how the speech had been received back in 1863. Lincoln's friend Ward Hill Lamon was responsible for the controversy, which only heightened interest in the address. The two men had been close. Lamon gave his name to a most likely ghost-written book about the common man of Illinois, and the public received it badly. The book seemed to miss Lincoln's greatness even as his apotheosis took wings. But that was who Lamon knew: a man.

The author stayed silent for years after that, but as the sanctification of the Gettysburg Address proceeded, he spoke. After all, he had been there, had had more to do with organizing the event than any person outside of Gettysburg. He had been the marshal of the day, he had introduced Lincoln. He knew. Ever fewer people would recall the president "as a politician and a partisan," Internal Revenue Commissioner George Boutwell wrote in 1885, but "these he was, first and always." Lamon, too, hated the "falsification of history." He vehemently objected to looking at Lincoln "not as a human being endowed with a mighty intellect and extraordinary virtues, but as a god."

He recalled no applause during Lincoln's Gettysburg speech, and no "hearty demonstrations" after it closed. He wrote of conversations with Everett, Seward, and above all Lincoln, all of whom agreed that "he has made a failure." "The speech will not *scour*," Lamon remembered the president saying. The marshal thought that the "speech fell on the vast audience like a *wet blanket.*" In the later version published after his death by his daughter, the statement would be attributed to Lincoln. In his anger at the deifiers, Lamon remembered words that may have never been spoken. But his overall conclusion was true: "the perfection, the intrinsic excellence" of the Gettysburg speech "seem to have escaped" most people in Lincoln's lifetime. And for years after that.

Upon reading Lamon in the 1890s, another old Lincoln friend, Henry Clay Whitney, was delighted: "I had supposed that the whole world except me deemed the Gettysburg speech the summum bonum of eloquence: I always deemed it *rot*. . . ." Writing to Herndon, Whitney called the speech "a fraud—an abortion" and "hogwash." By then, Isaac Arnold's biography of Lincoln not only perpetuated the legend of the speech having been written on the train to Gettysburg but also described "a thrill of feeling, like an electric shock" that overtook the crowd before the president had completed his first sentence. "All his hearers realized . . . that the words he was speaking would live as long as the language. . . ." At least Arnold had been among the few who recognized early great worth in Lincoln's words. Soon afterwards Noah Brooks's biography suggested that this might be growing into the new orthodoxy—if there could be one. He wrote that at first the oration of "the silver tongued Everett" outshone Lincoln's speech, but "in a few days" the American public "glorified it as one of the few masterpieces of oratory that the world has received."

Many eyewitnesses got into the discussion; the reporter of the *Boston Herald* had his say, as did the man for the *New York Times*, and so on. "The writer hereof was present, sitting on the platform, within ten feet of President Lincoln," wrote one. "Yet it is doubtful," wrote another, whether among the reporters present "a dozen could be found who would agree, even in essential points."

By this time, the words Lincoln had added to his speech at the National Cemetery, "under God," had taken on special significance for many. His religion—or lack of it—had spawned a bitter dispute quickly after his death. Gettysburg did represent a moment of growth in Lincoln's religious outlook; but for some not satisfied with his deep spirituality who wished to baptize him posthumously, it was not merely the turning point of the war but the moment of Lincoln's own new birth. " 'Then and there consecrated myself to Christ,' " one witness claimed to have heard Lincoln say. " 'I do love Jesus.' " From then on, this would be gospel truth for some. And so it has continued to this day. "When the clouds lifted above the carnage of Gettysburg," one divine declared in 1882, "he gave his heart to the Lord Jesus Christ." Hence his "matchless oration" and "under God." Such an interpretation would be especially important for Southern acceptance of Lincoln, including the embrace of the address.

In Gettysburg, on the sixteenth anniversary of the cemetery dedication, the Democratic paper saw fit to note briefly that though Lincoln's speech was his "most memorable" utterance, those close to him, including Seward and Everett, had been disappointed at the time of its delivery. The Republican *Star & Sentinel* put on its first page the defense against such calumny some years later, borrowing it from the *Philadelphia Press*, and including the words of former Congressman Edward McPherson who, too, by now remembered that Lincoln's speech left "every sensitive heart touched" and "every generous eye suffused. At the end there was but one feeling, and that of the rare exquisiteness of the appeal."

On the twenty-fifth anniversary of the battle, in 1888, seven thousand Blue and two hundred Gray veterans assembled in Gettysburg and heard the entire address for the first time at a public event since the 1860s. The local Republican paper published the speech, including the gushing commentary on it. The Democratic counterpart took another six years to reprint the entire speech.

Yet as late in the century as this, the Strobridge Lithograph Company of Cincinnati still considered it good business to publish "Abraham Lincoln and his Emancipation Proclamation." It showed in vibrant colors the American eagle and the American shield, Lincoln flanked by the flag on both sides, and the abridged text of the Proclamation with lily-white classical images of women representing Justice and Liberty.

The people of Gettysburg, too, still heard about the Emancipation Proclamation. It may have been a very white document to many of the white people of the town, showing a noble nation freeing a downtrodden alien race. Still, in the mid-eighties, Gettysburg's Republicans yet objected to how "enterprising Confederate masters of ours are hastening to rewrite history . . . discrediting every fact which does honor to the men who led the Union cause." Having "annulled" Reconstruction, the *Star & Sentinel* complained, the rebels now asserted that Lincoln signed the Emancipation Proclamation " 'with hesitating hand.' Next year, they will probably assert that Lincoln's signature to that immortal paper was a forgery." On Memorial Day, 1897, one white speaker could still affirm that "The Emancipation Proclamation was the most wonderful document ever signed by a single pen." But increasingly, black people were the ones most likely to remember that version of history.

Southern whites and more of the nation as a whole learned to forget slavery, or turn it into a benign institution. Did it play much of a role in history? Any role? Did Lincoln's document matter? Did Gettysburg's "new birth of freedom" have anything to do with such questions? Had not the Confederates fought heroically for their own rights? Were they not the children of the American Revolution? The legend of the noble Lost Cause grew as that of Emancipation faded.

Blacks and their white allies fought back—Frederick Douglass in the forefront. On the twentieth anniversary of the Emancipation Proclamation, New Year's Day, 1883, at a dinner held in his honor in Washington, Douglass told a distinguished assemblage of black leaders: "This high festival of ours is coupled with a day which we do well to hold in sacred and everlasting honor, a day memorable alike in the history of the nation, and in the life of the emancipated people . . . it is one of those days which may well count for a thousand years." Even if at times he had mixed thoughts about the Civil War president, the Proclamation was sacred.

Emancipation Day, a black celebration in some places, including Lincoln's Springfield, even in the antebellum years, recalled Haiti or the West Indies; indeed, it went back to the 1808 abolition of the transatlantic slave trade. During the Civil War it grew to great significance, and continued as a great black holiday into the twentieth century. Remembered on different days in different parts of the country because the news of Lincoln's act reached people at different times, the Proclamation was nearly always read on these festive occasions—the African-American founding document, their Magna Carta. For the long decades as oppression got worse, Lincoln's portrait adorned black homes, public places, and churches. As the importance of the Emancipation Proclamation receded among whites, as Jim Crow reigned, blacks firmly clung to the document.

Of course there was no single black voice that spoke for all, any more than there was a single white voice. As one century closed and another came, the shame of slavery, the pain of remembrance, the need to accommodate to the realities of the segregated world of a new age, the hope for the "progress of the race," Pan-Africanism, millennialism, and more, contended for a hearing among black people. Some, like W. E. B. DuBois, wished to scrutinize the Lincoln myth. But the force that placed the freedom document at the center of the memory of the Civil War era, and Emancipation Day, never died. In the year of the centennial of Lincoln's birth, a black minister's Emancipation Day sermon in Georgia entitled "Abraham Lincoln: Sent of God" vowed: "may God forget my people when they forget this day."

Some white churches, too, showed less willingness than the culture as a whole to abandon the Emancipator. For example, in Brooklyn's Plymouth Church, where Beecher had preached and Lincoln worshipped once, a stained-glass window with such an image commemorated the 1909 centennial of his birth. But for most white Americans who respected Lincoln, even in the South, the Gettysburg Address was growing into the sacred text. Blacks would claim the address, too, but the emphasis, the meaning most whites and blacks gave to it differed substantially. For the freed people and their descendants, the meaning of a "new birth of freedom" was unmistakable. With segregation and lynching the ugly order of the day, the *Baltimore Afro-American Ledger* noted sarcastically: "We are wondering whether Mr. Lincoln had the slightest idea in his mind that the time would ever come when the people of this country would come to the conclusion that by the 'People' he meant only white people."

Seeking healing from the bitterness of the Civil War, a deeply admirable, altogether legitimate goal went hand-in-hand with the re-subjugation of black people, as the historian David Blight has shown. This result was "both intentional and unseen." Forgetting blacks in the developing memory of Gettysburg was part of the larger national amnesia. Black participation in the military campaigns had been significant, though little of it took place with gun in hand, and that would be forgotten by the white majorities. And the Gettysburg that one newspaper in 1863 predicted would become the "Mecca" of American remembrance would by the late 1880s begin to become the "Mecca of American Reconciliation."

The first attempt to bring officers from both sides to Gettysburg had attracted two Confederates and forty-nine Yankees in 1869. Robert E. Lee flatly refused to come. It would be better to "obliterate the marks of Civil Strife" than preserve them, he wrote. The attempt to organize a Blue and Gray reunion in 1874 had to be abandoned, but by 1887, some success was achieved. Time, and much else, began to heal wounds. The older the soldiers got, the more genuinely they learned to respect each other's valor. "In our youth our hearts were touched with fire," said Oliver Wendell Holmes, Jr, giving voice to the aging soldiers of both sides. To share the fire is to share a great deal.

Economic interest also began to reconcile the sections. Politicians did their part. So did religion: after all, "Love thine enemy" was Christ's commandment. Had not Lincoln spoken before his death with "malice toward none"? Artists and writers added their might. As the years went by, a poem by Francis Miles Finch would come to voice the dominant American sentiment:

> No more shall the war-cry sever,
>   Or the winding rivers be red;
> They banish our anger forever
>   When they laurel the graves of our dead!
>   Under the sod and the dew,
>   Waiting for judgment day;—
>   Love and tears for the Blue,
>   Tears and love for the Gray.

Such words could melt many hearts.

Yet commemorating the dead could also open old wounds. The various forces for reconciliation could often pull in opposite directions. Gettysburg, where thousands died, might have become an eternal sore, a symbol of the horror of war, a past that hurt. But Americans slowly turned it into a monument to unity—a place that would give them a sense of achievement, where the nation came through a difficult test. The brothers who fought one another were brothers again, Americans with a great future. Everett, increasingly forgotten, had predicted that this would happen. Lincoln had, too. This was a remarkable achievement. In the process, however, part of history grew dim. A "new birth of freedom" grew lily-white for the majorities. The goal of black freedom that at least some in the North cherished to some degree was erased from the past and removed from the present: a terrible price on top of a terrible war.

The desire for reconciliation of the sections had been growing all along; but as the movement gathered speed in the 1880s, difficult subjects such as race or war guilt tended to disappear. Instead, fascination with the purely military aspect of the war rose to prominence. One of the sensations of the decade came from the romantic cycloramas that depicted the Battle of Gettysburg. People stood on a high platform surrounded by a gigantic circular oil painting with dioramas reaching toward them so they almost became part of the action. This popular form of nineteenth-century entertainment sidestepped the causes and consequences of the war by focusing on military action. The issues that divided in 1860 could still do so two decades later. The French artist Paul Phillippoteaux, working in the European tradition of battle panoramas, brought his first cyclorama to Chicago in 1883. By the end of the decade, investors had financed five such awe-inspiring paintings in the North.

The Gettysburg cycloramas, together with the memorials to the battlefield that began to appear in ever larger numbers about the same time— paintings, fiction, poetry, all the arts that focused on the battle—tended to portray heroes, sacrifice, and, in the end, glory. They made Gettysburg the crucial turning point where all hung in the balance, just as Stockton, Everett, and others had said in 1863. People understood that the clash might have gone the other way, making it all the more important.

One of the cycloramas showed Lincoln speaking; perhaps many did. It took some time for the focus on the battle to help bring attention to Lincoln's address. The two strengthened each other and, eventually, the relationship between battle and address would be reversed. First, the meaning of Lincoln's words needed to be sanitized, however, or at least given the understanding that some people had in 1863, those for whom "all men are created equal" and the "new birth of freedom" applied only to whites. Such an address could be made into a tool for reconciliation between the whites of the North and the South.

The *Century* magazine, slick-papered, loaded with lavish illustrations, reaching a large audience, played a part in ending the bitterness left by the war. In time, other publications would follow. Under the editorship of Richard Watson Gilder, the *Century* series of articles between 1884 and

1887 focused attention on the military aspect of the war, giving a platform to Confederate and Union generals alike. Here, too, causes and consequences were ignored. Yankees could glow in the knowledge that they had saved the Republic. The ex-Confederates could believe that slavery had nothing to do with the war, that their soldiers had fought bravely for Southern rights and lost only because of the "superior number and resources" of the North. Old enemies could now unite, twenty years after the war ended, on the bravery of the soldiers of both sides. *Century*'s approach worked, as it nearly doubled its circulation within a year. In 1888, the articles would be printed as a popular four-volume illustrated book: *Battles and Leaders of the Civil War*.

Gilder also hoped to contribute to the same cause with Lincoln. He convinced Nicolay and Hay, who were working on what would become their ten-volume history of the Civil War president, to allow the serialization of their writing in the magazine. Gilder thought that Lincoln's life would "help unite the North and South as never before," and of course make money, too. Problems such as Nicolay and Hay's belief, shared by many of the older generation in the North, that Davis and Lee deserved to hang, could be mitigated by editing.

Nicolay and Hay discussed Emancipation, but regarded the Proclamation as little more than a vehicle for saving the Union. The fire of their youth had waned. If the *Century* had a problem, it came not so much from the writers' partisan tone as their ponderous style. As readers began to depart, the magazine published less than half of Nicolay and Hay's text. But it was not coincidental that the *Century*, with its commitment to sectional reconciliation, brought out the first important authoritative article on the Gettysburg Address, written by John Nicolay.

In their 1890 *History*, the authors described Lincoln's task at Gettysburg—having to speak after Everett—as "a trying ordeal," but also indicated that he succeeded brilliantly "with simple words, in such living, original, yet exquisitely molded, maxim-like phrases that the best critics awarded it an unquestioned rank as one of the world's masterpieces of rhetorical art." When the "best critics" actually said this, the book left unexplained.

Nothing made clearer the change that had taken place than this ten-volume *History*. Back in November 1863, the two secretaries had enjoyed themselves the night before the big day—eating, drinking, doing politics, and on dedication day itself helping, taking in all that went on. Nicolay, al-most certainly present as Lincoln probably completed his speech on the morning of the 19th, wrote nothing about it afterwards. Hay wrote a great deal about the Gettysburg outing in his diary, and may have written an anonymous newspaper article about the dedication day; but he summarily dismissed Lincoln's "half dozen lines." Much had changed in a generation.

In his 1894 article, Nicolay firmly supported Speed's statement that Lincoln wrote half of his speech the day before leaving Washington, and then completed it in Gettysburg; Nicolay had the physical evidence of the first draft of the manuscript. The secretary-turned-historian contradicted himself about how Lincoln prepared for writing the speech, noting that Lincoln liked to arrange his thoughts "using great deliberation" before put-ting them on paper. But then Nicolay noted the president's "want of oppor-tunity even to think leisurely about what he might desire to say." Lincoln had had to attend to military matters and work on his Annual Message. In fact, there was "great uncertainty" about whether he would be able even to go to Gettysburg. On the other hand, Lincoln had hours to think about what he would say while participating in the ceremonies, not excluding the time it took Everett to orate. Earlier, Stoddard had also testified that Lincoln's "duties prevented elaborate preparation," something the third secretary could observe firsthand, but added what he could not observe since he did not go with Lincoln, that the speech was written on the way to Gettysburg.

Nicolay's article briefly described the train trip and dismissed any pos-sibility that the president worked on his speech on the way. The article noted the revelry of the town in the night, "enthusiasm so plentiful"; people having no place to sleep; the politics of speechifying, local and national, in-cluding the fate of Emancipation; and the upcoming presidential election. The next day, the parade to the cemetery was less impressive than expected since many people first went to look at the battlefield. Lincoln held the speech in his hand but spoke from memory, and the audience was "totally unprepared for what they heard" and did not realize its greatness. Not that people failed to appreciate the speech: they applauded repeatedly, the AP re-port showed.

But the bulk of Nicolay's article focused on comparing the different texts of Lincoln's speech, the careful attention given to making revisions. He defended Lincoln from the charge of plagiarism—that he borrowed the final line of his speech from others. Nicolay's article was not without its errors, but Gettysburg Address scholarship was underway. Before long it would pass from eyewitnesses to historical writers and has not yet stopped.

And so, by the end of the nineteenth century, the address had entered American culture fully. McGuffey's Readers included it, and the fiftieth volume of the Riverside Literature Series, which collected the best of Lincoln's writings, put the Gettysburg Address in its title and explained that when delivered, the great speech "instantaneously affected the country, whether people were educated or unlettered." In 1896, the press reported that the speech was cast in bronze for the first time. In 1900, *Harper's Weekly* published a drawing of the delivery of the address as its centerfold.

That Nicolay, and others, too, had begun to worry seriously about the correct text of Lincoln's speech measured its growing importance. People have strived to establish definitive texts since the beginning of sacred scriptures. The Gettysburg Address was on its way to becoming that. There may have been an element of iconoclasm involved, perhaps even questioning Lincoln's stature. A plagiarist? To make the notion ludicrous, Lamon, Nicolay, and numerous others turned up a lot of varied predecessors of the speech's concluding words—"a government of the people, by the people, for the people"—reaching all the way back to John Wycliffe's Bible.

Congress established the Gettysburg National Military Park in 1895 and directed that a bronze tablet with Lincoln's speech on it, as well as a "medallion likeness of President Lincoln," be placed at the cemetery. It would take some years for the monument to be put in place. But as the new century dawned, and the Grand Army of the Republic post in town celebrated Lincoln's birthday, the old veterans sang "America" and recited the Gettysburg Address.

By then, the old Confederacy and the white North had firmly shaken hands in peace. Arlington National Cemetery—Robert E. Lee's estate confiscated in Lincoln's day to bury the Union dead—now provided a section for Confederate dead. When in the 1880s Congress considered returning the captured Confederate battle flags to their respective state, an uproar from the Grand Army of the Republic, the Union's veterans' organization, stopped the action. The flag was so potent a symbol: so many had died carrying the Stars and Stripes in the war, so many trying to take the enemy's flag. Capturing a Confederate flag meant an automatic Medal of Honor for the brave Union soldier. Many of those men were still alive. Some were black. But by 1906 the flags were returned without much of a protest, at the same time that Congress required federal care of the Confederate dead in Northern cemeteries.

At the Gettysburg Cemetery, too, Confederates would presumably have been welcomed by then had their bodies not been removed to the South long before. In 1863, Lincoln had spoken clearly: "We are met on a great battle field of that war. We have come to dedicate a portion of it, as a final resting place for those who died here, that the nation might live." The soldiers of the Union died so that "the nation might live." Confederates were not allowed to be buried at the National Cemetery.

Reunion had changed the meaning of the war and so too the meaning of the address, even as it was moving to the fore of American memory and growing sacred. If the war had been necessary to create a united nation, if "all that was done was well done" by both sides, as President William Howard Taft said at a meeting of Blue and Gray veterans in 1909, if both had been right, if all who had died died for America, then Lincoln at Gettysburg spoke for all Americans. So Americans would be taught for generations to come.

The "new birth of freedom" referred henceforth not to a nation that had, "under God," ascended through Emancipation in a crucible of war and so was reborn, but rather to a nation that had been threatened by disunion in war but, "under God," was saved. This Gettysburg Address spoke of a war to save the Union, and its republican form of government created by the revolutionary fathers of '76, a "government of the people, by the people, for the people."

This had indeed been part of the message in 1863. Some had understood Lincoln's words solely in those terms even then. And why would the "new birth" even distantly refer to black folks, when Lincoln could be quoted from before the war saying that they should not vote or have civil rights? He could be quoted supporting colonizing the freedmen away from the United States. If Lincoln was to be the American saint, he would have to share American prejudices. The direction his words pointed in 1863 had to be changed; the address had to be cleansed to become a sacred document.

The Gettysburg speech came to be understood as addressed equally to Federal and Confederate soldiers, and also as a peace message. Indeed, it was said that a dove of peace flew up as Lincoln began to speak. When asked about this, Robert Todd Lincoln grumbled sarcastically about the confusion between "the helmet of Mars" and "a dove's nest."

Whatever writers aspiring to scholarship would say—and as the years went on their number kept growing—the little book that Americans read from 1906 onward came from the pen of Southern-born, Northern-based Mary Shipman Andrews. In *The Perfect Tribute*, Lincoln writes his speech on the piece of brown paper on the train, and at Gettysburg his shrill voice brings titters from the people and then total silence when his few words are done. But the heart of the story takes place in Washington, where a frantic boy collars the disheartened Lincoln, out for a walk. The boy's dying brother, a Confederate captain wounded at Gettysburg, now in a prison hospital, needs a lawyer to write his will. "I used to practice law," Lincoln says, and they go to the dying man.

The nameless lawyer drafts the will, and finds himself listening to the Confederate praising that man Lincoln's beautiful speech at Gettysburg. He tells the tall lawyer that the speech struck such a deep chord with the people that they could only offer a deeply reverent silence. "One might as well applaud the Lord's Prayer—it would be sacrilege." The captain shares that reverence, even if the speech might be wrong from his viewpoint. He predicts that, for years to come, both Southern and Northern children will recite the words of Lincoln. "I'd like to put my hand in his before I die." In his last convulsion the Confederate's hand shoots out and catches his visitor's hand, and then he is gone.

The story first appeared in *Scribner's* magazine, was soon after printed as a separate book, and continued to be reprinted in countless editions. Some were plain, some were fancy and leatherbound, all very popular. Assigned to schoolchildren decade after decade, *The Perfect Tribute* became the all-time Lincoln best seller. It was filmed twice, put on the Internet, and a century after its first publication, its influence continues to be felt. Back at the beginning of the twentieth century when Andrews was invited to a Lincoln Club, she declined, explaining, "my little book on Lincoln is all I know."

The logical extension of Andrews's and similar work was the popular print showing Lincoln at Gettysburg with head bowed before the grave of a Confederate soldier. The rebel flag sheltered the sacred grave. And before long popular prints gave way to popular films that carried the same message, but made ever uglier. For long nothing quite matched the artistry and the influence of D. W. Griffith's *Birth of a Nation* (1915), based on Thomas Dixon's popular novel *The Clansman*, with Lincoln as "the great heart" and the black man as the beast. As the President of the United States and historian Woodrow Wilson would say, this was "writing history with lightning."

The triumph of the Gettysburg Address and eclipse of the Emancipation Proclamation won an official stamp of approval from Congress itself. The year 1913 marked the passage of half a century since the Proclamation and the Battle of Gettysburg and the address. Though some states and cities held celebrations of the Proclamation, and congressional legislation to commemorate it received a hearing, in the end no support came from Washington.

In contrast, Congress, the War Department, and various states together provided money to create a memorable festival of reconciliation between the Blue and the Gray. Every living Civil War veteran from both sides was invited to return to Gettysburg, to live free in a "Great Camp" and celebrate together their mutual sense of honor, their devotion to duty, their courage, and what it had led to: a great united people, the greatest on the face of the earth. More than 50,000 surviving veterans came, as did at least as many spectators, to the "Peace Jubilee." Sally Myers, who had no time to go to the cemetery in 1863, still lived in Gettysburg. She had stopped teaching black children to placate local prejudices. She participated in the celebration. So did Nurse Hancock, who remained unmarried and independent. It was so very good to have peace and reunion. Unlike 1863, the trains ran fine, people had places to stay, and the picture of grizzled veterans in blue and gray shaking hands melted the heart. President Wilson came, if briefly. The Gettysburg Address was read. A nation reunited in spirit celebrated. Every living Civil War veteran had been invited. Everyone came—except for the black veterans of the war.

This is a bit of an oversimplification. All written history has some of that. As the thousands of Yankee and rebel soldiers celebrated together on the old battlefield, at the local hotel a nasty altercation took place. A man claiming to be the son of a Confederate general applied a "vile epithet" to Lincoln. A Union veteran, hearing it, struck the unrepentant rebel, who then went on a rampage, stabbing eight. The war was not over for all the people.

Much more than unhappy cultural politics was at work in the rise of the Gettysburg Address. If in Lincoln's day or immediately after only the very sensitive ears of an Emerson or a Stowe could hear the beauty of his language, as time went on the rest of the country caught up. The American language changed. Unadorned, direct speech better fit the sensibilities of 1900 than 1863.

Women contributed their share to the Lincoln cult, too. Elsie Singmaster, widowed at a young age, lived in Gettysburg and wrote about the battle. She did not love the war. She depicted its horrors and portrayed veterans bitter about their service. Her Union soldier, "Gunner Criswell," blinded at Gettysburg, given no pension, returns to the battlefield after a hard life to seek his own name among all those of the other soldiers engraved upon the Pennsylvania Monument. His name is missing.

Yet Singmaster of the bleak vision—some would say honest vision—who also gave voice to the unbearable burden carried by the women of the war, brightened up when it came to Lincoln. She has a grief-stricken, impoverished widow make her way to the National Cemetery on November 19, 1863, suffer through Everett, and then find deep consolation in Lincoln's words. The address speaks to the nation, but speaks also to one individual woman, turning her life around, salvaging it. Lincoln's words "pointed to the future for which there was a new task." Women, like men, "the people," distinguished the commander in chief, whom many had held responsible for the death of hundreds of thousands, from Gettysburg's mourner in chief, the nation's consoler.

To establish the definitive text of the address, smart people spent inordinate amounts of time on the various versions, arguing over them. Even the U.S. Senate became involved. At one point the *Army and Navy Register* reported with alarm that "The government came very near placing incorrect versions" of the speech that was to be set at the entrance of every National Cemetery in the country. CONGRESS IS TO STRAIGHTEN OUT ERRORS IN GETTYSBURG SPEECH, ran a headline in the *Philadelphia Evening Bulletin*; "Perhaps only the Lord's Prayer exceeds it as a familiar composition to American minds." A hundred different versions had been found, read another report—true enough, and more, if one went back to the newspapers of 1863. Robert Lincoln became deeply involved in establishing an "authorized" text. Though the variations were minor and should have been mostly of interest to scholars, settling on the definitive version grew into something of an obsession.

Lincoln's words at Gettysburg had always called for union, and since in some ways disunion still threatened the nation in the new century, albeit no longer along sectional lines, the Gettysburg Address could serve again as the call to union. Modernization, massive industries, the rise of the city, and millions of new immigrants divided the land. Lincoln united it, especially in his Gettysburg Address.

The Progressive movement, striving for the common man, for democratization, turned the Gettysburg Address into a manifesto. Facing the problems of the early twentieth century, its inequalities of wealth and power, the address provided inspiration. "People versus the Slave Power," the historian Merrill Peterson noted, became "People versus the Money Power." The cartoonist showed Lincoln taking Theodore Roosevelt by the hand. The reformers fought for antitrust and pro-labor laws, and for constitutional amendments that would permit the income tax, women's suffrage, and direct election of U.S. senators. Lincoln's words could help assimilate the masses of immigrants. Thousand upon thousand of them, as well as schoolchildren, memorized the brief prose poem. What better example could be put before them? However different the problems of the Progressive Age from Lincoln's, the reformers believed that they, too, strove for a democratic country where "all men are created equal" and where the "government of the people, by the people, for the people" would be a reality.

Among the reasons for the emergence of Lincoln as a national symbol and the rise to prominence of the Gettysburg Address were the abandonment of Reconstruction and the need to find a substitute for the Emancipation Proclamation; the growth of a more modern language; the need to Americanize immigrants; and, above all, the democratizing of Progressive politics. But the country's entrance upon the world scene at the end of the nineteenth century also played a central role. Success on the world stage required unity, especially when war came, as it did in 1898 and again in 1917.

The Gettysburg Address seemed to define perfectly what America stood for now around the globe. Did not Lincoln's speech end by referring to the whole "earth"? If in the 1860s the United States was to save the world by saving the democratic example at home through force of arms, in 1917 it would do the same by sending those arms abroad. This seemed like the logical extension of the address; perhaps it was. The United States would fight against authoritarianism and for democracy. If, especially in the Philippine adventure, racism was also involved, the part of the address that touched the issue had already been whitewashed. "If Lincoln were here today," one political leader explained in 1917, "his prayer would be verified and glorified into the prayer that all civilized nations shall have a new birth of freedom, and that government of the people, by the people, for the people, shall not perish from the earth." Men in uniform received via a "War Service Library" *Lincoln's Gettysburg Address*, a little booklet that also included his two inaugural addresses.

A war speech for a war time the address surely was U.S. Allies agreed and appealed to Lincoln, too. British prime minister David Lloyd George grew up in his shoemaker father's home with a portrait of the American president on the wall. He came to the United States as a hero and made his pilgrimage to Gettysburg, as well as to the other Lincoln sites. French prime minister Georges Clemenceau spoke of his grief as a student upon hearing of Lincoln's assassination. Together the Allies marched off to war with the words of the Civil War president on their lips.

Even before World War I came, Gettysburg Address statues began to dot the American landscape. Emancipation monuments did not disappear—Alfonso Pelzer's 1898 work in particular was quite popular, in part because of inexpensive duplications. One was erected in St. Cloud, Minnesota, as late as 1918, and another in Detroit in 1919. But Emancipation statues could also be baptized into Gettysburg Address memorials. Leonard Wells Volk's Lincoln atop the Soldiers' and Sailors' Monument in Rochester, New York, holds a large scroll, and may have been conceived in the early 1870s, if not earlier. By the time it was dedicated in 1892, or perhaps some years afterward, it would be understood as a Gettysburg Address statue. In Lancaster, Pennsylvania, an 1874 Soldiers' and Sailors' monument by Lewis Haldy later acquired a bronze tablet of the Gettysburg Address (and still later plaques for veterans of the two world wars and Vietnam). Soldiers' and Sailors' monuments put up in the twentieth century would often have the printed address on them. In 1911, Boston added Lincoln's words to the Volk head on Beacon Hill.

The turn of the century began the stream of specifically Gettysburg Address monuments. For example, Charles J. Mulligan's *Lincoln the Orator* for Rosamond, Illinois, of 1903, replicated for Chicago two years later, swings one arm high in a rhetorical gesture while the other hand holds a rolled document. For Francis E. Elwell's sculpture in East Orange, New Jersey, ground was broken on the anniversary of the address in 1910 and dedicated a year later. The text on the pedestal quotes the final words of the Address.

Gettysburg unveiled its first Lincoln in 1910 as part of the large Pennsylvania monument. The sculptor, Swiss-born J. Otto Schweitzer, has the orator's right hand extended forward, clutching a scroll, his gaze fixed firmly on the fields before him. Two years later, the Soldiers' National Cemetery finally got its monument that Congress had requested in 1895. It had taken so long in part because people argued about it—Gettysburg and Lincoln both aroused deep passions. The classical-style curved monument, designed by Louis R. Henrich of Boston, displays bundles of fasces and an axhead, ancient symbols of strength and unity, as well as stars for the states that stayed loyal. From its center, Henry Kirke Bush-Brown's large bust of a brooding, idealized Lincoln looks down, determined and tender, set off from the pinkish-beige of the granite base. On the right the text of the Gettysburg Address is engraved on a bronze plaque; on the left, David Wills's letter of invitation. This may have been the only monument on the globe dedicated to a speech until Lincoln's words got a second one at the National Cemetery in 1976, and a third in front of the Wills House, by Seward Johnson, in 1991.

Schoolchildren collected their coins to create monuments around the country to the Gettysburg Lincoln they knew from *The Perfect Tribute*. For the culture at large, even if a sculptor intended the hero to hold the Proclamation, the viewer was increasingly likely to see the Gettysburg Address, as happened with Volk. New Milford, Connecticut, Moberly, Missouri, and Long Beach, California, all erected statues with documents next to Lincoln. The sculptor could create an explicitly non-Gettysburg Lincoln, as did Andrew O'Connor for the Capitol in Springfield, Illinois, showing the man's farewell to his community; but the dedication concluded with Lincoln biographer Lord Charnwood proclaiming: "We here highly resolve that these dead shall not have died in vain." By then, World War I was raging.

At Philadelphia's Union League Club, another Schweitzer Lincoln showed him giving the address, face resolute, fist clenched. The *Ladies' Home Journal* gave its readers, together with a facsimile of the address, a variation on the image, but with one hand pointing to heaven. Numerous prints, from postcard size to large works, did the same. The Civil War president had said that the country went to war to save democracy for the world. Woodrow Wilson, his successor, added that the country went again to war "to make the world safe for democracy."

Now the cartoonists would show Lincoln taking Wilson by the arm: the champions of democracy, war presidents. Perhaps the cost of war made Tacoma's *Lincoln at Gettysburg* by Alonzo Lewis of 1930 a bit more contemplative. His Spokane Lincoln rests his eyes across a great battlefield.

The Lincoln Memorial in Washington, planned since 1913, was completed in 1922. Saint-Gaudens had been the first great sculptor to separate Lincoln from the Emancipation Proclamation. His successor, if he had one as a major American master, was Daniel Chester French. He created his first *Lincoln* for the Nebraska state capital, named after the president, and placed a huge Gettysburg Address behind him.

At the Lincoln Memorial, which instantly grew into the great American temple of democracy, the Gettysburg Address along with the Second Inaugural flanks the president on either side. The seated Lincoln, of white Georgia marble, his chair draped with the flag, clenches one fist: war president, defender of democracy. The other hand gently rests, and the face, too, speaks of a kind man. Sitting there, he reaches up to nineteen feet from toe to head; the pedestal raises the height to thirty feet. If Lincoln stood up twenty-eight feet into the sky, the beautiful white marble temple, with its thirty-six Doric columns—one for each state of the Union of 1865—would crumble. Henry Bacon, the architect, modeled his temple of Colorado Yule marble after the Parthenon in Greece, the birthplace of democracy. But this is the universal Lincoln made American, in the words of Langston Hughes: "a voice forever."

The theme of the Great Emancipator still continued. African Americans were invited to the dedication of the memorial—and made to sit in the rear. The president of the famed Tuskegee Institute, Robert Moton, was one of the speakers, though he must have made some quite nervous. Two ships had come to America, he explained, the *Mayflower* and a slave ship. The principles they represented were still fighting for the soul of the land. The other speakers, former president of the United States, now chief justice and chair of the Lincoln Memorial Commission, William Howard Taft, and President Warren G. Harding both spoke in a nationalistic vein. The poet Edwin Markham spoke of the people.

But the Second Inaugural engraved on the wall speaks for eternity of American slavery in beautiful, penitent terms. Above the Gettysburg Address, the murals by Jules Guerin show allegorical figures that represent Liberty, and at the center, the Angel of Truth bestowing freedom on slaves. Even if these were not images a black artist would have put there, the original chief meaning of "a new birth of freedom," however abused in 1920s America, was not forgotten.

Churches, too, continued to nurture the Emancipator image. Stained-glass windows with a sainted Lincoln appeared in various places, from the Polish National Catholic Church of Scranton, Pennsylvania, to the Central Woodward Christian Church of Detroit. Bartoli's marble Lincoln in Puerto Rico holds the Emancipation Proclamation. But it is the Gettysburg Address, understood as the voice of American democracy, that hovers over the culture. Monuments continued to rise throughout the 1920s and into the 1930s. The public sculptures often made the connection to the address explicit; at times it was left for the eye of the beholder to decide, as with Samuel Cashwan's Ypsilanti Lincoln of 1938, who holds a paper in his hand. The student-inspired work, however, was surely another upshot of *The Perfect Tribute* that the schools continued to assign routinely.

Art still both reflects and shapes broad American attitudes toward the Gettysburg Address today. The gamut ranges from heroic sculptures through smaller works of art, medals, musical records, down to postage stamps, toys, games, action figures, advertising, and other commercial products. Painters usually portrayed Lincoln at Gettysburg high above his audience, blacks almost never evident, flags, bigger or smaller, an important part of the design. But when the black artist William H. Johnson painted the subject, he placed a black Union soldier next to Lincoln, guarding him. He was not going to allow whites to steal the "new birth of freedom." More important for popular culture were the mass-produced pictures of the Gettysburg Address that began to appear at the start of the twentieth century, grew into an avalanche, and continue today. Many found their way to honored places on the walls of people's homes. The style of these prints evolved to reflect changing tastes and ranged from work that derived from medieval illuminated manuscripts to abstract.

The speech was not in the retrograde silent classic *Birth of a Nation*, which featured Lincoln as "the great heart." But earlier, in 1912, Frank McGlynn recited it with title cards in *Lincoln's Gettysburg Address*, and did so again in 1915. Ward Mack did so (from what are clearly the Malibu Hills) in *The Battle of Gettysburg* of 1913; Ralph Ince did so in 1922 in a film with the same title; as did George Billings in two productions in 1924, still in the silent era, still with title cards.

The first American film with a sound track came in 1927: *Lincoln's Gettysburg Address*. In the years that followed, some of the major actors of the country would recite the speech: Walter Huston; Raymond Massey in the 1935 version of *The Perfect Tribute*; Dame Judith Anderson in 1951; Henry Fonda in 1961; Robert Marsden in 1979; Charlton Heston in 1981 (and live in Gettysburg in 1984); Gregory Peck in 1982; Jason Robards, again in *The Perfect Tribute*, in 1990; and in the same year Sam Waterston in Ken Burns's television documentary *The Civil War*. Early in the twenty-first century, filmmaker Stephen Spielberg invited Liam Neeson to play Lincoln.

During the Great Depression and the New Deal, Lincoln continued to be central to the culture. Franklin Delano Roosevelt and his supporters fully adopted the Progressives' champion of democracy, turning him into the defender of the New Deal. If the Gettysburg Address had any economic implications that might have run counter to the New Deal vision, that mattered not.

Nineteen thirty-eight brought the last Blue and Gray reunion at Gettysburg. By then, the town had its Lincoln Fellowship—its chief duty to conduct public commemoration of the address. FDR came that year to speak to the some 100,000 people, with radio broadcasting to millions. A few of the veterans present were black and, at last, there were some blacks buried at the National Cemetery. The country again faced the likelihood of war, but did not like the idea at all. So the president showed that he was a man of peace by dedicating the Gettysburg Peace Memorial. Lincoln in his 1862 letter to Greeley had announced that "if I could save the Union without freeing *any* slave I would do it; and if I could save it by freeing *all* the slaves I would do it," though in private he had already made up his mind to issue the Emancipation Proclamation. Just as the Greeley letter protected Lincoln, Franklin D. Roosevelt at Gettysburg claimed his peace credentials, already expecting that he would go to war.

The nationalistic cast of the Gettysburg Address was emphasized as the United States became a world power. World War I had reinforced the trend and World War II completed it. In 1917, war bonds featured Lincoln's words from the address, and they did so again now, together with the image of the flag-raising on Iwo Jima. Historical analogies such as these always wobble, yet the fate of the world was indeed at stake in the 1940s. Perhaps the existence of the United States as "a government of the people, by the people, for the people" was also at stake. The Gettysburg Address lived.

Black freedom, on the other hand, and its Civil War memory, languished among the general public. But it was not lost. Lincoln the universal man could also be that of the black man. Carl Sandburg, poet of the common man, created in *Abraham Lincoln: The Prairie Years* (1926) a man that any hog butcher or field hand could call his own. He continued working for eleven years to produce *Abraham Lincoln: The War Years*, a four-volume, 2,500-page masterpiece with hundreds of illustrations. Published in 1940 as the United States was about to enter World War II, the book took the nation by storm. It "sometimes seemed the literary counterpart of the Lincoln memorial," wrote Merrill D. Peterson; the song of America.

The war president, the common man's president, was also the Gettysburg Lincoln. That place "was to Lincoln a fact in crimson mist." In the middle of Sandburg's labors on his great opus, he took time to publish *The People, Yes*—poetry that also touched on Lincoln, who was "of the people by the people for the people."

In 1942, the young critic Alfred Kazin called *The War Years* the "greatest of all American works of art, the people's memory of Lincoln." For a long time, it was. In the 1970s, *Sandburg's Lincoln* became a TV miniseries. By the 1980s, Gore Vidal would dismiss Sandburg with cynical contempt, and academics provided scholarly versions of his judgment. But as late as 2002, when after another American tragedy people would turn to Lincoln's words, some would still refer to Sandburg as the creator of "perhaps the most definitive work on Lincoln."

With World War II, "the painful immediacy" of Lincoln's Gettysburg Address, to quote a recording of Alexander Wolcott, seemed to grow obvious. "Have those words, at any time since they were first spoken, ever meant so much as they mean today?" Wollcott asked. Aaron Copland, perhaps the greatest of American composers, chose the greatest of Americans when commissioned in 1942 "to mirror the magnificent spirit of our country." He needed "the voice of Lincoln to help me when I was ready to risk the impossible," he explained. Copland adorned his work with Lincoln quotations, avoiding what he thought were well-known passages. He made one exception: the Gettysburg Address. *A Lincoln Portrait* quickly grew into a standard of American music and the part that summoned his words has been performed by actors, leaders, and writers, from Eleanor Roosevelt to John Hope Franklin. The work has also circled the globe—America's message to humanity.

As World War II ended, James Daugherty created a picture book, intended for the growing generation, that illustrated the words of "the brave men living and dead" by using GIs of the time. "A new nation" had in it a black man with scarred back but chains being broken. His finest successor in the genre, the artist Sam Fink, would later put African-Americans and whites together for "a new birth of freedom." President Harry S. Truman signed the joint resolution of Congress that designated November 19 as "Dedication Day" and suggested that the Gettysburg Address, the American creed of democracy, be read at "public assemblages" wherever the "flag flies." In subsequent years, the custom continued. Peace had come, but the cold war followed and took the theme further.

Now the foreign danger no longer came from fascism but from communism, and the contest grew ever more global. Lincoln's words continued to serve well. The sesquicentennial of his birth in 1959 had a significant international component. If scholars went abroad to lecture on Lincoln, and if the microfilm of his newly completed *Collected Works* was sent to every country, it was the Gettysburg Address that was translated into numerous languages and cast to the wind. The Lincoln Sesquicentennial Commission adopted as its official slogan: "Lincoln: Symbol of the Free Man."

The Civil War Centennial followed fast upon the 150th anniversary of Lincoln's birth, coinciding with the civil rights era. The period once again pulled Lincoln vigorously in opposite directions. The centennial celebrations claimed him, and also helped turn the Confederate flag into a segregationist symbol. The civil rights revolution and with it a second Reconstruction was underway.

Martin Luther King, Jr., demanded in 1963 a second Emancipation Proclamation and went to the Lincoln Memorial to give his "I have a dream" speech. From the time Marian Anderson sang on its steps in 1939, having been denied the use of the "whites only" hall of the Daughters of the American Revolution, the memorial could serve protest as much as the status quo, a temple where tensions grew palpable, "between celebration and confrontation, between commemoration and politics, between sacred and profane," in the words of the historian Scott A. Sandage. Dr. King's picture replaced Lincoln's on the walls of black homes. If in 1963 the finest of African-American historians, John Hope Franklin, published an important study of *The Emancipation Proclamation,* and *Ebony* magazine a laudatory article about the sixteenth president, five years after that one of its editors, Lerone Bennett, published his much-quoted article "Was Lincoln a White Supremacist?" and gave a resounding affirmative answer. Decades later, he issued a full-length book on the subject.

In Detroit in 1969, Alfonso Pelzer's *Lincoln,* which holds in hand the Emancipation Proclamation, erected against all odds in 1919, was pulled down by vandals. It was 1986 before schoolchildren raised most of the money needed to restore and rededicate the statue. Heading up the effort was the managing editor of the *Detroit Free Press* which, in 1863, had derided the Gettysburg remarks for daring to speak of equal rights.

The divisions about Lincoln did not develop solely along racial lines any more than in earlier days. If militants, black or otherwise, derided Lincoln, so did neo-Confederates. When at last Richmond put up a Lincoln statue in 2003, it was the latter group that protested. A plane flew over the dedication streaming the words of John Wilkes Booth: *"Sic semper tyrannis*—Thus ever to tyrants." When the Lincoln Prize board held its annual awards banquet in Richmond, it was picketed with some Confederate flags. If now the local people present at the Virginia events celebrated, they were predominantly white in a city with a large black majority. In 1865, when the president had gone there, the black population rejoiced, while most whites stared in icy silence from their windows.

But the emancipationist view of the Gettysburg Address came back into fashion. A. L. Van den Bergen's sculpture, dedicated in 1924, in Racine, Wisconsin, with another copy in Clinton, Illinois, was still identified in a 1952 survey as Lincoln holding in hand the Gettysburg Address. By the 1990s, the Smithsonian Inventory came to describe it as Lincoln holding either the Emancipation Proclamation or the Gettysburg Address. The momentum that had turned Emancipation Proclamation statues into Gettysburg Address statues in the 1890s swung the other way a century later.

The Abraham Lincoln Bicentennial Commission, appointed by Congress at the start of the twenty-first century, which included Congressman Jesse Jackson, Jr., and the African-American president of the Organization

of American Historians, James O. Horton, talked often about the "unfinished work" of the United States. The Lincoln scholar and co-chair of the
commission Harold Holzer summed up the dominant understanding beautifully: "The Gettysburg Address was the poetry to the Emancipation
Proclamation's prose."

Wendy Allen, a young painter who fell in love with Lincoln in Gettysburg and devoted her career to capturing him on her canvases, spoke for her
generation. In 2002, Allen's Lincoln was flanked on one side by Rosa Parks
and on the other by the moment of Reverend King's assassination.

Mainstream America at last got the forward-looking face of the Gettysburg Address right—at least in part. In that small Pennsylvania town, Lincoln spoke of "a new birth of freedom" for all people, black and white. Of
course, no idea moves unchanged through the years. Lincoln had not fore-
seen the particulars of the civil rights legislation with which his name
would later be linked. But his words had pointed that way. Lincoln, and
with him an ever greater part of the American people, interpreted the Declaration of Independence as "a standard maxim for free society, which
should be familiar to all, and revered by all; constantly looked to, constantly
labored for." It would never be "perfectly attained," but it carried the hope
that its influence would ever deepen, "augmenting the happiness and value
of life to all people of all colors everywhere." This was now "the unfinished
work."

At the opening of a major exhibit about slavery at the New-York Historical Society in the fall of 2005, the first African-American mayor of the
city, David Dinkins, quoted Lincoln glowingly with those very words and
this very meaning, as people streamed by to view the handwritten draft of
the Preliminary Emancipation Proclamation. About the same time a holiday sales catalogue out of Little Rock, Arkansas, advertised for a substantial sum a facsimile of the Gettysburg Address, "this stunning tribute to
those gallant soldiers North and South." Old ideas die hard.

Idealized heroes inspire people to action; historically accurate ones may
not. Scholarship filters down to the general public over the years to become
part of the common wisdom of the country. Distracting voices remain. But
the Gettysburg Address, sacred for generations, now has been granted
nearly miraculous powers—"the words that remade America." Yet the
words did not do that. How could a speech do that, especially one that was
not heard distinctly in its own day?

The address did highlight democracy, first of all by the political role it played in its time. The deeper message that helped Lincoln's words live, exalted popular government and the equality of people. They were meant to encompass all people, including black people, indeed the people of the world. But the message the speech carried went well beyond race relations. Americans of World Wars I and II understood that. Though neither war duplicated the circumstances of the Civil War, they did threaten the United States. The Gettysburg Address was, above all, a war speech. To the degree it was heard in 1863, it helped people come to terms with massive death. It gave courage and an the answer to the eternal question of the battlefield: Why? It was a war speech. One dares not forget that.

The sociologist Barry Schwartz has shown that the prestige of America's great historical figures had fallen significantly since the 1960s revolt against authority, including the authority of the past. Lincoln has not escaped. The American drive toward equality led, among scholars, to "history from the bottom up." In the culture as a whole, it led to the paradox of "Lincoln, a symbol of equality, being diminished by the very ideal he exemplifies."

Yet Schwartz also argues that the Gettysburg Address never lost any of its sovereign allure. Just as the Declaration of Independence, or at least its preamble, has not been diminished by Jefferson's partial fall from grace, so Lincoln's words have lived forcefully beyond the culture's flight from the heroes of the past. Perhaps so. But in the last decade of the twentieth century and the dawn of the twenty-first Lincoln has experienced a revival.

The beauty of the language of the Gettysburg Address, its poetry, has something to do with that. It lives on. The British poet and playwright John Drinkwater, at the start of the twentieth century, made Shakespeare and Lincoln kinsfolk, though one devoted his life to his art, the other to public life, finding time for only a few masterpieces. But the beauty of the language of the Gettysburg Address helps explain its glory over the years.

If the power of the words shines brightly, the uses to which they have been put, in the United States and around the world, also continue to reverberate. The address inspires creative genius—great sculptures and monuments, paintings, drawings, popular prints, cartoons, fiction, theater, poetry, humor, dance, music—all the facets of artistic life, enhancing the magic of Lincoln's words. The Internet throbs with Lincoln.

Nor is this limited to the United States. Myth, symbol, reality—the

Gettysburg Gospel is all that. Tolstoy called Lincoln a saint and recited words about him from a Muslim chief in the Caucasus: "He spoke with the voice of thunder; he laughed like the sunrise and his deeds were as strong as the rock and as sweet as the fragrance of the rose." About the same time Gandhi spoke in a like spirit: "though America was his motherland and he was an American, he regarded the whole world as his native land." Later in independent India, Jawaharlal Nehru kept a brass mold of Lincoln's right hand near him: "I look at it every day, and it gives me strength." Sun Yat-sen, the founder of modern China, could explain his goal as creating *the government of the people, by the people, for the people*. As Africa shook off colonial powers, the new independent countries, one after another, issued postage stamps with Lincoln on them.

And Nelson Mandela, South Africa's first postapartheid president, looked on Lincoln as a model and often acted like him. In Latin America, during a Caracas performance of Copland's *Lincoln Portrait* in the 1950s, when the final words came, "a government of the people, by the people— por el pueblo y para el pueblo," the audience erupted, and an American foreign service officer later explained this was the beginning of the end of a dictatorship. Students in Hungary in 1956, in Tehran in 1979, and on Tiananmen Square in 1989 called upon the same words. In the twenty-first century, when Pope John Paul II arrived in the United States, he knelt to kiss the soil and quoted Lincoln. Of course around the globe, as in the United States, the Gettysburg Address could be misused to support unsavory causes. But the American "saint's" words most often elevated people, and sometimes moved them to action. They still do.

The world's love of Lincoln's address focuses on the beauty of its language, its devotion to democracy, and above all its eternal promise of "a new birth of freedom" for all "the people." Shaded into the background is the other face of the speech, even more important to Americans in 1863— or at any time of great threat—the appeal to the use of force to defend democracy. Americans recognize fully that meaning of the Gettysburg Address when crises come. The understanding can be misused, but it can also give great strength. Lincoln gave a speech with a universal message, but its nationalist face cannot be ignored. And whatever sins may have been committed around the globe in the name of nationalism during the last two centuries, few doubt the justice of a democratic nationalism that means self-preservation. At times that requires force. Lincoln made that clear at Gettysburg.

But the Gettysburg Gospel does not exult in war. It illuminates the tragedy that is part of the "new birth": its message of sacrificial redemption is for humankind. Its good news Lincoln could not complete until the end of the war came into sight. As Garry Wills and so many others have pointed out, the Second Inaugural Address can be understood as the culmination of the Gettysburg Address.

The "unfinished work" looked to higher meanings, but its immediate concern was the bloodiest war of American history. In the spring of 1865, the president, who had entered the national stage in 1848 as a congressman opposing war, still had to acknowledge "the progress of our arms, upon which all else chiefly depends. . . ." "All dreaded" that war in 1861, and in 1865 still, "Fondly do we hope—fervently do we pray—that this mighty scourge of war may speedily pass away." But the world creates "offences," they must come, and for Americans, the great offense came with slavery. The war came as the punishment for the American sin. And terrible was the message of war:

> *Yet, if God wills that it continue, until all the wealth piled by the bond-man's two hundred and fifty years of unrequited toil shall be sunk, and until every drop of blood drawn with the lash, shall be paid by another drawn with the sword, as was said three thousand years ago, so still it must be said "the judgments of the Lord, are true and righteous altogether."*

Humankind could not abolish the "scourge of war"; Lincoln could not. But he would fight in the best tradition of humanity, struggle as counseled in the Western world by St. Augustine of Hippo in fourth-century North Africa, with mercy in his heart. He would carry the unbearable burden of war "with malice toward none; with charity for all; with firmness in the right, as God gives us to see the right." And then redemption would come, "a lasting peace, among ourselves, and with all nations." But, as history tells us, we must continue to seek that redemption until the end of time.

C H A P T E R   E I G H T

─────◆─────

CODA

The dawn comes in mist over the Hudson River. The day will be warm, not quite time for Indian summer. But long before dawn the bagpipers in their kilts begin their march toward ground zero. The music wails and drums beat. Awake, New York City, awake. Remember. Remember. Lights turn on, candles burn, windows open, flags wave, fists are raised, hands over hearts. Mile after mile from the five boroughs of the city the marchers head toward the sacred site.

By the time they reach ground zero, a huge crowd is assembled there. Thousands upon thousands fill the area. Some are relatives of people lost in the fall of the two towers. Most are not. "The families of the dead and the families of the living have joined," the *New York Times* reports. As the ceremonies are about to start, some two hundred construction workers arrive—"Thickly muscled men." A foreman leads them, holding up a large American flag. The men stand in silence.

In other parts of the United States, and in many countries around the globe, people remember. At the Pentagon outside of Washington. In the Pennsylvania countryside, where passengers brought down the plane intended to bring death to many more. In St. Paul's Cathedral in London. In the little tenth-century church in the village of Bellagio in Italy. Mozart's

Requiem rolls around each of the world's twenty-four time zones beginning at 8:46 a.m. local time, the moment when the first hijacked aircraft hit the north tower of the World Trade Center. Choirs in Canada, Brazil, Surinam, Haiti, and Honduras participate.

In Gettysburg, the evening brings crowds to what in the old days people called the Diamond. Now it is Lincoln Square. Farmers in overalls, policemen, volunteer firemen, field hands mostly from Mexico with feeble command of English, stylishly dressed office workers, businessmen, lawyers, doctors, nurses, families with children and grandparents, students from the College, the Seminary, professors. Candles in hand, they sing. On the curb before the Wills House, where Lincoln had stayed so long ago, his statue stands silently, the hand pointing to the room where he probably finished writing the Gettysburg Address.

Ceremonies are for "us the living," as Lincoln said long ago. At home and around the world they help people remember and help them go on living. At ground zero the rituals are unforgettable. The names of everyone who died there a year before are read, a litany of two and a half hours, a "story" that "had no verbs or adjectives . . . one epic paragraph."

When the reading starts, a gust of wind whips the dust out of the vast pit where towers stood. The winds will continue to blow, and by the end everyone will have dust in their eyes and mouth. Sacred music underscores the silence of the multitudes. *Ave Maria*. Pealing bells interrupt the reading of the names at the moments when hate struck the first tower, then when the tower fell, and again when the second did, too. Two great historic documents are read: one, the Declaration of Independence, begins: "We hold these truths to be self-evident, that all men are created equal. . . ." The mayor speaks of the martyrs, "they were us," and the president in Washington adds that "they did not die in vain."

People walk into the pit, seven stories deep, led by the relatives of the dead. One after another they descend into the depths and some linger there, picking up stones, leaving flowers, photos, whispered prayers and messages. A peace that passes all understanding fills the empty space. "When I first came," one woman recalls the ground zero of the year before, "it was such a horrible pile. I thought they could never take it away. Now it looks so empty and clean. It is almost beautiful." Nine-eleven, 2002. This too, is an unforgettable day.

But this chapter has gotten ahead of itself telling the story of a day of commemoration, for many a day of searching for closure. Let's step back and start at the beginning: A minute of silence commences the ceremonies. Then the governor of the state of New York breaks the stillness:

> *Four score and seven years ago our fathers brought forth on this continent, a new nation, conceived in Liberty, and dedicated to the proposition that all men are created equal.*
>
> *Now we are engaged in a great civil war, testing whether that nation, or any nation so conceived and so dedicated, can long endure. We are met on a great battle-field of that war. We have come to dedicate a portion of that field, as a final resting place for those who here gave their lives that that nation might live. It is altogether fitting and proper that we should do this.*
>
> *But, in a larger sense, we can not dedicate—we can not consecrate—we can not hallow—this ground. The brave men, living and dead, who struggled here, have consecrated it, far above our poor power to add or detract. The world will little note, nor long remember what we say here, but it can never forget what they did here. It is for us the living, rather, to be dedicated here to the unfinished work which they who fought here have thus far so nobly advanced. It is rather for us to be here dedicated to the great task remaining before us—that from these honored dead we take increased devotion to that cause for which they gave the last full measure of devotion—that we here highly resolve that these dead shall not have died in vain—that this nation, under God, shall have a new birth of freedom—and that government of the people, by the people, for the people, shall not perish from the earth.*

The ceremony is beamed around the globe. People who listen understand. Americans are saying, this is who we are.

THE PROGRAM AT THE SOLDIERS' NATIONAL CEMETERY, NOVEMBER 19, 1863

EVERETT'S ORATION

Address Delivered at the Consecration of the National Cemetery at Gettysburg on the 19th of November, 1863. *

It was appointed by Law in Athens, that the funeral obsequies of those who had fallen in battle should be performed at the public expense, and in the most honora-ble manner. Their bones were carefully gathered up from the funeral pyre, where their bodies were consumed, and brought home to the city: There for three days before the interment, they lay in state, beneath tents of honor, to receive the votive offerings of friends and relatives,—flowers, weapons, precious ornaments, painted vases, (wonders of art, which after two thousand years adorn the museums of {modern} Europe), the last tributes of surviving affection. Ten coffins of funeral cypress received the honorable deposit, one for each of the tribes of the city, and an eleventh in memory of the unrecognized, but not therefore, unhonored, dead, & of those whose remains could not be recovered. On the fourth day the mournful procession was formed {moved}; mothers, wives, sisters, daughters, led the way, and to them it was permitted by

---

* *From the manuscript at the Abraham Lincoln Presidential Library. Endnotes, pages 366–71, identify the more subtantive variations that appeared in the published official version: Address of the Hon. Edward Everett . . . (Boston: Little, Brown, 1864). The text is printed as it appears in the manuscript. Brackets [ ] in the text enclose passages that the official version omitted or replaced with the passages in the Notes. Double brackets [[ ]] indicate text Everett put in brackets. Braces {} identify text Everett crossed out in his manuscript.*

simplicity of ancient manners to utter aloud their lamentations for the beloved & the lost; the male relatives followed; citizens & strangers closed the train. Thus marshalled, they moved to the place of interment in that famous Ceramicus, the most beautiful suburb of Athens, which had been adorned by Cimon, the son of Miltiades, with walks & fountains, & columns; whose groves were filled with altars, shrines & temples; whose gardens were watered with streams from the neighboring hills, & shaded with the {illegible} and trees {olives} coeval with the foundation of the city; whose circuit enclosed

> . . . the olive grove of Academe,
> Plato's retirement, when the attic bird
> Trilled his thick warbled note the summer long;

whose pathways gleamed with the monuments of the illustrious dead, the work of the most consummate masters, that ever gave life to marble. There, beneath the overarching plane trees, upon a lofty stage erected for the purpose, it was provided by law, that a funeral oration should be pronounced, by some {distinguished} citizens of Athens, in the presence of the assembled multitude.

Such were the tokens of respect required by law to be paid at Athens, to the memory of those who had fallen in the cause of their country. To those alone who fell at Marathon, a peculiar honor was reserved. As the battle fought upon that immortal field was distinguished from all others in Grecian history for its influence over the fortunes of Hellas,—as it depended upon the event of that day, whether Greece should live, a glory and a light to all coming time, or should expire, like the meteor of a moment, to the honors awarded to its martyr-heroes were such as were bestowed by Athens on no other occasion; {for no other services or sacrifices}. They alone of all her sons were entombed upon the spot, which they had forever rendered famous. Their names were inscribed upon ten pillars erected upon the monumental tumulus which covered their ashes, (where, after six hundred years they were read by the traveler Pausanias), and although the columns, beneath the hand of barbaric violence & time, have long since disappeared, the venerable mound still marks the spot where they fought & fell:

> That battlefield, where Persia's victim horde,
> First bowed beneath the brunt of Hellas' sword.

And shall I, fellow citizens, who, after an interval of twenty three centuries, a youthful pilgrim from a world unknown to ancient Greece, have wandered over that illustrious plain, with feelings akin to those with which one treads on holy ground; have gazed with respectful emotion on the mound, which still protects the remains of those, who rolled back the tide of Persian invasion, & rescued the land of popular liberty, of letters, and arts from the ruthless foe, stand unmoved over the graves of our dear brethren, who but yesterday, on one of those all-important days which decide a nation's history,—a day on whose issue it depended, whether this august republican union, founded by some of the wisest statesmen that ever lived, cemented with the blood of some of the purest patriots that ever died, should perish or endure,—rolled back the tide of an invasion not less unprovoked, not less ruthless, than that which came to plant the dark banner of Asiatic despotism & slavery on the free soil Greece. Heaven forbid! And could I prove so insensible to every prompting of patriotic duty and affection, not only would you fellow-citizens, gathered many of you from distant states, who have come to take part in these pious offices of respect and gratitude,—You, respected fathers, brethren, matrons, sisters who sur-round me, cry out for shame, but the forms of brave & patriotic men who fill these honored graves would heave beneath the sod with indignation.

We have assembled, Friends, Fellow-citizens, at the invitation of the Execu-tive of the great & central State of Pennsylvania, seconded by the governors of nineteen States of the union, to pay the last tribute of respect to the brave men, who in the hard fought battles of the 1st, 2d, & 3d days of July last, laid down their lives for the country on the hillsides & plains spread out before us, & whose remains have been gathered into the cemetery, which we consecrate this day. As my eye ranges over the fields whose sods were so lately moistened by the blood of gallant & loyal men, I feel as never before, how truly it was said of old that it is sweet & becoming to die for one's Country. I feel as never before how justly, from the dawn of history to the present time, men have paid the homage of their gratitude & admiration to the memory of those, who nobly sacrifice their lives, that their fellow-men may live in safety. And of this tribute were ever due, when—to whom could it be more justly paid, than to those whose last resting place, we this day commend to the blessing of Heaven & of Men. For consider, my friends, what would have been the consequences to the country, to yourselves, and to all You hold dear, if those who sleep beneath our feet & their gallant comrades, who survive to serve their country on other fields of danger & death, had failed in their duty on those memorable days. Consider what, at this moment, would have been the condition of the United States, if that noble army of the Potomac, instead of gallantly and for the sec-ond time beating back the tide of invasion, had been itself driven from these well-contested heights; thrown back in confusion on Baltimore; or trampled, discomfited, scattered to the four winds. What, under these circumstances, would not have been the fate of the Monumental City, of Harrisburg, of

Philadelphia, of Washington,—the Capital of the union, each & every one of which, accordingly as it might have pleased an enemy, guided only by passion, flushed with victory, & confident of continued success to direct his course, would have lain at his mercy?

For this we must bear in mind, it is the great lesson of the war, indeed of every war, that it is impossible for a people without military organization, inhabiting the cities, towns, & villages of an open country, including of course the natural proportion of non-combatants of either sex & of every age, to withstand the inroad of a veteran army. What defence can be made by the inhabitants of villages mostly built of wood, of cities unprotected by walls, nay by a population of men, however high-toned & resolute, whose aged parents demand their care whose wives & children are clustering about them, against the charge of the war-horse whose neck is clothed with thunder, against flying artillery, & batteries of rifled cannon planted on every commanding eminence, against the onset of trained veterans led by skilful chiefs? No, my friends, army must be met by army; battery by battery, squadron by squadron, & the shock of organized thousands must be encountered by the firm breasts & valiant arms of other thousands, as well-organized & as skillfully led. It is no reproach, therefore, to the unarmed population of the country to say, that we owe it to the brave men who sleep in their beds of honor around us & their gallant surviving associates, not merely that your fertile fields, my friends of Pennsylvania & Maryland were redeemed from the presence of the Invader, but that your beautiful capitals were not given up to threatened plunder, perhaps laid in ashes—Washington seized by the enemy, and a blow struck at the heart of the nation.

Who that hears me has forgotten the thrill of joy, that ran through the country on the 4th of July,—happy day for the glorious tidings, & still more for the fall of Vicksburg, when the telegraph flashed through the land the assurance from the President of the United States, that the army of the Potomac had again smiten the invader. Sure I am that with the ascriptions of praise that rose to Heaven from twenty millions of freemen, with the acknowledgments that breathed from patriotic lips, throughout the length & breadth of America, to the surving officers and men who had rendered the country this inestimable service, there beat in every loyal bosom a throb of tender & sorrowful gratitude to the martyrs who had fallen & to those who still lay wounded & bleeding on the sternly contested field. Let a nation's fervent thanks make some amends for the sufferings of those who survive; would that that the heartfelt tribute could penetrate these honored graves!

[Let us contemplate for a few moments, my friends, the train of events, which culminated in the battles of the 1st, 2d & 3d of July, that we may comprehend, to their full extent, our obligations to the martyrs & surviving heroes of

the army of the Potomac.⌉ Of this stupendous rebellion, planned, as its origi-
nators boast, more than thirty years ago, matured & prepared for during an entire generation, finally commenced because, for the first time since the
adoption of the Constitution, an election of a President had been effected without the votes of the South, (which retained however the control of the two
other branches of the government), the occupation of the national capital, the
seizure of the public archives & of the treaties with foreign powers was an essential feature. This was in substance, within my personal knowledge in the
winter of 1860–61, admitted by one of the most influ⌈ential leaders of the rebellion, {several words crossed out are not legible, except for "dark project"}
and it was fondly thought that this object could be effected, by a bold & sudden
movement on the 4th of March 1861. There is abundant proof also that a
darker project was contemplated, if not by the responsible chiefs of the rebellion, Yet by nameless ruffians, willing to play a subsidiary & murderous part in
the treasonable drama. It was accordingly maintained by the rebel {Confeder-
ate} emissaries abroad, in the circles to which they found access, that the new
American minister ought not, when he arrived, to be received as the Envoy of
the United States, inasmuch as before that time, Washington would have been
captured, & the capitol of the Nation & the Archives & Monuments of the government would be in the Possession of the Confederates. In full accordance
also with this threat, it was declared by the rebel Secretary of War at Montgomery, in the presence of his colleagues, which the tidings of the assault on
Sumter were travelling over the wires on that fatal 12th of {May} April, that
before the end of May "the flag which now flaunted the breeze (as he expressed
it) would float over the dome of the capitol at Washington."

⌈⌈At the time this threat was made the rebellion was confined to the cotton-
growing States, and it was well understood by them, that the only hope of
drawing any of the other slave-holding states into the conspiracy was by
bringing about a conflict of arms, & "firing the heart of the South," by the effu-
sion of blood. This was declared by the Charleston press to be the object for
which Sumter was to be assaulted; and the emissaries sent from Richmond, to
urge on the unhallowed work, gave the promise, that with the first drop of
blood that should be shed, Virginia would place herself by the side of South
Carolina.

In pursuance of this original plan of the leaders of the rebellion, the capture
of Washington has been continually had in view, not merely for the sake of its
public buildings, as the capitol of the Confederacy, but as the necessary preliminary to the absorption of the border states, & for the moral effect in the eyes of
Europe of possessing the metropolis of the Union.

I allude to these facts, not perhaps enough borne in mind, as a sufficient refutation of the claim on the part of the South, that the war is one of self-defence, waged for the right of self-government. It is in reality a war originally levied by ambitious men in the cotton-growing States, for the purpose of drawing the Slave-holding border states into the vortex of the Conspiracy, first by sympathy, which in the case of Eastern Virginia, North Carolina, part of Tennessee & Arkansas succeeded, & then by force & for the purpose of subjugating Western Virginia, Kentucky, Eastern Tennessee, Missouri, & Maryland; and it is a most extraordinary fact, considering the clamors of the rebel chiefs on the subject of Invasion that not a soldier of the United States has entered the States last named, except to defend their union-loving inhabitants from the armies & guerillas of the Rebels.]]

In conformity with the designs alluded to on the city of Washington, and notwithstanding the disastrous results of the Invasion of 1862, it was determined by the rebel government last summer to resume the offensive in that direction. Unable to force the passage of the Rappahannock, where General Hooker, notwithstanding the reverse at Chancellorville in May, was strongly posted, the Confederate general resorted to Strategy. He had two objects in view. The first was, by a rapid movement Northward, & by manæuvring with Longstreet's corps on the East side of the blue ridge, to draw Hooker from his base of operations, thus leading him to uncover the approaches to Washington, & to throw it open to a raid by Stuarts' cavalry & enable Lee himself to cross the Potomac in the neighborhood of Poolesville & fall upon the Capital. This plan of operations was wholly frustrated. The design {plan} of the rebel General was promptly discovered by Hooker, & moving himself with great rapidity from Fredericksburg, he preserved unbroken the inner line, & stationed the various corps of his army at all the points protecting the approach to Washington, from Guilford up to Leesburg. From this vantage ground the rebel general in vain attempted to draw him. In the meantime, by the vigorous operations of Pleasonton's cavalry, the cavalry of Stuart, [though twice as numerous], was so crippled as to be disabled from performing the part assigned it in the campaign. In this manner General Lee's first objective, the defeat of Hooker's army [and the consequent capture of] Washington was baffled.

The second part of the Confederate plan, & which is supposed to have been undertaken in opposition to the views of General Lee, was to turn the demonstration toward the North into a real invasion of Maryland & Pennsylvania, in the hope that, in this way, General Hooker would be drawn to a distance from the capital; that some opportunity would be afforded of taking him at disadvantage, and after defeating his army, of making a descent upon Baltimore & Washington. This part of General Lee's plan, which was the repetition of that of 1862, was not less signally defeated, with what honor to the arms of the Union the heights on which we are assembled will forever attest.

Much time had been uselessly consumed by the rebel general, in his unavailing attempt to outmanæuvre General Hooker. Although he broke up from Fredericksburg on the 3d of June, it was not till the 24th, that the main body of his army entered Maryland, & instead of crossing the Potomac as he intended East of the Blue Ridge, he was compelled to do it at Shepherdstown & Williamsport, thus materially deranging his plan of campaign North of the river.

Stuart, who had been sent with his cavalry to the east of the Blue Ridge, to guard the passes of the mountains, to mask the movements of Lee, and to harass the Union general in crossing the river, having been very severely handled by Pleasonton at Beverly Ford, Aldie, and Upperville, instead of being able to retard General Hooker's advance, was driven himself away from his connection with the army of Lee, and cut off for a fortnight from all communication with it,—a circumstance to which General Lee, in his report, alludes more than once, with evident displeasure. Let us now rapidly glance at the incidents of the eventful campaign.

A detachment from Ewell's corps, under Jenkins, had penetrated, on the 15th of June, as far as Chambersburg. This movement was intended at first merely as a demonstration, and as a marauding expedition for supplies. It had, however, the salutary effect of alarming the country; and vigorous preparations were made, not only by the General Government, but here in Pennsylvania and in the sister States, to repel the inroad. After two days passed at Chambersburg, Jenkins, anxious for his communications with Ewell, fell back with his plunder to Hagerstown. Here he remained for several days, and then, having swept the recesses of the Cumberland valley, came down upon the eastern flank of the South Mountain, and pushed his marauding parties as far as Waynesboro. On the 22d the remainder of Ewell's corps crossed the river and moved up the valley. They were followed on the 24th by Longstreet and Hill, who crossed the Potomac at Williamsport & Shepherdstown, and pushing up the valley, encamped at Chambersburg on the 27th. In this way the whole rebel army, estimated at 90,000 infantry, upwards of 10,000 cavalry, & 4000 or 5000 artillery, making a total of 105,000 of all arms, was concentrated in Pennsylvania.

Up to this time no report of Hooker's movements had been received by General Lee, who having been deprived of his cavalry had no means of obtaining information. Rightly judging, however, that no time would be lost by the union army in the pursuit, in order to detain it on the eastern side of the mountains, in Maryland and Pennsylvania, & thus preserve his communications by the way of Williamsport, he had, before his own arrival at Chambersburg, divided

Ewell to send detachments from his Corps to Carlisle & York. The latter detachment under Early passed through Gettysburg on the 26th of June. You need not, fellow-citizen, that I should recall to you those moments of alarm and distress, precursors as they were of the trying scenes, which were so soon to follow.

As soon as General Hooker perceived that the advance of the Confederates into the Cumberland Valley was not a mere feint, to draw him away from Washington, he moved {himself} rapidly in pursuit. Attempts, as we have seen, were made to harass & retard his passage across the Potomac. These attempts were not only altogether unsuccessful, but so unskilfully made, as to place the entire federal army between the Cavalry of Stuart & the army of Lee. While the latter was massed in the Cumberland Valley, Stuart was East of the mountains, with Hooker's army between, & Gregg's cavalry in close pursuit. Stuart was accordingly compelled to force a march northward, which was destitute of all strategical character, & which deprived his chief of all means of obtaining intelligence.

⟦It is difficult to see, in these vagrant excursions of Ewell's divisions & Stuart's cavalry the traces of that eminent skill which is claimed for the rebel general. They had the effect, it is true, of spreading alarm through the country & harassing the unarmed population; but they did not deceive the union commanders, as to what must be his main object, if he had in reality any well conceived plan of operations, which is doubtful. The utmost he could expect {was} to accomplish was to attack the separate corps of Hooker's army before they could be concentrated, & then, if seconded by fortune, descend upon Baltimore & Washington. General Lee, however, states that his objects in directing the Raids on Carlisle & York were to keep the Union Army East of the Mountains, and preserve his own communications with Viriginia.⟧

⟦No time, (as we have seen, had been)⟧ lost by General Hooker in the pursuit of Lee. The day after the rebel army entered Maryland, the union army crossed the Potomac at Edward's ferry, & by the 28th lay {in} between Harper's ferry and Frederick. The enemy on that day was ⟦either⟧ massed at Chambersburg or moving on the Cashtown road, in the direction of Gettysburg, while the detachments from Ewell's corps, of which mention has been name, had reached the Susquehannah opposite to Harrisburgh & Columbia. That a great battle must soon be fought no one could doubt, but in the apparent absence of plan on the part of Lee, it was impossible to foretell the scene of the encounter. Whereever fought, consequences the most momentous hung upon the result.

In this critical & anxious state of affairs, General Hooker was relieved & General Meade was summoned to the chief command of the army, and it appears to my unmilitary judgment to reflect the highest credit upon him, upon his predecessor and upon the army of the Potomac, that a change could take place in the Chief Command on the eve of a battle,—the various corps necessarily moving on lines somewhat divergent & all [ignorance of the enemy], intended point of concentration,—not an hour's hesitation ensued in the advance of any portion of the entire force.

Having assumed the chief command on the 28th, General Meade directed his left wing under Reynolds upon Emmitsburg this right upon New Windsor, leaving Genl. French with 11,000 men to protect the Baltimore & Ohio Rail Road, & convey the public property from Harper's Ferry to Washington. Buford's Cavalry was then at this place & Kilpatrick's at Hanover, where he encountered and defeated the rear of Stuart's cavalry, who was roving the country in search of the main army of Lee. On the rebel side, Hill had reached {Cashtown} Fayetteville on the Cashtown road on the 28th, and was followed on the same road by Longstreet on the 29th. The eastern side of the mountain as seen from Gettysburg, was lighted up at night by the camp fires of the enemy's advance, & the country swarmed with his foraging parties. It was now too evident to be doubted, that the thunder cloud, so long gathering blackness, would soon burst on some part of the devoted vicinity of Gettyburg.

The 30th of June was a day of eventful preparation. At [11½] in the morning Buford passed through Gettysburg upon a reconnaissance in force, with his cavalry, upon the Chambersburg road. The information obtained by him was immediately communicated to Genl. Reynolds, & that gallant officer with the first corps moved from Emmitsburg to within six or seven miles of this place, & encamped on the right bank of Marsh's Creek. Our right wing meantime was moved to Manchester. On the same day the corps of Hill & Longstreet were pushed forward on the Chambersburg road & distributed in the vicinity of March's Creek. A reconnaissance was made by Genl. Pettigrew up to a very short distance from this place. Thus at [the close of] the 30th of June the greater part of the rebel force was concentrated against two corps of the union army; the former refreshed by two days passed in comparative repose, & deliberate preparation for the encounter, the latter fatigued by the rapidity of their {march} advance, separated by a march of one or two days from their supporting corps, and [ignorant] at what point they were to expect an attack.

And now the momentous day, a day to be forever remembered in the annals of the country, arrived. General Lee states, in his report, that he had not intended to fight a general battle so far from his base. But when we consider that Gen. Meade's army was between him & Baltimore & Washington, the main objects of his campaign; that his base was in Virginia, but the line of the Cumberland Valley, from which he was emerging by the Chambersburg road, it is not very apparent where he could have expected to fight a battle nearer his base, as every day's march carried him further from it.

Early in the morning on the 1st of July the conflict began. I need not say that it would be impossible to comprise, within the limits of the hour, such a narrative as would do anything like full justice to the all-important events of these three great days, or to the merit of the brave officers & men of every rank, of every arm of the service, & of every State, who bore their part in the tremendous struggle,—alike those who nobly sacrificed their lives for their country and those who survive, many of them scarred with honorable wounds,—the objects of our admiration and gratitude. The astonishingly minute & accurate accounts contained in the journals of the day, some of them prepared from personal observation by reporters who witnessed the scenes they describe, & the highly valuable 'Notes' of Professor Jacobs of the university in this place will abundantly supply the deficiency of my necessarily too condensed statement.

———————

Besides the sources of information mentioned in the text, I have been kindly favored with a memorandum of the operations of the three days drawn up for me, by direction of Major General Meade, by his aide Colonel Theodore Lyman, from whom also I have received other important communications relative to the campaign. I have received very valuable documents relative to the battle from Major General Halleck, Commander-in-Chief of the Army, & have been much assisted in drawing up the sketch of the campaign, [by the official reports] of the movements of every corps of the army, for each day, after the breaking up {movement} from Fredericksburg commenced. I have derived much assistance from Col. John B. Bachelder's oral explanations of his beautiful & minute drawing (about to be engraved) of the field of the three day's struggle. With the information derived from these sources, I have compared the statements in General Lee's official Report of the Campaign of the 31 July 1863; a well-written article purporting to be an account of the three days in the Richmond Enquirer of 22nd July, & the article on "the battle of Gettysburg & the campaign in Pennsylvania," by an officer [of the] British army in Blackwood's Magazine for September. The value of the information combined in this last essay may be seen by comparing the remark under date 27th of June, that "private property is to be rigedly protected" with the statement, in the next sentence but one, that "all the cattle & farm horses having been seized by Ewell, farm labor had come to a complete standstill." He also, under date of the 4th of July, speaks of Lee's retreat being encumbered by "Ewell's immense train of plunder." This writer informs us that, on the Evening of the 4th, he heard "reports coming in from the different <u>generals</u>, that the enemy (Meade's army) was retiring, & had been doing so all day long." At a consultation at Headquarters on the 6th between General Lee, Longstreet, Hill, & Wilcox, this writer was told by some one, whose name he prudently leaves in blank, that "the army had no intention at present of retreating for good & that some of the enemy's dispatches had been intercepted, in which the following words occur: "The noble but unfortunate army of the Potomac has again been obliged to retreat before superior numbers"!

[At ½ past 9 in the morning Buford's cavalry, dismounted as skirmishes, commenced the action at 10 oclock our artillery opened. General Reynolds at ½ past ten, after a conference with General Howard, hastened through Gettysburg to the field, while his men] moved up over the fields from the Emmitsburg road in front of McMillan's & Dr. Schmucker's under cover of Seminary [Hill]. [It is probable that the strength of the enemy to be encountered had been underrated by Genl. Reynolds, who] immediately found himself engaged with a force which greatly outnumbered his own. [The conflict was however sustained by him with spirit, till he fell at the head of his advance.] The command for a short time devolved on Genl. Doubleday, who was at length relieved by General Howard of the 11th Corps, with the divisions of Schurz & Barlow, the latter of whom received a severe wound. Thus strengthened, the advantage of the battle was for some time on the union side. The attacks of the rebels were repulsed & a large number of prisoners taken. At length, however, the reinforcement [of the rebels, by the divisions of Rodes & Early, advancing from Heidlersberg by separate roads, turned the fortunes of the day.] Our army, after contesting the ground for five hours, was obliged to yield to the force, which outnumbered them two to one, & toward the close of the afternoon, [retreated, with heavy loss,] to the heights where we are now assembled. [The first corps] passed through the outskirts of the town, & reached the hill, without serious loss or molestation. The eleventh corps, not being aware that the enemy had entered the town from the North, attempted to force their way through Washington & Baltimore streets, which they did with a heavy loss in prisoners.-

General Howard was not unprepared for this turn in the fortunes of the day. [Early in the morning discovering the superiority of the forces opposed to General Reynolds and himself, he had reflected on the probability of a retreat, & had perceived the advantageous position of Cemetery hill.] He [accordingly caused it to be occupied by Genl. Steinwehr, with the third division of the eleventh Corps, while batteries of heavy artillery were planted on the commanding points. Hither our brave men retired, overpowered but not dispirited,

& they were cheered in the evening by the arrival of General Slocum with the 12th Corps, & Genl. Sickles with part of the third. A feeble demonstration was made by the enemy at nightfall against our position, but they were swept back by our artillery & abandoned the attempt.]

Such was the fortune of the first day, commencing with success to our arms, followed by a reverse, but ending in the occupation of this all-important position. The principal losses of the three days occurred in the afternoon of this day, in the manner I have described, & could easily have been avoided, had it been known to our retreating troops, that the enemy were already in occupation of the town. To you, fellow-citizens of Gettysburg I need not attempt to portray the anxieties of the ensuing night. Witnessing as you had done with sorrow the [retreat] of our army through your streets, with a [heavy] loss of prisoners, mourning as you did over the brave men who had fallen, shocked with the widespread desolation around you, ignorant of the near approach of Genl. Meade, you passed the [anxious] hours of the night in [feverous] expectation.

Long before the dawn of the 2d of July the new commander had [arrived at the front.] Having received intelligence of the events in progress, [he had directed the remaining corps of the army to concentrate at Gettysburg with all possible dispatch, & leaving his Head Quarters at Taneytown at 10 P.M. he arrived on the field at one o'clock in the morning. Few were the moments given to rest, during the rapid watches of that brief midsummer's night, by officers or men, though half of our troops were exhausted by the conflict of the day, & the residue by the forced marches, which had brought them to the rescue.] The full moon shone down that night on a strange unearthly scene,—the silence of the graveyard broken by the heavy tramp of armed men; by the neigh of the warhorse; the harsh rattle of the wheels of artillery hurrying to their stations; the voice of the bugle, the roll of the drum, & all the indescribable tumult of preparation. The various corps of the army, as they arrived, were moved to their positions on the spot where we are assembled, & the ridges that extend south east & south west; batteries were planted, & hasty breastworks thrown up. [Hancock's corps, the 2d, did not come up, with the reserve artillery, till 6 o'clock in the morning, nor was it] till 2 oclock in the [P.M] that Sedgwick arrived with the 6th corps. He had marched 32 miles, since 9 o'clock in the {morning} Evening of the day before.—It was not till his arrival, that the union army attained an equality of numbers with that of the rebels [opposed to them on the opposite & parallel ridge & overlapping our own on either wing.]

And here I cannot but remark on the providential inaction of the rebel army. Had the contest been renewed [at dawn] on the 2d of July, with the first &

eleventh corps exhausted by the battle & the retreat; the 3d & the 12th weary from their forced march; & the 2d & 6th not yet arrived, nothing but a Miracle could have saved the army from [destruction.] Instead of this the day dawned, the sun rose, the cool hours of the morning passed, the forenoon wore away, without the slightest aggressive movement on the part of the enemy. Thus time was given for our last corps to arrive & take its place in the lines, & the rest of the army enjoyed a much needed half day's repose.

At length between three & four o'clock in the afternoon the work of death began. A signal gun from the hostile batteries was followed by tremendous cannonade along the rebel lines, & this by a heavy advance of infantry, brigade after brigade, commencing on the enemy's right against the left of our army, & so on to the left center. A forward movement of Genl. Sickles to gain a commanding position, from which to repel the rebel attack {advance} drew upon him a destructive fire from the enemy's batteries & a furious assault from Longstreet's & Hill's advancing troops. After a brave resistance, he was forced back, himself falling severely wounded. This was the critical moment of the second day; but the 5th and a part of the 6th corps, with portions of the 1st & [12th] were promptly brought to the support; the struggle was fierce & murderous, but by sunset the enemy was driven back in confusion. Important service was rendered toward the close of the day by Genl. Crawford's division of the 5th Corps, consisting of two brigades of the Pennsylvania reserves, of which one company was from this town & neighborhood. The rebel [general Barksdale fell at this juncture, this force was driven back {fast} with great loss in killed & prisoners.] At 8 o'clock in the Evening a desparate attempt was made by the enemy to storm the position of the 11th corps on cemetery hill, but here too, after a terrible conflict, he was repulsed with immense loss. Ewell on our extreme right, which had been weakened by the withdrawal of the troops sent over to support our left, had succeeded in gaining a foothold within a portion of our lines near Spangler's Spring. This was the only advantage obtained by the rebels, to compensate them for the disasters of the day, & of this they were soon deprived.

Such was the result of the second act of this Titanic drama; a hard fought anxious day, & with the exception of the slight reverse just named, dearly earned but uniform success to our arms, auspicious of a glorious termination of the final struggle. On these good omens the night fell.

[At dawn of the 3d,] General Geary returned to the position on the right; from which he had hastened the day before to strengthen [the left, & after a sharp & decisive action drove the enemy out of our lines, & recovered the ground which had been lost on the preceding day.]

Such was the cheering commencement of the third day's work and with it ended all further attempts of the enemy on our right. As on the preceding day, his efforts now mainly diverted against our left centre & left wing. From eleven till half past one o'clock, all was still; a solemn pause of preparation, as if both parties were nerving themselves for the supreme effort. At length the awful silence, more terrible than the wildest tumult of battle, was broken by the roar of near [300] pieces of artillery [on the two sides], joining in a cannonade of unsurpassed violence,—the rebel batteries along two thirds of their line pouring their fire upon Cemetery hill & the left center and left of our position. Having attempted in this way for two hours, but without success, to shake the steadiness of our lines, the enemy rallied his forces for a last grand assault. [His most determined efforts were directed against the position of Gibbon and Hancock.] Successive lines of infantry moved up with equal spirit & steadiness from their cover on the wooded crest of Seminary ridge, supported right and left by the choicest brigades [of the rebel army.] Our own brave troops received the shock with firmness; the ground was on both sides long & fiercely contested; till after "a determined & gallant struggle," as it is pronounced by General Lee, the rebel advance, consisting of two thirds of Hill's corps and the whole of Longstreet's including Pickett's division, the elite of his corps, which had not yet been under fire, & was now depended upon to decide the fortune of this last eventful day, was driven back with prodigious slaughter, discomfitted, & broken. [While these events were in progress at our left center, the enemy was driven by the Pennsylvania Reserves from a strong position on our extreme left, from which he was annoying our force on "Little Round Top"; {his battery takes}, & three hundred prisoners captured. In the terrific assault on our left center, Hancock & Gibbon were wounded, while in the rebel army Armistead, Kemper, Pettigrew, & Trimble were wounded, the latter also made prisoner, General Garnett killed,] & 3500 officers & men made prisoners.

These were the expiring agonies of the three days conflict, & with them the battle ceased. It was fought, on either side, with courage & skill, from the first cavalry skirmish on Wednesday morning to the fearful route of Friday afternoon, by every arm & every rank of the service, by officers & men by cavalry, artillery, & infantry. [The armies, after the first day, were numerically equal, if the union force had the advantage of a strong position, the confederates had that of choosing time & place, the prestige of former victories over the army of the Potomac & of the success of the first day. That so decisive a triumph, under circumstances like these, was gained by our troops I am inclined to ascribe, under Providence to the spirit of exalted patriotism that animated them, & the consciousness that they were fighting in a righteous cause.]

All hope of defeating our army & securing what general Lee calls "the valuable results" of such an achievement having vanished, he thought only of rescuing from destruction the remains of his shattered forces. In killed, wounded, & missing he had as far as can be ascertained suffered a loss of 37,000 men, rather more than a third of the force which he brought with him into Pennsylvania. Perceiving that his only safety was in rapid retreat, he commenced withdrawing his troops at daybreak on the 4th, throwing up field works [to protect the rear]. That day,—sad celebration of the 4th July for an Army of Americans,— was passed in hurrying forward his trains. The main army was in full retreat on the Cashtown & Fairfield roads by night fall, & moved with such precipitation that by daylight the following morning, the rearguard had left its position. The struggle of the two last days resembled in many respects the battle of Waterloo, & if at nightfall, General Meade, like the Duke of Wellington, had had the assistance of a powerful Allied army to take up the pursuit, the rout of the rebels would have been as complete as that of Napoleon.

[As General Lee employed a portion of his force on the 4th in throwing up earth works to protect the rear of his army on the retreat, his intentions that day were uncertain.] The moment his flight was discovered the following morning, he was pursued by our Cavalry [& a part of Sedgwick's Corps.] His rearguard was briskly attacked at Fairfield; a great number of wagons & ambulances were captured in the passes of the mountains, the country swarmed with his stragglers; & he literally emptied his wounded from the vehicles containing them into the farm houses on the road. General Lee, in his report, makes repeated mention of the Union prisoners whom he conveyed into Virginia, somewhat overstating their number. He mentions also that "such of his wounded as were in a condition to be removed" were forwarded to Williamsport. He does not mention, that the number not removed & left to the Christian care of the Victors was 7540, not one of whom failed of any attention which it was possible, under the circumstances of the case, to afford them; not one of whom was put upon Libby prison fare,—lingering death by starvation.—Heaven forbid, however, that I should claim any merit for behaving with common humanity.— Under the protection of the mountain ridge, whose passes are easily held even by a retreating army, Genl. Lee reached Williamsport in safety, & took up a strong position opposite to that place. Genl. Meade pursued with the main army by a flank movement through Middletown, Turner's pass having been secured by General French. The Union army came up with that of the rebels on the 12th, & found it securely posted on the heights of Marsh's run. His position was reconnoitred & preparations made for an attack on the 13th. The depth of the river, swollen by the recent rains, authorized the [hope that he] would be brought to a general engagement the following day. An advance was accordingly made by Gen. Meade but it was soon found that the rebels had escaped in the night, with such haste, that Ewell's corps forded the water, when it was breast high. The cavalry sent in pursuit captured three guns & a large number of prisoners.—In an action which took place [about this time], Gen. Pettigrew was mortally wounded. General Meade, in further pursuit of the enemy, crossed the Potomac at Berlin. Thus again covering the approaches to Washington, he compelled the rebels to pass the Blue ridge at one of the upper gaps, & in about six weeks from the commencement of the campaign, General Lee found himself [with about two thirds of his army, safe] on the south side of the Rappahannock.—

Such, most inadequately recounted, is the history of the ever memorable Three days & of the events immediately preceding & following. It has been pretended, in order to diminish the magnitude of this disaster to the rebel cause, that it was merely the repulse of an attack on a strongly defended position. The tremendous losses on both sides are a sufficient answer to this misrepresentation, & attested the courage & obstinacy, with which the three days battle was waged. [Not one] of the great conflicts of modern times has cost victors and vanquished so great a sacrifice. On the union side there fell in the whole campaign of Generals killed Reynolds, Weed, and Zook, & wounded General Barlow, Barnes, Butterfield, Doubleday, Gibbon, Graham, Hancock, Sickles, & Warren, while of officers below the rank of General & men there were 2834 killed, 13,709 wounded, & 6643 missing. On the Confederate side, there were killed on the field or mortally wounded Armistead, Barksdale, Garnett, Pender, Pettigrew & Semmes, & wounded Heth, Hood, Johnson, Kemper, Kimball & Trimble. Of officers below the rank of general & men there were taken prisoners including the wounded 13,621, an amount ascertained officially. Of the wounded in a condition to be removed, [the official estimate is about 13,000; of killed 5000, of stragglers as many more, forming a total of about 37,000, of which nearly 24,000 are exclusive of the wounded not taken prisoners.]

I must leave to others, who can do it from personal observation, to describe the mournful spectacle presented by these hillsides and plains at the close of the terrible conflict. It was a saying of the Duke of Wellington, that next to a defeat the saddest thing was a victory. The horrors of the battle field, after the contest is over,—the sights & sounds of Woe,—let me throw a pall over the scene, which no words can [reproduce] to those who have not witnessed it; on which no one who has witnessed it, & who has a heart in his bosom, can bear to dwell. One drop of balm alone, one drop of heavenly lifegiving balm,—mingles in this bitter cup of misery. Scarcely has the cannon ceased to roar; when the brethren & sisters of [charity], ministers of compassion, angels of pity, hasten to the field & the hospital, to moisten the parched tongue, to bind the ghastly wounds {of friend & foe} to soothe the parting agonies alike of friend & foe, to catch the last whispered messages of love from dying lips. "Carry this minia-

ture back to my dear wife, but do not take it from my bosom, till I am gone."—
"Tell my little Sister not to grieve for me, I am willing to die for my Country."—"Oh, that my mother was here.' "—When since Aaron stood between
the living & the dead was there ever a ministry like this? It has been said that it
is characteristic of Americans to treat women with a deference not paid to
them in any other country. I will not undertake to say whether this is so, but I
will say that since this terrible war has been waged, the women of the Loyal
States, if never before, have entited themselves to our highest admiration &
gratitude, alike those who at home, often with fingers unused to toil, often
bowed beneath their own domestic cares, have performed an amount of daily
labor not [less than hers who works for her] daily bread, & those who in the
hospital & the tent of the Sanitary Commission have rendered services, which
millions could not buy. Happily the labor & the service are their own reward.
Thousands of matrons & thousands of maidens have experienced a delight in
these homely toils and services compared with which the pleasures of the ball-
room & the operahouse are tame and unsatisfactory. This on earth is reward
enough; but a richer is in store for them. Yes, brothers, sisters of charity, forget
not, while you bind up the wounds of the poor sufferers,—the humblest perhaps that have shed their blood for the country,—[that the King of glory,
seated on the throne of the universe {glory}, will say to you] "Inasmuch as ye
did it, unto one of the least of these, my brethren, ye did it unto me."

And now, Friends, Fellow Citizens, as we stand among these honored
graves, the momentous question presents itself, [who is responsible for all this
suffering],—for this dreadful sacrifice of life,—the lawful & constitutional
government of the United States, or the ambitious men who have rebelled
against it? I say "rebelled," although Lord Russell, the British Secretary of
State for foreign affairs, in his recent temperate & conciliatory speech in Scot-
land, [intimates] that no prejudice ought to attach to that word, because our
English forefathers rebelled against Charles I and James II, and our American
fathers rebelled against George III. These certainly are venerable precedents,
but they prove only that it is just & proper to rebel against oppressive governments. {But} They do not prove that it was just & proper for the adherents of
the son of James II to rebel against George I, or [the adherents of] Charles Edward to rebel against George II; nor ought these dynastic struggles, little better than family quarrels, to be compared with this Monstrous Conspiracy
against the American Union. These precedents {precedents} do not prove,
that it was just and proper for the disappointed great men of the {south} cotton growing states to rebel against "the most beneficent government of which
history gives us any account," as the Vice-President of the Confederacy in November 1860 charged them with doing. They do not create a presumption even

in favor of the slaveholders of the South, who living under a government of which Mr. Jefferson Davis, in the Session of 1860—I said, that it was "the best government ever instituted by man, unexceptionably administered, & under which the people have been prosperous beyond comparison with any other people whose career is recorded in history" rebelled {not legible} against it, because their aspiring politicians, himself among the rest, were in danger of losing their monopoly of its offices.

What would have been thought by an impartial posterity of the American rebellion against George III, if the colonists had at all times been more than equally represented in parliament, and James Otis, & Patrick Henry, & Washington & Franklin and the Adamses, & Hancock & Jefferson & men of their stamp had, for two generations, enjoyed the confidence of the Sovereign & administered the government of the empire? What would have been thought of the rebellion against Charles I, if Cromwell & the men of his school had been the responsible advisers of that prince from his accession to the throne, & then, on account of a partial change in the ministry, brought his head to the block, & involved the country in a desolating war? What would have been thought of the whigs of 1688 if they had themselves composed the cabinet of James II, & been the advisers of the measures & the promoters of the policy, which drove him into exile? The puritans of 1640 & the whigs of 1688 rebelled against arbitary power, in order to establish constitutional liberty. If they had risen against Charles & James, because those monarchs favored equal rights, & in order themselves, "for the first time in the history of the world" to establish an oligarchy founded "on the cornerstone of slavery," they would truly have furnished a precedent for the rebels of the South, but their cause would not have been sustained by the eloquence of Pym or of Somers, nor sealed with the blood of Hampden or Russell.

I call the war which the South is waging against the Union a "rebellion" because it is one, & in grave matters it is best to call things by their right names. I speak of it as a crime, because The Constitution of the United States puts "rebellion" on a par with "invasion." The Constitution & Law, not only of England, but of every civilized country regard them in the same light; or rather they regard the rebel as far worse than the alien enemy. To levy war against the United States is the Constitutional definition of Treason, & that crime is, by every civilized government, regarded as the highest, which citizen or subject can commit. Not content with the sanctions of human justice, of all the crimes against the Law of the Land it is singled out for the denunciations of Religion. The Litanies of every church in Christendom, as far as I am aware, from the

Metropolitan Cathedrals of Europe to the humblest missionary chapel in the islands of the sea, concur with the Church of England in imploring the Sovereign of the Universe, by the most awful adjurations which the heart of man can conceive or his tongue utter, to deliver us from "sedition, privy conspiracy, & rebellion." And reason good; for while a rebellion against tyranny,—a rebellion designed, upon the ruins of arbitrary power, to establish free government on the basis of justice & truth, is an enterprize on which good men & angels may look with complacency, an unprovoked rebellion of ambitions even against a beneficent government, for the purpose,—the avowed purpose of establishing, extending & perpetuating any form of injustice & wrong is an imitation on earth of that first foul revolt of "the Infernal Serpent," [which emptied Heaven of one third part of its sons.]

Lord Bacon, "in the true marshalling of the Sovereign degrees of honor," assigns the first place to "the Conditores Imperiorum, {the} founders of States & Commonwealth," & truly to build up from the discordant elements of our nature; the passions, the interests, and the opinions of the individual man; the rivalries of family, clan, and tribe, the influences of climate, the accidents of peace & war accumulated for ages,—to build up from these often times warring elements a well compacted, prosperous & powerful state, if it were to be accomplished by one effort, or in one generation, would require a more than mortal skill. To contribute in some notable degree to this the greatest work of man, by wise & patriotic counsel in peace & loyal heroism in War, is as high as human merit can well rise, & far more than to any of those to whom Bacon assign this highest place of honor.—Romulus, Cyrus, Cæsar, Ottoman, Ismael,—is it due to our Washington, as the founder of the American union. And if to achieve or help to achieve this greatest work of man's wisdom & virtue gives title to a place among the chief benefactors, rightful heirs of the benedictions, of mankind, by equal reason shall the bold bad men, who seek to undo the noble work; "eversores Imperiorum" destroyers of States, who for base & selfish aids rebel against beneficent governments, seek to overturn wise constitutions, lay powerful republican Unions at the foot of foreign thrones, bring in civil & foreign war, anarchy at home, dictation abroad, desolation, ruin,—by equal reason, I say, Yes, a thousand fold stronger, shall they inherit the execrations of the ages.

[But to hide the deformity of the crime under the cloak of that sophistry, which makes the worse appear the better reason, we are told by the leaders of the rebellion, that, in our complex system of government, the separate states are "sovreign," & that the Central power is only an "agency," established by these sovreigns to manage certain affairs, which they could not so conveniently administer themselves. It happens unfortunately for this theory, that the federal constitution, (which has been adopted by the People of every State of the Union, as much as their own State Constitutions have been, & is declared to be paramount to them), no where recognizes the States as "Sovreigns," in fact that by their names, it does not recognize them at all; while the authority established by that instrument is recognized, in its text, not as an "agency," but as "the government of the United States." By that constitution, moreover, which purports in its preamble, to be ordained & established by "the People of the United States" it is expressly provided, that "the members of the State legislatures and all executive officers shall be bound by oath or affirmation to support this constitution." Now it is a common thing under all governments for an agent to be bound by oath to be faithful to his sovreign, but I never heard before of a Sovreign being bound to be faithful to his agency.]

[[Certainly I do not deny that the separate states are clothed with sovreign powers for the administration of local affairs. It is one of the most beautiful features of our mixed system of government, but it is equally true that, in adopting the federal constitution {government}, the states abdicated, by express renunciation, all the most important functions of National Sovreignty, & by one comprehensive self denying provision, gave up all right to contravene the Constitution of the United States. Specifically & by enumeration they renounced all the most important prerogatives of Independent States for peace & for war; the right to keep troops or ships of war in time of peace, or to engage in war unless actually invaded; to enter into any compact with another State or foreign power, to lay any duty on tonnage, or any impost on exports or imports without the consent of congress, to enter into any treaty, alliance, or confederation, to grant letters of marque & reprisal, and to emit bills of credit; while all these powers and many others are expressly vested in the general government. To ascribe to political communities, thus limited in their jurisdiction, the character of independent sovreignty, & to reduce an organization, clothed with all the transcendent powers of government to the name and condition of an "agency" of the States, proves nothing but that the logic of secession is on a par with its loyalty & patriotism.]]

[[Oh, but "the reserved rights"! and what of the reserved rights? {No such phrase occurs in the constitutions.} The amendment supposed to provide for reserved rights is constantly misquoted. By [the tenth amendment of the Constitution,]" the [powers] not delegated to the United States nor prohibited by it to the States are reserved to the States respectively or to the People." The "powers" reserved must of course be such as could have been but were not delegated to the States;—could have been but were not prohibited to the States;—but to speak of the [right] of an [individual] State to secede as a [power] that could have been delegated to the [United States] is simple nonsense.]]

[[But waiving this obvious absurdity, can it need a serious argument to prove, that there can be no right to enter into a new Confederation reserved under a Constitution, which expressly prohibits a state to enter into any treaty, alliance, or confederation or any agreement or compact with another state or a foreign power? How can a right be reserved to do the things expressly prohibited? To say that the State may, by enacting the preliminary force or secession, acquire the right to do the prohibited things,—to say for instance, that though the states, in forming the constitution, delegated to the United States & prohibited to themselves the power of declaring war, they reserved to each state the right of seceding & then [going to] war; that though they prohibited to the States, & delegated to the United States the entire treaty making power, they reserved to the [individual] states, to Florida, for instance, the right to secede & then to make a treaty with Spain, retroceding that Spanish colony, & surrendering to a foreign power the key to the gulf of Mexico,—to maintain propositions like these, with whatever affected seriousness it is done, appears to me egregious trifling.]]

Pardon me, my friends, for dwelling on these wretched sophistries. But it is these which conducted the armed hosts of rebellion to your doors, on the terrible & glorious days of July, & which have brought upon the whole land the scourge of an aggressive & wicked war,—a war which can have no other termination compatible with the permanent safety & welfare of the country, but the complete destruction of the military power of the enemy. I have, on other occasions, attempted to show that to yield to his demands & acknowledge his independence, thus resolving the Union at once into two hostile governments, with a certainty of further disintegration, would annihilate the strength and the influence of the country, as a member of the family of Nations; afford to foreign powers the opportunity & the temptation for disastrous & humiliating interference in our affairs, wrest from the middle & western states some of their great natural outlets to the sea & {some} of their most important lines of internal communications; deprive the commerce & navigation of the country of two thirds of our seacoast and of the fortresses which protect it;—not only so, but would enable each individual state, some of them with a white population not equal to a good sized Northern County,—or rather the dominant party in each state, to cede its territory, its harbor, its fortresses, the mouths of its rivers to any foreign power. It cannot be that the people of the loyal States,—that twenty two millions of brave & prosperous freemen,—will, for the temptation of a brief truce in an eternal border war, consent to this hideous National Suicide.

Do not think that I exaggerate the consequences of yielding to the demands of the leaders of the rebellion. I understate them. They require of us not only all the sacrifices I have named, not only to cede to them—a foreign and a hostile power—all the territory of the United States, at present occupied by the rebel forces, but the abandonment to them of the vast region which we have rescued from their grasp,—of Maryland, of a part of Eastern Virginia & the whole of Western Virginia, the sea coast of N. & South Carolina; Kentucky, Tennessee, & Missouri, Arkansas & the larger portion of Mississippi & Louisiana, in most of which, with the exception of lawless guerillas, there is not a rebel in arms, in all of which the great majority of the People are loyal to the Union. We must give back too the helpless colored population, thousands of whom are perilling their lives in the ranks of our armies, to a bondage rendered tenfold more bitter, by the momentary enjoyment of Freedom. Finally we must surrender every man in the Southern Country, white or black, who has moved a finger or spoken a word, for the restoration of the union,—to a reign of terror, as remorseless as that of Robespierre which has been the chief instrument by which the rebellion has been organized & sustained, & has already filled the prisons of the South with noble men, whose only crime is that they are not [traitors]. The South is full of such men. I do not believe there has been a day, since the election of M. Lincoln, when, if an ordinance of secession could have been fairly submitted to the mass of the people, in any single Southern State, a majority of ballots would have been given in its favor. No, not in South Carolina. It is not possible that the majority of the People, even of that State, if permitted, without fear or favor, to give a ballot on the question would have abandoned a leader like Petigru, & all the memories of the Gadsdens, the Rutledges & the Cotisworth Pinckneys [, to follow the {obvious} agitation & demagogues of the present day.]

Nor must we be deterred from the vigorous prosecution of the war, by the suggestion, continually thrown out by the rebels & those who sympathize with them, that however it might have been at an earlier stage, there has been engendered by the operations of the war, a state of mutual exasperation & bitterness, which, independent of all reference to the original nature of the matters in controversy, will forever prevent the restoration of the union, and the return of harmony between the two great sections of the country. This opinion I take to be entirely without foundation. {The tone of the rebel leaders & the rebel press was just as bitter, just as uncompromising before a gun was fired, as it is now.}

No man can deplore more than I do the miseries of every kind unavoidably incident to war. Who could stand on this spot & call to mind the scenes of July with any other feeling? A [ghastly vision] of what would ensue, if war should break out between North & South, has haunted me through life, & led me perhaps too long to tread in the path of hopeless compromise, in the fond endeavor to conciliate those, who were predetermined not to be conciliated. But it is not true, as is pretended by the rebels, & their sympathizers that the war {has been} has been carried on by the United States, without entire regard to those temperaments, which are enjoined by the Law of Nations, by our modern civilization, & by the spirit of Christianity. It would be quite easy to point out, in the recent military history of the leading European powers, acts of violence & cruelty, in the prosecution of their wars, to which no parallel can be found among us. In fact when we consider the peculiar bitterness, with which civil wars are almost invariably waged, we may justly boast of the manner in which the United States have carried on the contest. It is of course impossible to prevent the lawless acts of stragglers and deserters, or the occassional unwarrantable proceedings of subordinates on distant stations, but I do not believe there is, in all history, the record of a civil war of such gigantic dimensions, where too little has been done in the spirit of vindictiveness, as in the war by the Government & Commander of the United States; and this notwithstanding the provocation given by the rebel government by assuming the responsibility of wretches like Quantrall, refusing quarter to colored troops, selling into slavery free colored men from the North, who fall into their hands, covering the sea with pirates, & starving prisoners of war to death.

In the next place, if there are any present who believe, that, in addition to the effect of the military operations of the war, the confiscation acts & emancipation proclamations have embittered the rebels beyond the possibility of reconciliation, I would request them to reflect, that the tone of the rebel leaders and rebel press was just as bitter in the first months of the war, nay before {the war broke out} a gun was fired, as it is now. There were speeches made in Congress in the very last session before the rebellion so ferocious, as to show that their authors were under the influence of a real frenzy. At the present day, if there is any discrimination made by the Confederate press on the affected scorn, hatred & contumely with which every shade of opinion and sentiment in the loyal states is treated, the bitterest contempt is bestowed {not legible} upon those at the North, who still speak the language of compromise, & who condemn those measures of the Administration, which are supposed to have rendered the return of peace hopeless.

No, my friends, that gracious Providence which everrules all things for the best, from seeming evil still educing good, has so constituted our natures, that the violent excitement of the passions in one direction is generally followed by a reaction in the opposite direction, & the sooner for the violence. If it were not so, if anger produced abiding anger, if hatred caused undying hatred, if injuries inflicted & retaliated of necessity led to new retaliations, with forever accumulating compound interest of revenge, then the world, thousands of years ago, would have been turned into an earthly hell, and the nations of the earth would have been resolved into clans of furies & demons, each forever warring with his neighbor. But it is not so, all history teaches a different lesson. The wars of the roses in England lasted an entire generation, from the battle of St. Albans in 1455 to that of Bosworth field in 1485. Speaking of the former, Hume says "This was the first blood spilt in that fatal quarrel, which was not finished in less than a course of thirty years, which was signalized by twelve pitched battles, which opened a scene of extraordinary fierceness & cruelty; is computed to have cost the lives of eighty princes of the blood, & almost entirely annihilated the ancient nobility of England. The strong attachments, which, at that time, men of the same kindred bore to each other, & the vindictive spirit which was considered a point of honor, rendered the great families implacable in their resentments, & widened every moment the breach between the parties." Such was the state of things in England, under which an entire generation grew up, but when Henry VII, in whom the titles of the two houses were united went up to London after the battle of Bosworth field, he was every where received with joyous acclamations, as one ordained & sent from Heaven to put an end to the dissensions which had so long afflicted the Country.

The great "rebellion" in England of the seventeenth century, after long & angry premonitions, may be said to have begun with the calling of the long Parliament in 1640, & to have ended with the return of Charles II in 1660,— twenty years of discord, conflict & civil war,—of confiscation, plunder, havoc,—a proud hereditary peerage {not readable} trampled in the dust,—a national church overturned, its clergy beggared, its most eminent prelate put to death, a military despotism established on the ruins of a monarchy, which had subsisted seven hundred years and the legitimate sovreign brought to the block; the great families, which adhered to the king, proscribed, impoverished, ruined; prisoners of war sold to slavery in the West Indies;—in a word every thing that can embitter & madden contending factions. Such was the State of things for twenty years, & yet, by no gentle transition, but suddenly & "when the restoration of affairs appeared most hopeless," the son of the beheaded sovreign {monarch} was brought back to his father's bloodstained throne, with such "unexpressible & universal joy," as led the merry monarch to exclaim "he doubted it had been his own fault he had been absent so long, for he saw nobody that did not protest, he had ever wished for his return."—"In this wonderful manner," says Clarendon, "and with this incredible expedition, did God put an end to a rebellion, that had raged near twenty years, and had been carried on with all the horrid circumstances of murder, devastation, & parricide, that fire & sword, in the hands of the most wicked men in the world, could be instruments of, almost to the desolation of two kingdoms & the exceeding defacing & deforming of the third.—By these remarkable steps did the merciful hand of God, in this short space of time not only bind up & heal all those wounds, but even make the scar as undiscernable, as, in respect of the deepness, was possible, which was a glorious addition to the deliverance."— In Germany, the wars of the reformation & of Charles V in the 16th century, the thirty years war in the 17th century, the seven years war in the 18th century, not to speak of other less celebrated contests, entailed upon that country, [for three centuries,] all the miseries of intestine strife for more than three centuries. At the close of the last named war "an officer," say Archenholz, "rode through seven villages in Hesse, & found in them but one human being." More than Three hundred {petty} principalities, comprehended in the Empire, fermented with the fierce passions of proud & petty states; at the commencement of this period, the castles of robber counts frowned upon every hilltop; a dreadful secret tribunal froze the hearts of men with terror throughout the land; religious hatred mingled its bitter poison in the seething cauldron of provincial animosity,— but of all these deadly secular enmities between the States of Germany, scarcely the memory remains. There is no country in the world, in which the sentiment of national brotherhood is stronger.

In Italy on the breaking up of the Roman empire, society might be said to be resolved into its original elements,—into hostile atoms, whose only movement was that of mutual repulsion. Ruthless barbarians had destroyed the old organizations & covered the land with a merciless feudalism. As the new civilization grew up, under the wing of the Church, the noble families & the walled towns fell madly into conflict with each other, the secular feud of Pope & Emperor scourged the land; Province against province, City against city, Street against street waged relentless war with each other from father to son, till Dante was able to fill his imaginary hell with the real demons of Italian history. So ferocious had the factions become, that the great poet exile himself, the glory of his native city & of his native language, was, by a decree of the municipality, ordered to be burned alive, if found in the city of Florence. But these deadly feuds & hatreds yielded to political influences; the hostile cities were grouped into States, under stable governments; the lingering traditions of the ancient animosities died away gradually, & now Tuscan & Lombard, Sardinian & Neapolitan [join] in one cry for a united Italy.

In France, not to go back to the civil wars of the league in the 16th century & of the Fronde in the 17th, not to speak of the dreadful scenes throughout the Kingdom, which followed the revocation of the edict of Nantes, we have, in the great revolution which commenced at the close of the last century, seen the bloodhounds of civil strife let loose as rarely before in the history of the world. The reign of terror established at Paris, stretched its bloody Briarean arms to every city & village in the land, & if the most deadly feuds, which ever divided a people, had the power to cause permanent alienation & hatred, this surely was the occasion. But far otherwise the fact. In seven years from the fall of Robespierre, the strong arm of the youthful conqueror brought order out of the chaos of crime & woe; Jacobins, whose hands were scarce cleansed from the best blood of France met the returning emigrants, whose kindred they had dragged to the guillotine, in the Imperial antichambers; & when, after another turn of the wheel of fortune, Louis XVIII was restored to his throne, he took the regicide Fouché, who had voted for his brother's death, to his cabinet & confidence.

The people of loyal America will never take to their confidence or admit again to a share in their government the hardhearted men, whose cruel lust of power has brought this desolating war upon the land, but there is no personal bitterness felt even against them. They may live, if they can bear to live, after [wantonly causing so many thousand fellowmen] to die, they may live in safe obscurity beneath the shelter of the government they have sought to overthrow. Or they may fly to the protection of the governments of Europe; some of them are already there seeking, happily in vain, to obtain the aid of foreign powers in furtherance of their own {domestic} treason. There let them stay. The humblest dead soldier, that lies cold & stiff in his grave before us is an object of envy beneath the clods that cover him, in comparison with the living man, who is willing to grovel at the foot of a foreign throne, for assistance in compassing the ruin of his country.

But the hour is coming & now is, when the power of the leaders of the rebellion to delude & inflame must {will} cease. There is no bitterness on the part of the masses. The people of the South are not going to wage an eternal war for the wretched pretexts by which the rebellion is sought {attempted} to be justified. The bonds that unite us as one People, a substantial community of origin, language, belief, & law, (the four great ties that hold {whole} the societies of men together), common national & political interests; a common history; a common pride in a glorious ancestry; a common interest in this great heritage of blessings; the very geographical features of the country,—the mighty rivers that cross the lines of climate & thus facilitate the interchange of natural & industrial products, while the wonder working arm of the Engineer has leveled the mountain walls which separate the East & West, compelling your own Alleghanies, my Maryland & Pennsylvania friends, to open wide their everlasting gates to the chariot wheels of traffic & travel, these bonds of Union are of perennial force & energy, while the causes of alienation are imaginary, factitious & transient. The heart of the People north & south is for the Union. Indications too plain to be mistaken announce the fact, both in the East & the West of the States in rebellion. In North Carolina & Arkansas the fatal charm at length is broken. At Raleigh & Little Rock the lips of honest & brave men are at length unsealed, and an independent press is unlimbering its artillery. The weary masses of the people are yearning to see the dear old flag again floating upon their capitols, & they sigh for the return of the peace, prosperity, & happiness, which they enjoyed under a government whose power was felt only in its blessings.

And now, friends, fellow citizens of Gettysburg & Pennsylvania, & you from remoter states, let me again invoke your benediction, as we part, on these honored graves. You feel, though the occasion is mournful, that it is good to be here. You feel that it was greatly auspicious for the cause of the country, that the men of the East and the men of the West, the men of nineteen sister States, stood side by side on the peril{l}ous ridges of the battle. You now feel it a new bond of union, that they shall lie side by side, till a clarion louder than that which marshaled them to the combat, shall awake their slumbers. God bless the union;—it is dearer to us for the blood of these brave men shed in its defence. The spots on which they stood & fell; these pleasant heights; the fertile plain beneath them; the thriving village whose streets so lately rang with the strange din of war; the fields beyond the ridge, when the noble Reynolds held the advancing foe at bay, & while he gave up his own life, assured by his forethought & self sacrifice, the triumph of the two succeeding days; the little streams which wind through the hills, on whose banks in aftertimes the wandering ploughman will turn up, with the rude weapons of savage {undiscernable} warfare, the fearful missiles of modern artillery; the Seminary ridge, the peach orchard, cemetery, Culp & Wolf Hill, Round Top, Little Round Top, humble names, henceforward and dear & famous {Illustrious}, no lapse of time no distance of space shall cause you to be forgotten. "The whole Earth," said Pericles, as he stood over his fellow citizens, who had fallen in the first year of the Peloponnesian War, "the whole earth is the sepulchre of illustrious men." All time, he might have added, is the millennium of their glory. Surely I would do no injustice to the other noble achievements of the War, which have reflected such honor on both armies of the service, & have entitled the armies & the navy of the United States, their officers & men; to the warmest thanks & the richest rewards, which a grateful people can pay. But they, I am sure, will join us in saying, as we bid farewell to the dust of these martyr heroes, that whersoever throughout the civilized world the accounts of this great warfare are read, & down to the latest period of recorded time, in the glorious annals of our common country, there will be no higher page than that which relates <u>the Battles of Gettysburg</u>.

Programme of the Ceremonies at the Soldiers' National Cemetery

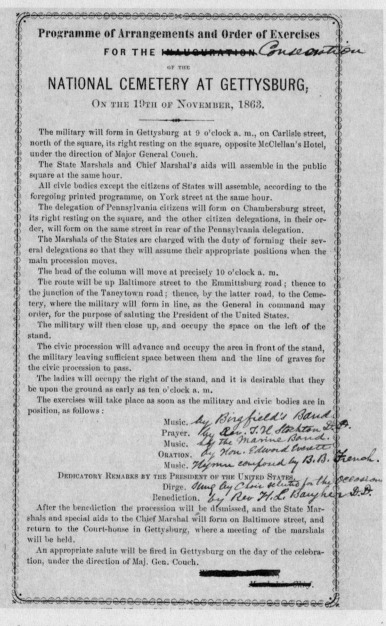

The order of exercises for the dedication ceremony on November 19, 1863, printed by Ward Hill Lamon, Lincoln's friend and chief marshal of the event. Listed most prominently is "Dedicatory Remarks by the President of the United States," with the "orator" of the day not so much as named. In his own copy, the miffed Everett crossed out the offending marshal's name at the bottom, wrote in the names of the participants, including that of the "Hon. Edward Everett," and most important, changed the heading from "Inauguration" of the cemetery to "Consecration." (Massachusetts Historical Society)

PRAYER

AT THE

DEDICATION OF THE NATIONAL CEMETERY AT GETTYSBURG,

Thursday, November 19th, 1863.

O God our Father, for the sake of Thy Son our Saviour, inspire us with Thy Spirit, and sanctify us to the right fulfilment of the duties of this occasion.

We come to dedicate this new historic centre as a National Cemetery. If all departments of the one Government which Thou hast ordained over our Union, and of the many Governments which Thou hast subordinated to our Union, be here represented; if all classes, relations, and interests of our blended brotherhood of people stand severally and thoroughly apparent in Thy presence; we trust that it is because Thou hast called us, that Thy blessing awaits us, and that Thy designs may be embodied in practical results of incalculable and imperishable good.

And so, with Thy holy Apostle, and with the Church of all lands and ages; we unite in the ascription:— "Blessed be God, even the Father of our Lord Jesus Christ, the Father of mercies, and the God of all comfort, who comforteth us in all our tribulation, that we may be able to comfort them which are in any trouble, by the comfort wherewith we ourselves are comforted of God."

In emulation of all angels, in fellowship with all saints, and in sympathy with all sufferers; in remembrance of Thy works, in reverence of Thy ways, and in accordance with Thy word; we laud and magnify Thine infinite perfections, Thy creative glory, Thy redeeming grace, Thy providential goodness, and the progressively richer and fairer developments of Thy supreme, universal, and everlasting administration.

In behalf of all humanity, whose ideal is divine, whose first memory is Thine image lost, and whose last hope is Thine image restored; and especially of our own nation, whose history has been so favored, whose position is so peerless, whose mission is so sublime, and whose future is so attractive; we thank Thee for the unspeakable patience of Thy compassion and the exceeding greatness of Thy loving-kindness. In contemplation of Eden, Calvary, and Heaven; of Christ in the Garden, on the Cross, and on the Throne; nay, more, of Christ as coming again in all-subduing power and glory; we gratefully prolong our homage. By this Altar of Sacrifice, on this Field of Deliverance, on this Mount of Salvation, within the fiery and bloody line of these "munitions of rocks," looking back to the dark days of fear and trembling, and to the rapture of relief that came after; we multiply our thanksgivings, and confess our obligations to renew and perfect our personal and social consecration to Thy service and glory.

O, had it not been for God! For lo! our enemies—they came unresisted, multitudinous, mighty, flushed with victory, and sure of success. They exulted on our mountains, they revelled in our valleys; they feasted, they rested; they slept, they awaked; they grew stronger, prouder, bolder every day; they spread abroad, they concentrated here; they looked beyond this horizon to the stores of wealth, to the haunts of pleasure, and to the seats of power, in our Capital and chief Cities. They prepared to cast the chain of Slavery around the form of Freedom, binding life and death together forever. Their premature triumph was the mockery of God and man. One more victory, and all was theirs! But, behind these hills was heard the feebler march of a smaller but still pursuing host. Onward they hurried, day and night, for God and their country. Foot-sore, way-worn, hungry, thirsty, faint—but not in heart, they came to dare all, to bear all, and to do all, that is possible to heroes. And Thou didst sustain them! At first they met the blast on the plain, and bent before it, like the trees in a storm. But then, led by Thy hand to these hills, they took their stand upon the rocks and remained as firm and immovable as they. In vain were they assaulted. All art, all violence, all desperation, failed to dislodge them. Baffled, bruised, broken, their enemies recoiled, retired, and disappeared. Glory to God, for this rescue! But, O, the slain! In the freshness and fulness of their young and manly life; with such sweet memories of father and mother, brother and sister, wife and children, maiden and friends; they died for us. From the coasts beneath the Eastern star, from the shores of Northern lakes and rivers, from the flowers of Western prairies, and from the homes of the Midway, and the Border, they came here to die for us and for mankind. Alas, how little we can do for them! We come with the humility of prayer, with the pathetic eloquence of venerable wisdom, with the tender beauty of poetry, with the plaintive harmony of music, with the honest tribute of our Chief Magistrate, and with all this honorable attendance: but our best hope is in Thy blessing, O, Lord, our God! O, Father, bless us! Bless the bereaved, whether present, or absent; bless our sick and wounded soldiers and sailors; bless all our rulers and people; bless our army and navy; bless the efforts for the suppression of the rebellion; and bless all the associations of this day, and place, and scene, forever. As the trees are not dead, though their foliage is gone, so our heroes are not dead, though their forms have fallen. In their proper personality, they are all with Thee. And the spirit of their example is here. It fills the air, it fills our hearts. And, long as time shall last, it will hover in these skies, and rest on this landscape; and the pilgrims of our own land, and from all lands, will thrill with its inspiration and increase and confirm their devotion to liberty, religion and God.

Our Father, who art in Heaven, hallowed be Thy name. Thy kingdom come. Thy will be done on earth as it is in heaven. Give us this day our daily bread, and forgive us our debts, as we forgive our debtors. Lead us not into temptation, but deliver us from evil; for Thine is the kingdom, the power, and the glory, for ever. Amen.

Invocation by the Reverend Thomas A. Stockton (Gettysburg National Military Park)

Signature of Reverend Stockton. (Boritt collection)

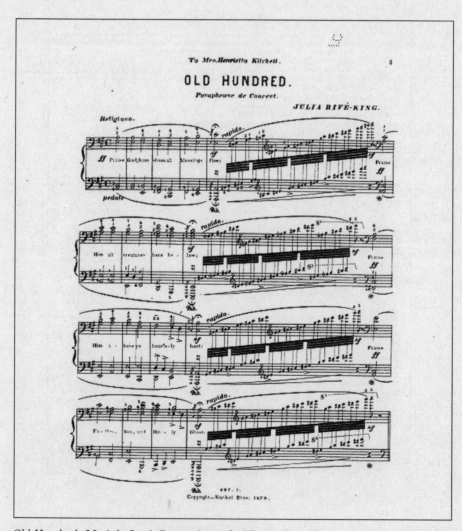

Old Hundred. *Music by Louis Bourgeois; text by Thomas Ken. This 1870 version is reproduced because most hymnbooks of nineteenth-century America printed only words and identified music by its traditional name or the meter. (Library of Congress)*

Note.

In the narrative portion of the following address, the printed text will be found to vary somewhat from the manuscript, especially in the account of the first day's battle. This arises from the circumstance, that the manuscript was written, before the appearance of Major General Meade's official report. The General had kindly favored me with a condensed narrative of the battle, in advance of the publication of his report, but the appearance of that important document enabled me to give some details with greater fullness and precision.

Verbal differences between the printed and written text will be found throughout the address, of which about one third was omitted in the delivery on account of its length.

Edward Everett.

Boston 21 March 1864.

Edward Everett's notes preface the manuscript of his Gettysburg Address sent as a gift to the New York Metropolitan Fair in the early spring of 1864. (Abraham Lincoln Presidential Library). The full text is printed on pages 207–33.

B.B.French.

Hymn
Composed at Gettysburg for the consecration, Nov. 19, 1863.

'Tis holy ground,—
This spot where in their graves
We place our country's braves,
Who fell in Freedom's holy cause
Fighting for liberties and laws.
    Let tears abound

    Here let them rest;
And summer's heat and winter's cold
Shall glow and freeze above this mold,—
A thousand years shall pass away,—
A nation still shall mourn this clay,
    Which now is blest.

    Here, where they fell,
Oft shall the widow's tear be shed,
Oft shall fond parents mourn their dead;
The orphan here shall kneel and weep,
And maidens, where their lovers sleep
    Their woes shall tell.

    Great God in heaven!
Shall all this sacred blood be shed?
Shall we thus mourn our glorious dead?
Oh, shall the end be wrath and woe,
The knell of Freedom's overthrow,
    A country riven?

    It will not be!
We trust, O God! thy gracious power
To aid us in our darkest hour.
This be our prayer,—"O Father! save
A people's freedom from its grave.
    All praise to thee!"

B.B.French.

199

Sheet music held by one of the singers at the National Cemetery on November 19, 1863. Words by Benjamin French; music by Wilson G. Horner. (Gettysburg National Military Park)

PRESIDENT LINCOLN'S ADDRESS.

The President then delivered the following dedicatory speech:

Fourscore and seven years ago our Fathers brought forth upon this Continent a new nation, conceived in liberty and dedicated to the proposition that all men are created equal. [Applause.] Now we are engaged in a great civil war, testing whether that nation, or any nation so conceived and so dedicated, can long endure. We are met on a great battle-field of that war. We are met to dedicate a portion of it as the final resting-place of those who here gave their lives that that nation might live. It is altogether fitting and proper that we should do this. But in a larger sense we cannot dedicate. We cannot consecrate, we cannot hallow this ground. The brave men, living and dead, who struggled here have consecrated it far above our power to add or detract. [Applause.] The world will little note nor long remember, what we say here, but it can never forget what they did here. [Applause.] It is for us, the living, rather to be dedicated here to the refinished work that they have thus so far nobly carried on. [Applause.] It is rather for us to be here dedicated to the great task remaining before us, that from these honored dead we take increased devotion to that cause for which they here gave the last full measure of devotion; that we here highly resolve that the dead shall not have died in vain; [applause] that the Nation shall under God have a new birth of freedom, and that Governments of the people, by the people and for the people, shall not perish from the earth, [Long continued applause.]

The Associated Press text of Lincoln's speech as it appeared in the New York Times, *November 20, 1863. Variations of this version reached more Americans in 1863 than any other.*

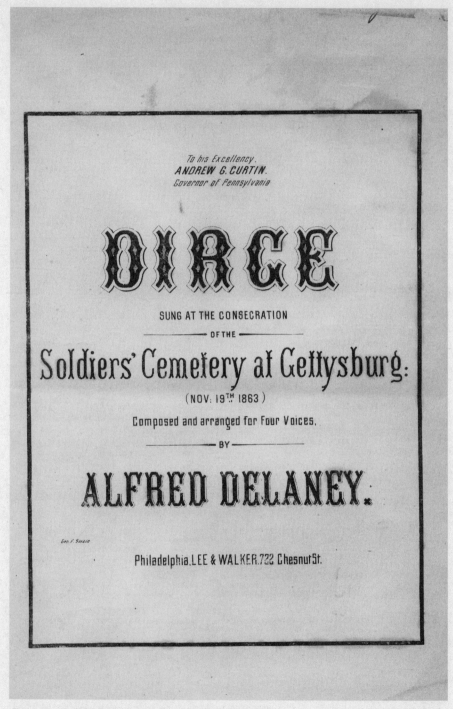

Front cover of the Dirge sung after Lincoln delivered his remarks. Music by James G. Percival; words by Alfred Delaney. (Gettysburg National Military Park)

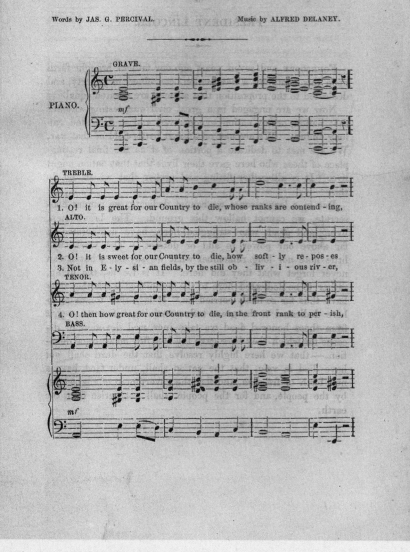

Musical notes and text of the Dirge *from the official version of the proceedings:* Address of the Hon. Edward Everett. *(Boston: Little, Brown, 1864) Boritt Collection.*

86 DIRGE, Continued.

Bright is the wreath of our fame; glo - ry a - waits us for aye;

War - ri - or youth on his bier, wet by the tears of his love,
Not in the Isles of the blest, o - ver the blue roll - ing sea;

Firm with our breast to the foe, vic - to - ry's shout in our ear;

Glo - ry, that nev - er is dim, Shin - ing on with a

Wet by a mother's warm tears; they crown him with
But on O - lym - pi - an heights shall dwell the de -

Long they our stat - ues shall crown, in songs our

cres.

DIRGE, Concluded. 87

light nev - er ending, Glo - ry, that nev - er shall fade, nev - er O!

garlands of ro - ses, Weep, and then joy-ous - ly turn, bright where he
vot - ed for - ev - er; There shall as - semble the good, there the wise,

mem-o - ry cherish; We shall look forth from our heaven, pleased the sweet

nev - er a - way!....

tri - umphs a - bove.....
val - iant, and free......

mu - sic to hear.....

BENEDICTION

BY

REV. H. L. BAUGHER, D. D.,

PRESIDENT OF PENNSYLVANIA COLLEGE, GETTYSBURG.

—◆—

O THOU King of kings and Lord of lords, God of the nations of the earth, who by Thy kind providence hast permitted us to engage in these solemn services, grant us Thy blessing.

Bless this consecrated ground, and these holy graves. Bless the President of these United States, and his Cabinet. Bless the Governors and the Representatives of the States here assembled with all needed grace to conduct the affairs committed into their hands, to the glory of Thy name, and the greatest good of the people.

May this great nation be delivered from treason and rebellion at home, and from the power of enemies abroad. And now may the grace of our Lord Jesus Christ, the love of God our Heavenly Father, and the fellowship of the Holy Ghost, be with you all. *Amen.*

THE END.

The concluding prayer by the president of the College from the official version of the proceedings. (Boritt Collection). Signature of H. L. Baugher (Gettysburg College)

A BEAUTIFUL HAND

FACSIMILES OF THE FIVE VERSIONS OF THE GETTYSBURG ADDRESS IN LINCOLN'S HAND

The president wrote out in his clear beautiful hand five copies of his Gettysburg speech. Apart from trying to improve style, he made two significant changes between his second and third copies, and so replicated what he actually said at Gettysburg. In the long last sentence in the copy he sent to the Metropolitan Fair in New York via Edward Everett, he not only included the words "under God" and moved them to a more felicitous place, but also changed the focus from the United States alone in "that this government of the people," etc., to the universal "that government of the people, by the people, for the people."

Executive Mansion,

Washington, , 186 .

Four score and seven years ago our fathers brought forth, upon this continent, a new nation, conceived in liberty, and dedicated to the proposition that "all men are created equal"

Now we are engaged in a great civil war, testing whether that nation, or any nation so conceived, and so dedicated, can long endure. We are met on a great battle field of that war. We have come to dedicate a portion of it, as a final resting place for those who died here, that the nation might live. This we may, in all propriety do. But, in a larger sense, we can not dedicate — we can not consecrate — we can not hallow, this ground — The brave men, living and dead, who struggled here, have hallowed it, far above our poor power to add or detract. The world will little note, nor long remember what we say here; while it can never forget what they did here.

It is rather for us, the living, to stand here,

First Draft, also known as the Nicolay Copy (Library of Congress)

ted to the great task remaining before us—
that, from these honored dead we take increased devotion to that cause for which
they have gave the last full measure of devotion— that we here highly resolve these
dead shall not have died in vain, that
the nation, shall have a new birth of freedom, and that government of the people by
the people for the people, shall not perish from the earth.

Four score and seven years ago our fathers brought forth, upon this continent, a new nation, conceived in Liberty, and dedicated to the proposition that all men are created equal.

Now we are engaged in a great civil war, testing whether that nation, or any nation, so conceived, and so dedicated, can long endure. We are met here on a great battle-field of that war. We have come to dedicate a portion of it as the a final resting place for those who here gave their lives that that nation might live. It is altogether fitting and proper that we should do this.

But in a larger sense we can not dedicate—we can not consecrate—we can not hallow this ground. The brave men, living and dead, who struggled here, have consecrated it far above our poor power to add or detract. The world will little note, nor long remember, what we say here, but can never forget what they did here. It is for us, the living, rather to be dedicated here to the unfinished work which they have, thus far, so nobly carried on. It is rather

Second Draft, or Hay Copy (Library of Congress)

for us to be here dedicated to the great
task remaining before us— that from these
honored dead we take increased devotion
to the *that* cause for which they here gave ~~g~~
the last full measure of devotion— that
we here highly resolve that these dead
shall not have died in vain; that this
nation shall have a new birth of freedom,
and that this government of the people, by
the people, for the people, shall not perish
from the earth.

57

Four score and seven years ago our fathers brought forth upon this continent, a new nation, conceived in Liberty, and dedicated to the proposition that all men are created equal.

Now we are engaged in a great civil war, testing whether that nation, or any nation so conceived, and so dedicated, can long endure. We are met on a great battle-field of that war. We have come to dedicate a portion of that field, as a final resting place for those who here gave their lives, that that nation might live. It is altogether fitting and proper that we should do this.

But, in a larger sense, we can not dedicate— we can not consecrate— we can not hallow— this ground. The brave men, living and dead, who struggled here, have consecrated it, far above our poor power to add or detract. The world will little note, nor long remember, what we say here, but it can never forget what they did here. It is for us, the living, rather, to be dedicated here to the unfinished work which they who fought here, have, thus far, so nobly advanced. It is rather for us to be here dedicated to the great task remaining before

New York Metropolitan Fair, or Everett Copy (Abraham Lincoln Presidential Library)

58

us— that from these honored dead we take increased devotion to that cause for which they here gave
the last full measure of devotion— that we here
highly resolve that these dead shall not have
died in vain— that this nation, under God,
shall have a new birth of freedom— and that
government of the people, by the people, for the
people, shall not perish from the earth.

Four score and seven years ago our fathers brought forth, on this continent, a new nation, conceived in Liberty, and dedicated to the proposition that all men are created equal.

Now we are engaged in a great civil war, testing whether that nation, or any nation so conceived, and so dedicated, can long endure. We are met on a great battle-field of that war. We have come to dedicate a portion of that field, as a final resting-place for those who here gave their lives, that that nation might live. It is altogether fitting and proper that we should do this.

But, in a larger sense, we can not dedicate— we can not consecrate— we can not hallow— this ground. The brave men, living and dead, who struggled here, have consecrated it, far above our poor power to add or detract. The world will little note, nor long remember what we say here, but it can never forget what they did here. It is for us the living, rather, to be dedicated here to the unfinished work which they, who fought here have thus far so nobly advanced. It is rather for us to be here dedicated to the great task remaining be-

fore us— that from these honored dead we take increased devotion to that cause for which they here gave the last full measure of devotion— that we here highly resolve that these dead shall not have died in vain— that this nation, under God, shall have a new birth of freedom— and that government of the people, by the people, for the people, shall not perish from the earth.

Baltimore Sanitary Fair, First Version, or Bancroft Copy (Cornell University)

Address delivered at the dedication of the cemetery at Gettysburg.

Four score and seven years ago our fathers brought forth on this Continent, a new nation, conceived in Liberty, and dedicated to the proposition that all men are created equal.

Now we are engaged in a great civil war, testing whether that nation, or any nation so conceived and so dedicated, can long endure. We are met on a great battle field of that war. We have come to dedicate a portion of that field, as a final resting place for those who here gave their lives that that nation might live. It is altogether fitting and proper that we should do this.

But, in a larger sense, we can not dedi-

Baltimore Sanitary Fair, Second Version, or Bliss Copy (The White House)

cate— we can not consecrate— we can not hallow— this ground. The brave men, living and dead, who struggled here, have consecrated it, far above our poor power to add or detract. The world will little note, nor long remember what we say here, but it can never forget what they did here. It is for us the living, rather, to be dedicated here to the unfinished work which they who fought here have thus far so nobly, advanced. It is rather for us to be here dedicated to the great task remaining before us— that from these honored dead we take increased devotion to that cause for which they gave the last full measure of devotion— that we here highly resolve that these dead shall not have died in vain— that this nation, under God, shall have a new birth of freedom— and that government of the people,

*by the people, for the people, shall not per-
ish from the earth.*

Abraham Lincoln.

November 19, 1863.

PARSING LINCOLN

LINE-BY-LINE COMPARISONS OF LINCOLN'S SPEECH:

1. What Lincoln Wrote
2. What People Read and Heard: A Sample
3. What Lincoln Read at Gettysburg
4. The Parunak Report: A Statistical Look at What Lincoln Read at Gettysburg

1. What Lincoln Wrote

1 First Draft (Nicolay)	Four score and seven years ago
2 Second Draft (Hay)	Four score and seven years ago
3 NY Metropolitan Fair (Everett)	Four score and seven years ago
4 Baltimore Sanitary Fair Copy # 1 (Bancroft)	Four score and seven years ago
5 Baltimore Sanitary Fair Copy # 2 (Bliss)	Four score and seven years ago
1 First Draft (Nicolay)	our fathers brought forth, upon this continent,
2 Second Draft (Hay)	our fathers brought forth, upon this continent,
3 NY Metropolitan Fair (Everett)	our fathers brought forth upon this continent,
4 Baltimore Sanitary Fair Copy # 1 (Bancroft)	our fathers brought forth, on this continent,
5 Baltimore Sanitary Fair Copy # 2 (Bliss)	our fathers brought forth on this continent,

1 First Draft (Nicolay)	a new nation, conceived in liberty,
2 Second Draft (Hay)	a new nation, conceived in Liberty,
3 NY Metropolitan Fair (Everett)	a new nation, conceived in Liberty,
4 Baltimore Sanitary Fair Copy # 1 (Bancroft)	a new nation, conceived in Liberty,
5 Baltimore Sanitary Fair Copy # 2 (Bliss)	a new nation, conceived in Liberty,
1 First Draft (Nicolay)	and dedicated to the proposition
2 Second Draft (Hay)	and dedicated to the proposition
3 NY Metropolitan Fair (Everett)	and dedicated to the proposition
4 Baltimore Sanitary Fair Copy # 1 (Bancroft)	and dedicated to the proposition
5 Baltimore Sanitary Fair Copy # 2 (Bliss)	and dedicated to the proposition
1 First Draft (Nicolay)	that "all men are created equal"
2 Second Draft (Hay)	that all men are created equal.
3 NY Metropolitan Fair (Everett)	that all men are created equal.
4 Baltimore Sanitary Fair Copy # 1 (Bancroft)	that all men are created equal.
5 Baltimore Sanitary Fair Copy # 2 (Bliss)	that all men are created equal.
1 First Draft (Nicolay)	Now we are engaged in a great civil war,
2 Second Draft (Hay)	Now we are engaged in a great civil war,
3 NY Metropolitan Fair (Everett)	Now we are engaged in a great civil war,
4 Baltimore Sanitary Fair Copy # 1 (Bancroft)	Now we are engaged in a great civil war,
5 Baltimore Sanitary Fair Copy # 2 (Bliss)	Now we are engaged in a great civil war,

1 First Draft (Nicolay)	testing whether that nation, or any nation
2 Second Draft (Hay)	testing whether that nation, or any nation,
3 NY Metropolitan Fair (Everett)	testing whether that nation, or any nation
4 Baltimore Sanitary Fair Copy # 1 (Bancroft)	testing whether that nation, or any nation
5 Baltimore Sanitary Fair Copy # 2 (Bliss)	testing whether that nation, or any nation
1 First Draft (Nicolay)	so conceived, and so dedicated, can long endure.
2 Second Draft (Hay)	so conceived, and so dedicated, can long endure.
3 NY Metropolitan Fair (Everett)	so conceived, and so dedicated, can long endure.
4 Baltimore Sanitary Fair Copy # 1 (Bancroft)	so conceived, and so dedicated, can long endure.
5 Baltimore Sanitary Fair Copy # 2 (Bliss)	so conceived and so dedicated, can long endure.
1 First Draft (Nicolay)	We are met on a great battle field of that war.
2 Second Draft (Hay)	We are met here on a great battle-field of that war.
3 NY Metropolitan Fair (Everett)	We are met on a great battle-field of that war.
4 Baltimore Sanitary Fair Copy # 1 (Bancroft)	We are met on a great battle-field of that war.
5 Baltimore Sanitary Fair Copy # 2 (Bliss)	We are met on a great battle field of that war.
1 First Draft (Nicolay)	We have come to dedicate a portion of it,
2 Second Draft (Hay)	We have come to dedicate a portion of it
3 NY Metropolitan Fair (Everett)	We have come to dedicate a portion of that field,
4 Baltimore Sanitary Fair Copy # 1 (Bancroft)	We have come to dedicate a portion of that field,
5 Baltimore Sanitary Fair Copy # 2 (Bliss)	We have come to dedicate a portion of that field,

1 First Draft (Nicolay)	as a final resting place for those
2 Second Draft (Hay)	as a final resting place for those
3 NY Metropolitan Fair (Everett)	as a final resting place for those
4 Baltimore Sanitary Fair Copy # 1 (Bancroft)	as a final-resting place for those
5 Baltimore Sanitary Fair Copy # 2 (Bliss)	as a final resting place for those

1 First Draft (Nicolay)	who died here, that the nation might live.
2 Second Draft (Hay)	who here gave their lives that that nation might live.
3 NY Metropolitan Fair (Everett)	who here gave their lives, that that nation might live.
4 Baltimore Sanitary Fair Copy # 1 (Bancroft)	who here gave their lives, that that nation might live.
5 Baltimore Sanitary Fair Copy # 2 (Bliss)	who here have their lives that that nation might live.

1 First Draft (Nicolay)	This we may,
2 Second Draft (Hay)	It is alltogether fitting
3 NY Metropolitan Fair (Everett)	It is alltogether fitting
4 Baltimore Sanitary Fair Copy # 1 (Bancroft)	It is alltogether fitting
5 Baltimore Sanitary Fair Copy # 2 (Bliss)	It is alltogether fitting

1 First Draft (Nicolay)	in all propriety do.
2 Second Draft (Hay)	and proper that we should do this.
3 NY Metropolitan Fair (Everett)	and proper that we should do this.
4 Baltimore Sanitary Fair Copy # 1 (Bancroft)	and proper that we should do this.
5 Baltimore Sanitary Fair Copy # 2 (Bliss)	and proper that we should do this.

1 First Draft (Nicolay)	But, in a larger sense, we can not dedicate-
2 Second Draft (Hay)	But in a larger sense we can not dedicate-
3 NY Metropolitan Fair (Everett)	But, in a larger sense, we can not dedicate,
4 Baltimore Sanitary Fair Copy # 1 (Bancroft)	But, in a larger sense, we can not dedicate,
5 Baltimore Sanitary Fair Copy # 2 (Bliss)	But, in a larger sense, we can not dedicate-

1 First Draft (Nicolay)	we can not consecrate- we can not hallow, this ground-
2 Second Draft (Hay)	we can not consecrate- we can not hallow this ground.
3 NY Metropolitan Fair (Everett)	we can not consecrate- we can not hallow- this ground.
4 Baltimore Sanitary Fair Copy # 1 (Bancroft)	we can not consecrate- we can not hallow- this ground.
5 Baltimore Sanitary Fair Copy # 2 (Bliss)	we can not consecrate- we can not hallow- this ground.

1 First Draft (Nicolay)	The brave men, living and dead,
2 Second Draft (Hay)	The brave men, living and dead,
3 NY Metropolitan Fair (Everett)	The brave men, living and dead,
4 Baltimore Sanitary Fair Copy # 1 (Bancroft)	The brave men, living and dead,
5 Baltimore Sanitary Fair Copy # 2 (Bliss)	The brave men, living and dead,

1 First Draft (Nicolay)	who struggled here, have hallowed it,
2 Second Draft (Hay)	who struggled, here, have consecrated it
3 NY Metropolitan Fair (Everett)	who struggled here, have consecrated it,
4 Baltimore Sanitary Fair Copy # 1 (Bancroft)	who struggled here, have consecrated it
5 Baltimore Sanitary Fair Copy # 2 (Bliss)	who struggled here, have consecrated it,

1 First Draft (Nicolay) — far above our poor power to add or detract.

2 Second Draft (Hay) — far above our poor power to add or detract.

3 NY Metropolitan Fair (Everett) — far above our poor power to add or detract.

4 Baltimore Sanitary Fair Copy # 1 (Bancroft) — far above our poor power to add or detract.

5 Baltimore Sanitary Fair Copy # 2 (Bliss) — far above our poor power to add or detract.

1 First Draft (Nicolay) — The world will little note,

2 Second Draft (Hay) — The world will little note,

3 NY Metropolitan Fair (Everett) — The world will little note,

4 Baltimore Sanitary Fair Copy # 1 (Bancroft) — The world will little note,

5 Baltimore Sanitary Fair Copy # 2 (Bliss) — The world will little note,

1 First Draft (Nicolay) — nor long remember what we say here;

2 Second Draft (Hay) — nor long remember, what we say here,

3 NY Metropolitan Fair (Everett) — nor long remember, what we say here,

4 Baltimore Sanitary Fair Copy # 1 (Bancroft) — nor long remember what we say here,

5 Baltimore Sanitary Fair Copy # 2 (Bliss) — nor long remember what we say here,

1 First Draft (Nicolay) — while it can never forget what they did here.

2 Second Draft (Hay) — but can never forget what they did here.

3 NY Metropolitan Fair (Everett) — but it can never forget what they did here.

4 Baltimore Sanitary Fair Copy # 1 (Bancroft) — but it can never forget what they did here.

5 Baltimore Sanitary Fair Copy # 2 (Bliss) — but it can never forget what they did here.

1 First Draft (Nicolay)	It is rather for us, the living, we here be dedicated
2 Second Draft (Hay)	It is for us, the living, rather to be dedicated here
3 NY Metropolitan Fair (Everett)	It is for us, the living, rather, to be dedicated here
4 Baltimore Sanitary Fair Copy # 1 (Bancroft)	It is for us the living, rather, to be dedicated here
5 Baltimore Sanitary Fair Copy # 2 (Bliss)	It is for us the living, rather, to be dedicated here

1 First Draft (Nicolay)	———————————————
2 Second Draft (Hay)	to the unfinished work which they have,
3 NY Metropolitan Fair (Everett)	to the unfinished work which they who fought here, have,
4 Baltimore Sanitary Fair Copy # 1 (Bancroft)	to the unfinished work which they who fought here have
5 Baltimore Sanitary Fair Copy # 2 (Bliss)	to the unfinished work which they who fought here have

1 First Draft (Nicolay)	———————————————
2 Second Draft (Hay)	thus far, so nobly carried on.
3 NY Metropolitan Fair (Everett)	thus far, so nobly advanced.
4 Baltimore Sanitary Fair Copy # 1 (Bancroft)	thus far so nobly advanced.
5 Baltimore Sanitary Fair Copy # 2 (Bliss)	thus far so nobly advanced.

1 First Draft (Nicolay)	———————————————
2 Second Draft (Hay)	It is rather for us to be here dedicated
3 NY Metropolitan Fair (Everett)	It is rather for us to be here dedicated
4 Baltimore Sanitary Fair Copy # 1 (Bancroft)	It is rather for us to be here dedicated
5 Baltimore Sanitary Fair Copy # 2 (Bliss)	It is rather for us to be here dedicated

1 First Draft (Nicolay)	to the great task remaining before us-
2 Second Draft (Hay)	to the great task remaining before us-
3 NY Metropolitan Fair (Everett)	to the great task remaining before us-
4 Baltimore Sanitary Fair Copy # 1 (Bancroft)	to the great task remaining before us-
5 Baltimore Sanitary Fair Copy # 2 (Bliss)	to the great task remaining before us-

1 First Draft (Nicolay)	that, from these honored dead we take increased devotion
2 Second Draft (Hay)	that from these honored dead we take increased devotion
3 NY Metropolitan Fair (Everett)	that from these honored dead we take increased devotion
4 Baltimore Sanitary Fair Copy # 1 (Bancroft)	that from these honored dead we take increased devotion
5 Baltimore Sanitary Fair Copy # 2 (Bliss)	that from these honored dead we take increased devotion

1 First Draft (Nicolay)	to that cause for which they here, gave
2 Second Draft (Hay)	to that cause for which they here gave
3 NY Metropolitan Fair (Everett)	to that cause for which they here gave
4 Baltimore Sanitary Fair Copy # 1 (Bancroft)	to that cause for which they here gave
5 Baltimore Sanitary Fair Copy # 2 (Bliss)	to that cause for which they gave

1 First Draft (Nicolay)	the last full measure of devotion-
2 Second Draft (Hay)	the last full measure of devotion-
3 NY Metropolitan Fair (Everett)	the last full measure of devotion-
4 Baltimore Sanitary Fair Copy # 1 (Bancroft)	the last full measure of devotion-
5 Baltimore Sanitary Fair Copy # 2 (Bliss)	the last full measure of devotion-

1 First Draft (Nicolay)	that we here highly resolve these dead
2 Second Draft (Hay)	that we here highly resolve that these dead
3 NY Metropolitan Fair (Everett)	that we here highly resolve that these dead
4 Baltimore Sanitary Fair Copy # 1 (Bancroft)	that we here highly resolve that these dead
5 Baltimore Sanitary Fair Copy # 2 (Bliss)	that we here highly resolve that these dead

1 First Draft (Nicolay)	shall not have died in vain;
2 Second Draft (Hay)	shall not have died in vain;
3 NY Metropolitan Fair (Everett)	shall not have died in vain—
4 Baltimore Sanitary Fair Copy # 1 (Bancroft)	shall not have died in vain—
5 Baltimore Sanitary Fair Copy # 2 (Bliss)	shall not have died in vain—

1 First Draft (Nicolay)	that the nation, shall have
2 Second Draft (Hay)	that this nation shall have
3 NY Metropolitan Fair (Everett)	that this nation, under God, shall have
4 Baltimore Sanitary Fair Copy # 1 (Bancroft)	that this nation, under God, shall have
5 Baltimore Sanitary Fair Copy # 2 (Bliss)	that this nation, under God, shall have

1 First Draft (Nicolay)	a new birth of freedom, and that government
2 Second Draft (Hay)	a new birth of freedom; and that this government
3 NY Metropolitan Fair (Everett)	a new birth of freedom—and that, government
4 Baltimore Sanitary Fair Copy # 1 (Bancroft)	a new birth of freedom, and that government
5 Baltimore Sanitary Fair Copy # 2 (Bliss)	a new birth of free,dom—and that government

1 First Draft (Nicolay)	of the people by the people for the people,
2 Second Draft (Hay)	of the people, by the people, for the people,
3 NY Metropolitan Fair (Everett)	of the people, by the people, for the people,
4 Baltimore Sanitary Fair Copy # 1 (Bancroft)	of the people, by the people, for the people,
5 Baltimore Sanitary Fair Copy # 2 (Bliss)	of the people, by the people, for the people,

1 First Draft (Nicolay)	shall not perish from the earth.
2 Second Draft (Hay)	shall not perish from the earth.
3 NY Metropolitan Fair (Everett)	shall not perish from the earth.
4 Baltimore Sanitary Fair Copy # 1 (Bancroft)	shall not perish from the earth.
5 Baltimore Sanitary Fair Copy # 2 (Bliss)	shall not perish from the earth.

2. What People Read and Heard: A Sample

In Lincoln's time people often read newspapers aloud to themselves, their families, and friends.

1 Associated Press: *N.Y. Tribune*	Four score and seven years ago
2 *The Philadelphia Inquirer*	Four score and seven years ago
3 *Chicago Times*	Four score and ten years ago
4 *Centralia Sentinel* (Illinois)	Ninety years ago
5 *Cincinnati Daily Gazette*	Four score and seven years ago

1 Associated Press: *N.Y. Tribune*	our fathers brought forth upon this continent
2 *The Philadelphia Inquirer*	our fathers brought forth upon this continent
3 *Chicago Times*	our fathers brought forth upon this continent
4 *Centralia Sentinel* (Illinois)	our fathers formed a Government
5 *Cincinnati Daily Gazette*	our fathers established upon this continent

1 Associated Press: *N.Y. Tribune*	a new Nation, conceived in Liberty,
2 *The Philadelphia Inquirer*	a new nation, conceived in liberty
3 *Chicago Times*	a nation consecrated to liberty
4 *Centralia Sentinel* (Illinois)	consecrated to freedom,
5 *Cincinnati Daily Gazette*	a Government subscribed in liberty

1 Associated Press: *N.Y. Tribune*	and dedicated to the proposition
2 *The Philadelphia Inquirer*	and dedicated to the proposition
3 *Chicago Times*	and dedicated to the proposition
4 *Centralia Sentinel* (Illinois)	and dedicated to the principle
5 *Cincinnati Daily Gazette*	and dedicated to the fundamental principle

1 Associated Press: *N.Y. Tribune*	that all men are created equal. [Applause.]
2 *The Philadelphia Inquirer*	that all men are created equal.
3 *Chicago Times*	that all men are created equal. [Cheers.]
4 *Centralia Sentinel* (Illinois)	that all men are created equal.
5 *Cincinnati Daily Gazette*	that all mankind are created free and equal by a good God— [applause]—

1 Associated Press: *N.Y. Tribune*	Now we are engaged in a great civil war,
2 *The Philadelphia Inquirer*	Now we are engaged in a great civil war,
3 *Chicago Times*	Now we are engaged in a great civil war,
4 *Centralia Sentinel* (Illinois)	and that we are engaged in a war
5 *Cincinnati Daily Gazette*	and now we are engaged in a great contest

1 Associated Press: *N.Y. Tribune*	testing whether that Nation or any Nation
2 *The Philadelphia Inquirer*	testing the question whether this nation or any nation
3 *Chicago Times*	testing whether that nation or any other nation
4 *Centralia Sentinel* (Illinois)	testing the question whether any nation
5 *Cincinnati Daily Gazette*	deciding the question whether this nation

1 Associated Press: *N.Y. Tribune* so conceived and so dedicated can long endure.

2 *The Philadelphia Inquirer* so conceived, so dedicated, can long endure.

3 *Chicago Times* so consecrated and so dedicated can long endure. [Cheers.]

4 *Centralia Sentinel* (Illinois) so formed can long endure,

5 *Cincinnati Daily Gazette* or any nation so conserved, so dedicated, can long remain.

1 Associated Press: *N.Y. Tribune* We are met on a great battle-field of that war.

2 *The Philadelphia Inquirer* We are met on the great battle-field of that war.

3 *Chicago Times* We are met on a great battle-field of that war,

4 *Centralia Sentinel* (Illinois) and come to dedicate

5 *Cincinnati Daily Gazette* We are met on a great battlefield of the war

1 Associated Press: *N.Y. Tribune* We are met to dedicate a portion of it

2 *The Philadelphia Inquirer* We are met to dedicate it, on a portion of the field

3 *Chicago Times* here, to dedicate a portion of that field

4 *Centralia Sentinel* (Illinois) a portion of a great battle-field of that war

5 *Cincinnati Daily Gazette* We are met here to dedicate a portion of that field

1 Associated Press: *N.Y. Tribune* as the final resting-place of those

2 *The Philadelphia Inquirer* set apart as the final resting place

3 *Chicago Times* as a final resting place for those

4 *Centralia Sentinel* (Illinois) to those who had died

5 *Cincinnati Daily Gazette* as the final resting place of those

1 Associated Press: *N.Y. Tribune*	who here gave their lives that that nation might live.
2 *The Philadelphia Inquirer*	of those who gave their lives for the nation's life; but the nation must live,
3 *Chicago Times*	who here gave their lives that the nation might live.
4 *Centralia Sentinel* (Illinois)	that the nation might live.
5 *Cincinnati Daily Gazette*	who have given their lives that it might live.

1 Associated Press: *N.Y. Tribune*	It is altogether fitting and proper that we should do this.
2 *The Philadelphia Inquirer*	and it is altogether fitting and proper that we should do this.
3 *Chicago Times*	It is altogether fitting that we should do this;
4 *Centralia Sentinel* (Illinois)	————————————————
5 *Cincinnati Daily Gazette*	It is altogether fitting and proper that we should do this,

1 Associated Press: *N.Y. Tribune*	But in a larger sense we cannot dedicate,
2 *The Philadelphia Inquirer*	In a larger sense we cannot dedicate,
3 *Chicago Times*	but, in a large sense, we cannot dedicate-
4 *Centralia Sentinel* (Illinois)	He could not dedicate,
5 *Cincinnati Daily Gazette*	but in a large sense we cannot dedicate,

1 Associated Press: *N.Y. Tribune*	we cannot consecrate, we cannot hallow this ground.
2 *The Philadelphia Inquirer*	we cannot consecrate, we cannot hallow this ground in realty.
3 *Chicago Times*	we cannot consecrate-we cannot hallow this ground.
4 *Centralia Sentinel* (Illinois)	consecrate or hallow that ground,
5 *Cincinnati Daily Gazette*	we cannot consecrate, we cannot hallow this ground.

1 Associated Press: *N.Y. Tribune*	The brave men living and dead
2 *The Philadelphia Inquirer*	The number of men, living and dead,
3 *Chicago Times*	The brave men, living and dead,
4 *Centralia Sentinel* (Illinois)	————————————————
5 *Cincinnati Daily Gazette*	The brave men, the living and the dead

1 Associated Press: *N.Y. Tribune* who struggled here have consecrated it
2 *The Philadelphia Inquirer* who struggled here have consecrated it
3 *Chicago Times* who struggled here, have consecrated it
4 *Centralia Sentinel* (Illinois) for it was consecrated
5 *Cincinnati Daily Gazette* who struggled here, have consecrated it

1 Associated Press: *N.Y. Tribune* far above our power to add or detract. [Applause.]

2 *The Philadelphia Inquirer* far above our poor attempts to add to its consecration.

3 *Chicago Times* far above our power to add or to detract.
4 *Centralia Sentinel* (Illinois) above our power to add or detract.
5 *Cincinnati Daily Gazette* far above our power to add to or to detract from the work. [Great applause.]

1 Associated Press: *N.Y. Tribune* The world will little note
2 *The Philadelphia Inquirer* The world will little know
3 *Chicago Times* The world will little heed
4 *Centralia Sentinel* (Illinois) The world would
5 *Cincinnati Daily Gazette* ———————————————————

1 Associated Press: *N.Y. Tribune* nor long remember what we say here,
2 *The Philadelphia Inquirer* and nothing remember of what we see here,
3 *Chicago Times* or long remember what we say here;
4 *Centralia Sentinel* (Illinois) not long remember what we said there,
5 *Cincinnati Daily Gazette* Let us long remember what we say here,

1 Associated Press: *N.Y. Tribune* but it can never forget what they did here. [Applause.]

2 *The Philadelphia Inquirer* but we cannot forget what these brave men did here.

3 *Chicago Times* but it can never forget what they did here. [Tremendous applause.]

4 *Centralia Sentinel* (Illinois) but it could never forget what was done there,

5 *Cincinnati Daily Gazette* but not forget what they did here. [immense applause.]

1 Associated Press: *N.Y. Tribune*   It is for us, the living, rather to be
                                                 dedicated here

2 *The Philadelphia Inquirer*   We owe this offering to our dead.

3 *Chicago Times*   It is for us rather, the living to be dedicated
                                                 here

4 *Centralia Sentinel* (Illinois)   and it was rather for it to be dedicated

5 *Cincinnati Daily Gazette*   It is for us rather, the living, to be
                                                 dedicated here

1 Associated Press: *N.Y. Tribune*   to the refinished work that they have

2 *The Philadelphia Inquirer*   ————————————————————

3 *Chicago Times*   to the important work that they have

4 *Centralia Sentinel* (Illinois)   on that spot to the work

5 *Cincinnati Daily Gazette*   to the unfinished work that they have

1 Associated Press: *N.Y. Tribune*   thus far so nobly carried on. [Applause.]

2 *The Philadelphia Inquirer*   ————————————————————

3 *Chicago Times*   thus far so nobly carried forward.

4 *Centralia Sentinel* (Illinois)   they had so nobly carried forward

5 *Cincinnati Daily Gazette*   thus far so nobly carried forward.
                                                 ["Good," and great applause.]

1 Associated Press: *N.Y. Tribune*   It is rather for us to be here dedicated

2 *The Philadelphia Inquirer*   ————————————————————

3 *Chicago Times*   It is rather for us here to be dedicated

4 *Centralia Sentinel* (Illinois)   ————————————————————

5 *Cincinnati Daily Gazette*   It is for us here to be dedicated

1 Associated Press: *N.Y. Tribune*   to the great task remaining before us,

2 *The Philadelphia Inquirer*   ————————————————————

3 *Chicago Times*   to the great task remaining before us,

4 *Centralia Sentinel* (Illinois)   ————————————————————

5 *Cincinnati Daily Gazette*   to the great task remaining before us,

1 Associated Press: *N.Y. Tribune*   that from these honored dead we take
                                                 increased devotion

2 *The Philadelphia Inquirer*   We imbibe increased devotion

3 *Chicago Times*   that those who have died shall not have
                                                 died in vain,

4 *Centralia Sentinel* (Illinois)   ————————————————————

5 *Cincinnati Daily Gazette*   for us to to renew our devotion

1 Associated Press: *N.Y. Tribune*   to that cause for which they here gave
2 *The Philadelphia Inquirer*   to that cause for which they here gave
3 *Chicago Times*   ————————————————————————
4 *Centralia Sentinel* (Illinois)   ————————————————————————
5 *Cincinnati Daily Gazette*   to that cause for which they gave

1 Associated Press: *N.Y. Tribune*   the last full measure of devotion;
2 *The Philadelphia Inquirer*   the last full measure of devotion;
3 *Chicago Times*   ————————————————————————
4 *Centralia Sentinel* (Illinois)   ————————————————————————
5 *Cincinnati Daily Gazette*   the full measure of their devotion.

1 Associated Press: *N.Y. Tribune*   that we here highly resolve that the dead
2 *The Philadelphia Inquirer*   we here might resolve
3 *Chicago Times*   ————————————————————————
4 *Centralia Sentinel* (Illinois)   ————————————————————————
5 *Cincinnati Daily Gazette*   Here let us resolve that what they have
    done

1 Associated Press: *N.Y. Tribune*   shall not have died in vain [applause];
2 *The Philadelphia Inquirer*   that they shall not have died in vain;
3 *Chicago Times*   that those who have died shall not have
    died in vain,
4 *Centralia Sentinel* (Illinois)   that they might not have died in vain,
5 *Cincinnati Daily Gazette*   shall not have been done in vain;

1 Associated Press: *N.Y. Tribune*   that the nation shall, under God, have
2 *The Philadelphia Inquirer*   that the nation shall, under God, have
3 *Chicago Times*   but that the nation shall endure
4 *Centralia Sentinel* (Illinois)   ————————————————————————
5 *Cincinnati Daily Gazette*   that the nation shall, under God, have

1 Associated Press: *N.Y. Tribune*   a new birth of freedom; and that
    Governments
2 *The Philadelphia Inquirer*   a new birth of freedom, and that the
    Government
3 *Chicago Times*   and that government
4 *Centralia Sentinel* (Illinois)   and that Government
5 *Cincinnati Daily Gazette*   a new birth offered; that the Government

1 Associated Press: *N.Y. Tribune*	of the people, by the people, and for the people,
2 *The Philadelphia Inquirer*	of the people, for the people, and for all people,
3 *Chicago Times*	by the people, and of the people,
4 *Centralia Sentinel* (Illinois)	for and of the people, based upon the freedom of man
5 *Cincinnati Daily Gazette*	of the people, founded by the people,

1 Associated Press: *N.Y. Tribune*	shall not perish from the earth. [Long-continued applause.]
2 *The Philadelphia Inquirer*	shall not perish from earth.
3 *Chicago Times*	shall not perish from the earth.
4 *Centralia Sentinel* (Illinois)	may not perish from off the face of the earth.
5 *Cincinnati Daily Gazette*	shall not perish.

3. *What Lincoln Read at Gettysburg*

Historians and buffs have debated for more than a century whether Lincoln used the First or Second Draft as his reading copy at the National Cemetery. Some even speculated, perhaps a little loosely, about some versions that no longer exist. Though no one can offer inconvertible truths, the Second Draft is closest to the texts taken down by reporters at the time. Chapters 4 and 5 discuss the drafts, and this part of the Appendix provides some additional evidence on the subject.

Students of history must often rely on probabilities, as do statisticians. Comparisons of the first two drafts with the version provided by the Associated Press, which journalists much later remembered was copied from Lincoln's own speaking copy (though the reporters also took shorthand notes), clearly identifies the Second (Hay) Draft, as much closer to the printed reports than the First (Nicolay) Draft. The AP version was read in some form by more people in 1863 than any other. But some historians believe that a version taken down by another journalist, Charles Hale, a member of the Massachusetts delegation and a nephew of Edward Everett, that few saw at the time, comes closer to what Lincoln actually said. A computer-generated analysis of character and word-level differences, performed by Dr. H. Van Dyke Parunak and Dr. Anita Gene Parunak of Ann Arbor, strongly indicates that the Second Draft (Hay) is almost as close to both the AP and the shorthand (Hale) transcriptions as these two are to each other, while the First Draft (Nicolay) is as far from

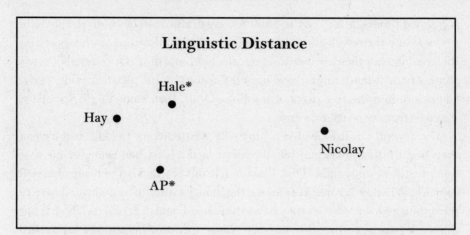

Linguistic Distance

Which is the delivery speech? *Of the five versions of the Gettysburg Address, three have been put on paper after delivery. Two other versions (Nicolay and Hay) cannot be dated from contemporary sources, though scholars place one or more before delivery. One of the two (Hay) closely resembles the two contemporary versions from reporters (AP and Hale), that also closely resemble each other. Under such circumstances the layperson with common sense will ask "what is the debate about?"*

The dots above represent linguistic distance and are arranged in 2D space so that the geometrical distances among them are, approximately, proportional to the differences in the report. Getting 4 points exactly situated at prespecified distances would require 3 dimensions, not 2. There is no independent meaning to the x or y axes. Dots representing character or word distances produce similar results. For asterisks see Parunak Report, Table 4.

them as it is from the Second Draft. Technically, one should be cautious about drawing conclusions from sums of differences that are not statistically independent of one another—but the differences are so strong as to allay qualms. Indeed, a separate linguistic analysis performed by the Parunaks at the author's request produced the same conclusion.

The likelihood remains that having written the first part of his speech in Washington, Lincoln finished his First Draft in the evening in Gettysburg, and then hurriedly wrote his Second Draft the next morning—as discussed in chapters 4 and 5. Nicolay remembered that at a later date the president had asked him and Hay to examine the AP version of his speech and help produce from it a corrected copy. If this was done, that copy appears to be either the New York Metropolitan Fair or the Baltimore Sanitary Fair copy. The hypothesis that Lincoln wrote out the Second Draft after returning from Gettysburg and that the corrections in that copy represent an attempt to replicate the AP version, is invalidated by the absence of some changes in the Second Draft and, most important, by the failure to include the words "under God." Neither Lincoln's developing religious sensibility nor his acute political instincts would have permitted leaving out the widely reported words. By contrast, the suggested timetable for the First and Second drafts, matches both the physical evidence and the recollections indicating that Lincoln worked on the speech on the evening, and then also wrote it out the next morning. Of course Nicolay's recollection, at least, might have been influenced by the physical evidence: he had before him the two parts of the First Draft, that, some might speculate, survived from two separate drafts.

The Second Draft looks like a hurriedly written copy. Lincoln had a clear, even beautiful handwriting, but this draft is the least handsome of his five, though still quite legible. That Lincoln left out words also indicates hurried copying. When he wrote: "It is for us, the living, rather to be dedicated here to the unfinished work which they have, thus far, so nobly carried on," he left out the word "work" so that the sentence read, "dedicated here to the unfinished which they . . ." Lincoln did insert "work" to make the sentence intelligible, but as he rushed on, presumably on the morning of the 19th, he left out "us" from "the great task remaining before us," and he repeated the word "gave" so that, until he made amends, his sentence read "they here gave gave the last full measure of devotion." Other corrections in the Second Draft in turn suggest someone attempting to improve not only cadence but also phrasing, in modest ways, but finding that the original wording was better.

1 First Draft (Nicolay)	Four score and seven years ago
2 Second Draft (Hay)	Four score and seven years ago
3 Associated Press: *NY Tribune*	Four score and seven years ago
4 Hale Report	Fourscore and seven years ago,

1 First Draft (Nicolay)	our fathers brought forth, upon this continent,
2 Second Draft (Hay)	our fathers brought forth, upon this continent,
3 Associated Press: *NY Tribune*	our fathers brought forth upon this continent
4 Hale Report	our fathers brought forth upon this continent

1 First Draft (Nicolay)	a new nation, conceived in liberty,
2 Second Draft (Hay)	a new nation, conceived in Liberty,
3 Associated Press: *NY Tribune*	a new Nation, conceived in Liberty,
4 Hale Report	a new nation, conceived in liberty

1 First Draft (Nicolay)	and dedicated to the proposition
2 Second Draft (Hay)	and dedicated to the proposition
3 Associated Press: *NY Tribune*	and dedicated to the proposition
4 Hale Report	and dedicated to the proposition

1 First Draft (Nicolay)	that "all men are created equal"
2 Second Draft (Hay)	that all men are created equal.
3 Associated Press: *NY Tribune*	that all men are created equal.
4 Hale Report	that all men are created equal.

1 First Draft (Nicolay)	Now we are engaged in a great civil war,
2 Second Draft (Hay)	Now we are engaged in a great civil war,
3 Associated Press: *NY Tribune*	Now we are engaged in a great civil war,
4 Hale Report	Now we are engaged in a great civil war,

1 First Draft (Nicolay)	testing whether that nation, or any nation
2 Second Draft (Hay)	testing whether that nation, or any nation,
3 Associated Press: *NY Tribune*	testing whether that Nation of any nation
4 Hale Report	testing whether that nation- or any nation,

1 First Draft (Nicolay)	so conceived, and so dedicated, can long endure.
2 Second Draft (Hay)	so conceived, and so dedicated, can long endure.
3 Associated Press: *NY Tribune*	so conceived and so dedicated can long endure.
4 Hale Report	so conceived and so dedicated- can long endure.

1 First Draft (Nicolay)	We are met on a great battle field of that war.
2 Second Draft (Hay)	We are met here on a great battlefield of that war.
3 Associated Press: *NY Tribune*	We are met on a great battle-field of that war.
4 Hale Report	We are met on a great battle-field of that war.

1 First Draft (Nicolay)	We have come to dedicate a portion of it,
2 Second Draft (Hay)	We have come to dedicate a portion of it
3 Associated Press: *NY Tribune*	We are met to dedicate a portion of it
4 Hale Report	We are met to dedicate a portion of it

1 First Draft (Nicolay)	as a final resting place for those
2 Second Draft (Hay)	as a final resting place for those
3 Associated Press: *NY Tribune*	as the final resting-place of those
4 Hale Report	as the final resting-place of those

1 First Draft (Nicolay)	who died here, that the nation might live.
2 Second Draft (Hay)	who here gave their lives that that nation might live.
3 Associated Press: *NY Tribune*	who here gave their lives that that nation might live.
4 Hale Report	who have given their lives that that nation might live.

1 First Draft (Nicolay)	This we may,
2 Second Draft (Hay)	It is altogether fitting
3 Associated Press: *NY Tribune*	It is altogether fitting
4 Hale Report	It is altogether fitting

1 First Draft (Nicolay)	in all propriety do.
2 Second Draft (Hay)	and proper that we should do this.
3 Associated Press: *NY Tribune*	and proper that we should do this.
4 Hale Report	and proper that we should do this.

1 First Draft (Nicolay)	But, in a larger sense, we can not dedicate-
2 Second Draft (Hay)	But in a larger sense we can not dedicate—
3 Associated Press: *NY Tribune*	But in a larger sense we cannot dedicate,
4 Hale Report	But, in a larger sense, we cannot dedicate,

1 First Draft (Nicolay)	we can not consecrate—we can not hallow, this ground—
2 Second Draft (Hay)	we can not consecrate—we can not hallow this ground.
3 Associated Press: *NY Tribune*	we cannot consecrate, we cannot hallow this ground.
4 Hale Report	we cannot consecrate, we cannot hallow, this ground.

1 First Draft (Nicolay)	The brave men, living and dead,
2 Second Draft (Hay)	The brave men, living and dead,
3 Associated Press: *NY Tribune*	The brave men living and dead
4 Hale Report	The brave men, living and dead,

1 First Draft (Nicolay)	who struggled here, have hallowed it,
2 Second Draft (Hay)	who struggled here, have consecrated it
3 Associated Press: *NY Tribune*	who struggled here have consecrated it
4 Hale Report	who struggled here, have consecrated it,

1 First Draft (Nicolay)	far above our poor power to add or detract.
2 Second Draft (Hay)	far above our poor power to add or detract.
3 Associated Press: *NY Tribune*	far above our power to add or detract.
4 Hale Report	far above our power to add or to detract.

1 First Draft (Nicolay)	The world will little note,
2 Second Draft (Hay)	The world will little note,
3 Associated Press: *NY Tribune*	The world will little note
4 Hale Report	The world will very little note

1 First Draft (Nicolay)	nor long remember what we say here;
2 Second Draft (Hay)	nor long remember, what we say here,
3 Associated Press: *NY Tribune*	nor long remember what we say here,
4 Hale Report	nor long remember what we say here;

1 First Draft (Nicolay)	while it can never forget what they *did* here.
2 Second Draft (Hay)	but can never forget what they did here.
3 Associated Press: *NY Tribune*	but it can never forget what they did here.
4 Hale Report	but it can never forget what they did here.

1 First Draft (Nicolay)	It is rather for us, the living, we here be dedicated
2 Second Draft (Hay)	It is for us, the living, rather to be dedicated here
3 Associated Press: *NY Tribune*	It is for us, the living, rather to be dedicated here
4 Hale Report	It is for us, the living, rather, *to be dedicated,* here,

1 First Draft (Nicolay)	————————————————
2 Second Draft (Hay)	to the unfinished work which they have,
3 Associated Press: *NY Tribune*	to the refinished work that they have
4 Hale Report	to the unfinished work that they have

1 First Draft (Nicolay)	————————————————
2 Second Draft (Hay)	thus far, so nobly carried on.
3 Associated Press: *NY Tribune*	thus far so nobly carried on.
4 Hale Report	thus far so nobly carried on.

1 First Draft (Nicolay)	————————————————
2 Second Draft (Hay)	It is rather for us to be here dedicated
3 Associated Press: *NY Tribune*	It is rather for us to be here dedicated
4 Hale Report	It is rather for us to be here dedicated

1 First Draft (Nicolay)	to the great task remaining before us—
2 Second Draft (Hay)	to the great task remaining before us—
3 Associated Press: *NY Tribune*	to the great task remaining before us,
4 Hale Report	to the great task remaining before us;

1 First Draft (Nicolay)	that, from these honored dead we take increased devotion
2 Second Draft (Hay)	that from these honored dead we take increased devotion
3 Associated Press: *NY Tribune*	that from these honored dead we take increased devotion
4 Hale Report	that from these honored dead we take increased devotion

1 First Draft (Nicolay)	to that cause for which they here, gave
2 Second Draft (Hay)	to that cause for which they here gave
3 Associated Press: *NY Tribune*	to that cause for which they here gave
4 Hale Report	to that cause for which they here gave

1 First Draft (Nicolay)	the last full measure of devotion—
2 Second Draft (Hay)	the last full measure of devotion—
3 Associated Press: *NY Tribune*	the last full measure of devotion;
4 Hale Report	the last full measure of devotion;

1 First Draft (Nicolay)	that we here highly resolve these dead
2 Second Draft (Hay)	that we here highly resolve that these dead
3 Associated Press: *NY Tribune*	that we here highly resolve that the dead
4 Hale Report	that we here highly resolve that these dead

1 First Draft (Nicolay)	shall not have died in vain;
2 Second Draft (Hay)	shall not have died in vain;
3 Associated Press: *NY Tribune*	shall not have died in vain;
4 Hale Report	shall not have died in vain;

1 First Draft (Nicolay)	that the nation, shall have
2 Second Draft (Hay)	that this nation shall have
3 Associated Press: *NY Tribune*	that the nation shall, under God, have
4 Hale Report	that the nation shall, under God, have

1 First Draft (Nicolay)	a new birth of freedom, and that government
2 Second Draft (Hay)	a new birth of freedom; and that this government
3 Associated Press: *NY Tribune*	a new birth of freedom; and that Governments
4 Hale Report	a new birth of freedom, and that government

1 First Draft (Nicolay)	of the people by the people for the people,
2 Second Draft (Hay)	of the people, by the people, for the people,
3 Associated Press: *NY Tribune*	of the people, by the people, and for the people,
4 Hale Report	of the people, by the people, for the people,
1 First Draft (Nicolay)	shall not perish from the earth.
2 Second Draft (Hay)	shall not perish from the earth.
3 Associated Press: *NY Tribune*	shall not perish from the earth.
4 Hale Report	shall not perish from the earth.

4. The Parunak Report: A Statistical Look at What Lincoln Read at Gettysburg

H. Van Dyke Parunak, Anita Gene Parunak, and Gabor Boritt

THE BIG PICTURE

History has preserved two drafts of Lincoln's Gettysburg address that may have served as the reading copy: the "First Draft" ("Nicolay"), and the "Second Draft" ("Hay"). We also have two good independent stenographic transcriptions of the words that Lincoln spoke, "AP" and "Hale." We wish to compare the drafts with the transcriptions, to see which draft Lincoln read at Gettysburg.

We can count the differences between two texts. The fewer differences, the more similar the texts are. What might we expect to find?

We can count the differences between each draft and each transcription. If one draft has fewer differences from the transcriptions than the other, it is more likely to be the draft that Lincoln read. We can also compare the two drafts with each other, and the two transcriptions with each other. We expect that the two drafts will differ at many points, because they are different versions of the speech. We expect that the two transcriptions will have fewer differences between them than the two drafts, because both stenographers heard the same speech. Indeed, much later, one who claimed to be the AP reporter recalled copying the manuscript from which Lincoln spoke. We take this recollection with caution and treat the AP text as an independent transcription. Differences between the texts reflect misreporting.

We will count differences in three ways: in terms of characters, words, and semantic units. Consider characters. We can change one text into another by repeatedly performing one or another of three operations: delete a character, insert a character, or replace one character by another. The difference between two texts is the smallest number of operations needed to turn one into the other.

Table 1 shows the differences among our texts[1] in terms of characters, Table 2 in terms of words, and Table 3 in terms of semantic units. The names of drafts are in regular font, and those of transcriptions are in *italics*.

Table 1: Character-based edit distances between texts

	Nicolay	Hay	AP*	Hale
Nicolay	0	203	198	199
Hay		0	30	33
AP*			0	23
Hale*				0

Table 2: Word-based edit distances between texts

	Nicolay	Hay	AP*	Hale
Nicolay	0	51	54	53
Hay		0	14	14
AP*			0	12
Hale*				0

Table 3: Distances between texts based on linguistic units

	Nicolay	Hay	AP*	Hale
Nicolay	0	18	15	14
Hay		0	6	5
AP*			0	6
Hale*				0

Each table shows three boxes. The upper-left box compares the two drafts. The lower-right box compares the two transcriptions. The larger box in the middle compares each of the drafts with each of the transcriptions. In all three tables, as we expected,

---

[1] *AP* and Hale* are versions of AP and Hale modified to correct for extemporaneous changes that Lincoln introduced as he was speaking. The next section describes how we identify these. The AP text is taken from the* New York Tribune, *Nov. 20, 1863; the Hale text from* Address of His Excellency John A. Andrew, to the Two Branches of the Legislature of Massachusetts, January 8, 1864 *(Boston: Wright & Potter, 1864), p. lxxii. The Nicolay and Hay texts come from Lincoln's original manuscripts. http://www.loc.gov/exhibits/gadd/gadrft.html*

- there are more differences between the two drafts than between the two transcriptions;
- Nicolay is about as different from the transcriptions as it is from Hay, (and even more different in Table 2) showing that it is very unlikely to be the copy that Lincoln read;
- Hay is about as close to the transcriptions as they are to each other (and even closer in Table 3) showing that it is likely to be the copy that Lincoln read.

FURTHER DETAILS

This section offers further details supporting the analysis described above.

DID LINCOLN EXTEMPORIZE?

This analysis supposes that the reading draft, like the transcriptions, is an accurate record of what Lincoln said. There is evidence that Lincoln sometimes deviated from his prepared text. At five points in the speech, the two transcriptions agree with one another, but differ from the drafts. Table 4 summarizes these differences.

The agreement of both transcriptions against the drafts implies that whichever draft Lincoln used, he deviated as recorded in the transcriptions.[2] It would be misleading to include these deviations in our measure of the distance of a draft from a transcription. So, in addition to comparing the drafts with AP and Hale, we also compare them with modified versions of AP and Hale (AP* and Hale*), in which these extemporaneous changes are removed.

Table 4: Agreements of transcriptions against the drafts (likely extemporaneous changes)

DRAFTS	TRANSCRIPTIONS
We *have come* to dedicate	We *are met* to dedicate
a final resting place	*the* final resting place
our *poor* power to add or detract	our power to add or detract
the . . . work *which* they have[3]	the . . . work *that* they have
nation shall have	nation shall, *under God,* have

---

[2] *In fact, we are certain from other reports that Lincoln said "poor power." For the correction we describe in the text, whether this change was spoken makes no difference; the modified texts AP* and Hale* have "poor."*

[3] *Nicolay lacks this line entirely, but both transcriptions agree against Hay.*

These examples show that Lincoln was not a slave to his written text, and it is likely that he extemporized elsewhere in the speech as well. But we cannot identify such changes before we have identified the reading text. Thus the draft that is closest to the transcriptions may not be quite as close to them as they are to one another.

If we substitute the word "unfinished," which Lincoln certainly used, for the erroneous "refinished" of the AP report that appeared in the *New York Tribune*, the AP, Hale, and the Second (Hay) draft are even closer to each other.

It might be possible to argue that there were other versions of Lincoln's speech that are lost, but it is best for historians to rely on the available factual evidence, texts that survive, rather than on speculation. Fertile imaginations can produce an almost infinite number of variations.

DISTANCE MEASURES

We explore three measures. The first is based on a character-by-character analysis of the two texts. The second is based on differences at the level of words. The natural semantic units of text are sometimes phrases or clauses rather than words, so we define a third measure that attempts to capture changes at the level of semantic units.

Character-Based Edit Distance

Our first measure is the character-based edit distance, sometimes called the Levenshtein distance,[*] which is widely used in modern information-processing applications. Imagine that we have one text in a word processor that supports three operations: delete a character, insert a character, and replace one character by another. The character-based edit distance between this text and another is the fewest number of operations that we would have to perform to change our text into the other. In measuring this distance, we first remove all capitalization, punctuation, and extra spaces from the texts, since these are not reliably recovered by a transcriber.

Word-Based Edit Distance

We can define a word-based version of the Levenshtein distance by imagining that our word processor operates on whole words, not characters. Now the op-

---

[*] *Vladimir I. Levenshtein,* Binary codes capable of correcting deletions, insertions, and reversals, *Doklady Akademii Nauk SSSR, 163(4):845–848, 1965 (Russian). English translation in Soviet Physics Doklady, 10(8):707–710, 1966. Convenient references include www.levenshtein.net/, www.nist.gov/dads/HTML/Levenshtein.html, http://en.wikipedia.org/wiki/Levenshtein_distance.*

erations that we count to define the distance between two versions are the number of words (not characters) that must be inserted, deleted, or changed. The absolute distances between texts using this measure are much lower because we are counting the number of changed words, not the number of changed characters, and each word has several characters.

Linguistic Units

Our third distance measure is less objective than the previous two, but conforms more closely to how language works. Characters and words in natural language text are not independent of one another. For example, if one inserts a "q" in English text, one must also insert a "u" following it; if one inserts the word "of," one must also insert either an article or a noun after it. Thus counting characters or words that change between texts is likely to over-count. In this third measure, instead of counting the insertion or change of characters or graphical words, we count the following kinds of changes:

- insertion of a word or phrase in one version that is not in another, counting the entire inserted phrase as a single change
- change of singular to plural
- replacement of a word or phrase by a synonymous word or phrase
- transposition (inversion of the order of two words or phrases).

DETAILED NUMERICAL COMPARISONS

The following tables give the full comparisons among the texts. In the case of character- and word-based distances, they include the difference measured as a percentage of the text.[5] Table 5 gives the lengths of the texts in characters and words, after elimination of punctuation.

Table 5: Lengths of Texts

	Nicolay	Hay	AP	Hale	AP*	Hale*
Characters	1243	1398	1397	1402	1393	1398
Words	239	266	265	266	264	265

For example, in Table 6, the entry "203 15%" in the row labeled "Nicolay" and the column labeled "Hay" means that the smallest number of character insertions, deletions, or replacements needed to change Nicolay into Hay or vice-

---

[5] *The percentage reported is the geometric mean of two ratios: the number of operations divided by the length of one text, and the number of operations divided by the length of the other text.*

versa is 206, which represents 15% of the length of the text. We list only the distances in the upper half-matrix, since those in the lower half are the same (that is, the distance between Hay and *AP* is the same as the distance between *AP* and Hay).

Table 6: Character-based edit distances between versions

	Hay	**AP**	**Hale**	**AP***	**Hale***
Nicolay	203	220	221	198	199
	15%	17%	17%	15%	15%
Hay		57	60	30	33
		4%	4%	2%	2%
AP			23	27	50
			2%	2%	4%
Hale				50	27
				4%	2%
AP*					23
					2%

Table 7: Word-based edit distances between versions

	Hay	**AP**	**Hale**	**AP***	**Hale***
Nicolay	51	60	59	54	53
	20%	24%	23%	21%	21%
Hay		21	21	14	14
		8%	8%	5%	5%
AP			12	7	19
			5%	3%	7%
Hale				19	7
				7%	3%
AP*					12
					5%

The third table, dealing with linguistic units, differs from the first two in two ways.

1. Linguistic units vary in length depending on the nature of the change, so it isn't possible to compute a percentage measure of the change.
2. We have not computed the changes between the original and modified versions of the transcriptions.

Table 8: Distances between versions based on linguistic units

	Hay	AP	Hale	AP*	Hale*
Nicolay	18	19	18	15	14
Hay		11	10	6	5
AP			7		
AP*					6

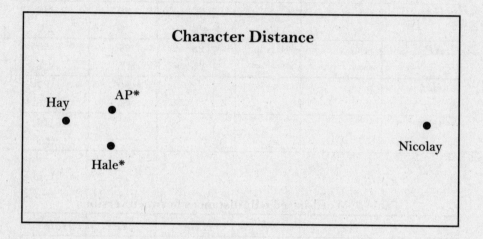

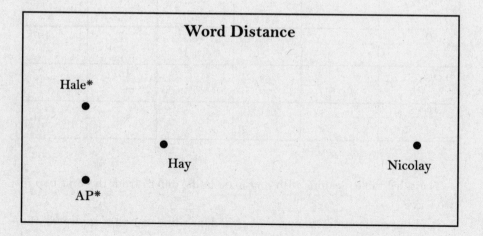

DOLLAR SIGNS

A Brief Look at the Monetary Afterlives
of the Five Versions of the Gettysburg Address

First Draft (Nicolay)

The First Draft of Lincoln's speech, often called the Nicolay Copy, has an adventurous post-creation history. Probably the president wrote the first part in Washington, with a pen, on Executive Mansion stationery, and the second part in pencil, at the Wills House in Gettysburg, on the evening of November 18. But we do not know for certain (see chapter 4). Lincoln's first secretary, John G. Nicolay, recalled in 1885 that he was with the president at the Wills House on the morning of the 19th, the day of the cemetery dedication, when he wrote out his speech. If this was the Second Draft, did Nicolay put away the no longer needed First Draft, so that it stayed in his possession until his death in 1901? Not very likely. Or did the First Draft stay with the Lincoln papers? Nicolay and Hay carefully packed up the papers in 1865, after the assassination, and Supreme Court Justice David Davis, overseeing the estate, had them locked away until 1874, when they went to Nicolay in Washington. The papers stayed with him until his death in 1901, but he shared them with Hay while the two worked on their ten-volume study of the Lincoln presidency. In 1885, we know, Nicolay wrote of the address that "the original ms. is now lying before my eyes." Nicolay's daughter, Helen, turned Lincoln's papers over to Hay upon her father's death, and inadvertently included the Gettysburg Address with them—and possibly the Second Draft as well. Thereafter, the manuscripts stayed hidden for years as Helen Nicolay, Robert Lincoln, and others searched in vain for the increasingly valuable documents. They had become part of Hay's collection; he already owned a copy of Lincoln's Second Inaugural Address, as well as Lincoln's secret 1864 memo that predicted his defeat in that year's presidential election. Hay thus had assembled a small collection that Martin P. Johnson, the finest scholar of the subject, says "in monetary and historical value, was perhaps the most important ever assembled." It is open to question what right, if any, Hay had to copies of the Gettysburg Address.

After his death in 1905, the whereabouts of the First Draft continued to remain unknown to the public even as news of the existence of the Second Draft surfaced. In 1916, at last, avoiding possible scandal, the Hay family presented both the First and Second drafts to the American people as represented by the Library of Congress. They have been there ever since, with a brief interlude during World War II when "the Gettysburg Address and the Second Inaugural found refuge in the Bullion Depository at Fort Knox, Kentucky."

Second Draft (Hay)

Lincoln wrote the Second Draft, also known as the Hay Copy, in ink on the same lined paper as the second page of the first draft, (see chapter 5). If so, this was the reading copy, though we cannot be fully certain about either matter. Nor do we know for certain how the manuscript ended up with Hay who, as Lincoln's young second secretary, was far from flattering about the speech in his diary: "The President, in a firm free way, with more grace than is his wont said his half dozen lines of consecration, and the music wailed and we went home through the crowded and cheering streets. And all the particulars are in the daily papers." It is possible that the manuscript of the speech came to Hay from Helen Nicolay with the other Lincoln papers, in 1901. The public did not know until 1909 that this version existed, when it was published for the first time in facsimile. Earlier, when Hay had been asked for a copy of the speech, he supplied the text Lincoln had sent to Alexander Bliss in 1864 for reproduction purposes. Along the way, various people attempted to buy the address, including one of the richest men of the time, the banker J. P. Morgan, who rarely failed to obtain what he wished for and reputedly offered the unheard-of sum of $50,000. That amount would have been "the highest price ever offered for a literary manuscript"—in today's dollars, close to $1 million, though any such calculation can only be inexact. Helen Hay Whitney, John's daughter, wrote in 1907 to manuscript dealer George Sidney Hellman that she was "surprised by the market value but its value to us is so much greater that there will never be now or at any other time, the slightest chance of it going into any other hands." Helen thus upheld the passionate commitment of her father, who wrote Robert Lincoln in 1888 (in all probability even before he possessed any copies of the address) that he owned a "few" Lincoln manuscripts, "which are very precious to me." These, he added, "I shall try to make an heirloom in my family as long as any of my blood exists with money enough to buy breakfast." Family heirlooms they remained until 1916, when the Hays made their gift to the Library of Congress. That institution has guarded the address jealously ever since.

New York Metropolitan Fair Copy (Everett)

After a copy of the Emancipation Proclamation brought the great sum of $3,000 for Chicago's Northwestern Sanitary Fair in the fall of 1863, the largest single figure obtained there for the support of Union soldiers, one could expect additional requests for Lincoln manuscripts. Some of the elite, who organized such fairs, found Lincoln's Gettysburg remarks beautiful, and indeed, Edward Everett and Mrs. Hamilton Fish requested a copy from the president for the New York Sanitary Fair. Lincoln obliged them, sending Everett a revised manuscript. Though the sale was advertised, no evidence exists that the item was sold. Much later, a $1,000 price surfaced. Why the speech did not sell remains uncertain (see chapter 6), but a Boston merchant who was an acquaintance of Everett's, Carlos Pierce, became the owner. After his death in 1870, his widow sold it to her sister-in-law, Mrs. Henry Keyes, and the document long remained in her family. The specifics of the financial transactions that occurred along the way are unknown. With the onset of the Great Depression in 1929, the owner at the time, Senator Henry Wilder Keyes of New Hampshire, sold it to a manuscript dealer, Thomas Madigan, for $100,000. "Before me as I write lies the most precious American manuscript, literary or historical—and it is both— which has not yet found its way into a public institution," wrote the exultant Madigan. Senator Keyes's son later remembered a little sadly that his father "reluctantly felt obliged to sell it because of the financial strains of many years of public service at a salary inadequate to meet the expenses expected of him." Madigan in turn sold it to a Chicago banker, James C. Ames, for $150,000. After Ames's death in 1943, his heirs offered the document to the Illinois State Historical Library for a modest $60,000. Under the leadership of the state's Superintendent of Public Instruction, Vernon L. Nickell, Illinois schoolchildren collected $50,000 and department store magnate Marshall Field added $10,000. The manuscript, together with what is likely to have been the text that Everett brought to Gettysburg, is now at the Abraham Lincoln Presidential Library.

Baltimore Sanitary Fair Copy, No. 1 (Bancroft)

Lincoln came to write the fourth copy of his speech for the same reason as the third, this time for the Baltimore Fair, held to raise money for soldiers. However, George Bancroft, who made the request for the manuscript, ended up keeping the copy. His stepson, Alexander Bliss, had originally returned the speech to the White House because, having been written on both sides of a sheet, it turned out to be unsuitable for reproduction in the *Autograph Leaves of Our Country's Authors*—the original reason for the request (see chapter 6). Bliss had hoped to give this copy to his stepfather, and wrote to Nicolay: "I therefore beg that you will *return it with the new copy.*" His wish was granted (see description of next copy). The document stayed in the Bancroft family until Cornell University professor Wilder D. Bancroft sold it in 1929 to Thomas Madigan for somewhere around $90,000–$100,000. The appraised value was $100,000. As the Great Depression deepened, Madigan had to sell for half the amount he had paid a few years earlier. "It is an American historical document of great value," he wrote to the Lincoln scholar Louis Warren, "that in better times would command a very high price." An Indianapolis dealer, Arthur Zinkin of the Meridian Bookshop, obtained the document in 1935, apparently on behalf of the wife of a former drug company executive of that city, Nicholas Noyes, and the couple presented it to Cornell University in 1949. There it remains to this day.

Baltimore Sanitary Fair Copy, No. 2 (Bliss)

When the first Baltimore Fair copy failed to serve the purpose Bancroft had intended, his stepson, Alexander Bliss, asked for still another copy and sent to the White House, at Secretary Nicolay's request, the ruled paper that Lincoln was to use so that the speech could be lithographed. Lincoln wrote out the speech and it arrived in Baltimore in good order. This was the only copy that, at the urging of his Baltimore correspondents, Lincoln dignified with a title: "Address delivered at the dedication of the cemetery at Gettysburg," a rare full signature, and the date: "November 19, 1863." It seems likely that the speech was not offered for sale at the Baltimore Fair; after all the president had been requested to make a copy for reproduction purposes and not for the selling of the actual manuscript. The Bancroft and Bliss families thus ended up with two copies.

This final draft, generally considered the standard text, remained in the Bliss family until 1949. Along the way, or so a story goes, Thomas Madigan offered $100,000 for this copy, too, but when he proceeded to examine the document with care, the owners felt insulted and refused to sell. The Bliss descendants did sell, finally, at a Parke-Bernet auction in 1949, and the draft was listed as "the most important American historical document ever offered for public sale" in the United States. Experts predicted a sale price "as high as $125,000," but times were lean, and the piece brought a disappointing $54,000. However, even that price set "a new high record for the sale of a document at public auction," according to the *New York Times*, although private sales had brought much larger sums. The promise that in time the document would go to a public institution in the United States accompanied its purchase by Cuban businessman Oscar Cintas, a former ambassador to Washington. After his death in 1957, the Castro government claimed Cintas's properties, but he had willed the Gettysburg Address to the people of the United States with the proviso that it should be kept at the White House. There it went in 1959, and there it remains to this day.

Forgeries

As the years went by and the value of historical documents increased, forgeries inevitably turned up. In 1963, David C. Mearns wrote from the Library of Congress to Ralph Newman, a Lincoln expert and the owner at the time of the Abraham Lincoln Bookshop in Chicago, that he had before him the "stats" of a "newly discovered" Gettysburg Address. First in the keeping of one John Carter, it was next consigned for sale at Sotheby's, and then turned up as the property of "Chris R. Ring, of Rome's Via degli Orti Flavani." Mearns was dubious about the document's authenticity. "I never confided my uneasiness to anyone else, but you chaps are different," he told Newman. In time, this "simulated" Gettysburg Address appears to have disappeared.

Manuscript dealers fantasize about discovering unknown copies of the address—the road to untold riches. Even scholars do—the road to new knowledge and fame. This author has done so too, in private, and confessed in an earlier note. Garry Wills's popular *Lincoln at Gettysburg* postulated that at one time another copy of the address may have existed, sent to Lincoln's Gettysburg host, David Wills. Wills did indeed ask for a copy, though no evidence exist that he ever received one, nor did he ever claim in his various reminiscences that he did; in fact, he appears to have directly denied anything of the sort. Edward McPherson, who knew Wills well, also categorically denied that Lincoln had sent a manuscript to his Gettysburg host.

Garry Wills had warned that if this text existed, "the hunt for it among his [DW's] papers is useless," but postulated the likelihood of such a draft. Then, even as he must have been researching and writing, one turned up—at least what purported to be the second page of the Gettysburg Address. The circumstances of the appearance of this document are mysterious.

On February 11, 1991, a respected Lincoln collector and artist, Lloyd Ostendorf, announced that he had obtained the second part of a newly discovered copy for which he had bartered some valuable items from his collection. The original owner refused to be identified and wags immediately declared that as soon as this new discovery was authenticated, the missing first page would turn up. That never happened, because in spite of various tests (some of which seemed favorable) and the fact that some esteemed people in the field, including the historian Frank Klement, appeared to accept the document as genuine, the scholarly consensus registered strong skepticism. When the Ostendorf estate was auctioned off, the document was excluded from the sales catalogue. Like its predecessors, it disappeared from public sight, though it remains on the private market.

Early in the twenty-first century, by which time less significant Lincoln documents, even important fragments are fetching seven figures, the value of a copy of the Gettysburg Address must be in the many millions. "Would it achieve a record price as the most valuable American manuscript or document sold?" one expert wondered aloud, and answered yes. "Would it eclipse the Da Vinci manuscript that [Bill] Gates paid over $30 million for? Probably." But we cannot expect to see the sacrilege of any of the five copies being put up for sale unless one of the revered institutions that owns them faces bankruptcy. In 2005, the earliest pamphlet printing of the address from the Forbes Collection sold for over $300,000 at Christie's. Two other copies repose in two old institutions, while a third copy disappeared from a venerable third library.

Every so often Lincoln scholars are brought copies of the address with request for authentication. The standard procedure is simple: Compare the newly discovered document against the facsimiles of the five copies Lincoln made—which are readily available from the Library of Congress on the Internet or in printed form. If the match is exact, the document is a forgery.

NOTES

ABBREVIATIONS

ACHS: Adams County Historical Society

ALPLM: Abraham Lincoln Presidential Library and Museum

CHP: Cornelia Hancock Papers, W. L. Clemens Library, University of Michigan, Ann Arbor

GC: Gettysburg College

GNMP: Gettysburg National Military Park

LM: Lincoln Museum, Fort Wayne, Indiana

LOC: Library of Congress

LP: Lincoln Papers, Library of Congress

MMMP: Michael Murray Miller Papers, Gilder Lehrman Collection on deposit at the New-York Historical Society

NA: National Archives

OR: *The War of the Rebellion: A Compilation of the Official Records of the Union and Confederate Armies*, 127 vols., index, and atlas (Washington: GPO, 1880–1901). Series 1, vol. 27, pt. 3

PSA: Pennsylvania State Archives

RG: Record Group

Preface

Page

1 *Ward Hill Lamon, Lincoln's friend:* Draft of Lamon's Reminiscences about the Gettysburg Address, c. 1885–86, Ward Hill Lamon Collection, LN 2442, folder 8, The Huntington Library, San Marino, Calif.; cf. Dorothy Lamon, ed., *Recollections of Abraham Lincoln by Ward Hill Lamon* (Chicago: McClurg, 1895), pp. 167–77; *Philadelphia Times*, Oct. 4, 1887; *Washington Critic*, Feb. 18, 1888.

1 *The eldest son of the president:* Robert Todd Lincoln to Bell F. Keys, December 16, 1885, in William E. Barton, *Lincoln at Gettysburg: What He*

Intended to Say; What He Said; What He Was Reported to Have Said; What He Wished He Had Said (Indianapolis: Bobbs, Merrill, 1930), p. 107.

2   *The Alabama-born writer:* The story first appeared in *Scribner's Magazine*, vol. 40, no. 1 (July 1906): 17–24, and frontispiece.

2   *Edward Everett tells Anson:* Louis A. Warren, *Lincoln's Gettysburg Declaration: "A New Birth of Freedom"* (Fort Wayne, IN: Lincoln National Life Foundation, 1964), pp. 61–63.

2   *At the other end looms:* Garry Wills, *Lincoln at Gettysburg: The Words That Remade America* (New York: Simon & Schuster, 1992).

2   *It is not surprising:* Warren wrote explicitly where others showed more circumspection. "It is regrettable," he commented in 1964 about *The Perfect Tribute,* "that American Youth for over half a century have received the impression that the finest oration in our language, was belatedly, hurriedly, and even slovenly written on a railroad train. The story is a travesty on how masterpieces are created"—*Lincoln's Gettysburg Declaration*, p. 63.

3   *David C. Mearns:* David C. Mearns, "Unknown at This Address," in Allan Nevins, ed., *Lincoln and the Gettysburg Address* (Urbana: University of Illinois Press, 1964), p. 133.

3   *Kent Gramm:* Kent Gramm, *November: Lincoln's Elegy at Gettysburg* (Bloomington: Indiana University Press, 2000), pp. 18, 121; cf. Edwin Black, "The Ultimate Voice of Lincoln," *Rhetoric and Public Affairs*, vol. 3, no. 1 (2000): 49–57.

3   *The novelist John Steinbeck:* John Steinbeck to Lyndon Baines Johnson, May 28, 1966, Lyndon Baines Johnson Presidential Library. I'm indebted to James A. Percoco for providing a copy of this letter.

4   *The sun comes out:* Sarah Sites Rogers, ed., *The Ties of the Past: The Gettysburg Diaries of Salome Myers Stewart, 1854–1922* (Gettysburg: Thomas, 1996), p. 154.

4   *A soldier will later add:* William Kepler, *Three Months' and Three Years' Service from April 16th, 1861, to June 22nd, 1864, of the Fourth Regiment of Ohio Volunteer Infantry in the War for the Union Service* (Cleveland: Leader, 1886), p. 132.

Chapter One: After Battle

Page

5   *A nurse writes of carcasses:* E.B.S. to My Dear ——, July 15, 1863, in Mrs. Edmund A. Souder, *Leaves from the Battle-field of Gettysburg. A Series of Letters from a Field Hospital and National Poems* (Philadelphia: Caxton

Press, 1864), p. 23 (cited hereafter as *Leaves*). We do not know the exact number of men present. The most respected study speaks of close to 164,000 in the two armies—John W. Busey and David G. Martin, *Regimental Strengths and Losses at Gettysburg*, 4th ed. (Hightstown, NJ: Longstreet House, 2005). However, this work does not take into account the non-combatant support personnel, a large number and mostly African-American in the Confederate army, and largely so in much more modest numbers in the Union army—Kent Masterson Brown, *Retreat from Gettysburg: Lee, Logistics, and the Pennsylvania Campaign* (Chapel Hill: University of North Carolina Press, 2005); Scott Hartwig to Boritt, Dec. 12, 2005; If we combine the 5,098 Union dead from *Regimental Strengths and Losses* with the 4,649 Confederate dead listed in Robert K. Krick, compiler, *The Gettysburg Death Roster: The Confederate Dead at Gettysburg* (Dayton, Ohio: Morningside, 1981), we arrive at 9,747 dead, still surely an understated number.

5 *The town took pride:* Pennsylvania College, long known as Gettysburg College and officially that since the early twentieth century.

7 *Disinfecting chloride of lime:* An old-fashioned historical term, chloride of lime is calcium hypochlorite, $Ca(OCL)_2$, containing chlorine, which makes the compound a disinfectant.

7 *The townspeople try "to extinguish":* E.B.S. to My Dear ——, July 15, 1863, in *Leaves*, p. 17; cf. F. M. Stoke to J. M. Stoke, Oct. 26, 1863, copy, Special Collections, Gettysburg College. It should be pointed out that these Notes mostly cite contemporary primary sources whenever possible since the book was created from them. The secondary sources, the work of historians, which also played a large role in creating this book, are acknowledged and discussed in the Bibliographical Note.

7 *Sarah Broadhead, a wife:* Sarah M. Broadhead, *The Diary of Lady of Gettysburg, Pennsylvania from June 15 to July 15, 1863* (n.p., [1864]), July 11, 1863), p. 22; cf. *Adams Sentinel*, Gettysburg, July 7, 1863, hereafter *Sentinel; Star & Banner*, Gettysburg, July 9, 1863, hereafter *Star*; Robert E. Housch, "The Gettysburg Civilians, 1860–1865, What Was Killing Them Before and After the Battle." Paper presented at the meeting of the Adams County Historical Society, Gettysburg, Pa., March 1, 2005.

7 *When strangers approach the town:* E.B.S. to My Dear——, July 15, 1863, in *Leaves*, p. 22; cf. Stoke to Stoke, Oct. 26, 1863; John B. Linn, "Journal of my trip to the battlefield at Gettysburg," July 7, 1863, Typescript, Hospitalization, Gettysburg National Military Park (hereafter GNMP).

7 *On July 13, the Broadheads' house:* Broadhead, *Diary of Lady*, July 13, 1863, p. 23.

7   *He wishes "the whole land":* M. Jacobs, "Later Rambles Over the Field of Gettysburg," *United States Service Magazine* 1 (January/February 1863): 66–67.

8   *"We had a severe trial":* G.R.F. to Editor [father], July 10, 1863, in *Lewistown Gazette,* July 15, 1863. Frysinger served in the 36th Pennsylvania Emergency Militia.

8   *"The whole town":* EWF (Eliza W. Farnham) to Mrs. Kirby, July 7, 1863, in *Santa Cruz (Calif.) Common Sense,* Aug. 22, 1874; Diary of William Quesenbury Claytor, July 1863, North American Women's Letters and Diaries, www.alexanderstreet2.com/nwldlive/.

9   *Newspapers that seem loath: Philadelphia Public Ledger,* July 15, 1863.

9   *Looking back in September 1863:* U.S. Christian Commission, *Second Report of the Committee of Maryland, Sept. 1, 1863* (cited hereafter as *Christian Commission Report*), U.S. Christian Commission Records, National Archives, Washington, DC, hereafter NA.

9   *The more measured tones:* Report of Edward P. Vollum to William A. Hammond, July 25, 1863, U.S. War Department, *The War of the Rebellion: Official Records of the Union and Confederate Armies,* 127 vols. (Washington, DC: Government Printing Office, 1881–1901, hereafter as OR), 27:1, 28. All references are to Series 1, unless otherwise noted.

9   *Jonathan Letterman, the medical director:* Report of Jon. A. Letterman to S. Williams, Oct. 3, 1863, OR, 27:1, 195–96.

10   *Even as the fighting went on:* Mrs. John Harris to Mrs. J[oel Jones], July 2, 1863, in *Fifth Semi-Annual Report of the Ladies' Aid Society of Philadelphia with Letters and Extracts from Letters from the Secretary of the Society. . . .* (Philadelphia: Sherman, 1863, hereafter *Letters*), p. 12.

10   *Crimsoned it was:* Jonathan Letterman, M.D., *Medical Recollections of the Army of the Potomac* (New York: Appleton, 1866), p. 157. The one exception was Dr. John McNully, the medical director of the Twelfth Corps, who disobeyed orders (or never received them) and so was much better prepared.

10   *"It was absolutely necessary":* George G. Meade to L. Montgomery Bond, April 8, 1864, *Sanitary Commission Bulletin,* April 15, 1864, 369.

10   *"What! Take away surgeons":* Andrew B. Cross, *Battle of Gettysburg and the Christian Commission* (Baltimore, n.p., 1865), pp. 15, 16, NA.

10   *A distraught Ohio army doctor:* H[arry] M[McKindree] McAbee to Edwin Stanton, n.d., in Kepler, *Three Months' and Three Years' Service,* p. 193.

10   *The official medical report:* Report of Jon A. Letterman to S. Williams, Oct. 3, 1863, OR, 27:1, 198.

11   *As for Dr. McAbee:* War Department Special Order No. 415; CMSR
      (Compiled Military Service Record) of Harry McKindree McAbee,
      NA; Ronald R. Maust, *Grappling with Death: The Union Second Corps
      Hospital at Gettysburg* (Dayton, OH: Morningside, 2001), pp. 779,
      900–09. Maust's work informs this chapter.

11   *Lee's medical director:* L[afayette]. Guild to Med[ical]. Directors Office
      [John M. Cuyler, Hunter McGuire, J. W. Powell], ANVa, July 3, 1863,
      War Department Collection of Confederate Records, Ch. VI, vol. 641,
      Medical Department, Letters Sent, Medical Director's Office, Army of
      Northern Virginia, 1862–63, NA. The letter is misplaced between two
      July 10 items; cf. A. N. Dougherty, July 5, 1863, quoted in Maust, *Grap-
      pling with Death*, pp. 334–35. Brown makes a case for what the Confed-
      erate army did. Cf. *Richmond Daily Dispatch*, Sept. 30, 1863.

11   *One of the Gettysburg papers: Star*, July 30; also *Sentinel*, July 18, 1863.
      The actual number of Confederate wounded left behind came to nearly
      7,000.

11   *But the Sanitary Commission's report:* Gordon Winslow to J. H. Douglas,
      July 22, 1863; J. H. Douglas, Aug. 22, 1863, in *Report of the Operations of
      the Sanitary Commission During the Battles of Gettysburg* (New York:
      William C. Bryant, 1863), pp. 21–22, 24.

11   *Christian Commission delegates digging: Christian Commission Report*,
      pp. 21, 107; cf. Report of John M. Cuyler to William H. Hammond, July
      27, 1863, OR, 27:1, 24.

12   *When Nurse Harris:* Harris to Mrs. J., *Letters*, p. 12.

12   *"How many volunteer surgeons":* Hammond to Curtin, July 5, 1863; cf. J. R.
      Smith to John M. Cuyler, July 6, 1863, RG112, Entry 7, Vol. 4, Letters
      and Endorsements Sent to Medical Officers ("Military Letters"), NA.

12   *General Robert C. Schenck:* OR, 27:3, 504.

12   *"The army has left Gettysburg":* Farnham to Kirby, July 7, 1863.

12   *On July 9, Nurse Harris:* Harris to Husband, July 9, 1863, *Letters*,
      p. 13.

12   *As disaster engulfed Gettysburg: Philadelphia Inquirer*, July 6, 1863;
      Lutheran Observer, Aug. 21, 1863.

12   *When civilian doctors finally:* Report of John M. Cuyler to William A.
      Hammond, July 27, 1863, OR, 27:3, 25.

12   *By October, however:* Report of Jon. A. Letterman to S. Williams, Octo-
      ber 3, 1863, ibid., 197.

12   *Reverend Henry Bellows, head:* Bellows to William A. Hammond, quoted in
      William Quentin Maxwell, *Lincoln's Fifth Wheel: The Political History of
      the United States Sanitary Commission* (New York: Longmans, 1956), p. 211.

13   *To his own people:* Henry W. Bellows to Frederick L. Olmstead, July 8, 1863, ibid.

13   *A friend would later note:* Farnham to Kirby, July 7, 1863.

13   *"I never saw men":* John M. Cuyler to William A. Hammond, July 27, 1863, OR, 27:3, 25. Lacking knowledge of bacteriology and antisepsis, surgeons were fighting a losing battle.

13   *A nurse would write:* Cornelia Hancock to Mother, Aug. 17, 1863, Cornelia Hancock Papers, W. L. Clements Library, University of Michigan, Ann Arbor (cited hereafter as CHP). Hancock's letters are reproduced less than accurately in Henrietta Stratton Jaquette, ed., *South After Gettysburg: Letters of Cornelia Hancock from the Army of the Potomac, 1863–1865* (Philadelphia, University of Pennsylvania Press, 1937), and though this book cites the manuscripts, endnotes also refer to the Jaquette edition for easy access.

13   *One doctor recorded in his diary:* John H. Brinton Diary, July 5, 1863, D.G. Brinton Thompson, ed., "From Chancellorsville to Gettysburg," *Pennsylvania Magazine of History and Biography* 89 (July 1965): 313.

13   *"Anxiety is constant":* J. H. Douglas, Aug. 22, 1863, *Operations of the Sanitary Commission,* p. 25.

13   *"Language as profane":* Christian Commission Report, pp. 33, 34; cf. Stoke to Stoke, Oct. 26, 1863.

14   *Robert G. Harper:* J. D. Bongless, et al. to H. W. Raymond, July 11, 1863, in *Sentinel,* July 14, 1863.

14   *Men helped, too:* Fanny Buehler, "Recollections of the Great Rebel Invasion and One Woman's Experience during the Battle of Gettysburg," manuscript copy, p. 17, ACHS.

14   *The Christian Commission report later: Christian Commission Report,* p. 22.

14   *"Never did we see men":* Cross, *Christian Commission,* p. 19.

14   *When the battle arrived:* H. J. Watkins, "Gettysburg War Incidents," *The Spectrum* (Gettysburg College, 1902): 182.

14   *Old Dorm was hit: Philadelphia Public Ledger,* July 7, 17, 1863; *Lutheran Observer,* July 31, 1863; "College Hospital in Gettysburg," *Land We Love,* 2 (February 1867): 290–94; Davis Garber to P[hilip] M. Bikle, March 5, 1877, *Pennsylvania College Monthly* 1 (December 1877): 297.

14   *In the Baugher home: Lutheran Observer,* July 31, 1863.

15   *Nurse Emily Souder spoke:* E.B.S. to My Dear ——, July 15, 1863, *Leaves,* pp. 14–15.

15   *When Sally Myers was called: Salome Myers Stewart Diaries,* p. 152 (July 2, 1863). Since my son, Jake Boritt's, documentary film *Adams County, USA* also has this scene, I should add that he found it first.

15   *Sarah Broadhead also kept a diary:* Broadhead, *Diary of Lady*, July 5, 7, 13, 1863, pp. 17, 19, 23.

15   *Nurse Sophronia Bucklin watched:* Sophronia E. Bucklin, *In Hospital and Camp: A Woman's Record of Thrilling Incidents. With an Introduction by* S.L.C. (Philadelphia: Potter, 1869), pp. 156–57.

15   *The* Compiler *later reported: Compiler*, Gettysburg, Aug. 17, 1863. Cross, *Christian Commission*, p. 26, appears to report on the same woman.

15   *The newspaper wrote of potions: Compiler*, Aug. 10, 1863.

16   *Visiting Nurse Cornelia Hancock:* Hancock to Cousin, July 7, 1863; Hancock to Sister, July 8, 1863, CHP; also in Jaquette, ed., *South After Gettysburg*, pp. 7–8, 12.

16   *"The sights and sounds":* E.B.S. to Mary C——, July 16; to Mrs. J. Heulings, July 16; to Brother, July 20; to Sister, July 22; to Friends, July 22; to Brother, July 29, 1863, in *Leaves*, pp. 23, 26, 36, 43, 42, 63–64.

16   *Professor Jacobs would write:* Jacobs, "Later Rambles Over the Field of Gettysburg," p. 168.

16   *Writing to wives:* Hancock to Cousin, July 7, 1863; CHP, also in Jacquette, ed., *South After Gettysburg*, p. 8.

16   *He could "take a man's leg off":* Ohio surgeon quoted in *Leaves*, p. 13.

16   *Nurse Souder managed:* E.B.S. to Mary C——, July 16, 1863, ibid., p. 26.

17   *In the midst of the horror:* D.A.W. to R. G. Harper, July 9, 1863, *Sentinel*, July 21, 1863.

17   *"Uncle Sam is very rich":* Hancock to Sister, July 8, 1863; CHP; also in Jacquette, ed., *South After Gettysburg*, p. 9.

17   *As strong Mary Livermore:* Mary Livermore, *My Story of the War* (Hartford, CT: Worthington, 1891), p. 130; Bellows quote at p. 128.

18   *Its workers, the "angels":* [Georgeanna Woolsey], *Three Weeks at Gettysburg* (New York: Anson D. F. Randolph, 1863), p. 7.

18   *"Refrigerating cars":* Charles J. Stille, *History of the United States Sanitary Commission* (Philadelphia: Lippincott, 1866), pp. 379, 381.

18   *"Lee's army had taken": Christian Commission Report*, pp. 35–36; *Indianapolis Daily Journal*, July 23, 1863.

18   *As one medical director told:* Hancock to Sister, Aug. 31, 1863, CHP; also in Jacquette, ed., *South After Gettysburg*, p. 24.

18   *The Sanitary Commission's Reverend Bellows: New York Times*, July 16, 1863.

18   *In private, however:* George Templeton Strong, *Diary of the Civil War*, Allan Nevins and Milton Halsey Thomas, eds. (New York: Macmillan, 1962), pp. 589, 311.

19 *"From this source":* Christian Commission Report, p. 59; George E. Leakin's report, pp. 77; 42; W. B. Canfield's report, p. 94.

19 *One delegate wrote:* ibid., p. 107; cf. Edward P. Smith, *Incidents Among Shot and Shell. The Only Authentic Work Extant Giving the Many Tragic and Touching Incidents that Came Under the Notice of the United States Christian Commission During the Long Years of the Civil War* (n.p.: Edgewood, 1868), pp. 159–89; the book was also published under the title *Incidents of the United States Christian Commission* (Philadelphia: Lippincott, 1869).

19 *The townspeople felt that:* Sentinel, July 21, 1863.

19 *"Whoever aids them":* Broadhead, *Diary of Lady,* July 9, 1863, p. 21.

19 *"Blessed, pure, angelic":* Compiler, Oct. 6, 1863.

19 *When Reverend Bellows arrived:* Chelsea Telegraph and Pioneer, March 5, 1864. Later, someone remembered evidently the same barn and noticed "with horror, as I assisted at the dressing of a bleeding wound, that the blood of the patient filtered through the cracks and knot-holes of the floor and dripped upon the sufferers below"—H. S. Peltz, "Two Brass Buttons," *Compiler,* March 15, 1887. Peltz's recollection, however, contains many errors.

20 *When the floods came:* Charles H. Merrick to wife, July 10, 1863, William P. Palmer Collection, Western Reserve Historical Society, Cleveland, Ohio.

20 *Later, the official report:* Justin Dwinelle, Final Report of Wounded in Second Corps Hospital, Aug. 10, 1863, copy, Union Field Hospital Vertical File, GNMP.

20 *"I fear I should be very hard":* Charles S. Wainwright, *A Diary of Battle—The Personal Journals of Col. Charles S. Wainwright—1861–1865,* Allan Nevins, ed. (New York: Harcourt, Brace, 1962), p. 253.

20 *One young rebel officer:* Woolsey, *Three Weeks at Gettysburg,* pp. 16, 10.

20 *They generally did:* M. Jacobs, "The Battle of Gettysburg," *Evangelical Review* 15 (1864): 243.

20 *One visitor overheard:* Cross, *Christian Commission,* p. 20. Cf. *Report of the General Agent of the State of New York for the Relief of Sick, Wounded, Furloughed and Discharged Soldiers* (Albany, Comstock, 1864), 47–49.

20 *A visitor from New Hampshire:* Joseph H. Foster, "Visit to the Battlefield, July 26, 1863," in Michael J. Birkner and Richard E. Winslow III, eds., *Adams County History,* 11 (2005): 41–42.

21 *Nurse Hancock felt relieved:* Hancock to Sallie, Aug. 8, 1863, CHP; also in Jaquette, ed., *South After Gettysburg,* p. 17.

21   *Nurse Broadhead was happy:* Broadhead, *Diary of Lady*, July 11, 1863, p. 22.

21   *And Nurse Souder noted:* E.B.S. to My Dear ——, July 15; to Mrs. S. F. Ashton, July 27, 1863; to Margaret, July 20, 1863, *Leaves*, pp. 17, 59, 34.

21   *They got equal treatment:* Woolsey, *Three Weeks at Gettysburg*, p. 23.

21   *With the Patriot Daughters:* The Patriot Daughters of Lancaster, *Hospital Scenes After the Battle of Gettysburg* (Philadelphia: Henry B. Ashmead, 1864), p. 28.

21   *One could sense:* Woolsey, *Three Weeks at Gettysburg*, p. 23.

21   *Rebs would report:* Joseph T. Durkin, ed., *John Dooley, Confederate Soldier; His War Journal* (Washington, DC: Georgetown University Press, 1945), p. 111; cf. Decimus et Ultimus Barziza, *Adventures of a Prisoner of War, 1863–1864* (Austin: University of Texas Press, 1964), p. 54; *Christian Commission Report*, p. 29; Edmund J. Raus, Jr., ed., *Ministering Angel: The Reminiscences of Harriet A. Dada, a Union Army Nurse in the Civil War* (Gettysburg: Thomas, 2004), p. 34.

21   *"Sixty or seventy rebel officers":* *Sentinel*, Sept. 15, 1863.

21   *One reb with the unforgettable name:* Barziza, *Adventures*, p. 58.

22   *A visiting pastor recounted:* L. O. Sloan to G. S. Griffith, July 22, 1863, *German Reformed Messenger*, July 29, 1863.

22   *The scene was common:* E. W. Hutter, "Four Days Spent on the Battlefields of Gettysburg," *Star*, July 30, 1863; cf. L. O. Sloan to [G. S.] Dr. Griffith, n.d., *Lutheran Observer*, Aug. 14, 1863; Frank B. Nickerson to Kepler, n.d., in Kepler, *Three Months' and Three Years' Service*, pp. 193–94.

22   *Then there was the rebel lieutenant:* Durkin, ed., *John Dooley*, pp. 119–20; cf. Smith, *Incidents Among Shot and Shell*, pp. 176–89.

22   *Union and Confederate soldiers lying:* E.B.S. to Mrs. J. Huelings, July 16; to Margaret, July 20; to Friends, July 22, 1863, *Leaves*, pp. 24, 36, 47–48.

22   *Though the attempt was made:* Cross, *Christian Commission*, p. 28.

22   *Nurse Harris claimed:* Harris to Mrs. J., July 10, 1863, *Letters*, pp. 13–14.

22   *After one of these young nurses:* [Mrs. R. P. McCormick], *The Banishment of Miss Euphemia Goldsborough, Looking Back to the Days of 1863* (n.p., n.d. [1898?]), p. 2, Typescript, GNMP.

22   *Another woman would write of:* Jane Boswell Moore, "An Incident at Gettysburg," *Christian Commission Report*, pp. 104–05.

23   *Would that we:* Jane Boswell Moore to G.S. Griffith, et al., Aug. 1863, *Lutheran Observer*, Sept. 25, 1863.

23   *Cornelia Hancock wrote to her sister:* Hancock to Sister, July 8, 1863; Hancock to Mother, July 26, Aug. 14, 1863, CHP; also in Jaquette, ed., *South*

After Gettysburg, pp. 11, 15, 18; cf. Mrs. Edwin Price letter, n.d., *Christian Commission Report,* 98; E.B.S. to Dear Friends, July 22; to Margaret, July 20, 1863, *Leaves,* pp. 51, 38; Broadhead, *Diary of Lady,* July 7, 1863, p. 19.

23   *At summer's end, their great adventure:* Bucklin, *In Hospital and Camp,* pp. 192–93.

23   *One woman would remember:* Harriet Bayly, "A Woman's Story," *Star & Sentinel,* Sept. 25, 1888.

23   *Nurse Woolsey reported that children:* Woolsey, *Three Weeks at Gettysburg,* p. 14.

23   *The Democratic proprietors: Sentinel,* July 14; *Star,* July 20, 1863. See also *Compiler,* July 13, 20, 27, Aug. 17, Oct. 9, 1865; *Sentinel,* July 21, Aug. 11, 1863; *Star,* July 16, 23, Aug. 13, 1863; Mrs. Tillie (Pierce) Alleman, *At Gettysburg or What a Girl Saw and Heard of the Battle. A True Narrative* (New York: W. Lake Borland, 1889; 1994 reprint by Butternut and Blue), p. 26; David S. Sparks, ed., *Inside Lincoln's Army: The Diary of Gen. Marsena Rudolph Patrick, Provost Marshall General, Army of the Potomac* (New York: Yoseloff, 1964), pp. 268–69; cf. John C. Wills, "Reminiscences of the Three Days Battle of Gettysburg at the 'Globe Hotel,' " p. 26, GNMP.

24   *Josephine Forney:* Josephine Forney Roedel Diary, LOC.

24   *One report in the* Sentinel: "Touching Incident of the Battle-Field," *Sentinel,* July 28, 1863.

24   *The other Republican paper: Star,* Aug. 6, 1863.

24   *The issue of the* Sentinel: *Sentinel,* July 28, 1863.

24   *One Virginia colonel:* William S. Christian to wife, [July 1863], in Frank Moore, ed., *The Rebellion Record: A Diary of American Events,* 12 vols. (New York: Putnam, 1861–63; Van Nostrand, 1864–68), 7:325; *Pittsburgh Evening Chronicle,* July 28, 1863. The original of the Christian letter does not exist and so its reliability can be questioned.

25   *Victims or their descendants:* Gettysburg Claim Files, NA; summary copies at GNMP, which also has a summary of Pennsylvania claims.

25   *When Mrs. Leister returned:* J. T. Trowbridge, "The Field of Gettysburg," *Atlantic Monthly* (November 1865): 623.

26   *In town, one young woman: Sentinel,* July 7, 1863.

26   *He became famous: Harper's Weekly,* Aug. 22, 1863.

26   *People said that the Reserves': Star,* July 9, 16; *Sentinel,* July 14, 1863; *Compiler,* July 13, Aug. 3, 1863; *New York Times,* July 14, 1863. And people never quite gave up the claim: Crawford to T. T. Locke, July 10, 1863, *OR,* 27:1, pp. 653; Crawford to J. W. Fisher, Dec. 22, 1863; Crawford to

M. Jacobs, Dec. 1863, Samuel Wylie Crawford Papers, No. 3, LOC; H. N. Minnigh, *History of Company K. 1st (Inft,) Penn'a Reserves* (Duncansville, PA: Home Print, 1891), 1:25; S. M. Jackson in John P. Nicholson, et al., eds., *Pennsylvania at Gettysburg: Ceremonies at the Dedication of the Monuments Erected by the Commonwealth of Pennsylvania*, 2 vols. (Harrisburg, PA: Ray, 1904), 1:73, 112, 258, 279.

26   *The newspapers told their story: Star*, July 16; *Compiler*, Aug. 3, 1863.

26   *He described how for two endless days:* M. Jacobs, *Notes on the Rebel Invasion of Maryland and Pennsylvania and the Battle of Gettysburg. . . .* (Philadelphia: Lippincott, 1864), p. 37.

27   *Jacobs overheard rebel soldiers':* Ibid.

27   *Their boys fought: Star*, July 16, also Aug. 6; *Compiler*, Aug. 3, 1863.

27   *At the hospitals, people talked:* Emily [Souder] to Mrs. S. F. Ashton, July 27, 1863, in *Leaves*, p. 60.

27   *The newspapers listed: Star*, July 9; *Sentinel*, July 14; *Compiler*, July 20, 1863. All three newspapers reported the exact same words. Hamilton, in fact, did not lose his leg.

27   *"An amiable youth": Compiler*, Aug. 3; *Sentinel*, July 28, 1863. McGrew Pension File, NA. The Pension File erroneously dates McGrew's death to August 26. Listing him as nineteen years old, the 1860 Census also calls into question the precise age as reported at McGrew's death.

27   *A poem appeared: Sentinel*, Aug. 25, 1863; see also *Star*, Aug. 27, 1863. The initials N.N.N. identified the author. The only living member of the company whose name began with an "N" was Private Wilson E. Nailor (Naylor), musician. Did he write the poem? He had signed up in 1861 at age sixteen pretending to be nineteen. Wounded in the battle, after the war he became a dentist—Minnigh, *History of Company K*, p. 31; Pension File of Wilson A. Nailor, NA.

28   *If the town suffered:* For a sample of the censure, see *New York Times*, July 7, 9; *Philadelphia Daily Evening Bulletin*, July 9; *New York Herald*, July 10.

28   *The visitor who spoke:* Trowbridge, "The Field of Gettysburg," p. 623.

28   *Even the charitable Christian Commission: Christian Commission Report*, p. 25.

28   *One reporter complained: Indianapolis Daily Journal*, July 23, 1863, p. 2.

28   *One officer became so disgusted:* Wainwright, *A Diary of Battle*, p. 254.

29   *Nurse Woolsey called local farmers:* Woolsey, *Three Weeks at Gettysburg*, p. 13.

29   *Even a local paper: Star*, Sept 3, 1863. "Dutch" is a corruption of the word *Deutsch*, meaning "German."

29   *To one visitor, "the appearance":* Cross, *Christian Commission*, p. 25.

29   *People came "in Swarms":* Sparks, ed., *Inside Lincoln's Army*, p. 268.

29   *A New York reporter wrote: New York Herald,* July 8, 1863.

29   *A minister watched "a young lad":* Sloan to Griffith, n.d. [August 1863].

29   *At one point, General Schenck: Christian Commission Report,* p. 38.

29   *Later, one men would recall:* Nathaniel Lightner account; Provost Guards Diary, GNMP; "In the Hospitals of Gettysburg, July, 1863," *Harrisburg Telegraph,* Sept. 16, 20, 1907; *Personal Memoirs of John H. Brinton, Civil War Surgeon,* foreword by John Y. Simon (Carbondale: Southern Illinois University Press, 1996 [completed 1891]), pp. 243–44.

29   *Gettysburg was raked over: New York Times,* July 9, 1863; cf: *New York Times,* July 1, 4, 1863; *Philadelphia Inquirer,* July 3, 11, 1863; *Lancaster Daily Express,* Pa, July 10, 13, 1863; *Philadelphia North American,* July 10, 1863; *New York Herald,* July 10, 1863; *Boston Evening Transcript,* July 14, 1863; *New York Tribune,* July 17, 1863; *Pottsville Miners' Journal,* Aug. 15, 1863. See also: William Watson letter, July 7, 1863, in Paul Fatout, ed., *Letters of a Civil War Surgeon* (West Lafayette, Ind.: Purdue University Studies, 1961), p. 70; John West Haley, July 6, 1863, in Ruth L. Silliker, ed., *The Rebel Yell & Yankee Hurrah: The Civil War Journal of a Maine Volunteer* (Camden, Me.: Down East Books, 1985), p. 108; Charles Francis Adams, Jr. to John Quincy Adams, July 12, 1863, in Worthington Chauncey Ford, ed., *A Cycle of Adams Letters* (2 vols., Boston: Houghton Mifflin, 1920), 2:45; Wainright, *Diary,* pp. 228–30, 254, 256, 259; Dunn Brown [Samuel W. Fiske] to *Springfield Republican,* MA, July 13, 1863, in Stephen W. Sears, ed., *Mr. Dunn Browne's Experiences in the Army: The Civil War Letters of Samuel W. Fiske* (New York: Fordham University Press, 1998), pp. 119–20; "Field of Gettysburg," pp. 616–17.

30   Harper's Weekly *added insult to injury: Harper's Weekly,* July 11, 1863.

30   *The people of Gettysburg: Sentinel,* July 21, 1863.

30   *"Ignorant, drunken": Star,* July 16, 1863.

30   *A "card of thanks":* Ibid., July 30, Aug. 20, 1863. And see for example *Sentinel,* July 14, 16, Aug. 4, 11, 18; *Star,* Aug. 8, 20; cf. *Brooklyn Eagle,* July 15; *Lutheran and Missionary,* July 16; *Philadelphia Public Ledger,* July 17; *National Republican,* July 18; *New York Times,* July 18, 24, 27; *New York Tribune,* July 24; *Chicago Tribune,* July 21; *Sunday School Times,* Philadelphia, July 25; *Lutheran Observer,* July 31, 1863; *Christian Recorder,* Aug. 15; John F. Seymour to Editor of the *Utica Morning Herald,* n.d., *Sanitary Commission Report,* Nov. 1, 1863, 43–44; "Four

Days at Gettysburg," *Harper's New Monthly Magazine,* 165 (Feb. 1864), 387–88.

30   *Still, when Lorenzo Crounse: Sentinel,* July 11, 1865.

30   *Crounse would backtrack enough: New York Times,* July 10, 1865.

30   *The rival* New York Tribune: *New York Tribune,* July 6, 1865.

30   *If Gettysburg received some:* Broadhead, *Diary of Lady,* July 13, 1863, p. 23.

30   *After battle, Gettysburg:* F. M. Stoke to J. M. Stoke, Oct. 26, 1863.

Chapter Two: Rebirth

Page

31   *"A splendid Camp":* Hancock to Sally, Aug. 8; to niece, Aug. 31, 1863, CHP; also in Jaquette, ed., *South After Gettysburg,* pp. 17, 24; "A Young Quakeress Goes to War," p. 4.

31   *"A beautiful spot":* Cross, *Christian Commission,* p. 19.

31   *"a thing of wonder":* G. Winslow to L. H. Steiner, Sept 25, 1863, *Operations of the Sanitary Commission.*

31   *"You little know":* "A Soldier" to Hancock, July 21, 1863, CHP; also in Jaquette, ed., *South After Gettysburg,* p. 13.

31   *"It is wonderful how the eyes":* E.B.S. to Mrs. Margaret Souder, July 20, 1863; cf. E.B.S. to Mrs. M. L. Thacher, July 22, 1863, Souder, *Leaves,* pp. 34, 49; Diary of E[uphemia] Mary Goldsborough, typescript, GNMP.

31   *It did no harm:* Hancock to Sallie, Aug. 8, 1863, CHP; also in Jaquette, ed., *South After Gettysburg,* p. 4.

32   *"When This Cruel War":* Woolsey, *Three Weeks at Gettysburg,* p. 7.

32   *At the end of July, Eliza Jane Miller:* Eliza Jane (Lile) Miller to Michael Murray Miller, July 30, 1863, Michael Murray Miller Papers, Gilder Lehrman Collection, on deposit at the New-York Historical Society (cited hereafter as MMMP). This collection of papers represents half of the surviving correspondence between the couple, with the other half in private hands and unavailable.

33   *"sad pathos in the voices":* Patriot Daughters, *Hospital Scenes,* 32.

33   *But by the second half of July:* Sloan to Griffith, July 29, 1863; John Rupp to sister, July 19, 1863, Adams County Historical Society: "we had no Sunday services."

33   *They cooked for the wounded:* Woolsey, *Three Weeks at Gettysburg,* pp. 6–7, 18–19.

34   *The Christian Commission reported: Christian Commission Report,* pp. 19, 26.

34 *"It was a grand sight"*: Operations of the Sanitary Commission, p. 18.

34 *Yet when they left:* Miller to Miller, Aug. 16, 1863, MMMP; cf. Annie Sheads to Mary Corwin, March 4, 1864, GNMP: "Our town is quite dull this winter."

34 *"A person is just like a slave"*: Miller to Miller, Sept. 8, 1863.

34 *In September, the "noble"*: Sentinel, Sept. 22, 1863.

34 *Nurse Hancock had left by then:* Hancock to Mother, Sept, 1863; W.H.H. to Hancock, Sept. 28, 1863, CHP; also in Jaquette, ed., *South After Gettysburg*, pp. 24, 26.

34 *Patriotic designs and evergreens:* Sentinel, Sept. 22, 1863.

35 *After a "bright and balmy day"*: Mrs. H. [Mrs. William H. Holstein (Anna Morris Ellis)], *Three Years in Field Hospitals of the Army of the Potomac* (Philadelphia: Lippincott, 1867), p. 50.

35 *A "fantastically dressed company"*: Sentinel, Sept. 22, 29, 1863; Nurse Dada's reminiscences, based on her contemporary letters, spoke of the party as "a great day" for the soldiers, "long to be remembered by all"— Raus, Jr., ed., *Ministering Angel*, p. 36.

35 *"appeal from the ballot to the bullet"*: To James C. Conkling, Aug. 26, 1863, in Roy P. Basler, ed., Marion Dolores Pratt and Lloyd A. Dunlap, asst. eds., *The Collected Works of Abraham Lincoln*, 9 vols., 2 suppl. vols. (New Brunswick, NJ: Rutgers University, 1953–55, 1974, 1990), 6:410. Hereafter *Collected Works of Lincoln*.

35 *"Forcible and Characteristic"*: Sentinel, Sept. 8, 1863; *Star*, Sept. 10, 1863; *Compiler*, Sept. 14, 1863.

35 *A few weeks later, the* Star: *Star*, Sept. 24, 1863.

36 *David McConaughy proposed:* Sentinel, July 28, 1863.

36 *Now he also suggested:* C. P. Krauth, H. L. Baugher, etc., to D. McConaughy, Aug. 18, 1863, McConaughy Papers, Gettysburg College Library; *Sentinel*, Sept. 8, 1863; cf. Sept. 15; *Star*, Sept. 17, 1863.

36 *"The heart sickened"*: "The National Cemetery," *Report Soldiers' National Cemetery*, p. 63.

36 *Skulls "kicked around"*: Stoke to Stoke, Oct. 26, 1863.

36 *"And this, too, on Pennsylvania"*: "The National Cemetery," *Soldiers' National Cemetery*, p. 62.

36 *Public appeals ensued:* Andrew Cross to the Patriotic of the Land, July 25, 1863, in Andrew B. Cross, *The War. Battle of Gettysburg and the Christian Commission* (n.p., 1865), p. 60. This publication binds together two pamphlets.

36 *The idea "suggested itself"*: "The National Cemetery," in *Report of the Select Committee Relative to the Soldiers' National Cemetery, Together with the*

Accompanying Documents, as Reported to the House of Representatives of the Commonwealth of Pennsylvania, March 31, 1864 (Harrisburg: Singerly & Myers, 1864), p. 63. Hereafter *Soldiers' National Cemetery.*

36 *a "happy inspiration of patriotism":* Newark Daily Mercury, N.J., Nov. 16, 1863.

37 *To design the burying grounds:* Ibid.

37 *He was "at the head":* Compiler, Oct. 5, 1863.

38 *and obtained the support:* David Wills to Andrew Curtin, Aug. 17, 1863, *Soldiers' National Cemetery,* p. 67.

38 *In Gettysburg, Saunders would shape:* Wills to Curtin, Aug. 17, 1863, *Soldiers' National Cemetery,* p. 67.

38 *By mid-October, the people: Star,* Oct. 15, 1863; see also Oct. 8; *Compiler,* Oct. 19, 1863. The *Philadelphia Inquirer,* Oct. 13, 1863, published Wills's description of the program, which was identical to what actually took place, with Lincoln included. The major exception was the poet Longfellow who, in the end, must have demurred.

38 *As late as November 16:* A. Curtin to Morton McMichael, Nov. 16, 1863, Andrew Curtin Papers, Pennsylvania State Archives. Hereafter PSA. Actually the letter ends with the words "the President will go direct by Baltimore." But other evidence makes clear that Lincoln was not certain about going until two days before the event (see chapter 4) and so the last part of the sentence remains unquoted to avoid suggesting that the Baltimore route was in question.

38 *"It is doubtful whether":* Everett to Wills, Sept. 26, 1853, *Soldiers' National Cemetery,* p. 69; Everett to Wills, Oct. 2, 1863, copy, GNMP.

39 *"An ode or dirge": Star,* Oct. 15, 1863.

39 *The poet was interested:* Henry Wadsworth Longfellow to George Washington Greene, Nov. 12, 1863, in Andrew Hilen, ed., *The Letters of Henry Wadsworth Longfellow,* 4 vols. (Cambridge, MA: Harvard University Press, 1972), 4:366.

39 *Not much later he would decline:* Longfellow to Israel Washburn, Dec. 22, 1863, in ibid., 4:375.

40 *He declined the Gettysburg invitation:* Benjamin Brown French Diary, Nov. 6, 1863, Library of Congress. The manuscript has been used, however, the edition of the diary in book form is accurate and is cited hereafter for easier reference: Donald B. Cole and John Jay McDonough, eds., *Witness to the Young Republic: A Yankee's Journal, 1828–1870* (Hanover, NH: University Press of New England, 1989), p. 432 (Nov. 6, 1863, cited hereafter as French Diary); W. C. Bryant to Wills, Oct 16, 1863, David Wills Papers, LOC. The correspondence with the other

three poets does not appear to survive. Wills, *Lincoln at Gettysburg*, p. 3, n. 10, claims it is at the Library of Congress, but neither staff nor I were able to locate it.

39   *The digging up of bodies:* Wills to Curtin, Aug. 17, 1863, *Soldiers' National Cemetery*, p. 68.

39   *"The affair will be":* Sentinel, Sept. 15, 1863.

39   *The "National sepulchre:"* Curtin to Wills, Aug. 31, 1863, *Soldiers' National Cemetery*, p. 68.

39   *Governor F. J. Pierpont of the new state:* F. J. Pierpont to Gov. Curtin, Edward Salomon to Gov. Curtin, Alex Ramsey to Gov. Curtin, Nov. 13, 1863, PSA. This collection has twenty-seven telegrams, letters, and an order to or from Curtin. I'm very grateful to the PSA staff for finding these lost documents. However, it is evident from William H. Work to Lloyd A. Dunlap, Aug. 10, 1961, David C. Mearns Papers, LOC, that another twenty-six related items are missing.

42   *The words "immense concourse":* Star, Nov. 12, 1863; cf. *Compiler*, Nov. 9, 15, 1863.

42   *"fast filling up":* Star, Nov. 12, 19, 1863.

42   *A Copperhead hotel keeper:* Ibid., Nov. 19, 1863.

42   *The "Stirring Speech":* Ibid., Nov. 12, 19, 1863.

43   *On October 27:* The following paragraphs are based on the reports to the Pennsylvania legislature by David Wills, March 21, 1864, Samuel Weaver, March 19, 1864, and James S. Townsend, n.d., in *Soldiers' National Cemetery*, pp. 6–9, 39–42. See also *Report of the Joint Special Committee on the Burial of Massachusetts Dead at Gettysburg Together with the Oration of Edward Everett, at the Consecration of the National Cemetery, and Other Matters in Relation Thereto* (Boston: Farwell, 1863); *Sentinel*, Sept. 22, 1863.

43   *There were also individual graves:* Foster, "Visit to the Battlefield," p. 42.

44   *If the dead were "well buried":* Stoke to Stoke, Oct. 26, 1863, GC.

45   *When you open a grave:* Weaver Report, *Soldiers' National Cemetery*, pp. 39, 40; Stoke to Stoke, Oct. 26, 1863, GC.

46   *Some fields where rebels fell:* Ibid.; cf. Francis T. Hoover for Jane Ann Hedley, Sept. 25, 1863, Rare Manuscript Collection, Carl A. Kroch Library, Cornell University.

46   *Yet, bit by bit:* Sentinel, Feb. 2, 1864; cf. March 22, 1864; *Compiler*, April 11, 1864.

46   *When news of "the exposed":* Andrew Curtin to David McConaughy, Nov. 7, 1863, McConaughy Papers.

46   *Some discussion took place:* Mrs. A. T. Mercer to Rufus Benjamin Weaver,

Aug. 16, 1866, quoted in James K. P. Scott, *The Story of the Battles of Gettysburg* (Harrisburg, PA: Telegraph Press, c. 1927), p. 35. General Meade also suggested the decent burial of Confederates in 1870. Russell Bartlett, *The Soldiers' National Cemetery at Gettysburg* (Providence, R.I.: Providence Press, 1874), p. 86. This volume should not be confused with the book first identified on p. 305 or n. 37.

46   *But as for the National Cemetery:* "The National Cemetery at Gettysburg," *Hours at Home* 2 (December 1865): 183.

46   *A white boy, Leander Warren:* Leander H. Warren, "Recollections of the Battle of Gettysburg," typescript, n.d. [1926?], ACHS; Frassanito, *Early Photography*, pp. 167–69.

47   *But, as Nurse Souder told:* Emily [Souder] to Brother, July 29, 1863, *Leaves*, pp. 63–64.

47   *"Quite a boy":* Miller to Miller, Nov. 8, 1863.

47   *Between October 1863 and the following:* Townsend Report, *Soldiers' National Cemetery*, pp. 40–41.

47   *"Words would fail to describe":* Report of David Wills, March 21, 1864, ibid., p. 7.

48   *"Maine: Unknown":* List of Articles, ibid., pp. 144–53 passim.

Chapter Three: Lincoln Comes to Gettysburg

Page

49   *But Lincoln only smiled:* James B. Fry in Allen Thordike Rice, ed., *Reminiscences of Abraham Lincoln by Distinguished Men of his Time* (New York: North American Review, 1888), p. 403.

49   *Wills, who had already invited:* David Wills to William H. Seward, Nov. 2, 1863, William H. Seward Papers, microfilm, LOC; Wills to Seward, Nov. 14, 1863, Gideon Welles Papers, LOC. The Welles Papers also contain Wills's invitation to the Secretary of the Navy, indicating that he used the same language in the various invitations.

50   *Once Lincoln had made his decision:* Lincoln to Salmon P. Chase, Nov. 17, 1863, *Collected Works of Lincoln*, 7:15; Howard K. Beale, ed., *The Diary of Gideon Welles* (3 vols., New York: W. W. Norton, 1960), 1:480.

50   *"I do not like this arrangement":* To Edwin Stanton [Nov. 17, 1863], *Collected Works of Lincoln*, 7:16 (Dec. 1863).

50   *But their ten-year-old son Tad was ill:* Everett to Lincoln, Nov. 20, 1863, Abraham Lincoln Papers, LOC.

50   *The Baltimore & Ohio had arranged:* Baltimore American and Commercial Advertiser, Nov. 19, 1863.

51   *A young Englishwoman:* [Isabella S. Trotter], *First Impressions of the New World* (London: Longman, 1859), pp. 141–45. See also Trotter quoted in John H. White, Jr., *The American Railroad Passenger Car* (Baltimore: Johns Hopkins University Press, 1978), pp. 346–47. Garrett had an even more luxurious director's car built in 1872 that would be also used by other presidents—ibid., pp. 348–49.

52   *Gettysburg built an Italianate villa: Compiler,* Dec. 6, 1858; May 16, 1859; cf. *Sentinel,* Sept. 27, 1858.

52   *By the end of the Civil War:* Henry Holly, *Country Seats* (New York, 1865), p. 76. The book was actually written in 1861.

53   *"The Engine is to weigh": Compiler,* March 7, May 9, 1859.

53   *Later, all too many would claim:* Warren, *Lincoln's Gettysburg Declaration,* p. 61.

53   *The people of Gettysburg were familiar: Star,* Aug. 27, 1863.

53   *A British visitor, Lord Wharncliffe: Pacific Appeal,* Dec. 5, 1863; *New York Times,* Nov. 20, 1863.

54   *Lincoln and Johnson had traveled together: New York Herald,* Feb. 20, 1861.

54   *As the president tried to find a job:* Lincoln to Welles, March 16, 1861, *Collected Works of Lincoln,* 4: 288.

54   *He characterized Johnson as:* Lincoln To Whom It May Concern, March 7, 1861, *Collected Works of Lincoln,* 4:277; Lincoln to Gideon Welles, March 16, 1861, 288; Lincoln to Salmon P. Chase, Nov. 29, 1861, 5:33; Recommendation for William H. Johnson, Oct. 24, 1862, 574.

54   *Johnson was not shy:* Memorandum Concerning William H. Johnson, Dec. 12, 1862, ibid., 6:8; Lincoln to Chase, Nov. 29, 1861.

54   *Johnson landed a job:* "William Johnson, Lincoln's First Body Guard," in John E. Washington, *They Knew Lincoln* (New York: Dutton, 1942), pp. 127–34; quotation at p. 100. See also Roy P. Basler, "Did President Lincoln Give the Smallpox to William H. Johnson?" *Huntington Library Quarterly* 35 (May 1972): 279–84; and Benjamin Quarles, *Lincoln and the Negro* (New York: Oxford University Press, 1962), pp. 194–95.

54   *Lincoln took along Johnson:* Lincoln to S. Yorke At Lee, Sept. 30, 1862, *Collected Works of Lincoln,* 5:446; cf. 6:69.

54   *A curt note went to the Treasury:* Lincoln to S. Yorke At Lee, Nov. 18, 1863, *Collected Works of Lincoln: Supplement,* pp. 210–11.

55   *The French minister:* Hay Diary, 111–12 (Nov. 18, 1863); *New York Evening Post,* Nov. 18, 1863.

55   *Lincoln had tried to force Chase:* Lincoln to Chase, Nov. 1863, *Collected Works of Lincoln,* 7:15.

55   *The confident U.S. Treasurer:* James G. Smart, ed., *A Radical View: The*

"Agate" Dispatches of Whitelaw Reid, 1861–1865, 2 vols. (Memphis, TN: MSU Press, 1976), 2:152. Thaddeus Stevens also received credit for the witticism—David Herbert Donald, *Lincoln* (New York: Simon & Schuster, 1995), p. 665, n. 463.

56   *Lincoln had "strongly urged":* Beale, ed., *Welles Diary*, 1:480 (Dec., 1863).

56   *The press reported that Lincoln:* Newark *Daily Mercury*, Nov. 17, 1863.

56   *Attorney General Edward Bates wrote cryptically:* Howard K. Beale, ed., *The Diary of Edward Bates, 1859–1866* (Washington, DC: Government Printing Office, 1933), p. 316 (Nov. 19, 1863).

56   *Lincoln himself noted:* To Elihu B. Washburne, Oct. 26, 1863, *Collected Works of Lincoln*, 6:540.

56   *The Democratic press did not know: Cincinnati Enquirer*, Nov. 24, 1863. The three most important influences on this section are Menahem Blondheim, *News Over the Wires* (Cambridge, MA: Harvard University Press, 1994), and Blondheim's " 'Public Sentiment is Everything': The Union Public Communications Strategy and the Bogus Proclamation of 1864," *Journal of American History* 89 (December 2002): 869–99; and Richard J. Carwardine, "Abraham Lincoln and the Fourth Estate: The White House and the Press During the Civil War," *American Nineteenth Century History*, 7 (March 2006): 1–27. I'm indebted to Professor Carwardine for sharing his manuscript before publication and to Professor Blondheim for commenting on parts of this and some other chapters.

57   *The* Chicago Tribune: *Chicago Tribune*, Nov. 20, 1863, clipping in Mearns Papers, Box 146, LOC. The *Tribune* copied the report of the *Washington Republican*. Careful researcher Josephine Cobb of the Library of Congress, famed among scholars for her discovery of Lincoln's face in a Gettysburg photograph, attempted to create a list of people who traveled on the president's train but gave up the project: "I distrusted the reminiscences after it seemed that everybody was on board . . . I checked the names of many who were probably on the train with him but found no mention of the trip among their papers. It didn't seem to be important until many years later"—Josephine Cobb to Lloyd A. Dunlap, n.d., typed notation on Dunlap to Cobb, June 26, 1961, Mearns Papers, Box 146, LOC. After finding Cobb's notation, I stopped attempting the same task.

57   *The Republican press would so dominate:* John Russell Young, *Men and Memories: Personal Reminiscences* (2 vols., New York: Tennyson Neely, 1901), ed. May D. Russell Young, vol. 1, p. 64.

57   *It may be true, as some claimed:* Michael Burlingame, ed., *Lincoln's Jour-*

nalist: John Hay's Anonymous Writings for the Press, 1860–1864 (Carbondale: Southern Illinois University Press, 1998), p. 177.

57   *After the Republican losses:* Lincoln to Carl Schurz, Nov. 10, 1862, *Collected Works of Lincoln,* 5:493–94.

58   *To take the pulse of the country:* Carpenter, *Six Months at the White House,* p. 281.

58   *"I do not often decline":* To John Milderborger, Nov. 11, 1863, *Collected Works of Lincoln,* 7:10.

58   *As Wills had written the president:* David Wills to Abraham Lincoln, Nov. 2, 1863, Lincoln Papers.

58   *He had done so repeatedly:* To James C. Conkling, Aug. 26, 1863, *Collected Works of Lincoln,* 6:410.

59   *Traveling in the United States:* Goldwin Smith, "President Lincoln," *Macmillan's Magazine,* 2 (February 1865): 301.

59   *Close to one third:* Charles Johanningsmeier, *Fiction and the American Literary Marketplace: The Role of Newspaper Syndicates, 1860–1900* (Cambridge: Cambridge University Press, 1997), p. 2; cf. Patricia Okker, *Social Stories: Magazine Novel in Nineteenth-Century America* (Charlottesville: University of Virginia Press, 2003), pp. 9–28.

59   *To assist them, Lincoln added:* William O. Stoddard, "White House Sketch No. 2," *New York Citizen,* Aug. 25, 1866, in Michael Burlingame, ed., *Inside the White House in War Times* (Lincoln: University of Nebraska Press, 2000), p. 148.

60   *Though the time of the "official":* Harrisburg *Patriot and Union* quoted in *Compiler,* Aug. 24, 1863.

60   *He believed that "No man":* Chauncey M. Depew in Rice, ed., *Reminiscences of Abraham Lincoln,* p. 436.

60   *Forney was routinely described:* See, e.g., the *Compiler,* Nov. 9, 18, 21, 1863; *Pittsburgh Post,* Nov. 23, 1863; and John W. Forney to Lincoln, May 12, 1863, Lincoln Papers.

60   *The lieutenant leading the Marine Band:* Henry Clay Cochran, "With Lincoln to Gettysburg, 1863," *Military Order of the Loyal Legion of the United States, Commandery of the State of Pennsylvania, Abraham Lincoln* (Philadelphia, 1907), 88.

61   *Hay would later report:* Hay to William Herndon, Sept. 5, 1866, in Douglas L. Wilson and Rodney O. Davis, eds., *Herndon's Informants: Letters, Interviews, and Statements About Abraham Lincoln* (Urbana: University of Illinois Press, 1998), p. 330.

61   *As Nicolay wrote to the editors:* Nicolay to *Chicago Tribune,* June 19, 1863, in Michael Burlingame, ed., *With Lincoln in the White House: Letters,*

Memoranda, and Other Writings of John G. Nicolay, 1860–1865 (Carbondale: Southern Illinois University Press, 2000), p. 116.

61   *Then the train arrived at Camden Station:* J. P. Kennedy Diary, Nov. 19, 1863, Peabody Institute Library.

61   *Another observer thought:* Cochran, "With Lincoln to Gettysburg, 1863," p. 9.

61   *Ambassador Mercier reported to Paris:* Mercier to Thouvenal, Feb. 25, March 1, 1861, quoted in Daniel B. Carroll, *Henry B. Mercier and the American Civil War* (Princeton: Princeton University Press, 1971), p. 44.

61   *Now newspaper reported military: National Intelligencer,* Washington, Nov. 19, 1863.

61   *B&O president John Garrett: Baltimore American and Commercial Advertiser,* Nov. 19, 1863. William Prescott Smith was responsible for Lincoln's schedule.

62   *After one dining experience: Philadelphia Engineer,* Dec. 8, 1860, quoted in White, *The American Railroad Passenger Car,* p. 314.

62   *When the train went through a deep cut:* Wayne MacVeagh, "Lincoln at Gettysburg," *Century* 79 (November 1909): 21.

62   *At one stop a little girl:* E. W. Andrews in Rice, ed., *Reminiscences of Abraham Lincoln,* p. 511.

62   *The Pennsylvania had "some matters":* MacVeagh, "Lincoln at Gettysburg," p. 20.

62   *Hay thought the young politician:* Michael Burlingame and John R. Turner Ettlinger, eds. *Inside Lincoln's White House: The Complete Civil War Diary of John Hay* (cited hereafter as *Hay Diary*) (Carbondale, IL: Southern Illinois University Press, 1997), pp. 111, 113; cf. MacVeagh, "Lincoln at Gettysburg," pp. 21–22.

62   *In the night MacVeagh's companion:* Young, *Men and Memories,* vol. 1, p. 61.

63   *Wills's invitation specifically requested:* Wills to Lincoln, Nov. 2, 1863, Lincoln Papers.

63   *One traveler would remember:* Andrews in Rice, ed., *Reminiscences of Abraham Lincoln,* pp. 510–11.

63   *But Lincoln did not need to speak:* Speech at the Great Central Sanitary Fair, June 16, 1864, *Collected Works of Lincoln,* 7:394.

63   *"The knowledge of death":* "When Lilacs Last in the Dooryard Bloom'd," in Michael Moon, ed., *Leaves of Grass and Other Writings* (New York: W. W. Norton, 2002), p. 281.

63   *Afterwards he wrote to Ellsworth's parents:* To Ephralm and Phoebe Ellsworth, May 25, 1861, *Collected Works of Lincoln,* 4:386.

63 *Back in July, victory in battle: Washington Daily Morning Chronicle,* July 8, 1863. Martin Johnson called attention to this version of the speech in Forney's paper, suggesting that it provides the most accurate transcript of Lincoln's words and that he probably prepared for "the longest extemporaneous speech to a serenading party" during his presidency—Johnson, "Lincoln Greets the Turning Point of the Civil War, July 7, 1863," *Lincoln Herald,* vol. 106, no. 3 (Fall 2004): 106. Cf. Response to Serenade, July 7, 1863, *Collected Works of Lincoln,* 6:319–20.

64 *It would have been "painfully tedious": Baltimore American and Commercial Advertiser,* Nov. 20, 1863; cf. *Philadelphia Press,* Nov. 21, 1863.

64 *A Philadelphia paper had reported: Philadelphia Inquirer,* Oct. 13, 1863.

64 *"Upwards of one hundred": Baltimore Clipper,* Nov. 18, 1863.

64 *"Crowds have gone from here":* J. P. Kennedy Diary, Nov. 19, 1863.

64 *"Interminable trains": Philadelphia Inquirer,* Nov. 21, 1863.

64 *Trains broke down: Philadelphia Public Ledger,* Nov. 23, 1863; *Lancaster (Pa.) Daily Express,* Nov. 25, 1863.

64 *One reporter traveled the distance: Cincinnati Daily Commercial,* Nov. 23, 1863.

64 *Nurse Emily Souder, returning:* E.B.S. to Cousin, Nov. 20, 1863, *Leaves,* p. 134.

64 *Luckily, the rains had stopped: Cincinnati Daily Commercial,* Nov. 23, 1863.

64 *The angry Cincinnati newsman:* Ibid.

66 *On the train to Gettysburg:* E.B.S. (Souder) to cousin, Nov. 20, 1863, *Leaves,* pp. 135–36.

66 *With others: Indianapolis Daily Journal,* Nov. 23, 1863.

66 *"Long before the hour": Hanover Spectator,* Nov. 27, 1863.

66 *Or, as the Democratic paper: Hanover Citizen,* Nov. 26, 1863.

67 *Lincoln appeared to have been less: Hanover Spectator,* Nov. 27, 1863.

67 *He hesitated until:* The words of M. J. Alleman, Pastor of St. Mark's Lutheran Church, Hanover, are based on a persistent oral tradition in the Hanover, Pennsylvania, area. See, e.g., the eyewitness recollections George D. Gitt, November 1933, in Rufus Rockwell Wilson, *Intimate Memories of Lincoln* (Elmira, NY: Primavera, 1945), pp. 476–77; W. H. Long to Frederick S. Weiser, April 12, 1948; cf. John Henry Schmuck, typescript, n.d., copies in author's collection. See also "Lincoln in Hanover," *Hanover Herald,* Feb. 13, 1909; George R. Prowell, "Fifty Years Ago," *Hanover Record Herald,* Nov. 18, 1913; and Prowell, "Lincoln Spoke Here," *Hanover Record Herald,* Feb. 11, 1922.

67 *Lincoln may have muttered something:* For long, some people maintained that Lincoln used such words on the way to Gettysburg, indicating that

he had not known ahead of time that he would have to speak there. This tradition maintains that he wrote his speech on the train. The germ of the tale appears to have reached print immediately after Lincoln's death "from a gentleman who rode with him to Gettysburg"—*New York Evening Post*, May 3, 1865. Isaac N. Arnold, in *The History of Abraham Lincoln and the Overthrow of Slavery* (Chicago: Clark, 1866), p. 328, gave the story its first appearance in book form. Some went so far as to suggest that Lincoln spoke extemporaneously. The possibility, perhaps probability, arises that Lincoln indeed uttered some such words, but they referred to the Hanover Junction stop. Could the words have been transposed in people's memories? Nor is it impossible that Lincoln went into seclusion soon after the junction to think about his words for the following day. Cochrane's recollection is that Lincoln did this just *before* the junction. Cochran, "Lincoln," p. 10.

67 *Now he provides one of his:* Hanover Spectator, Feb. 12, 1863; The Hanover Centennial Committee, *Official Program of the Centennial of Incorporation of the Borough of Hanover Pennsylvania* (Hanover: Centennial Committee, 1915), p. 36.

67 *A young boy gave Lincoln an apple:* Philadelphia Inquirer, Nov. 21; *Hanover Citizen,* Nov. 26; *Hanover Spectator,* Nov. 27, 1863. The "speech" is not in the *Collected Works of Lincoln,* and a plaque at Hanover gives a much-cleaned-up version from memory that only loosely resembles the original. In addition to the contemporary report, the above reconstruction also relies on the following oral traditions: Amelia M. Ehrehart to Frederick S. Weiser, Sept. 18, 1950, and Aug. 1, 1951 (copies of portions of letters in the author's possession). See also Weiser to Gabor Boritt, Aug. 1, 2005. One eyewitness, then a boy, would recall that Lincoln departed "leaving the crowd in a disappointed condition"— Spangler to Weiser, Sept. 1950.

68 *The end of the trip approached:* Washington Daily Morning Chronicle, Nov. 21, 1863.

68 *Earlier in the day: The Sanitary Commission of the United States Army: A Succinct Narrative of Its Works and Purposes* (New York: U.S. Sanitary Commission, 1864), p. 161.

68 *The members of the press:* Young, *Men and Memories,* vol. 1, p. 59.

68 *The crowds had been there:* Cincinnati Daily Commercial, Nov. 23, 1863.

68 *Some got tired of waiting:* E.B.S. to Cousin, Nov. 20, 1863.

68 *"Passage had almost to be forced":* Cincinnati Daily Commercial, Nov. 23, 1863.

68 *As Lincoln shook the general's hand: Collected Works of Lincoln,* 6:328.

68   *Well, he was here now:* Everett Diary, Nov. 18, 1863, Massachusetts Historical Society, microfilm. Hereafter Everett Diary.

68   *"shimmering moonlight":* Philadelphia Inquirer, Nov. 21, 1863.

Chapter Four: Carousing Crowds

Page

69   *Josephine Forney Roedel:* Roedel Diary, Nov. 18, 1863.

69   *"Our old town is roused up":* Henry Sweeney to Brother, Nov. 29, 1863, typescript, GNMP, pp. 8–18b. See also *Compiler,* Nov. 9, 1863.

70   *"I suppose there will be a great time":* Miller to Miller, Nov. 14, 19, 1863.

70   *One household was told:* Mary Hunt Carson to Mother, Nov. 21, 1863, copy in the author's possession.

70   *A local sergeant:* Perhaps Bigham may have served in the evening and at night, and Rebert in the morning, as they recalled—H. P. Bigham Memo, n.d., in John B. Horton, *Sgt. Hugh Paxton Brigham: Lincoln's Guard at Gettysburg* (Gettysburg: Horner, 1994); Rebert in Orton H. Carmichael, *Lincoln's Gettysburg Address* (New York: Abingdon, 1917), pp. 87–88.

70   *He proposed that the marshals: Star,* Nov. 19, 1863.

70   *He suggested to Governor Curtin:* Ward H. Lamon to A. G. Curtin, Nov. 16, 1863; General Order No. 47, PSA; cf. *Philadelphia Public Ledger,* Nov. 18, 1863.

71   *"This will be a task":* French Diary, p. 431 (Nov. 6, 1863).

71   *On November 13, French:* Ibid. p. 432 (Nov. 14, 1863). John G. Stephenson, the Librarian of Congress, accompanied them to Gettysburg but got sick and could not participate in the work.

72   *For nearly four days:* French Diary, p. 433 (Nov. 22, 1863).

72   *Mrs. Harriet Ann Harper regaled her guests:* Ibid.

72   *As many as fifty wounded:* Cross, *Christian Commission,* pp. 15, 16; see also Andrew B. Cross to W. H. Seward, Nov. 23, 1863, Seward Papers.

72   *"The hills [are] alive":* Cincinnati Daily Commercial, Nov. 23, 1863.

72   *Assigning seats was a delicate:* Everett to Wills, Nov. 9, 1863, Wills Papers, contains explicit instructions about Everett's needs.

72   *In the area where the hospital tents:* Bucklin, *In Hospital and Camp,* pp. 192–93; E.B.S. to Cousin, Nov. 20, 1863, *Leaves,* p. 137.

73   *People kept coming: Philadelphia Inquirer,* Nov. 17, 1863.

73   *"The tranquility of the little town":* E.B.S. to Cousin, Nov. 20, 1863, *Leaves,* p. 137.

73   *Rumors surrounded:* Remarks at the dinner to Captain Winslow of the

Kearsapc, Nov. 15, 1864, in Edward Everett, *Orations and Speeches on Various Occasions,* 4 vols. (Boston: Little, Brown, 1850–68), 4:744.

73   *And though the press:* Young, *Men and Memories,* vol. 1, p. 59.

74   *Loud voices called: New York Times,* Nov. 21, 1863.

74   *Later, the Democratic* Compiler: *Compiler,* Nov. 23; *Sentinel,* Nov. 24; *Star,* Nov. 26, 1863.

74   *In 118 or so words:* The "address," to use the word of the *Star,* is reconstructed from several newspaper versions. The *Star's* report came on Nov. 26, 1863. *The Compiler* appeared on Nov. 23, and the *Sentinel* on Nov. 24. For the *New York Tribune's* Nov. 20 version, see *Collected Works of Lincoln,* 7:16–17.

75   *That his opponents would fault him: Buffalo Daily Courier,* Nov. 21, 1863.

75   *Local butcher Harvey Sweeney:* Harvey Sweeney to brother, Nov. 29, 1863.

76   *"I am now sixty years old": Soldiers' National Cemetery,* pp. 189–90; *New York Times,* Nov. 21, 1863; *Philadelphia Press,* Nov. 20, 1862; *Sentinel,* Nov. 24, 1863. The reaction to the speech is reconstructed from several sources. See also: *Courier & Freeman,* Potsdam, NY, Nov. 25, 1863; *Daily Freeman,* Montpelier, VT, Nov. 21, 1863; *Daily Sentinel & Times,* Bath, ME, Nov. 20, 1863; *Ballston Journal,* Ballston Spa, NY, Nov. 24, 1863; *Malone Palladium,* NY, Nov. 26, 1863; *Rutland Daily Herald,* Nov. 20, 1863.

77   *Hay complained in his diary: Hay Diary,* p. 111 (Nov. 18, 1863).

77   *Democratic papers would later suggest: Philadelphia Age,* Nov. 21, 1863, quoted in the *Compiler,* Dec. 14, 1863.

77   *Nurse Souder at least:* E.B.S to Cousin, Nov. 20, 1863, *Leaves,* p. 138.

77   *And one of John Forney's reporters:* Young, *Men and Memories,* vol. 1, pp. 60, 59.

77   *The* New York Tribune *reporter: New York Tribune,* Nov. 25, 1863; *Chicago Tribune,* Nov. 25, 1863.

78   *Not surprising, the notion:* Smith, "President Lincoln"; cf. *Pittsburgh Post,* Nov. 23, 1863; R. C. McCormick, April 29, 1865, in *New York Evening Post,* May 3, 1865; Warren Scrapbook, 2:41, LM.

78   *On the day of the cemetery's dedication:* W. Farquhar to —— Boos, May 26, 1921, ADS Catalogue, 1990, quoted in John M. Taylor, *William Henry Seward, Lincoln's Right Hand* (New York: HarperCollins, 1991), p. 224.

78   *But the Secretary of State:* Everett to Wills, Jan. 2, 1864, Wills Papers.

78   *In the end the* Sentinel: *Sentinel,* Dec. 1, Nov. 2; *Star,* Nov. 26, 1863.

78   *None recorded his "most eloquent": Compiler,* Nov. 23, 1863.

78   *Much later it would be recalled:* Andrews in Rice, ed., *Reminiscences of Abraham Lincoln,* pp. 512–13. This recollection, however, appears to

confuse the Seymour speech that evening with the one he gave the next day.

79 *Indeed, the Republican* Sentinel*: Sentinel,* Nov. 10, 17, 1863.

79 *Even after Lincoln gave his address: Philadelphia Age,* Nov. 20, 1863.

79 *If the Republicans found: Sentinel,* Nov. 24, 1863; *Compiler,* Nov. 23, 1863.

79 *A few weeks earlier, leading:* E. D. Morgan, Hiram Barney, Ira Harris, Thurlow Weed, Abram Wakeman, and A. M. Palmer to J. W. Forney, Oct 9, 1863, John Wien Forney Papers, LOC.

79 *Getting a band in Gettysburg: Hay Diary,* pp. 112–13 (Nov. 18, 1863).

79 *Then he appeared:* Ibid. For a sample of newspaper reports about the Forney speech, see: Albany *Atlas and Argus,* Nov. 20, 1863; *Bangor Daily Whig and Courier,* Nov. 23, 1863; *Boston Daily Journal,* Nov. 20, 1863; *Boston Herald,* Nov. 20, 1863; *Buffalo Daily Courier,* Dec. 3, 1863; *Buffalo Morning Express,* Nov. 20, 1863; *Chicago Tribune,* Nov. 21, 1863; *Cincinnati Daily Commercial,* Nov. 23, 1863; *Cincinnati Daily Gazette,* Nov. 21, 1863; *Compiler,* Nov. 23, 1863; *Hanover Citizen,* PA, Dec. 17, 1863; *Daily Eastern Argus,* ME, Nov. 20, 1863; *New Yorker Staats-Zeitung,* Nov. 20, 1863; *New York Times,* Nov. 21, 1863; *New York Tribune,* Nov. 20, 1863; *New York World,* Nov. 21, 1863; *Philadelphia Inquirer,* Nov. 20, 1863; *Age,* Nov. 20, 1863; *Philadelphia Press,* Nov. 20, 1863; *Philadelphia Public Ledger,* Nov. 20, 1863; *Pittsburgh Post,* Nov. 23, 1863; *Portland Advertiser,* Nov. 24, 1863; *Providence Daily Journal,* Nov. 20, 1863.

80 *Later, John Nicolay, who like other revelers:* John G. Nicolay, "Lincoln's Gettysburg Address," *Century,* 47 (February 1894): 601; Nicolay Memos, Dec. 14, 15, 19, etc., Nicolay Papers, LOC.

80 *Perhaps around 11 p.m.:* French Diary, p. 434 (Nov. 22, 1863). The sequence of the evening is uncertain. French's diary suggests that Lincoln and Seward spent their hour together before Seward spoke. In any case, it is almost certain that Lincoln knew what was in Seward's speech. Wills wrote several very similar versions of what happened in his house that evening, three of which, at least, survive. In a letter to Nicolay dated Jan. 19, 1894, Wills explained: "Years ago I wrote out the facts . . . and they were published in some of the newspapers." He enclosed a typed account of Lincoln's visit—*Lincoln Lore* 1437 (November 1957). See also "Statement Given by Judge Wills to Charles M. McCurdy, About 1890," copy, Wills Papers; Wills to William H. Shoemaker, Feb. 12, 1909, in Isaac Markens, *Lincoln's Masterpiece* (New York: Isaac Markens, 1913), p. 12. Edward McPherson to Editor of *The Nation,* Aug. 31, 1875. *Nation,* Sept. 9, 1875, also provides an early description obviously based on Wills's account.

80   *if Lincoln had not read Seward's:* Wills remembered that Lincoln carried with him some sheets of paper and came back with the same—Wills Memo.

80   I can't speak to-night: *Baltimore American and Commercial Advertiser,* Nov. 20, 1863.

80   *Lincoln made two copies: Collected Works of Lincoln,* 7:17–18. The editors call this the "first draft."

81   *James Speed, who did not know: Daily Louisville Commercial,* Nov. 12, 1879, reprinted with minor variations in the *Illinois State Journal,* Nov. 17, 1879. Speed repeated much the same in a letter to the *New York Times,* April 20, 1887. The excellent skeptical scholar David C. Mearns correctly called this, from among the many recollections and theories, "the transparently truthful report"—Mearns, "Unknown at This Address," p. 133. Cf. David C. Mearns and Lloyd A. Dunlap, eds., *Long Remembered: The Gettysburg Address in Facsimile* (Washington: Library of Congress, 1963), p. [3]. The first scholar of the subject, John G. Nicolay, also "strongly" vouched for "the correctness" of Speed's words, though Nicolay provided confusing evidence as well. "Lincoln's Gettysburg Address," p. 597.

81   *Lincoln's "wonderful facility."* Joshua Speed, *Reminiscences of Abraham Lincoln and Notes of a Visit to California* (Louisville: John P. Morton, 1884).

81   *Much later, telling his story:* Copy of William Saunders Journal, 1898, p. 6, LOC. The memoir is not always accurate.

81   *A number of others claimed:* Wills made the claim for the evening of the 18th: see note *Perhaps around 11 p.m.* on p. 318. Governor Curtin made the same claim, see note *He protested vigorously* on pp. 321–22, and he added that he had gone out among the crowds ahead of Lincoln, but no newspaper or diarist noticed. Curtin also claimed to have given Lincoln the paper—envelopes that the governor cut open—to write his speech on, and having done so on the train to Gettysburg. Curtain was not on the Lincoln train, however. Horatio C. King to Editor of the *New York Times,* June 29, 1913, in *New York Times,* July 1, 1913. Finally, William Slade, if we believe his daughter, claimed to have listened to Lincoln reading his speech in his room at the Wills House—Washington, *They Knew Lincoln,* p. 112. But Slade did not go to Gettysburg. See note on *Wills's memory was good enough* on pp. 320–21.

81   *Several men remembered:* Noah Brooks, "Personal Reminiscences of Lincoln," *Scribner's Monthly* 15 (February 1878): 565; *Abraham Lincoln: The Nation's Leader in the Great Struggle through which was Maintained the*

Existence of the United States (New York: Putnam, 1888), pp. 377–79; Brooks to Richard Watson Gilder, Feb. 3, 1894, in Michael Burlingame, *Lincoln Observed: Civil War Dispatches of Noah Brooks* (Baltimore: Johns Hopkins University Press, 1998), 89; "Personal Reminiscences of Abraham Lincoln," *Century* 49 (January 1895): 465; Herbert Mitgang, ed., *Washington, D.C., in Lincoln's Time* (Chicago: Quadrangle Books, 1971), pp. 252–53.

82   *Hay mentioned who: Hay Diary,* p. 109 (Nov. 8, 1863).

82   *The physical impossibility:* see note on *several men remembered* at p. 318.

82   *Annoyed by the uncritical:* Mearns, "Unknown at This Address," p. 123.

82   *That may be a little strong:* Brooks to the Rev. Isaac P. Langworthy, Washington, DC, May 10, 1865, privately printed, quoted in Wayne C. Temple, *Abraham Lincoln: From Skeptic to Prophet* (Mahomet, Mayhaven, 1995), 313. However wrong, Brooks should receive credit for consistency. In 1872, he wrote to the Reverend J. A. Reed about Lincoln's religion: "I never tried to draw anything like a statement of his views from him, yet he freely expressed himself to me as having 'a hope of blessed immortality through Jesus Christ' "—J. A. Reed, *Scribner's Monthly* 6, no. 340 (July 1873). I am indebted to Wayne C. Temple for calling my attention to this statement.

83   *The second aspirant: Philadelphia Times,* Oct. 4, 1887; *Washington Critic,* Feb. 18, 1888; Draft of Lamon's Reminiscence; Lamon, ed., *Recollections* pp. 172–79.

83   *The marshal was still: Washington Daily Morning Chronicle,* Nov. 18, 1863.

83   *The Stanford professor and great:* Don E. Fehrenbacher and Virginia Fehrenbacher, comps. and eds., *Recollected Words of Abraham Lincoln* (Stanford: Stanford University Press, 1996), p. 289. Others, too, had claimed to have seen Lincoln's speech, if we believe secondhand reports, among them John D. Defrees and Simon Cameron, but they deserve no consideration even if Warren, *Lincoln's Gettysburg Declaration,* pp. 53–54, credits them.

83   *his 239 words:* This is the word count of the "first draft." Other versions vary a little.

83   *Wills's memory was good enough:* David Wills's Statement to Charles M. McCurdy, c. 1890. Wills said that "After spending part of the evening in the parlors he retired to his room. He had his colored servant, William, with him" and sent him to get Wills. "Nibbie" Slade, the daughter of William Slade, of the White House staff, much later would claim that his father was the "William" who accompanied Lincoln to Gettysburg and was with him when he completed his speech. "After writing a sen-

tence or so he would pause, and read the piece to Slade. He would then say, 'William how does that sound?' "—Washington, *They Knew Lincoln*, p. 112. Since it was William Johnson, however, who went with Lincoln to Gettysburg, is it possible that he told the above about himself and then, after his death, the Slades took it over? Wills may have also claimed that Lincoln read his speech to him, but on the morning. This, at least, was the recollection of R. S. Chilton, who maintained that Wills confided to him in 1868—*New York Times*, July 23, 1881, citing the *Toronto Mail*. Others who remembered Lincoln writing that evening, in addition to Wills and Curtin, included Edward McPherson, though his accounts are clearly influenced by Wills—McPherson to Editor, Aug. 31, 1875, 21 (Sept. 9, 1875): 164; *Illinois State Journal*, Springfield, Nov. 17, 1879; also MacVeagh, "Lincoln at Gettysburg," pp. 21–22. Of course, people could repeat each other. By 1887, McPherson wrote frankly that "I know, personally, nothing of the circumstances under which it [Lincoln's speech] was prepared. I believe, however, that it was prepared after he got to Gettysburg and in his bedroom"—McPherson statement, April 15, 1887, copy, Mearns Papers.

84   *Everett would record in his diary:* Everett Diary, Nov. 19, 1863. His "lodger" suggests visitors, and though we can not be certain, it is reasonable to think in terms of forty-four people in the house that had probably twelve available rooms. Counting: four rooms on each of the three floors plus the kitchen extension with the servant's quarters, makes for thirteen rooms one of which served as a store room and a kitchen. (To complicate matters, Wills owned the adjacent two-story building, too, but none of it was likely to be available or to be included by Everett.) In the Wills house proper, Lincoln and Everett had their own rooms and perhaps the Wills family squeezed into one room for the night. That puts a few more than four people into each of the nine remaining rooms, not an improbable number for the time. If some people stayed in the attic, that would have accommodated a large number, reducing the crowding in the rooms below. Elwood W. Christ's chapter in the *David Wills House: Historic Structure Report for the Borough of Gettysburg and the National Park Service* by ICON Architecture, Inc., and John Bowie Associates (2002), GNMP; Christ to Boritt, March 31, 2006.

84   *He protested vigorously:* Everett Diary, Nov. 18, 1863. The governor later also remembered spending a little time alone with the president in his room, before going into the night, far from impossible though Everett does not note it, and some of the above reminiscing is dubious. Andrew

G. Curtin speaking to Horatio King, May 1885, *Washington Critic*, Feb. 18, 1888; King, *Turning Out the Light* . . . (Philadelphia, Lippincott, 1895), 238; Curtin to King, March 6, 1888, Horation King Papers, LC; Curtin to John G. Nicolay, Apr. 7, 1892, Nicolay Papers.

84 *"I did not get to bed":* Everett Diary, Nov. 18, 1863.

85 *A Baltimore correspondent: Baltimore American and Commercial Advertiser,* Nov. 20, 1863.

85 *"There was so many people":* Susan Holabaugh White to Alonzo V. White, Nov. 20, 1863, typescript of original, GNMP, pp. 10–16.

85 *A Philadelphia "lady": Philadelphia Daily Evening Bulletin,* Nov. 21, 1863.

85 *Others felt lucky: Washington Evening Chronicle,* Nov. 21, 1863; *Star & Banner,* Dec. 6, 1863; *Springfield (Ohio) Republic,* Nov. 27, 1863; Saunders Journal, pp. 6–7.

85 *A reporter wondered: Philadelphia Inquirer,* Nov. 21, 1863.

85 *Reporter John Russell Young:* Young, *Men and Memories,* vol. 1, p. 59.

85 *The fortunate had rooms:* Nicolay, "Lincoln's Gettysburg Address," p. 601; cf. Daniel Alexander Skelly, *A Boy's Experiences During the Battles of Gettysburg* (Gettysburg: Skelly, 1932), p. 26.

86 *Earlier in the day: Washington Daily Morning Chronicle,* Nov. 21, 1863; French Diary, p. 434 (Nov. 22, 1863).

87 *But the quiet folk: American and Commercial Advertiser,* New York, Nov. 20, 1863.

87 *In Harrisburg, "on the way": Indianapolis Daily Journal,* Nov. 21, 1863.

87 *But this was Gettysburg: Cincinnati Daily Commercial,* Nov. 23, 1863.

87 *By 1865, the* New York Herald: *New York Herald,* July 6, 1865.

87 *Like others, Hay "drank": Hay Diary,* pp. 111–12 (Nov. 18, 1863).

87 *"Handsome as a peach":* Young, *Men and Memories,* vol. 1, p. 59.

87 *A little more than three months:* Hay to Nicolay, Aug. 7, 1863, in Michael Burlingame, ed., *Lincoln's Journalist, John Hay's Anonymous Writings for the Press, 1860–1864* (Carbondale: Southern Illinois University Press, 1998), xxi. When Forney's paper admitted that Hay wrote something for it, he was not identified as Lincoln's secretary—*Daily Morning Chronicle,* June 1, 1863. The *Chronicle* article is not in the above collection, but Burlingame called my attention to the initials "J.H."

88 *One of the local papers: Star,* Nov. 26, 1863.

88 *150,000 people being present:* The local estimates put the crowd on the 19th between 15,000 to 30,000. Much of the press said the same, though 50,000 was not uncommon. The numbers ranged from 12,000 to the occasional 150,000, the last probably a misprint: *Compiler,* Nov. 23, 1863; *Boston Journal,* Nov. 23, 1863; *Courier & Freeman,* Potsdam, NY, Nov. 25,

1863; *Daily Sentinel & Times*, Bath, ME, Nov. 21, 1863; *Missouri Republican*, Nov. 21, 1863; *Fremont Journal*, OH, Nov. 27, 1863. Everett's *Diary* for November 19 noted that thirty-eight people lodged at the Wills house. We don't know whether he included in this number the six people who lived there. If not, the inhabitants of the house grew more than six-fold; if so, more than five-fold. If most homes had the same proportion of guests, then Gettysburg's nearly 2,500 people grew that night to somewhere between 13,000 to 16,000 people. But it is also clear that many homes crowded people in tighter, literally body to body on the floors, in the style of the "spooning" soldiers. Stables could accommodate the needy; churches and schools got filled; the College and the Seminary provided space; so did houses in outlying areas, as well as barns and other buildings not normally used for sleeping; the old hospital ground's tents housed soldiers; others slept in railroad cars, carriages, wagons, and many found no place to sleep at all. On the other hand, how many folks refused to have any guests, the temptation of money notwithstanding? Which commercial space accommodated no one? Still, all in all, fifteen thousand for the night of Nov. 18, seems a rather low figure, and from early dawn on people continued streaming into town in large numbers.

88   *Josephine Forney Roedel, too, wrote:* Roedel Diary, Nov. 19, 1863.

88   *Another letter from Gettysburg: Lancaster Daily Express*, Nov. 24, 1863.

88   *But clearly friendly correspondents: Philadelphia Public Ledger*, Nov. 23, 1863.

88   *The* New York World, *New York World*, Nov. 20, 1863.

88   *The* Daily Courier *of Buffalo: Buffalo Daily Courier*, Nov. 21, 1863.

88   *Pickpockets worked the crowds: Lancaster Daily Express*, Nov. 24, 1863. The *Star*, Nov. 26, 1863, reported on two or three pickpockets getting caught.

89   *He was there "to help": Washington Daily Morning Chronicle*, Nov. 19, 1863.

90   *His host, David Wills:* David Wills Statement, n.d., typescript enclosed in Oliver R. Barrett to Charles Moore, April 11, 1927, Wills Papers.

90   *Similarly, Nicolay would be:* John G. Nicolay to Richard Watson Gilder, Sept. 19, 1885; cf Nicolay, "Lincoln's Gettysburg Address," pp. 601–02; James A. Rebert suggested the same in 1891, quoted in Carmichael, *Lincoln's Gettysburg Address*, pp. 87–88.

90   *Sometime during the evening:* Telegram at the GNMP.

90   *"John Brown's body":* The words are taken from C. A. Brown, revised by Willard A. Heaps, *The Story of Our National Ballads* (New York, 1960), pp. 166–67.

Chapter Five: The Gettysburg Gospel

Page

91   *A glorious sun spread: Star*, Dec. 3, 1863; *Philadelphia Evening Bulletin*, Nov. 20, 1863. The various contradictory reports about the weather should be ignored in favor of Baltimore's *American and Commercial Advertiser*, Nov. 20, 1863.

91   *The beauty of the land: Sentinel*, Nov. 24, 1863.

91   *"Their mute disappearance is eloquent"*: Ibid.

92   *The president and Secretary of State:* Lincoln and Seward's touring is reported in, e.g., the *Washington Daily Chronicle*, Nov. 21, 1863.

92   *Back in the Diamond:* Ibid.

92   *"My friends—No one":* Farewell Address at Springfield, Ill., Feb. 11, 1861, *Collected Works of Lincoln*, 4:190–91.

93   *"It has long been a grave question":* Response to Serenade, Nov. 10, 1864, ibid., 8:100–101.

93   *Three days later, Hay noted: Hay Diary*, p. 248 (Nov. 11, 1864).

94   *Many years later:* Isabella F. Keyes to Hay, July 11, 1904, Hay Papers.

94   *The theory that the second draft:* Second Draft, *Collected Works of Lincoln*, 7:18–19. Mearns and Dunlap, *Long Remembered*, p. [7–10], make a case for what the *Collected Works of Lincoln* calls the "Second Draft" having been written after Lincoln had returned to Washington. Among other things, they ignore the above consideration. See also Mearns's typescript speculations in his papers, as well as the subsequent debunking of his and Dunlap's theory and a case made for the "Second Draft" being the reading copy by the staff of the Illinois State Historical Society— Clyde C. Walton to Foster Cannon, April 20, 1964 with 12pp. enclosure, "We have examined Cannon's evidence. . . . ," LOC, Box 148 (also advanced by Barton, *Lincoln at Gettysburg*). This memo fails to take into consideration the point about the absence of "under God" in the Second Draft, perhaps reflecting skepticism about Lincoln's religion as well as a lack of understanding of the importance of the Evangelical community to politics. The best—but hardly good—claim for Lincoln having written the second version after returning to Washington was written nearly eight years after Hay's death: Nelson Thomasson to Elihu Root, Feb. 21, 1913, copy enclosed with Clara S. Hay to Helen Nicolay, Feb. 28, 1913, Nicolay Papers, LOC; cf. Nicholson and Lambert referred to in "We have examined Cannon's evidence," 7; *New York Times*, June 29, 1913; "Chronology," Mearns Papers, LOC. See also Appendix C #3: "What Lincoln Read at Gettysburg;" and C #4: "The Parunak Report."

94   *Liberty Hollinger, then a young girl:* Mrs. Jacob A. Clutz [Liberty Augusta Hollinger], *Some Personal Recollections of the Battle of Gettysburg* (Gettysburg, 1925), p. 19, ACHS.

94   *"The best course for the journals":* Pittsburgh *Daily Commercial*, Nov. 23, 1863; cf. Charles Baum, *Reminiscences*, Dec. 17, 1935, Special Collections, Gettysburg College.

94   *The people greeted him: Washington Daily Morning Chronicle*, Nov. 21, 1863.

95   *Josephine Roedel:* Roedel Diary, Nov. 19, 1863.

95   *After a while the marshals: Washington Daily Morning Chronicle*, Nov. 21, 1863.

95   *One reporter noted that flags:* Ibid.; *Philadelphia Evening Bulletin*, Nov. 20, 1863.

95   *From a far part of the line: Star*, Dec. 3, 1863.

95   *"Like Saul of old he towered":* Sweeney to Brother, Nov. 29, 1863.

96   *People bowed to the president:* White to White, Nov. 20, 1863.

96   *"Hurrah for Old Abe": Star*, Dec. 3, 1863.

96   *The* New York Times *was less impressed:* Nov. 21, 1863. The *Times* saw a "slim" procession for the above reasons; the *Chicago Tribune* saw one "superior" to anything "ever witnessed in this country," Nov. 21, 1863.

96   *"It was a clear autumn day":* E.B.S. to Cousin, Sept. 20, 1863, *Leaves*, p. 23.

96   *An Indianapolis reporter: Indianapolis Daily Journal*, Nov. 23, 1863.

96   *Nor was Sally Myers very sure: Stewart Diaries*, p. 167 (Nov. 19, 1863).

96   *The bands played somber:* Winfield Scott to David Wills, Nov. 19, 1863; George G. Meade to David Wills, Nov. 13, 1863; S. P. Chase to David Wills, Nov. 16, 1863, all in *Revised Report Made to the Legislature of Pennsylvania Relative to the Soldiers' National Cemetery at Gettysburg* (Harrisburg: Singerly, 1867), pp. 187–89.

96   *When it grew clear: Springfield Republic*, Nov. 30, 1863.

97   *"Father of Moses":* Numerous newspapers reported these words. The text that Stockton prepared, however, and that many newspapers reported stated: "Father of mercies."

97   *The many who died: American Commercial & Advertiser*, Baltimore, Nov. 20; *Armstrong Democrat*, Kittanming, PA, Nov. 27, 1863; *Ashtabula Weekly Telegraph*, OH, Dec. 5, 1863; *Boston Daily Courier*, Nov. 23, 1863; *Boston Journal*, Nov. 20, 23, 1863; *Chicago Times*, Nov. 21, 1863; *Cincinnati Daily Commercial*, Nov. 21, 23, 1863; *Cincinnati Daily Gazette*, Nov. 21, 1863; *Christian Recorder*, Philadelphia, Nov. 21, 1863; *Cleveland Plain Dealer*, Nov. 20; *Evening Bulletin*, Philadelphia, Nov. 20, 1863; *Franklin Reposi-*

tory, PA, Dec. 9, 1863; *Harrisburg Daily Telegraph*, Nov. 20, 1863; *Hartford Evening Press*, Nov. 20, 1863; *Illinois State Journal*, Nov. 20, 1863; *Indiana State Sentinel*, *Nov. 20, 1863; Missouri Democrat*, Nov. 23, 1863; *Newark Daily Mercury*, Nov. 20, 1863; *New York Times*, Nov. 20, 1863; *New York Tribune*, Nov. 20, 1863; *New York World*, Nov. 20, 1863; *Philadelphia Inquirer*, Nov. 20, 1863; *Philadelphia Press*, Nov. 20, 1863; *Providence Daily Journal*, Nov. 20, 1863; *Public Ledger*, Philadelphia, Nov. 20, 1863; *Sacramento Daily Union*, Dec. 18, 1863; *Summit County Beacon*, Akron, OH. Dec. 3, 1863; *Washington County People's Journal*, Greenwich, NY, Nov. 26, 1863, *Washington Morning Chronicle*, Nov. 20, 1863.

97   *As Reverend Stockton finished: Daily Ohio State Journal*, Nov. 23, 1863.

97   *One of the carousers, however: Sentinel*, Nov. 24; *Compiler*, Nov. 30; *Star*, Dec. 3, 1863; *Hay Diary*, p. 113 (Nov. 19, 1863). As if in reply to Hay, the *Chicago Tribune*, on Nov. 21, 1863, noted: "few indeed were the hearts however obdurate, that did not unite with him."

98   *Much later, John Russell Young:* Young, *Men and Memories*, vol. 1, pp. 63, 61.

98   *He traveled from Maine:* $70,000 would perhaps be equal to something more than $2.1 million in the early twenty-first century. Scholars disagree about the exact amount.

98   *Years later, the famed author:* Richard H. Dana, Jr., *An Address upon the Life and Services of Edward Everett; Delivered before the Municipal Authorities and Citizens of Cambridge, February 22, 1865* (Cambridge, MA: Sever, 1865), p. 53. Everett, *Orations and Speeches on Various Occasions*, 4:3–17, describes his Washington oration tour. Here the interpretation of George B. Forgie, *Patricide in the House Divided: A Psychological Interpretation of Lincoln and His Age* (New York: W. W. Norton, 1979), pp. 168–72, is followed. See also Marling, *George Washington Slept Here* pp. 78–79.

99   *"He is evidently a person":* Everett Diary, Feb. 15, 1861.

99   *"Something of a compliment":* Everett to Sidney Everett, Oct. 29, 1861, Everett Papers, Massachusetts Historic Society.

99   *In 1862, hoping to send him:* To Whom It May Concern, Sept. 24, 1862, *Collected Works of Lincoln*, 5:437–38; Everett Diary, Sept. 24, 1862.

99   *Nor did he like the idea:* Everett to Salmon P. Chase, Aug. 14, 1862, Everett Papers.

99   *Would he speak about the Constitution:* Some expected that kind of performance exactly—*Brooklyn Daily Eagle*, Nov. 20, 1863. Everett later wrote that Gettysburg was his "first public address" that gave "the hopeful view" of the war.

99   *"The power of hope"*: Fragment on Free Labor [Sept. 17, 1859?], *Collected Works of Lincoln*, 3:462.

100   *Even Forney's paper: Forney's War Press*, Nov. 21, 1863.

100   *He also asked General-in-Chief Henry Halleck:* Everett to Halleck, Sept. 26, 1863, Everett Paper.

100   *He repeatedly discussed the battle:* Everett Diary, Nov. 2, 6, 11, 13, 1863. Nov. 11, 1863, is the first reference to his "Gettysburg Address."

100   *Professor Jacobs would earn special thanks:* Ibid., Nov. 17, 1863.

101   *The scholar from Harvard:* Ibid.

101   *As a young man, Everett had tramped:* Wills, *Lincoln at Gettysburg*, pp. 41–62, informs this paragraph, and more, even if the conclusions here are different.

102   *Two chief authoritative versions:* Manuscript of Edward Everett's Oration, November 19, 1863, ALPLM; and the official version: *Address of Hon. Edward Everett at the Consecration of the National Cemetery at Gettysburg, 19th November, 1863 with the Dedicatory Speech of President Lincoln and the Other Exercises of the Occasion; Accompanied by an Account of the Undertaking and of the Arrangement of the Cemetery Grounds, And by a Map of the Battle-field and a Plan of the Cemetery. Published for the Benefit of the Cemetery Fund* (Boston: Little, Brown, 1864). See also the pamphlet of Everett's speech that almost certainly predates the official version: *An Address Delivered at the Consecration of the National Cemetery at Gettysburg, 19th November, 1863, by Edward Everett* (Boston: Little, Brown, 1864), Boritt Collection; and "Address of the Hon. Edward Everett," *Revised Report*, 208n; "National Cemetery at Gettysburg," *Orations and Speeches on Various Occasions by Edward Everett*, 11th ed. (4 vols., Boston: Little, Brown, 1886), 4:622–69.

102   *In a "Note" that accompanied:* Everett Manuscript, "Note, 21 March 1864."

102   *Other differences between the manuscript:* For example, and crucial to dating the manuscript, the first paragraph of the official version (evidently inspired by Everett being in Gettysburg, perhaps by the moment he began to speak at the cemetery) is not in the newspaper versions that were based on the printing of the handwritten copy sent to the press before the speech was delivered.

102   *In addition to Everett's corrections:* "Note"; cf. Everett Diary, Nov. 19, 1863, explaining, "I omitted a good deal."

102   *"Every word . . . must have been heard": Star*, Nov. 26; *New York World*, Nov. 20; *New York Times*, Nov. 20, 1863.

102   *On the other hand: Indianapolis Daily Journal*, Nov. 23, 1863.

103   *The* Washington Chronicle *guessed:* Nov. 21, 1863.

103   *"Standing beneath this serene sky":* Except for this paragraph, the quotations from Everett's speech come from the manuscript copy. See Appendix A for variations in the official version.

103   *But Everett's magic: Daily Missouri Democrat,* Nov. 23, 1863.

103   *Nurse Souder politely noted:* E.B.S. to Cousin, Nov. 20, 1863, *Leaves,* p. 139.

103   *Nurse Bucklin spoke more forcefully:* Bucklin, *In Hospital and Camp,* p. 196.

103   *The ceremonies "had to us":* Holstein, *Three Years in Field Hospitals,* p. 54.

108   *Everett had been given:* Everett Diary, Nov. 4, 1863.

110   *("To bind up the nation's wounds"):* Second Inaugural Address, March 4, 1864, *Collected Works of Lincoln,* 8:333.

110   *"Our strife pertains to ourselves":* Annual Message to Congress, Dec. 1, 1862, *Collected Works of Lincoln,* 5:529.

111   *Weeks after delivering his address:* Everett to W. S. Wait, Dec. 17, 1863; Everett to W. E. Cramer, Dec. 14, 1863, Everett Papers.

111   *Sitting on the platform:* Forney quoted in Paul Revere Frothingham, *Edward Everett: Orator and Statesman* (Boston: Houghton Mifflin, 1925), p. 457.

112   *Even as the applause came:* Everett Diary, Nov. 19, 1863.

112   *The* New York World *remarked: New York World,* Nov. 20, 1863.

112   *Lincoln had listened intently: Chicago Tribune,* Nov. 21, 1863.

112   *"This holy ground":* Ibid.

112   *When Lincoln arrived: Washington Morning Chronicle,* Nov. 20, 1863.

113   *"Four score and seven years ago":* The Address Delivered at the Dedication of the Cemetery at Gettysburg, Nov. 19, 1863, *Collected Works of Lincoln,* 7:17–23, reproduces various texts with various hypotheses about what Lincoln may have actually said. Other possibilities also exist. Here the most widely published version from AP is quoted, from the most widely read paper of the time, the *New York Tribune,* Nov. 20, 1863, with two variations from what the editors of the *Collected Works* call the "second draft," and some refer to as the Hay Copy, which most likely was the text from which Lincoln spoke. If somehow this was not the actual paper he used, it was the text that he read. Some consider the version of Charles Hale that appeared in the *Address of his Excellency John A. Andrew, to the Two Branches of the Legislature of Massachusetts, January 8, 1864* (Boston: Wright & Potter, 1864), lxxii, the equal of the AP version, and some consider it superior. However, the differences are minute and the AP text—transcription, telegraph, and typesetting errors notwithstanding—went out to the whole country and beyond. With two exceptions described later the variations of the five texts in

Lincoln's hand tend to be minor and mostly of interest to scholars. The Appendices includes both the handwritten versions of the speech and a word-by-word comparison of the texts (see pp. 245–264). In the first sentence of the speech, quoted here, the AP, as it appears in the *Tribune* (but not the *Times,* e.g., Nov. 20, 1863) used a capital "N" for nation, but a lower-case "n" is followed here since all of Lincoln's drafts used it.

113   *The crowd applauded:* Joseph I. Gilbert who much later recalled having been the AP reporter at Gettysburg also recalled that there was no applause. "Lincoln in 1861," *Nineteenth Annual Convention, National Shorthand Reporters' Association. Proceedings of the Annual Meeting . . . Cleveland, Ohio . . . [August 13–16, '17]* (La Porte, Ind., Chase & Shepherd, 1917), pp. 131–40. For Gilbert see also Appendix C, Part 3, and note *"Comparisons,"* on p. 372. Journalist John Russell Young remembered much the same. *Philadelphia Star,* July 25, 1891; *Men and Memories,* vol. 1, p. 70 (see also chapter 7 for Lamon), but the AP dispatch included applause six times that Young conjectured was stuck in by the "more than generous" reporter. When hostile reports carried the speech they often included applause and some papers like the *Pittsburgh Gazette,* Nov. 21, 1863, in addition to noting "applause" and "immense applause," mentioned the speech being interrupted with shouts of "Good, good." Of course, as with so many other aspects of Lincoln at Gettysburg, recollections about applause directly contradict each other and must be kept at arms' length. Barton collected many of these in *Lincoln at Gettysburg,* pp. 163, 173, 176, 179, 181–82, 184, 187, 188–89, 191, 192, 193, 198, 200, and 202. Barton is far from complete. See, e.g., the speech of William H. Tipton, who was thirteen years old in 1863: *Presentation and Unveiling of the Memorial Tablets Commemorating the Lincoln and Burns Event* (Gettysburg: Presbyterian Church, 1914), p. 32. The Ostendorf Collection included a letter that some credit but appears to be a forgery, Robert to "dear Wife," Nov. 20, 1863, that speaks of "light applause." Copy in author's possession.

113   *He had been invited to make:* Wills to Lincoln, Nov. 2, 1863, Lincoln Papers.

113   *first prepared speech:* Lincoln would give only three more prepared speeches: at the 1864 Baltimore Fair; the Second Inaugural Address; and his last speech before his assassination. Following his reelection to the presidency, Lincoln also wrote down his "Response to a Serenade," Nov. 10, 1864, *Lincoln's Collected Works,* 8:100–101, but after having given an impromptu response to a Nov. 8 serenade which, in turn, his secretary, John Hay, wrote down "to prevent the 'loyal Pennsylvanians'

getting a swing at it themselves." *Hay Diary*, p. 248 (Nov. 11, 1864). Presumably, the president wrote out the November 10 serenade response from Hay's text.

113   *Facing the horrendous casualties:* Response to Serenade, July 7, 1863, *Collected Works of Lincoln*, 6:319–20. Some believe that this off-the-cuff response to a serenade celebrating the Independence Day victories at Gettysburg and Vicksburg, indicated that by November 19 Lincoln has been thinking for months about making the speech he gave at Gettysburg. On July 7, in the midst of his response, according the press reports he said: "Gentlemen, this is a glorious theme, and the occasion for a speech, but I'm not prepared to make one worthy of the occasion." The comment appears to be thrown in as an apology for a rambling speech and not an announcement of a forthcoming one by a president who had not prepared a speech since his Inaugural Address. Lincoln did not know that he would go to Gettysburg until it was nearly time to go.

113   *"Near eighty years ago":* Speech at Peoria, Illinois, Oct. 16, 1854; Eulogy on Henry Clay, July 6, 1852, *Collected Works of Lincoln*, 2:275, 121.

114   *Even over the short run:* Nicolay, "Lincoln's Gettysburg Address," p. 597.

114   *Lincoln's friend James C. Conkling: Oration of Hon. James C. Conkling, Delivered in Springfield, Ill. July 4th, 1857* (Springfield, Ill., 1857), 1. The pamphlet is in the ALPLM. We do not know whether Lincoln was present when Conkling delivered the oration, though it is unlikely that he did not see the printed speech. I'm indebted to Kim Bauer of the ALPLM for calling the speech to my attention. Don E. Fehrenbacher, *Lincoln in Text and Context: Collected Essays* (Stanford: Stanford University Press, 1987), p. 285, raises the possibility that Galusha Grow's July 4, 1861, inaugural speech as Speaker of the U.S. House of Representatives, which referred to the Declaration of Independence "Four score years ago," caught Lincoln's eye, though the Speaker either miscounted or a clerk mistyped what should have been "four score and five years ago."

114   *Everett concluded his July 4, 1860:* Edward Everett, *Oration Delivered Before the City authorities of Boston, on the Fourth of July, 1860* (Boston: Rand & Avery, 1860), pp. 47–48.

115   *"They have a right to claim it":* Speech at Chicago, Ill., July 10, 1858, *Collected Works of Lincoln*, 2:501–02.

115   *Seward had already spoken:* Unknown to William H. Seward, Nov. 24, 1863, copy, Seward Papers.

115   *"They would probably help":* To Michael Hahn, March 13, 1864, *Collected Works of Lincoln*, 7:243.

115 *As an ambitious young man:* Address Before the Young Men's Lyceum of Springfield, Ill., Jan. 27, 1838, *Collected Works of Lincoln,* 1:114.

115 *Soon after issuing the Proclamation:* J. W. Forney to Lincoln, Dec. 20, 1862, Lincoln Papers.

116 *He recorded Lincoln saying:* Carpenter, *Six Months at the White House,* pp. 90, 269.

116 *Now he would be remembered:* Joshua Speed to William Herndon, February 1866, in Wilson and Davis, eds., *Herndon's Informants,* p. 197.

117 *"Now we are engaged":* Once again the *Tribune* uses capital "N"s for "Nation," but not Lincoln, or the *New York Times,* etc.

117 *In his July 4, 1861, war message:* Message to Congress in Special Session, July 4, 1861, *Collected Works of Lincoln,* 4:439.

117 *The United States was:* Ibid., 5:537.

118 *"far above our poor power":* The AP missed the word "poor," as did others, though it appears in all of Lincoln's drafts as well as in other newspaper reports. It is therefore inserted into the text quoted here. See for ex.: *Age,* Philadelphia, Nov. 20, *Ohio Statesman,* Columbus, Nov. 22, 1863; *Ohio Repository,* Canton, Nov. 25, 1863; *Fremont Journal,* Nov. 27, 1863.

118 *The reporter, noting the faces:* Isaac Jackson Allen in *Ohio State Journal,* Nov. 23, 1863. He would later write that Lincoln reached hearts that Everett could not. Some believe that the report may have been colored by Allen's hopes for a presidential appointment that came in 1864 in the form of the consulship in Bangkok—Isaac Jackson Allen Autobiography, 1904, LOC. However, Allen would repeat his exact words seventeen years later: I.J.A. to Editor, *Cincinnati Commercial,* Nov. 12, 1879.

119 *"Their fall was not in vain":* Mason Locke Weems, *The Life of Washington,* ed. Marcus Cunliffe (Cambridge, MA: Harvard University Press, 1962), p. 124.

119 *The applause quieted:* The "second draft" had "this government" and did not include "under God." The AP report in the *Tribune* used the plural "Governments" with a capital "G."

119 *He was a nationalist:* Address to New Jersey Senate, Trenton, NJ, Feb. 21, 1861, *Collected Works of Lincoln,* 4:235.

120 *A born-again nation:* The phrase "born again," a synonym for "new birth," or the theological term "regeneration," had been in common use since the transatlantic Evangelical awakenings of the eighteenth-century. In contrast to being born as a babe, new birth—often a moment of sudden conversion—offered spiritual blessings here and now and eternal life in the future.

120   *At a less than conscious level:* Compare Lincoln's words with a Bible Concordance—www.biblegateway.com. "Four score," for example, appears thirty-five times.

120   *He jotted down for himself perhaps:* Mediation on the Divine Will [Sept. 2, 1862?], *Collected Works of Lincoln,* 5:403. Second Inaugural Address, March 4, 1865, ibid., 333.

121   *In his own copy, Everett:* See Appendix A. Decades later Lamon still wrote about the "celebration of the National Cemetery," then crossed the word out and replaced it with "dedication"—Lamon's Recollections, Draft. "Inauguration" also remained in circulation.

121   *It was "the people's government":* Charles Wiltse and Alan R. Berolzheimer, eds., *The Papers of Daniel Webster: Speeches and Formal Writings* (Dartmouth, NH: Dartmouth College 1986), 1:339–40. Herndon wrote that "Lincoln thought that Webster's great speech in reply to Haynes was the very best speech that was ever delivered"—Herndon to Jesse W. Weik, Jan. 1, 1886, Herndon-Weik Collection, LOC, and that Lincoln consulted it when preparing his "House Divided" speech as well as his First Inaugural. See Paul M. Angle, ed., *Herndon's Life of Lincoln: The History and Personal Recollections of Abraham Lincoln as Originally Written by William H. Herndon and Jesse W. Weik* (New York: Fawcett, 1961), pp. 376, 324.

122   *The chief goal was to bind:* This paragraph is informed by Blondheim, *News Over the Wires.*

122   *The College folk did arrive in strength:* For Hopkins, see Pennsylvania Board of Trustees Minutes, Aug. 13, 1863, Gettysburg College; cf. *Star,* July 2, 1868. His funeral would be conducted by professors and attended by the whole student body. Until that ocassion in 1868 the College people had been only in one such procession: when Lincoln came. The recollection about "a group" of black people, "off to one side," loudly calling out their Amens, is not credible in the absence of contemporary evidence. "Recollections of Mr. Gitt," Wilson, ed., *Intimate Memories,* 479.

122   *At the end of Lincoln's remarks: Sentinel,* Nov. 24, 1863; *New York Times,* Nov. 20, 1863.

122   *The Massachusetts delegation: Report of the Joint Special Committee on the Burial of Massachusetts Dead at Gettysburg,* p. 20.

123   *Many felt that they stood on a sacred spot: Armstrong Democrat,* Kittanning, PA. Nov. 27, 1863.

123   *The singers came mostly from the local: Sentinel,* Nov. 24, 1863.

123   *The Reverend Baugher: Address of Hon. Edward Everett,* p. 88; for another version, see *Boston Daily Journal,* Nov. 20, 1863.

123   *They had been "wounden":* White to White, Nov. 20, 1863; cf. "The National Cemetery," *Soldiers' National Cemetery,* p. 66.

123   *Descending from the platform: Washington Chronicle,* Nov. 21, 1863; *Washington National Intelligencer,* Nov. 25, 1863.

124   *If he understood that "something": Baltimore American and Commercial Advertiser,* Nov. 20, 1863.

124   *Along the route back to town: Indianapolis Daily Journal,* Nov. 23, 1863.

124   *"Is it Crolius?":* E.B.S. to Cousin, Nov. 20, 1863, *Leaves,* p. 140.

125   *They "lingered until the shades": Washington Chronicle,* Nov. 21, 1863.

125   *Drayman and photographer William Weaver:* Samuel Weaver to William Weaver, Nov. 25, 1863, NA.

125   *Nurse Souder's group, too, went:* E.B.S. to Cousin, Nov. 20, 1863, *Leaves,* pp. 141–42.

125   *The Reverend H. N. Pohlman of Albany: Gettysburg, Lincoln's Address and Our Educational Institutions* (York, PA: Board of Education of the General Synod of the Evangelical Lutheran Church in the United States, 1907), pp. 14–15.

125   *The* Sentinel *sympathized: Sentinel,* Nov. 24, 1863.

126   *Handshake after handshake:* Gregory M. Caputo, Robert E. Dye, M.D. Professor of Medicine at the Pennsylvania State University Milton S. Hershey Medical Center College of Medicine provided the information about variola minor.

126   *Handshaking done, Lincoln: Sentinel,* Nov. 24, 1863.

126   *The wounded veteran: Cincinnati Daily Commercial,* Nov. 23, 1863.

126   *"It seemed difficult":* E.B.S. to Cousin, Nov. 20, 1863, *Leaves,* p. 142.

126   *New York's Governor Seymour reviewed: New York World,* Nov. 20, 1863; *American and Commercial Advertiser,* New York, Nov. 20, 1863.

126   *A German paper in Milwaukee: Der Milwaukee See-Bote,* Nov. 25, 1863: "Die Rede soll viele seiner Freunde überrascht und in Erstaunen gesetzt haben."

127   *Another, in Ohio, claimed: Columbus Westbote,* Nov. 26, 1863: "Governeur Seymour von New York hatte bereits am Morgen auf sturmisches Rufen des Publkums, auf offener Strasse sprechen mussen" (. . . ended up speaking in the open, on the street).

127   *The* Tazewell County Republican*: Tazewell County Republican,* Nov. 27, 1863.

127   *John Russell Young would much later:* Young, *Men and Memories,* vol. 1, p. 65.

127   *Lincoln would be remembered:* E. W. Andrews in Rice, ed., *Reminiscences of Abraham Lincoln,* p. 514.

127   *"I don't think he would have been":* W . . . to Sister, Nov. 23, 1863, copy, GNMP, pp. 10–18.

127   *But the president:* Cochrane, "Lincoln," p. 9.

128   *now had "a grievous headache":* Isaac Jackson Allen Autobiography, p. 26.

128   *Johnson bathed his forehead:* MacVeagh, "Lincoln at Gettysburg," p. 22.

128   *"The power of the President":* Indianapolis Daily Journal, Nov. 25, 1863. The editor was Berry R. Sulgrove.

128   *There are people out there: Hanover Spectator,* Nov. 27, 1863.

128   *"Some wretched junction":* William Everett, *The Knapsack,* Dec. 17, 1863, published for Boston Sanitary Fair, Mearns Papers.

128   *"The amount of blasphemy": Harrisburg Weekly Press and Union,* Nov. 21, 1863.

129   *Only days after the consecration: Cincinnati Daily Commercial,* Nov. 23, 1863.

Chapter Six: Echoes

Page

130   *He could not come:* Miller to Miller, Nov. 14, Nov. 19, 1863, MMMP.

130   *At home, Sally Myers: Stewart Diaries,* p. 167 (Nov. 20, 1863).

130   *The railroads had already received: Indianapolis Daily Journal,* Nov. 23, 1863.

130   *"Six mortal, long": Washington Daily Chronicle,* Nov. 21, 1863.

130   *Some had come prepared: Baltimore American and Commercial Advertiser,* Nov. 18, 1863.

131   *A Philadelphia paper: Philadelphia Daily Evening Bulletin,* Nov. 20, 1863.

131   *Some feared a second night: Hardin County (Ohio) Democrat,* Nov. 27, 1863.

131   *Proof sheets had been distributed:* Everett Diary, Nov. 14, 1863.

131   *This was not the exact speech:* Ibid., Nov. 19, 1863.

132   *The praise seems to have stuck:* Henry C. Robinson to McClellan, June 17, 1864, George B. McClellan Papers, LOC.

132   *But back in November 1863: Washington Evening Chronicle,* Nov. 20, 1863.

133   *The* Chronicle *then went on: The Gettysburg Solemnities* (Washington, DC: *Washington Chronicle,* 1863). For the announcement of the publication, see *Sentinel,* Nov. 24; *Compiler,* Nov. 30, 1863; *Washington Daily Chronicle,* Nov. 20, 21, 1863.

133   *The* Chicago Tribune: *Chicago Tribune,* Nov. 24, 1863; cf. praising Everett in Rep. press: *Albany Evening Journal,* Nov. 21, 1863; *American Standard,* Jersey City, NJ, Nov. 20, 1863; *Bangor Daily Whig & Courier,*

Nov. 21, 1863; *Boston Daily Courier,* Nov. 23, 1863; *Boston Daily Journal,* Nov. 20, 1863; *Boston Herald,* Nov. 20, 1863; *Camden Democrat,* NJ, Nov. 28, 1863; *Courier & Freeman,* Nov. 25, 1863; *Cleveland Plain Dealer,* Nov. 20, 1863; *Franklin Repository,* PA, Nov. 25, 1863; *Kennebec Journal,* Dec. 4, 1863; *Malone Palladium,* NY, Dec. 3, 1863; *Missouri Republican,* Nov. 23, 1863; *Monmouth Herald & Inquirer,* NJ, Dec. 10, 1863; *National Standard & Salem County Advertiser,* Dec. 9, 1863; *New Jersey Journal,* Elizabeth, Nov. 24, 1863; *New York Evening Post,* Nov. 20, 1863; *National Intelligencer,* Nov. 20, 1863; *Paterson Weekly Press,* NJ, Nov. 28, 1863; *Sentinel & Freedom,* Nov. 24, 1863; *Sacramento Daily Union,* Dec. 18, 1863; *Stockton Daily Independent* (Ca.) Nov. 23, 27, 1863; *Summit County Beacon,* Dec. 3, 1863; *Troy Daily Whig,* NY, Nov. 20, 1863.

133   *If the orator thought: Chicago Times,* Nov. 24, 1863; cf. *Richmond Dispatch,* Nov. 27, 1863; *Staunton Vindicator,* Dec. 4, 1863; *Liberator,* Jan. 1, 1864.

133   *The* New York World*: New York World,* Nov. 21, 24, 1863.

133   *The unkindest cut:* Nov. 20, 1863. Everett noted in his diary, Nov. 28, 1863, that he had been "vilified" in England by the *Saturday Review,* on account of his son, William, not being in uniform.

133   *Partisan criticism:* Everett Diary, Nov. 25, Dec. 16, 23, 1863; see also Nov. 27.

133   *Not until after the death: Harper's Weekly,* Dec. 5, 1863; July 22, 1865; see also March 11, 1865.

133   *But now to one reporter: Philadelphia Press,* Nov. 24, 1863; cf. *Daily Eastern Argus,* Dec. 1, 1863; *Delaware Republican & Visitor,* Delhi, NY, Nov. 28, 1863; *Evening Post,* Hartford, CT., Nov. 21, 1863.

133   *In his diary, Everett had written:* Everett Diary, Oct. 22, 1863.

134   *The* Chronicle *admired:* Nov. 27, 1863; cf. *Amesbury (Mass.) Villager,* Nov. 26, 1863.

134   *Boston echoed by comparing: Boston Daily Journal,* Nov. 20, 1863.

134   *Milwaukee praised the broad grasp: Milwaukee Sentinel,* Nov. 25, 1863.

134   *On the very day of his oration:* Everett Diary, Nov. 19, 1863.

134   *Not unexpected, the* New York Herald*: New York Herald,* Nov. 20, 1863; cf. *Providence Daily Post,* RI., Nov. 28, 1863.

134   *And William Cullen Bryant's: New York Evening Post,* Dec. 2, 1863.

134   *A letter from an army officer:* Everett Diary, Dec. 24, 1863.

134   *"Truly disgusting":* Ibid.; cf. Dec. 26, 1863.

134   *Complaints about his history:* Everett to Wills, Nov. 25, 1863, Wills Papers.

134 *As if knowing:* David Wills to Edward Everett, Nov. 25, 1863, GNMP. The letter is also printed in *Revised Report*, pp. 184–86.

134 *Everett also continued:* Brig. Gen. James C. Rice, "The Rebel Invasion of Pennsylvania: The Truth Regarding Some Important Facts," *New York Times,* Nov. 28, 1863; Everett to Jacobs, Nov. 28, Dec. 18, 1863, Everett Papers; Samuel Wylie Crawford to Jacobs, Dec. 1863, Crawford Papers, LOC.

134 *He recorded in his diary:* Everett Diary, March 12, 1864.

135 *General Hooker, in turn:* Ibid., March 5, 1864.

135 *When Everett prepared his final text:* Everett to Wills, Dec. 14, 1863, *Revised Report,* 186; Everett Diary, March 5, 1864.

135 *Everett felt good about his work:* Everett to W. S. Wait, Dec. 17, 1863, Everett Papers.

135 *Of course he knew that this aspect:* So it was: see, e.g., *Richmond Daily Dispatch,* Nov. 25, 1863, copied all over the Confederacy; *Staunton Vindicator,* Dec. 4, 1863; *Chicago Times,* Nov. 24, 1863; *Cincinnati Enquirer,* Nov. 30, 1863; *Newark Daily Journal,* NJ, Dec. 12, 1863.

135 *The "official" version of the dedication:* Everett to F[rederick] W[illiam] Seward, Jan. 22, 1863, Seward Papers; Everett Diary, Dec. 1, 1863; Jan. 2, 1864.

135 *He also interceded:* Everett Diary, Dec. 23, 1863; *Address of his Excellency John A. Andrew, to the Two Branches of the Legislature of Massachusetts, January 8, 1864* (Boston: Wright & Potter, 1864).

135 *At least eight expanded editions:* Jay Monaghan, *Lincoln Bibliography* (2 vols., Springfield, IL: Illinois State Historical Library, 1943), 1:47–48, lists various printings.

135 *The pamphlet crossed the Atlantic:* Everett to Charles Francis Adams, Jan. 5, 1864, in Frothingham, *Edward Everett: Orator and Statesman,* p. 458.

135 *In February, Everett was apparently:* Everett to F. W. Seward, Feb. 12, 1864, Seward Papers.

135 *In May, Everett's diary recorded:* Everett Diary, May 3, 1864.

136 *In July, he thanked the Secretary of State:* Everett to Seward, July 9, 1864, Seward Papers.

136 *"I have looked for a letter":* Miller to Miller, Nov. 22, 25, 1863.

137 *Nor did most other soldiers:* This is not only the author's finding but also that of his colleagues who had looked at the question. See extensive Boritt correspondence. One caveat might be added to the above conclusion: very few newspapers published in Union military camps survive for late 1863, but if these commented on Lincoln's Gettysburg remarks, they made no impression on the men.

138   *The* Hartford Courant *printed: Hartford Courant,* Nov. 20, 30, Dec. 11, 1863; cf. "Mr. Lincoln's 'Style,' " the *Times* of London cited in *Recorder and Democrat,* Catskill, N.Y., Oct. 22, 1863.

138   *The front page of the* Times: *New York Times,* Nov. 20, 1863.

138   *"President Lincoln was there": Steubenville Weekly Herald.*

138   *In Gettysburg the* Sentinel: Nov. 24, 1863; cf. *New Hampshire Sentinel,* Nov. 26, 1863.

138   *When the Republican press commented: Pittsburgh Daily Dispatch,* Nov. 23, 1863; cf. *Agitator,* Wellsboro, PA, Dec. 2, 1863; *Ashtabula Weekly Telegraph,* OH, Dec. 5, 1863; *Baltimore Sun,* Nov. 20, 1863; *New Brunswick Freedonian,* NJ, Nov. 21, 1863; *Stockton Daily Times,* CA, Nov. 23, 1863; *Troy Daily Times,* NY, Nov. 21, 1863.

138   *Forney's* Philadelphia Press: Nov. 21, 1863.

138   *Another of his papers: Forney's War Press,* Dec. 5, 1863.

139   *In Ohio, an editor perhaps hoping: Daily Ohio State Journal,* Nov. 23, 1863; cf. *Summit County Beacon* Akron, OH, Dec. 3, 1863.

139   *Still others sent:* James M. Scovel to Lincoln, Nov. 23, 1863, Lincoln papers, LOC.

139   *The* Providence Journal: Nov. 20, 1863.

139   *The* Daily Republican *of Springfield:* Nov. 21, 1863; cf. *Rutland (Vt.) Daily Herald,* Nov. 23, 1863; *St. Johnsbury (Vt.) Caledonian,* Nov. 27, 1863; *Peoria* (Ill.) *Transcript,* Dec. 9, 1863. Though not the editor of the paper, the assessment may have come from Josiah G. Holland, himself a master of the language and soon to be a Lincoln biographer.

140   *Like some other papers: Terre Haute Daily Wabash Express,* Dec. 3, 1863. The paper found room to print Lincoln's Annual Message, which was twenty-seven times as long (6,245 words): Dec. 11, 1863.

140   *Indeed, perhaps because the magazine's: Harper's Weekly,* Dec. 5, 12, 1863. Presumably the praise came from William Curtis, the editor. Cf. *Frank Leslie's Illustrated News,* Dec. 5, 1863.

140   *Although the* Boston: *Boston Evening Transcript,* Nov. 21, 1863.

140   *Many years later:* Young, *Men and Memories,* vol. 1, p. 64.

140   *The War Department had decided:* White, *The American Railroad Passenger Car,* pp. 367–70. No president after that would have a private railroad car. They would depend on railroad magnates for their transportation without much protest from reformers about the subject. Only the arrival of the jet airplane changed things.

141   *Lincoln spoke:* Adam Gurowski, *Diary* (3 vols., New York: Burt Frankin, 1968 reprint of vols. 1 and 2 published in 1862 and vol. 3 in 1866), vol. 3, p. 33 (Nov. 21, 1863).

141   *The same issue of a Baltimore paper: Baltimore County Advocate*, Nov. 28, 1863; cf. *Philadelphia News* quoted in *Washington Star*, Nov, 24, 1863; *Baltimore American and Commercial Advertiser* quoted in *Washington Star*, Dec. 2, 1863.

141   *In Ohio, the* Fremont: Nov. 27, 1863.

141   *The* Toledo Blade *did the same: Daily Toledo Blade*, Dec. 4, 1863.

141   *On the day the president rode: Daily Wabash Express*, Nov. 18, 1863.

141   *In New Jersey, the* Hudson: *Hudson County (Hoboken, N.J.) Democrat*, Nov. 28, 1863.

141   *In Illinois, the* Freeport Bulletin: Nov. 25, Dec. 10, 17, 24, 1863.

141   *Democratic papers often gave: Rochester (N.Y.) Daily Union and Advertiser*, Nov. 21, 1863.

141   *The paper that had been suppressed: Chicago Times*, Nov. 23, Dec. 2, 1863.

141   *But the* Chicago Times *would match:* See Dec. 4, 5, 7, 10, 11, 14, 16, 17, 21, 23, 28, and 31, 1863; the quotation is from Dec. 14, 1863.

142   *In Ohio, the "Copperhead": Crisis (Ohio)*, Nov. 25, 1863.

142   *Detroit's* Free Press: *New York World*, Nov. 27, 1863; *Detroit Free Press*, Nov. 27, 1863; *Indiana State Sentinel*, Dec. 7, 1863.

142   *That blacks were as good: Cheshire (Keene, N.H.) Republican*, Nov. 25, 1863.

142   *The reporter of the* Boston: *Boston Advertiser*, Nov. 23, 1863.

142   *In Lincoln's home state: Centralia (Ill.) Sentinel*, Nov. 26, 1863.

142   *"Ninety years ago" also appeared: Hardin County Republican*, Nov. 27, 1863; *Pittsburgher Volksblatt*, Nov. 21, 1863: "Vor neunzig Jahren schufen. . . ."

142   *The* Chicago Times *started:* Nov. 22, 1863.

142   *In Cincinnati, the* Daily Gazette: Nov. 21, 1863. The version of the *Chicago Tribune*, Nov. 21, 1863, is the same until: "mankind are created equal by a good God, and now we are engaged in a great contest. We are contesting the question whether this nation, or any nation, or any nation so conceived, so dedicated can longer remain," etc.

142   *That very language: Illinois State Journal*, Nov. 23, 1863.

143   *"Our Father": Rochester Daily Union Advertiser*, N.Y., Nov. 21, 1863.

143   *"Now, we are engaged": Detroit Free Press*, Nov. 21, 1863.

143   *"Can longer remain": Chicago Tribune*, Nov. 21, 1863; *Sterling Republican Gazette*, Nov. 28, 1863.

143   *"The dead will little heed": Sacramento Daily Union*, clipping, n.d. [Nov.–Dec. 1863].

143   *The* Steubenville Weekly: Nov. 25, 1863.

143   *"The world will little note": Philadelphia Inquirer*, Nov. 20, 1863; *Frank Leslie's Illustrated News*, Dec. 5, 1863.

143   *"We owe this offering": Philadelphia Inquirer,* Nov. 20, 1863; *Toledo Blade,* Nov. 21, 1863; *Pittsburgh Post,* Nov. 23, 1863.

143   *The* New York Times: Ibid; *New York Times,* Nov. 20; *New York Tribune,* Nov 20, 1863.

143   *A not uncommon conclusion: Cincinnati Daily Gazette,* Nov. 21, 1863.

143   *The* Cincinnati Daily Commercial: Nov. 21, 1863, which printed a better version on Nov. 23, 1863; *Hardin County Republican,* Nov. 27, 1863.

143   *"That the Government the people founded": Sterling Republican Gazette,* Nov. 28, 1863.

143   *It changed the last part: Christian Recorder,* Nov. 28, 1863. Italics are not in the original; "all" was simply slipped in. The paper may have simply copied from the *Philadelphia Inquirer,* Nov. 20, 1863.

143   *The* Recorder *also quoted:* Nov. 21, 1863.

144   *The German papers: Pittsburgher Volksblatt,* Nov. 21, 1863; *Freiheits Freund und Courier,* Pittsburgh, Nov 21, 1863; St. Louis *Westliche Post,* Nov. 25, 1863.

144   *Pennsylvania's* Pittsburgher: *Pittsburgher Volksblatt,* Nov. 21, 1863; *Freiheits Freund und Courier,* Pittsburgh, Nov. 21, 1863. The phrasings respectively were: *dass alle Menschen mit gleichen Rechten / dass alle Menschen gleich geschaffen sein.* My student Jay Hagerman called this example to my attention.

144   *It went with the more conservative: Westliche Post,* Nov. 25, 1863; cf. *Bauren Freund,* Pennsburg, Pa., Nov. 24, 1863.

144   *Other vital words:* See, e.g., *Pittsburgher Volksblatt, Freiheits Freund und Courier,* and *Westliche Post,* respectively, translating "government of the people": Volksregierung/selbsteingestze volksthümliche [Regierung]/die Regierung des Volkes.

144   *Though the* Westliche Post: Dec. 9, 1863: "Eines erlichen Bürgers von ordinärer Begabung."

144   *Its chief rival in the West: Illinois Staats-Zeitung,* Nov. 21, 1863: "Die Rede von dem Achtb. Edward Everett, die feierliche Todtenklage des Chors und der Weihespruch vom Praesidenten Lincoln werden sich wuerdig den Annalen des Krieges anschliessen."

144   *Neither did the most important: New Yorker Staats-Zeitung und Harold,* Nov. 20, 1863. The Catholic press, often catering to immigrants whether in German or English, appears to have paid no attention to Lincoln's speech. See, e.g., *New York Kirchen-Zeitung* or the *Catholic Register.* The same was true of the Spanish Press as illustrated by *Rio Abaje Daily Press* in the Arizona and New Mexico territories.

145   *The* Maine Farmer: Nov. 19, 1863; *Bath Daily Sentinel and Times,* Nov. 20, 21, 1863. I'm indebted to my student and volunteer assistant, Ashley Towle, for these wonderful examples.

145   *In New Castle, Indiana: New Castle Courier,* Dec. 3, 1863.

145   *He might have agreed:* Everett Diary, Nov. 11, 1863.

145   *In one issue that copied: Compiler,* Dec. 7, 14, 1863, reprinting an article from the Philadelphia *Age.* History, too, right to our own time, would mostly forget Seward's important speech.

145   *In nearby Harrisburg: Harrisburg Patriot and Union,* Nov. 24, 1863.

145   *The local Republican paper: Daily Telegraph,* Nov. 24, 1863.

146   The New York Tribune: *New York Tribune,* Nov. 26, 1863.

146   *The unkindest attack on Lincoln: Richmond Daily Dispatch,* Nov. 25, 1863.

146   *Echoed a Cincinnati voice: Cincinnati Daily Enquirer,* Nov. 29, 1863.

146   *The Philadelphia* Age *cried:* Nov. 20, 1863; cf. *York (Pa.) Gazette,* Nov. 24, 1863; *Cincinnati Enquirer,* Nov. 26, 30, 1863.

146   *Others, too, commented: Ebensburg (Pa.) Democrat and Sentinel,* Dec. 2, 1863.

146   *"His excellency appeared": Pittsburgh Post,* Nov. 23, 1863.

146   *The Dutch ambassador:* J. W. Schulte Nordholt, ed., "The Civil War Letters of the Dutch Ambassador," *Journal of the Illinois State Historical Society,* 54 (Winter 1961): 366–67.

146   The Times *in London:* Dec. 3, 4, 1863.

146   *People would later have it:* Lamon's Reminiscences; Lamon, *Recollection* p. 173.

146   *However, the next day:* Everett to Lincoln, Nov. 20, 1863, Lincoln Papers.

146   *In his diary:* Everett Diary, Nov. 20, 1863.

147   *Lincoln replied on the same day:* Lincoln to Edward Everett, Nov. 20, 1863, *Collected Works of Lincoln,* 7:24–25.

147   *Hay noted in his diary: Hay Diary,* pp. 113–14 (Nov. 19, 1863). Curiously, some believe that because a draft of Lincoln's speech ended up among Hay's papers, he must have requested Lincoln to make it for him. For the "second" or "Hay copy" see chapter 5 and Appendix C, Parts 3 and 4.

147   *But Frank Haskell:* Frank Haskell, Nov. 20, 1863, in Frank L. Byrne and Andrew I. Weaver, eds., *Haskell of Gettysburg. His Life and Civil War Papers* (Madison: State Historical Society of Wisconsin, 1970), p. 234.

147   *Haskell and his commander:* John Gibbon, *Personal Recollections of the Civil War* (New York: Putnam, 1928), p. 184. Gibbon wrote his recollections in the 1890s. Among other papers, the *Sentinel,* Nov. 24, 1863, reported the Gibbon "party" riding over the battlefield.

148   *A main reason for the creation:* Wills to Lincoln, Nov. 2, 1863, Lincoln Papers. LC.

148   *Frank Haskell, however, wrote:* Haskell, Nov. 20, 1863, in Byrne and Weaver, eds., *Haskell of Gettysburg,* p. 234.

148   *Haskell, however, complained:* Ibid.

148   *"President Lincoln is not a polished speaker":* Union Vedette, Jan. 1, 1864; cf. *Boston Transcript,* Nov. 20, 1863; see also *Deseret News,* Nov. 25, 1863. I am indebted to my student, Skye Montgomery, for finding this newspaper.

149   *The Presidential Proclamation:* Proclamation of Thanksgiving, October. 3, 1863, *Collected Works of Lincoln,* 6:496–97.

149   *It spoke not of a "new birth":* Annual Message to Congress, Dec. 8, 1863, ibid., 7:50.

149   *Had he not told Frederick Douglass:* "Our Work is Not Done," in Philip S. Foner, ed., *Life and Writings of Frederick Douglass* (4 vols., New York: International Publishers, 1952), 3:385. Douglass quoted Lincoln's comment from their August 10, 1863, meeting at the White House in a speech to the Annual Meeting of the American Antislavery Society, Philadelphia, Dec. 3–4, 1863.

149   *He concluded his address:* Annual Message, *Collected Works of Lincoln,* 7:53. This paragraph is indebted to David W. Blight, *Race and Reunion: The Civil War in American Memory* (Cambridge, MA: Harvard University Press, 2001), pp. 15–18. Blight maintains that Douglass "had given his own Gettysburg Address many times over during the war. . . . On the level of ideology, Douglass was the President's unacknowledged alter ego, the intellectual godfather of the Gettysburg Address" (p. 15). I am less certain that Lincoln, or the North, was very familiar with Douglass's speeches.

149   *The Republican* Berkshire: *Berkshire County Eagle,* Dec. 17, 1863.

149   *The Raleigh, North Carolina: Raleigh Weekly Standard,* Dec. 16, 1863.

150   *On the other hand: Coshocton* (Ohio) *Democrat,* Dec. 16, 1863. cf: *Argus and Patriot,* Montpelier, VT, Dec. 17, 1863; *New York Daily Reformer,* Watertown, NY, Dec. 8, 1863; *Rutland Daily Herald,* VT., Dec. 9, 10, 1863; *Caledonian* (St. Johnsbury, VT), Dec. 18, 1863; *Burlington* (VT) *Sentinel,* Dec. 11, 18, 1863; *Courier & Freeman,* Potsdam, NY, Dec. 16, 1863; *Daily Freeman,* Montpelier, VT, Dec. 10, 1863; *Kennebec Journal,* Dec. 18, 1863; *New York Daily Reformer,* Dec. 10, 1863; *New Jersey Chronicle,* Jersey City, Dec. 16, 1863; *Salem Press,* Dec. 15, 1863; *Washington County People's Journal,* Jan. 21, 1864; *Ballston Journal,* NY, Ballston Spa, Dec. 15, 1863; *Ohio Repository,* Canton, OH, Dec. 9,

1863; *Princeton Standard*, NJ, Dec. 11, 1863; *Somerset Messenger*, Dec. 17, 1863.

150 *In February 1864, he was asked:* Later, even the finest historians would try to prove the immediate success of Lincoln's speech through the "many" copies he made of the address. See, e.g., Merrill D. Peterson, *Lincoln in American Memory* (New York: Oxford University Press, 1994), p. 115; Donald, *Lincoln*, p. 465. It bears repeating that the record shows that Lincoln was asked twice to donate handwritten versions of his speech to charity. As early as 1894, Nicolay, "Lincoln's Gettysburg Address," 605, wrote of Lincoln having made "a half dozen or more" copies, but also explained that the number "cannot now be confidently stated," and the only examples he could point to were the ones that exist to this day. Wishful thinking about lost copies, which this author has indulged in too, privately, appear to be just that; newfound forgeries must be also dismissed.

150 *"The manuscript of my":* Everett Diary, March 15, 1864. Everett to Lincoln, Jan. 30, 1864, Lincoln Papers, which requested the president's speech, also referred to "my Gettysburg Address" and Lincoln's "dedicatory Remarks." For Everett's repeated references to his "Gettysburg Address," see Everett Diary, Nov. 11, Dec. 16, 18, 21, 1863; Apr. 7, May 3, 1864; Everett to Frederick Seward, Jan. 27, 1864. Everett was also asked for his "address at Gettysburg" for the Great Western Sanitary Fair, but by then he had promised it to New York—Everett to George McLaughlin, Dec. 17, 1863, in Charles Brandon Boyton, *History of the Great Western Sanitary Fair* (Cincinnati: Vent, 1864), p. 160.

150 *Lincoln indeed had agreed:* Lincoln to Everett, Feb. 4, 1864, *Collected Works of Lincoln*, 7:167–68; Everett to Lincoln, March 3, 1864, Lincoln Papers; Everett to Mrs. Hamilton Fish, March 18, 1864, Everett Papers, Julia K. Fish to Lincoln, n.d., Lincoln Papers. See also Everett to Mrs Hamilton Fish, Jan. 22, 26, 28, 1864, copies, Mearns Papers, Box 147, Folder "3rd Draft"; Nicolay to Abby A. Stevens, March 4, 1864, Lincoln Papers.

150 *Presumably to help try to sell:* Miller & Matthews to Lincoln, March 23, 1864, Lincoln Papers. None appear to have survived.

150 *Yet in advertising: Boston Daily Advertiser*, Apr. 6, 1864.

151 *"Herewith is the copy":* Lincoln to George Bancroft, Feb. 29, 1864, *Collected Works of Lincoln*, 7:212.

151 *The editor of the volume then complained:* John P. Kennedy to Lincoln, March 3, 1864; John G. Nicolay to Kennedy, March 7, 1864; Alexander Bliss to Nicolay, March 7, 1864; Final Text, 7:22–23, Lincoln Papers.

152 *Instead of being sold:* Mearns and Dunlap, *Long Remembered*, passim. See

also a full folder of letters about the manuscript and the fair, Mearns Papers, Box 147, Gettysburg Address Provenance, Third Draft, "Everett Copy."

152 *If the "Address . . .":* Boston Daily Advertiser, April 6, 1864; *The Catalogue of Articles Contained in Museum of Curiosity Shop of the Metropolitan Fair,* Mearns Papers, 147, folder Provenance of the Third Draft "Everett Copy."

152 *Much more than the generally:* John P. Kennedy, ed., *Autograph Leaves of Our Country's Authors* (Baltimore: Cushings & Bailey, 1864). Even decades later when people looked for the text of the speech, they pointed to this volume. See, e.g., Edward McPherson to John G. Nicolay, Nov. 28, 1893, Nicolay Papers; Robert Todd Lincoln to James B. Aleshire, May 5, 1909, Mearns Papers, Box 147.

153 *For Philadelphia's June 1864: President Lincoln's Emancipation Proclamation,* Leland-Boker "authorized" edition, the Gilder Lehrman Collection, on deposit at the New-York Historical Society.

153 *Lincoln acknowledged wanting:* A. H. Hoge and D. P. Livermore to Lincoln, Nov. 26, 1863, Lincoln Papers, Series 1. See also D. P. Livermore to Lincoln, Oct 11, 1863, and Isaac N. Arnold to Lincoln, Oct. 27, 1863, ibid. Lincoln wrote to Livermore on Oct. 26: "I had some desire to retain the paper; but if it shall contribute to the relief or comfort of the soldiers that will be better"—*Collected Works of Lincoln,* 6:540; see also 7:75, Dec. 17, 1863. In the 1871 Chicago fire, the Proclamation burned. The $3,000 of 1863 perhaps equals $90,000 in early twenty-first-century dollars.

153 *The original having been defaced:* Sherman to George McLaughlin, Dec. 15, 16, 1863, in Boynton, *History of the Great Western Sanitary Fair,* pp. 212–13.

153 *The folks out west:* John McLaughlin to Sherman, Dec. 14, 1863, John Sherman Papers, LOC.

153 *The state had also sent a special train: Washington Daily Chronicle,* Nov. 21, 1863.

154 *Cincinnati "Autograph Committee":* Boynton, *History of the Great Western Sanitary Fair,* pp. 212–14.

154 *It would have been too much:* Everett Diary, Jan. 18, March 15, Feb. 2, 1864.

154 *"Among free men, there can be":* Lincoln to James C. Conkling, Aug. 26, 1863, *Collected Works of Lincoln,* 6:409–10.

154 *Even his impromptu remarks:* Response to Serenade, July 7, 1863, ibid., 6:320.

154 *As the North had celebrated:* Lincoln to George G. Meade, July 14, 1864, ibid., 6:327–28.

155 *James Speed, Lincoln's Attorney General: Daily Louisville Commercial,* Nov. 12, 1879; *Illinois State Journal,* Nov. 17, 1879. Speed repeated much the same in a letter to the *New York Times,* April 20, 1887.

155 *Lincoln's son Robert:* Robert Todd Lincoln to Horatio King, March 1, 1888, LOC; Robert T. Lincoln to Isaac Markens, Nov. 5, 1913, Robert Todd Lincoln Papers, Chicago Historical Society. The second letter also appears in Paul M. Angle, ed., *A Portrait of Abraham Lincoln in Letters by His Oldest Son* (Chicago: Chicago Historical Society, 1968), p. 6.

155 *Judge Advocate General:* Holt quoted by Horatio King, *Washington Critic,* Feb. 18, 1888.

155 *By the spring of 1865:* Memorandum Concerning the Duchess of Argyll, March 22, 1865, *Collected Works of Lincoln,* 8:372.

155 *As far as Everett: Hay Diary,* p. 114 (Nov. 20, 1863). Yet even the great orator could use the reassurance. After reading the attack on him in the *New York Herald,* Everett wrote in a letter that "I suppose it is better to be abused than praised" from such quarters, but added a postcript: "The President has written me a letter warmly approving my address"— Everett to Robert Bonner, Nov. 25, 1863, Edward Everett Papers.

156 *Thanks to Everett's efforts:* Monaghan, *Lincoln Bibliography,* 1:47–49.

156 *The* American Literary Gazette *praised:* July 1, 1864.

156 *One of the campaign biographies:* Wm. M[akepeace] Thayer, *The Character and Public Services of Abraham Lincoln, President of the United States* (Boston: Walker, Wise, 1864), pp. 16–17.

156 *Wills's report to the Pennsylvania legislature: Revised Report,* pp. 239, 264, 11. Reports were issued in 1864, 1865, and 1867. Lincoln's address appeared, respectively, on pp. 110, 212, and 233.

156 *Though the program of the 1865 dedication:* "Oration," ibid., pp. 264–65.

157 *Among individual items:* Ibid., pp. 255–62.

157 *During the 1864 presidential campaign: Harper's Weekly,* Dec. 5, 12, 1863; April 23, 1864. Presumably the praise came from George William Curtis, the editor.

157 *But excepting the card:* Jay Monaghan, *Lincoln Bibliography* (2 vols., Springfield: Illinois State Historical Society, 1943), 1:49, item 198. Frank Williams, Chief Justice of Rhode Island, is updating Monaghan, but we should not expect dramatic results for early printings of the Gettysburg Address.

157 *That at least some people were talking:* Lynn Clyde Surles, ed., *Voices from Lincoln's Time* (Hubertus, WI: Belman, 1997), p. 21.

157   *The Oxford professor Goldwin Smith:* Smith, "President Lincoln," p. 302; cf. *Westminster Review*, Sept. 6, 1866 (clipping, Gettysburg Address Scrapbook), put together by Louis Warren, 3:6 (vol. 3, file 6), LM; John Malcolm Forbes Ludlow, *President Lincoln Self-pourtrayed* (London: Bennett, 1866), 149, said of Lincoln's speech that it "appears to me simply one of the noblest extant specimens of human eloquence."

158   *In late March of 1865:* Adams to Charles Francis Adams, March 7, 1865, in Worthington Chauncey Ford, ed., *A Cycle of Adams Letters* (2 vols. New York: Houghton, 1920), 2:257.

158   *In 1866, Ernest Duvergier de Hauranne:* The full statement: "Je ne crois pas que l'éloquence moderne ait jamais rien produit de plus élevé que le discours prononcé par lui sur la tombe des soldats morts à Gettysburg. Il atteint la simplicité grandiose, le souffle austère et patriotique de l'antiquité, mais on y sent en . . . même temps l'émotion d'une âme humaine et chrétienne en face des horreurs de la guerre civile"—de Hauranne, "Huit Mois en Amérique: Lettres et Notes de Voyage, 1864–1865," *Revue des Deux Mondes*, 61, Jan. 15, 1866, pp. 489–90, trans. by Laurence Gregorio. For a different translation, see that of Ralph H. Bowen, ed., *A Frenchman in Lincoln's America. Huit Mois en Amérique: Lettres et Notes de Voyage, 1864–1865*, 2 vols. (Chicago: Lakeside, 1975), 2:348.

158   *And surely from France:* This, too, is a subject looking for its explorers. At least Everett's speech appeared in German—Everett to Seward, July 9, 1864, Seward Papers.

158   *In one of the hundreds of interviews:* Daniel W. Wilder to William H. Herndon, Nov. 24, 1866, in Wilson and Davis, eds., *Herndon's Informants*, p. 419.

158   *In 1867, a Gettysburg hospital nurse:* Holstein, *Three Years in Field Hospitals*, p. 54. The hospital had closed, Holstein concluded, so as there was "nothing more to be done at Gettysburg, we gladly turned our faces homeward. . . ."

158   *A Christian Commission publication:* Lemuel Moss, *Annals of the United States Christian Commission* (Philadelphia: Lippincutt, 1868, p. 22.

158   *Joshua Speed labeled it:* J. F. Speed to Herndon, Dec. 6, 1866, in Wilson and Davis, eds., *Herndon's Informants*, pp. 499–500.

158   *His brother, James: Daily Louisville Commercial,* Nov. 12, 1879.

158   *called it "world-renowned": The Martyr's Monument. Being the Patriotism and Political Wisdom of Abraham Lincoln as Exhibited in His Speeches, Messages, Orders, and Proclamations, from the Presidential Canvas of 1860 Until His Assassination, April 14, 1865* (New York: American News Company, 1865), iii–iv, p. 220.

158   *Ralph Waldo Emerson:* Emerson, "Abraham Lincoln, Remarks at the Funeral Services Held in Concord, April 19, 1865," in *Abraham Lincoln* (Cleveland: Chautauqua Press, 1899), p. 80.

158   *Among other places: Union Vedette,* July 4, 1865.

159   *Isaac Arnold, in a book:* Arnold, *The History of Abraham Lincoln,* pp. 422–23.

159   *Harriet Beecher Stowe:* Harriet Beecher Stowe, *Men of Our Times* (Hartford, CT, 1868), p. 80.

159   *James Russell Lowell:* James Russell Lowell, "Ode Recited at the Harvard Commemoration, July 21, 1865," in J. D. McClatchy, ed., *Poets of the Civil War* (n.p. Library of America, 2005), p. 42.

159   *Most prophetical, Senator Sumner:* "Promises of the Declaration of Independence, and Abraham Lincoln. Eulogy . . . ," June 1, 1865, in Charles Sumner, *His Complete Works,* 20 vols. (New York: Negro University Press, n.d. [1969 reprint of 1900 ed.]), 12:296, 271–72.

159   *The many sermons preached:* See, e.g., *Sermons Preached in Boston on the Death of Abraham Lincoln* (Boston: Tilton, 1865); *Our Martyred President, Abraham Lincoln. Voices from the Pulpit of New York and Brooklyn. . . .* (New York: Tibbals & Whiting, 1865). Other sermons may yet turn up that mention Lincoln's speech. For a long list of post-assassination sermons by Northern ministers, as well as an analysis of them, see David B. Chesebrough, *"No Sorrow like Our Sorrow": Northern Protestant Ministers and the Assassination of Abraham Lincoln* (Kent, OH: Kent State University Press, 1994). The Lincoln Museum in Fort Wayne has 151 sermons. For what appears to be the first statement of Lincoln's supposed conversion in Gettysburg, see *Freeport [Illinois] Weekly Journal,* Dec. 7, 1864. However, the *Independent,* March 16, 1865, reached many more people: "When I left home to take this Chair of State I requested my countrymen to pray for me; I was not then a Christian. When my son died, the severest trial of my life, I was not a Christian. But when I went to Gettysburg, and looked upon the graves of our dead heroes, who had fallen in defense of their country, I then and there consecrated myself to Christ. *I do love Jesus."* Cf. David Brainerd Williamson, *Illustrated Life, Services, Martyrdom, and Funeral of Abraham Lincoln. . . .* (Philadelphia: Peterson, 1865), p. 269.

159   *Some might see the most revealing:* J. G. Butler, *The Martyr President* (Washington: McGill & Witherow, 1865). See also Phillips Brooks, *The Life and Death of Abraham Lincoln: A Sermon Preached at the Church of the Holy Trinity, Philadelphia, Sunday Morning, April 23, 1865* (Philadelphia: Ashmead, 1865), p. 24; Richard Eddy, *The Martyr to* Liberty. *Three Ser-*

mons Preached in the First Universalist Church, Philadelphia, Sunday, April 16th, Wednesday, April 19th, and Thursday, June 1st (Philadelphia: H. W. Smith, 1865); and Jeffrey Reuben, The Mission of Abraham Lincoln (Philadelphia: Bryson, 1865).

159   Yet at Lincoln's funeral: Our Martyred President, pp. 393–410; Cheesbrough, Northern Protestant Ministers, pp. 126–38.

159   A sermon preached and published: D. T. Carnahan, Oration on the Death of Abraham Lincoln (Gettysburg: Aughinbaugh, 1865).

160   Did Bancroft ask: Our Martyred President, pp. 383–92.

160   If the abolitionist William Lloyd Garrison's Liberator: Liberator, May 19, 1865, New York Evening Post, May 3, 1865.

160   Poetical tributes, too: Poetical Tributes to the Memory of Abraham Lincoln (Philadelphia: Lippincott, 1865).

160   But the eulogy delivered: W. E. Guthrie, Oration on the Death of Abraham Lincoln. Addressed to the American People (Philadelphia: Pennington, 1865).

160   The fame of the battle grew: This conclusion is based on an examination of the Gettysburg newspapers, 1865–1900, that almost never recalled the Gettysburg Address around its anniversary or that of the battle until very late in the century.

160   Much the same appears: See, e.g., the New York Times, 1865–1900. The stories begin to start up in the 1880s.

160   "Bunker Hill speaks": Chicago Tribune, Nov. 24, 1863.

161   "More than any other single event": Ibid.

161   As people left the place: Baltimore American and Commercial Advertiser, Nov. 20, 1863.

161   "An altar will rise": Sentinel, Nov. 24, 1863.

161   In Gettysburg, the Sentinel: Ibid., Nov. 24, Dec. 1, 1863.

161   Hundreds of thousands: Daily Missouri Democrat, Nov. 23, 1863; cf. W. to Dear Sister, Nov. 23, 1863.

162   French deeply respected: French Diary, pp. 434–35 (Nov. 22, 1863).

162   And without intending to make: Ibid.

Chapter Seven: Gloria

Page

163   French stayed an extra day: French Diary, pp. 436–37 (Nov. 22, 1863).

163   French wandered off by himself: Ibid.

163   A New York Times reporter: New York Times, Nov. 21, 1863; cf. Stoke to Stoke, Oct. 26, 1863. People would long remember the scene, e.g.,

Thomas Livermore, *Days and Events, 1860–1866* (Boston: Houghton Mifflin, 1920), p. 60.

164   *A three-months' soldier:* Trowbridge, "The Field of Gettysburg," p. 623.

164   *Before French could leave:* French Diary, pp. 436–37 (Nov. 22, 1863).

164   *As late as the 1880s:* Burial Registers, Superintendent's Monthly Report, May 1882, GNMP.

164   *"In less than 10 minutes":* French Diary, p. 437 (Nov. 22, 1863).

164   *The local papers gave:* Ibid.; *Compiler*, Nov. 23, 1863; *Star*, Nov. 26, 1863. Albertus McCreary, *Gettysburg: A Boy's Experiences of the Battle* (Gettysburg: Albertus McCreary, 1909), pp. 20–21, remembered a woman who lived across from the accident site telling him that the boy who was killed, Allen Frazer, came out to warn the stranger that hitting a shell was dangerous business. The stranger was Russell M. Briggs, who came to get his son, Corporal George E. Briggs, 72nd Pennsylvania, who had died on July 18—*Compiler*, Nov. 23, 1863. See also *Stewart Diary*, p. 167 (Nov. 20, 1863). For other reports on accidents, see e.g., *Sentinel*, July 7, 28, Sept. 8; *Lancaster Daily Express*, Nov. 24, 1863; *Three Months*, pp. 13–14.

164   *Now on November 20:* See, e.g., *Lancaster (Pa.) Daily Express*, Nov. 24; *Cincinnati Daily Times*, Nov. 27; *Portland (ME) Advertiser*, Nov. 28, 1863.

164   *Reading it in the:* Miller to Miller, Nov. 25, 1863, MMMP.

164   *The men of Company K:* Alexander L. C. Woods Pension File, Co. K., NA.

164   *"Why in the name of common sense":* Miller to Miller, Sept. 15, 1861, quoted in Frassanito, *Early Photography*, p. 89. The book has an excellent description of the ordnance-related accidents around Gettysburg.

165   *"If only these Six months":* Miller to Miller, Nov. 25, 1863, MMM.

165   *one hundred copies for two dollars:* Ballston Journal, Nov. 26, 1863.

165   *create this "Union Thanksgiving":* Sarah Josepha Hale to Lincoln, Sept. 28, 1863, Lincoln Papers.

167   *"hath nevertheless remembered mercy":* Proclamation of Thanksgiving, Oct. 3, 1863, *Lincoln's Collected Works*, 6:496–7.

167   *Battle of Chattanooga: Sentinel*, Oct. 6, Dec. 1, 1863.

167   *his Proclamation, or his Hymn, or both:* See for example: *Atlas and Argus*, Albany, NY., Oct. 7, Nov. 26, 1863; *Albany Morning Express*, NY, Oct. 6, 1863, Nov. 19, 1863; *Ohio Democrat*, Nov. 6, 27, 1863; *Albany Evening Journal*, published the Proclamation twice, Oct. 5, Nov. 19, 1863, (also the Gettysburg speeches of Seward, Lincoln, and Seymour, once, Nov. 20, 1863); *Canajoharie Radii and Tax-Payers Journal*, Canajoharie, NY, Nov. 19, 1863; *Mohawk Valley and Register*, Nov. 19, 1863; *Recorder and Democrat*, Catskill, NY, Oct. 8, Nov. 19, 1863; *Reporter and Tribune*,

Washington, PA, Nov. 25, 1863; *Daily Whig,* Troy, NY, Oct. 6, 1863; *Co-hoes Cataract,* Cohoes, NY., Nov. 21, 1863; *Maine Farmer,* Nov. 26, 1863, has the Hymn, but not the speech; *Ocean Emblem,* Nov. 3, 26, 1863, both the Proclamation and the Hymn, not the speech. Very few papers printed the Gettysburg speech but not the Proclamation, e.g.: *Bloomville Mirror,* NY, Dec. 1, 1863. A most evenhanded approach came in the *Toledo Blade,* Nov. 21, 1863, which gave its lead editorial to Thanksgiving, followed by a report on Gettysburg. On the top of the next column came the *President's Hymn,* and below it "Mr. Lincoln remarks" at Gettysburg. On Nov. 24 it repeated the printing, and on Nov. 26, "NATIONAL THANKSGIVING DAY!" the lead went to the Thanksgiving Proclamation, reinforced by the Proclamation of the governor, and also that of George Washington. Cf. *Dayton Daily Journal,* Nov. 20, 1863. Even when a paper refused to print either the Gettysburg speech or the Thanksgiving Proclamation, it would note the president's call and report on Thanksgiving activities: *Neuer Anzeiger des Westens,* Oct. 8, 1863; *Cincinnati Daily Times,* Nov. 20, 21, 24, 1863 (it is possible that reports appeared in missing issues). The same paper paid much attention to Lincoln's Annual Message, Nov. 21, Dec. 8, 10, 1863. Cf. *Democratic Union,* Sandusky, OH, Nov. 26, Dec. 3, 17, 1863; *Wyandot Pioneer,* Upper Sandusky, OH, Nov. 27, 1863.

167 *She knew that he was:* Interview with Mary Todd Lincoln [September 1866], in Wilson and Davis, eds., *Herndon's Informants,* p. 360.

168 *In time the faithful:* Like his wife, Lincoln's son Robert "gave no credence whatever" to such tales. "My old secretary, now deceased, used to amuse himself greatly in tracing the origin of such things"—Robert T. Lincoln to Isaac Markens, June 21, 1915, in Angle, ed., *A Portrait of Abraham Lincoln,* p. 10.

168 *"Major General Schenck":* To Robert C. Schenck, Nov. 20, 1863, *Collected Works of Lincoln,* 7:26.

168 *"Major General Meade":* To George G. Meade, Nov. 20, 1863, ibid., 7:25. To get a glimpse of the continued stream of Lincoln's stays of executions and at the same time sense the impact the discovery of these documents had at the time, see Ida M. Tarbell, *The Life of Abraham Lincoln . . . ,* 2 vols. (New York: Doubleday, 1900), 2:400ff.

169 *News of his contagious illness: Sentinel,* Dec. 22, 29, 1863.

169 *Republican papers:* See, e.g., *Rutland Daily Herald,* Vermont, Dec. 9, 1863; *Der Milwaukee See-Bote,* Nov. 25, 1863.

169 *The* Richmond Dispatch*:* Dec. 8, 1863.

169 *Then, on November 28: Washington Star,* Nov. 28, 1863; *Washington Morn-*

ing Chronicle, Nov. 28, 1863; cf. *Chicago Tribune,* Dec. 3, 14, 15. *Lincoln Day by Day,* 3:222–26, follows the alternating reports of work and illness. Cf. Hay Diary, p. 118 (Nov. 26, 1863); Beale, ed., *Bates Diary,* pp. 316, 319 (Nov. 17, Dec. 1, 1863).

169 *On December 4, he telegraphed her:* To Mary Todd Lincoln, Dec. 5, 6, 7, *Collected Works of Lincoln,* 7:34–35.

170 *Lincoln and his son both recovered:* The newspapers called Tad's illness "scarletina," e.g. *Washington Star,* Nov. 28, 1863, but most likely it, too, was a mild version of smallpox.

170 *A* Chicago Tribune *reporter:* Jan. 19, 1864. See also Basler, "Did President Lincoln Give the Smallpox to William H. Johnson?" pp. 279–84.

170 *Johnson was "very bad":* Chicago Tribune, Jan. 19, 1864.

170 *The story of how he took care:* Thayer, *Lincoln,* pp. 21–22.

170 *In the cold January of 1864:* DeWitt C. Morris to E. S. Randolph, June, 1864, *Collected Works: Supplement,* pp. 210–11n.

171 *The profits would go: Baltimore American and Commercial Advertiser,* Nov. 26, 1863.

171 *At the dedication of the Cemetary's Soldiers' Monument:* Oration of Hon. O. P. Morton in Bartlett, *Soldiers' National Cemetery,* pp. 88–102; *Sentinel,* July 9, 1869.

171 *Bayard Taylor, the poet:* Taylor, "Dedication Ode," in Bartlett, *Soldiers' National Cemetery,* pp. 103–09. Gettysburg, and later Harvard, Professor Richard Marius quipped that Taylor's was "an act approximate to setting Beethoven's Ninth to music"—Marius, ed., *The Columbia Book of Civil War Poetry* (New York: Columbia University Press, 1994), p. 402.

171 *Having been reminded: New York Times,* July 2, 1869; *Star & Sentinel,* Gettysburg, July 2, 1869 (the *Star* and the *Sentinel* merged in 1867).

171 *"Their fall was not in vain":* Weems, *The Life of Washington,* p. 124.

171 *For example,* New York Times*:* Henry J. Raymond, *The Life and Public Services of Abraham Lincoln* (New York: Derby & Miller, 1865), pp. 412–13, 420–21.

171 *Phoebe A. Hanaford's:* Mrs. P. A. Hanaford, *Abraham Lincoln: His Life and Public Services* (Boston: Russell, 1865), pp. 150, 179.

172 *David Brainerd Williamson's:* David Brainerd Williamson, *Illustrated Life, Services, Martyrdom, and Funeral of Abraham Lincoln . . .* (Philadelphia: Peterson, 1865), pp. 144, 149–50, 152. Both Hanaford and Williamson preferred the July Proclamation, though the later one is also included in Williamson.

172 *The most popular:* J. G. Holland, *The Life of Abraham Lincoln* (Springfield,

MA: Gurdon Bill, 1866), pp. 423, 426. This survey excludes Arnold, *The History of Abraham Lincoln*, pp. 422–23, which gave high praise to the address, as would Arnold's 1885 biography.

172 *By 1870, so much had been placed:* Andrew Boyd, *A Memorial Lincoln Bibliography: Being an Account of Books, Eulogies, Sermons, Portraits, Engravings, Medals, Etc., Published Upon Abraham Lincoln* . . . (Albany, NY: Andrew Boyd, 1870), p. 20. There are two editions of the book; one includes blank pages for collectors to add their own findings.

172 *Edward McPherson's oft-printed:* Edward McPherson, *The Political History of the United States During the Great Rebellion* (Washington, DC: Philip & Solomons, 1865), pp. 333–37.

172 *His chapter on Lincoln: Forney in Anecdotes of Public Men* (New York: Harper, 1873), pp. 168–76. This was still a step ahead from 1863, when Forney's *Washington Chronicle* immediately advertised the pamphlet of EVERETT'S GREAT ORATION without mentioning Lincoln's name—Nov. 21, 1863.

173 *Horace Greeley's very popular:* Horace Greeley, *The American Conflict: a history of the great rebellion in the United States of America, 1860–65; its causes, incidents, and results: intended to exhibit expecially its moral and political phases, with the drift and progress of American opinion respecting human slavery, from 1776 to the close of the war for the Union,* 3 vols. (Hartford, CT: Case; Chicago: Sherwood, 1864–67). The Mearns Papers contain reference to an unpublished speech by Greeley that speaks highly of Lincoln, with the claim that it was given in the late 1860s but not published until 1891—"Greeley's Estimate of Lincoln. An Unpublished Address by Horace Greeley," *Century* 42 (July 1891): 371n, 380.

173 *Greeley had plenty of conflicts:* Thomas P. Kettell, *History of the Great Rebellion* . . . (Hartford, CT: L. Stebbins; Cincinnati: F. A. Howe, 1865).

173 *Nor did R. G. Horton's:* R. G. Horton, *A Youth's History of the Civil War in the United States* (New York: Van Everie, 1867).

173 *In 1870, however, John William Draper's:* John William Draper, *History of the American Civil War,* 3 vols. (New York: Harper, 1870), p. 152.

173 *By 1874, in Benson J. Lossing's:* Benson J. Lossing, *The Pictorial Field Book of the Civil War,* 3 vols. (Hartford, CT: Belknap, 1874), 3:80.

173 *This historian had immediately:* Benson J. Lossing to D. McConaughy, Sept 14, 1863, McConaughy Papers.

173 *Immigrants who learned:* J. T. Headley, *Die Grosse Rebellion: Eine Geschichte des Burgerkrieges in den Ver Staaten* 2 vols., Hartford, CT: Hurlbut, Williams, & Compagie; Slogau: Karl Flemming, 1863–65, 2:285.

173   *Washington's National Lincoln Monument:* James Harlan, *National Lincoln Monument Association; incorporated by act of Congress, March 30th, 1867* (Washington, DC: National Lincoln Monument Association, 1867); *The National Lincoln Monument Association, organization and design, proceedings of the Board of Managers, plan and prospects, progress of the work, representative men selected, appeal to the public, appendix* (Washington, DC: National Lincoln Monument Association, 1870); Peterson, *Lincoln in American Memory,* pp. 53–55.

173   *In the end, nothing came:* Papers of the Lincoln National Monument Association, LM; James Caroll Power, *Abraham Lincoln . . . with a History and Development of the Lincoln National Monument* (Springfield, 1875).

174   *Henry Kirke Brown's:* The discussion of Lincoln sculpture in this chapter relies on personal inspections, and the sometimes contradictory information in the Inventories of American Painting and Sculpture, Smithsonian American Art Museum (cited hereafter as Smithsonian Inventories); Donald Charles Durman, *He Belongs to the Ages* (Ann Arbor, MI: Edwards, 1951); and F. Lauriston Bullard, *Lincoln in Marble and Bronze* (New Brunswick, NJ: Rutgers University Press, 1952).

174   *The bronze Lincoln stands:* In 1879, a copy was erected in Boston.

175   *David Gilmour Blythe:* Harold Holzer shared with me thirty-three popular prints about the Emancipation Proclamation; twelve of these reproduced the text and integrated it into a Lincoln image. See also Holzer, " 'Prized in Every Liberty Loving Household': The Image of the Great Emancipator in the Graphic Arts," in Holzer, *Lincoln Seen and Heard* (Lawrence: University of Kansas Press, 2000), pp. 7–33.

175   *If there ever was a boring:* This is a play on one of the most cited disparaging comments about the Emancipation Proclamation—Richard Hofstadter, *The American Political Tradition and the Men Who Made It* (New York: Knopf, 1948), pp. 129, 131.

175   *"Four score and seven years":* Some claims have been made that the painting was shown at the Centennial Exhibit, in Philadelphia, but I could find no evidence of it. See, e.g., *The Masterpieces of the Centennial International Exhibition,* 3 vols. (Philadelphia: Gebbie & Barrie, c. 1876–78; New York: Garland, 1977).

175   *a schoolbook for speakers:* John D. Philbrick, *The Primary Union Speaker, Containing Original and Selected Pieces for Declamation and Recitation in Primary Schools* (Boston: Taggard & Thomson, 1866).

175   *In 1878, the* New York Times*:* New York Times*,* Oct. 15, 1878.

175   *and the following year Bicknell:* Albion H. Bicknell, *Published in Connection with the Exhibition of the Historical Painting* Lincoln at Gettysburg

(Boston: Doll & Richards, 1879), inside cover page, 3, 5. The painting in oils, 1876, 108 x 216 inches, has been in the Malden Public Library in Massachusetts since the 1880s. The small version, also in oil, 1881, 25.25" x 40.5", is at Lafayette College. See also *New York Times*, Oct. 15, 1878.

176 *The enterprise failed:* Bicknell had done a Lincoln portrait in 1868, already, but after the failure, he did not return to Lincoln until the twentieth century, when he did portraits in 1905 and 1913. It is possible that there are unaccounted-for works as well.

176 *The forward-looking* Nation: Aug. 26, 1875.

176 *The magazine compared: New York Times,* April 17, 1875; *Nation,* Sept. 9, 1875, p. 284; *Congregationalist,* Sept. 16, 1875, p. 294; cf. *Washington Post,* May 31, 1878; *New York Times,* May 27, 1880; William H. Lambert, "Variations in the Reports of the Gettysburg Address," p. 638.

176 *Lincoln called the founding fathers:* Address Before the Young Men's Lyceum of Springfield, Ill., Jan. 27, 1838; Speech at Chicago, Ill., July 10, 1858; Speech at Peoria, Ill., Oct. 16, 1854, *Collected Works of Lincoln,* 1:115; 2:266, etc. A substantial literature has grown from Robert Bellah, "Civil Religion in America," *Deadalus,* 96 (Winter 1967): 21, http://hirr.hartsem.edu/Bellah/articles_5.htm; see esp. Pauline Maier, *American Scripture: Making the Declaration of Independence* (New York: Knopf, 1998).

177 *Unveiled in 1887:* Peterson, *Lincoln in American Memory,* p. 64; Smithsonian Inventories; Durman, *Statues;* Bullard, *Marble and Bronze.*

177 *However, by 1877: Compiler,* July 5, 1877.

177 *A year later, President Rutherford Hayes:* President Hayes Address, May 30, 1878, clipping, Gettysburg Scrapbook, 1:44, LM.

177 *an account of the battle: Star & Sentinel,* July 4, 1878, May 30, 1883.

177 *Lamon gave his name:* Ward H. Lamon, *The Life of Abraham Lincoln: From His Birth to His Inauguration as President* (Boston: Osgood, 1872). See also Benjamin Thomas, *Portrait for Posterity* (New Brunswick, NJ: Rutgers University Press, 1947), pp. 29–69; Rodney O. Davis, "Lincoln's 'Particular Friend' and Lincoln Biography," *Journal of the Abraham Lincoln Association,* 19 (Winter 1998): 21–37.

177 *Internal Revenue Commissioner:* George S. Boutwell in Rice, ed., *Reminiscences of Abraham Lincoln,* p. 134.

177 *He vehemently objected:* Lamon, *Recollections,* pp. 173, 169. The same account first appeared in the press: Ward Lamon, "Lincoln's Gettysburg Speech," newspaper clipping, LM. The clipping is dated by hand 1886, but it first appeared in 1879. See also *Star & Sentinel,* Nov. 20, 1879; I. J.

A. to Editor, *Cincinnati Commercial*, Nov. 12, 1879; Lamon, Reminiscences, draft.

178   *The marshal thought that the "speech":* Reminiscences, draft; Lamon, ed., *Recollections*, pp. 173–74. These words would be repeated endlessly all over the United States. For a rare newspaper clipping, see *Dakota Territory*, Oct. 21, 1889, Gettysburg Address Scrapbook, 3:6.

178   *Upon reading Lamon:* Whitney quoted in Thomas, *Portrait for Posterity*, p. 176.

178   *Writing to Herndon:* Whitney to William Herndon, March 6 [1897?], Herndon-Weik Papers, LOC.

178   *By then, Isaac Arnold's biography:* Isaac N. Arnold, *The Life of Abraham Lincoln* (Chicago: Jensen, McClurg, 1885), pp. 328–29. Not much later a correspondent confessed that "when the President began speaking I was a Democrat, when he finished I was a republican. . . ." W.C.K., "Lincoln at Gettysburg."

178   *Soon afterwards Noah Brooks's biography:* Brooks, *Lincoln*, p. 379.

178   *Many eyewitnesses got into: Boston Herald*, July 7, 1887; *New York Times*, July 7, 1887; cf. July 3, 1887. Contradictions by eyewitnesses would continue until the last ones died. See, e.g., Gettysburg Address Scrapbook, 1:6.

179   *" 'Then and there consecrated' ": Freeport [Illinois] Weekly Journal*, Dec. 7, 1864.

179   *"When the clouds lifted":* John H. Barrows, "Religious Aspects. Abraham Lincoln's Career," in Osborn H. Oldroyd, ed., *The Lincoln Memorial: Album Immortelles. . . .* (Boston: Guernsey, 1882), p. 508. It was also claimed by a woman visitor that Lincoln said Gettysburg changed him and that he intended "to make a public religious profession"— Raymond, *Life of Lincoln*, p. 732.

179   *In Gettysburg, on the sixteenth anniversary: Compiler*, Nov. 20, 1879.

179   *The Republican* Star & Sentinel: *Star & Sentinel*, May 30, 1883, quoting the *Philadelphia Press*, 1879. About the same time James Speed also recalled immediate positive reactions to the speech—*Illinois State Journal*, Nov. 17, 1879.

179   *The local Republican paper published: Star & Sentinel*, July 10, 1888; cf. *New York Times*, July 3, 1888.

179   *The Democratic counterpart: Compiler*, May 29, 1894.

179   *Yet as late in the century as this:* http://memory.loc.gov/service/ pnp/cph/3b50000/3b53000/3b53000/3b53030r.jpg (Abraham Lincoln and his Emancipation Proclamation, Strobridge Lith. Co., Cincinnati, c. 1888).

180   *Still, in the mid-eighties: Star & Sentinel,* Aug. 17, 1886. That Lincoln regretted issuing the Emancipation Proclamation was evident in 1863 already among Democrats, June 1, 1897.

180   *On the twentieth anniversary: Washington Bee,* Jan. 6, 1883, quoted in David Blight, *Beyond the Battlefield: Race, Memory, and the American Civil War* (Amherst: University of Massachusetts Press, 2002), p. 302.

180   *Emancipation Day:* See, e.g., *New York Times,* Jan. 1, 2000.

180   *Remembered on different days:* William Wiggins, *O Freedom! Afro-American Emancipation Celebrations* (Knoxville: University of Tennessee Press, 1987); cf. Mitch Kachun, *Festivals of Freedom: Memory and Meaning in African American Emancipation Celebrations, 1808–1915* (Amherst: University of Massachusetts Press, 2003); Blight, *Race and Reunion,* p. 369; Guelzo, *Emancipation Proclamation,* p. 244.

181   *As one century closed:* Blight, *Race and Reunion,* pp. 300–80.

181   *In the year of the centennial: Atlanta Constitution,* Jan. 2, 1909, quoted in ibid., 337.

181   *For example, in Brooklyn's:* Peterson, *Lincoln in American Memory,* p. 219.

181   *With segregation and lynching: Baltimore Afro-American Ledger,* July 5, 1913, quoted in Blight, *Race and Reunion,* p. 390.

181   *Seeking healing from the bitterness:* Blight, *Race and Reunion,* p. 3.

181   *Forgetting blacks in the developing:* Brown, *Retreat from Gettysburg;* Creighton, *The Colors of Courage: Gettysburg's Forgotten History, Immigrants, Women, and African Americans in the Civil War's Defining Battle* (New York: Basic Books, 2005); James M. Paradis, *African Americans and the Gettysburg Campaign* (Lantham, MD: Scarecrow, 2005).

181   *And the Gettysburg that one newspaper:* Luther W. Minnigh, *Gettysburg: What They Did Here* (1892; 1920); Blight, *Race and Reunion,* p. 199.

182   *Robert E. Lee flatly refused:* R. E. Lee to D. McConaughy, Aug. 5, 1869, David McConaughy Papers, Gettysburg College.

182   *"In our youth our hearts":* "An address delivered for Memorial Day, May 30, 1884, at Keene, NH, before John Sedgwick Post No. 4, Grand Army of the Republic," www.people.virginia.edu/~mmd5f/memorial.htm.

182   *As the years went by:* J. D. McClatchy, ed., *Poets of the Civil War* (n.p.: Library of America, 2005), 137.

182   *Yet commemorating the dead:* Neff, *Honoring the Civil War Dead,* passim.

183   *One of the sensations:* GNMP, Vertical Files, 12–1, contains a wealth of information on the subject. With the coming of the motion picture, the cycloramas disappeared. The one restored to its original state for the Gettysburg National Battlefield Museum is the second of the Phillippoteaux paintings that opened in Boston in 1884. See also Amy J. Kin-

sel, " 'From These Honored'. Gettysburg in American Culture, 1863–1938," PhD Dissertation, Cornell University, 1992, pp. 468–77; Harold Holzer, "Saving the 'Imax of its Day,' " *American Heritage* (September 2005): 38–45.

183   *One of the cycloramas:* Copy of photograph by Allen & Rowell, Boston, in author's possession. The Gettysburg mural, by Keith Rocco, at the Abraham Lincoln Presidential Library and Museum, which opened in 2005, also pictures the battle and Lincoln together.

183   *The* Century *magazine:* See Blight, *Race and Reunion*, pp. 164–68, 173–87.

184   *Gilder thought that Lincoln's life:* Gilder to Edmund Gosse, Nov. 2, 1885, in Peterson, *Lincoln in American Memory*, p. 169.

184   *But it was not coincidental:* John G. Nicolay, "Lincoln's Gettysburg Address," *Century*, 47 (February 1894): 596–608. The same issue contained William H. Lambert, "Variations in the Reports of the Gettysburg Address," 636–38; a third article on Lincoln; one on Stonewall Jackson—and a chapter of Mark Twain's *Pudd'nhead Wilson*. The Nicolay Papers contain a substantial Gettysburg Address file, presumably collected for this article.

184   *In their 1890* History: John G. Nicolay and John Hay, *Abraham Lincoln: A History*, 10 vols. (New York: Century, 1890), vol. 8: 199, 202. Nicolay appeared to have written this chapter. Schedule of chapters, Nicolay Papers.

185   *Hay wrote a great deal: Hay Diary*, pp. 113–14 (Nov. 19, 1863). One J. H., reporting for the *Washington Daily Chronicle*, Nov. 21, 1863, wrote that the speech "glittered with gems."

185   *Earlier, Stoddard had also testified:* William O. Stoddard, *Abraham Lincoln, the True Story of a Great Life* (New York: Fords, Howard & Hulbert, 1884), p. 412.

185   *But the bulk of Nicolay's article:* That the question of plagiarism had bothered both Nicolay and Hay for some time is clear; see, e.g., John Hay to John Nicolay, Jan. 25, 1887, Nicolay Papers. The issue was widely discussed in the press then, e.g., *Woodland (Calif.) Daily Democrat*, Feb. 14, 1896, and continued into the twentieth century—Gettysburg Address Scrapbook, 2:6.

186   *McGuffey's Readers: McGuffey's Alternate Sixth Reader, 1889*, copy of page in Mearns Papers; *The Gettysburg Speech and Other Papers by Abraham Lincoln* (Boston: Houghton Mifflin, 1888), p. 37.

186   *In 1896, the press reported:* "Cast in Bronze," clipping from the *Boston Journal*, May 31, 1896, Warren Scrapbook, 6:91, 93. *Chicago Tribune*,

Jan. 29, 1905, reported that such a tablet would be presented to every school in Chicago.

186 *In 1900* Harper's Weekly: A. I. Keller in *Harper's Weekly*, Feb. 10, 1900.

186 *To make the notion ludicrous:* The Wycliffe analogy has been accepted in the past by gullible scholars such as Gabor Boritt, ed., *Of the People, By the People, For the People and Other Quotations by Abraham Lincoln* (New York: Columbia University Press, 1996), p. xiv. The opposite side of the coin is claiming for someone credit for inspiring Lincoln. For example, in Washington a bronze tablet at Dupont Circle commemorates a speech given before the Ohio legislature by Lajos Kossuth, the Hungarian freedom fighter whom Lincoln admired. "The spirit of our age is democracy.—All for the people and all by the people. Nothing about the people without the people.—That is democracy, and that is the ruling tendency of the spirit of our age."—*Ohio State Journal*, Feb. 7, 1852.

186 *Congress established the Gettysburg:* The statute is reprinted in Henry Sweetser Burrage, *Gettysburg and Lincoln: The Battle, the Cemetery, and the National Park* (New York: Putnam, 1906), p. 214. See also Wayne Craven, *The Sculptures at Gettysburg* (Gettysburg: Gettysburg National Military Park, 1982), pp. 32–34.

186 *But as the new century dawned: Star & Sentinel*, Feb. 13, 1900.

186 *When in the 1880s Congress:* Blight, *Race and Reunion*, pp. 352, 356; Neff, *Honoring the Civil War Dead*, pp. 222ff.

187 *If the war had been necessary: New York Times*, May 20, 1909.

187 *Indeed, it was said:* R. T. Lincoln to Isaac Markens, Aug. 17, 1914, in Angle, ed., *A Portrait of Abraham Lincoln*, p. 9.

188 *In* The Perfect Tribute: Mary Raymond Shipman Andrews, *The Perfect Tribute* (New York: Scribner, 1906), pp. 25, 40, 47.

188 *The story first appeared: Scribner's*, 40 (1906): 17–24.

188 *Assigned to schoolchildren:* Since publishers hold their sales figures in confidence and typically lose their records, the above is an educated guess. See also Peterson, *Lincoln in American Memory*, p. 115.

188 *Back at the beginning:* Andrews to Judd Stewart, n.d., Judd Stewart Collection, Huntington Library.

188 *For long nothing quite matched: Birth of a Nation* (1915); see also Griffith, *Abraham Lincoln*, 1930, Digitview DVD, 2004; Thomas Cripps, *Slow Fade to Black: The Negroes in American Films, 1900–1942* (New York: Oxford University Press, 1977), pp. 41–69; and Richard Schickel, *W. D. Griffith: An American Life* (New York: Simon & Schuster, 1984), pp. 212–302.

189   *The year 1913 marked the passage:* Blight, *Race and Reunion*, pp. 368–72;
       Guelzo, *Lincoln's Emancipation Proclamation*, pp. 244–45.

189   *Every living Civil War veteran:* Blight, *Race and Reunion*, pp. 6–12,
       383–87; *New York Times*, June 29, 1913; Guelzo, *Lincoln's Emancipation
       Proclamation*, pp. 244–45.

189   *A man claiming to be the son:* "Eight Stabbed at Local Hotel," *Gettysburg
       Times*, July 3, 1913; "Stabbed at Gettysburg," *New York Times*, July 3,
       1863.

190   *The American language:* Kenneth Cmiel, *Democratic Eloquence: The Fight
       Over Popular Speech in Nineteenth-Century America* (Berkeley: University
       of California Press, 1990), pp. 95–97, 116–17.

190   *Elsie Singmaster, widowed:* Elsie Singmaster, *Gettysburg Stories of the
       Red Harvest and the Aftermath* (Boston: Houghton Mifflin, 1913),
       pp. 89–107. See also Kinsel, "From These Honored Dead," pp. 389–401.

190   *She has a grief-stricken:* Singmaster, *Gettysburg Stories*, p. 85.

190   *At one point the Army: Army and Navy Register*, n.d. [1909?]; *Phila-
       delphia Evening Bulletin*, Feb. 20, 1913. Clippings are in the *Scrapbook*,
       ALPLM, that may have belonged to John P. Nicholson and contains
       letters and newspaper clippings (1905–1920) connected with the
       movement to place bronze tablets engraved with the Gettysburg
       Address at every national cemetery. The ALPLM also had letters
       collected by Robert Todd Lincoln on the subject in a "Gettysburg
       Address" file. See, e.g., Robert T. Lincoln to Helen Nicolay, March 7,
       April 16, 1908; Helen Nicolay to Lincoln, Nov. 9, 1908; "An Act To
       establish a national military park at Gettysburg, Pennsylvania"
       [1909]; William H. Lambert to Lincoln, May 15, 1909; Geo. Peabody
       Wetmore to Lincoln, Feb. 20, 1913; Judd Stewart to Lincoln, June 17,
       1914; Isaac Markens to Lincoln, Nov. 22, 27, 1915. For additional
       examples, see Box 147 of Mearns Papers, e.g., Henry S. Burrage
       to John Hay, Oct. 29, 1904; Helen Nicolay to Clara Stone Hay, Dec. 12,
       1908; John P. Nicholson to Sec. of War, April 20, 1909; Robert T.
       Lincoln to Gen. James B. Aleshire, May 5, 1909; John P. Nicholson
       to Elihu Root, Feb. 13 and 17, 1913. All these letters are copies of
       originals—David C. Mearns to Lloyd A. Dunlap, June 20, 1961. See
       also Helen Nicolay to George Peabody Wetmore, Feb. 25, 1913;
       Clara S. Hay to Helen Nicolay, Feb. 28, 1913, enclosing Thommasson
       to Root, Feb. 21, 1913; Helen Nicolay to Clara S. Hay, March 3,
       1913; Clara S. Hay to Elihu Root, March 7, 1913; Root to Hay,
       March 12, 1913, Elihu Root Papers, LOC, *Congressional Record*, Feb. 12,
       1920.

191   *"People versus the Slave Power":* Peterson, *Lincoln in American Memory,* p. 163.

191   *The cartoonist showed: New York Mail and Express,* Aug. 3, 1904, in Barry Schwartz, *Abraham Lincoln and the Forge of National Memory* (Chicago: University of Chicago Press, 1992), p. 129; the section on pp. 107–43 is excellent on the Progressives and sees democratization as their chief goal. See also Peterson, *Lincoln in American Memory,* pp. 164–67.

192   *"If Lincoln were here today":* Speech of Joseph Choate, Apr. 23, 1917, quoted in Peterson, *Lincoln in American Memory,* pp. 198–99.

192   *Men in uniform received: Lincoln's Gettysburg Address and First and Second Inaugural Addresses* (New York: Doubleday, 1918), with "War Service Library" bookplate, LM.

192   *British prime minister David Lloyd George:* Richard J. Carwardine, *Working with Conscience: Acceptance Speech for the Lincoln Prize* (Gettysburg: Gettysburg College, 2005), pp. 14–17.

192   *Even before World War I:* Bullard, *Lincoln in Marble and Bronze,* pp. 92, 152.

192   *In Lancaster, Pennsylvania:* Smithsonian Inventory: Anonymous, Corinth, N.Y., 1908; Karl Schneider, Urbana, Ill, 1911; George Tilton, Newburyport, Mass., 1913; Edward A. Pryor, Atlantic, Iowa, 1919; W. H. Mullins Co., Elkader, Iowa, n.d.

192   *The turn of the century began:* Bullard, *Lincoln in Marble and Bronze,* pp. 120, 142, 159, 163, and 207.

193   *Gettysburg unveiled its first:* Craven, *Sculptures at Gettysburg,* pp. 32–35; *New York Times,* Dec. 20, 1903. The second monument, erected by the state of Kentucky, has the Gettysburg Address in Lincoln's hand on bronze tablets that sit on granite; for Johnson, see Gabor Boritt and Harold Holzer, "Lincoln in 'Modern' Art," in Boritt, ed., *The Lincoln Enigma: The Changing Faces of an American Icon* (New York: Oxford University Press, 2001; paperback, 2002 (only this latter edition has page numbers for the art section of the book), pp. 76–77.

193   *The* Ladies' Home Journal: Single page from the *Ladies' Home Journal* (June 1917), author's collection.

194   *Woodrow Wilson, his successor:* War Message, April 2, 1917, www.lib.byu.edu/~rdh/wwi/1917/wilswarm.html.

194   *Now the cartoonists would show: Philadelphia Press,* may 1917, Feb. 1918, reproduced in Schwartz, *Lincoln and the Forge of Memory,* pp. 233, 235.

194   *The Lincoln Memorial in Washington:* Christopher A. Thomas, *The Lincoln Memorial and American Life* (Princeton: Princeton University Press, 2002).

194   *But this is the universal:* Langston Hughes, "Lincoln Monument: Washington," in Marius, ed., *The Columbia Book of Civil War Poetry*, p. 366.

195   *Stained-glass windows:* Peterson, *Lincoln in American Memory*, pp.
219–21.

195   *But it is the Gettysburg:* The address is on the stone base of the anonymous sculptor's 1921 bronze in Fremont, Nebraska. Racine, Wisconsin, also erected a bronze by an anonymous artist in 1923, scroll in
hand and quotation from the address on its granite base. This was not
enough for the town, for a year later A. L. Van Den Bergen's bronze
was dedicated, speech in hand. When Clinton, Illinois, erected the same
statue in 1931, however, local pride replaced the words with those uttered locally, some of them apocryphal. But George F. Waters's statue
in Portland, Oregon, portrays Lincoln as he finished speaking at Gettysburg. If Isidore Konti's 1929 Yonkers Lincoln holds the Second Inaugural, at the dedication it was the Gettysburg Address that was read.
In the same year, in Austin, Illinois, a relief by an anonymous artist
showed Lincoln at Gettysburg. Max Kalish's 1932 work for Cleveland
has the address chiseled below it on three panels.

195   *Painters usually portrayed Lincoln:* Among them, N.C. Wyeth, Jean Leon
Gerome Ferris, Fletcher C. Ransom, Violet Oakley, James Edwin
McBurney, and Leon Bracker.

195   *But when the black artist:* Boritt and Holzer, "Lincoln in 'Modern' Art,"
pp. 168–69.

195   *The style of these prints:* See, e.g., J. R. Rosen, Edward Gentile, James
Daugherty, Sam Fink, Richard Wengenroth, Mort Kunstler, and
Michale Albert—author's collection.

195   *The speech was not in the retrograde:* Mark S. Reinhart, *Abraham Lincoln
on Screen: A Filmography of Dramas and Documentaries Including Television, 1903–1998* (Jefferson, NC: McFarland, 1999); Reinhart, *A Century
of Abraham Lincoln on Screen* (Redlands, CA: Lincoln Memorial Shrine,
2001). I am indebted to Richard Sloan for sharing his knowledge of
film.

196   *Nineteen thirty-eight brought the last:* For a souvenir booklet, see *Visit
Gettysburg: Blue and Gray Reunion, 75th Anniversary Battle of Gettysburg,
1938* (Pennsylvania State Commission, 1938).

196   *Lincoln in his 1862 letter:* Lincoln to Horace Greeley, Aug. 22, 1862, *Collected Works of Lincoln*, 5:388. Scholars do not fully agree when FDR realized that war was likely.

196   *The nationalistic cast:* For a strong case for such an interpretation, see
Arthur M. Schlesinger, Jr., "War and the Constitution: Abraham Lin-

coln and Franklin D. Roosevelt," in Boritt, ed., *Lincoln the War President: The Gettysburg Lectures* (New York: Oxford University Press, 1992), pp. 145–78.

196   *In 1917, war bonds:* The Lincoln Museum has a fine collection. See also Schwartz, *Lincoln and the Forge of Memory*, p. 242.

197   *Carl Sandburg, poet:* Carl Sandburg, *Abraham Lincoln: The Prairie Years*, 2 vols. (New York: Harcourt, Brace, 1926).

197   *It "sometimes seemed":* Peterson, *Lincoln in American Memory*, p. 307. The treatment of Sandburg relies heavily on Peterson.

197   *That place "was to Lincoln":* Sandburg, *The War Years*, 2:460. James Hurt, "Sandburg's *Lincoln* within History," *Journal of the Abraham Lincoln Association*, 20 (Winter 1999): 65, calls Sandburg's Lincoln "a secular scripture."

197   *In the middle of Sandburg's labors:* Carl Sandburg, *The People, Yes* (New York: Harcourt, Brace, 1936), 134. Also in *Poetry X*, Feb. 21, 2005; http://poetry.poetryx.com/poems/11025/.

197   *In 1942, the young critic:* Alfred Kazin, *On Native Grounds: An Interpretation of Modern American Prose Literature* (New York: Reynal & Hitchcock, 1942), p. 508.

197   *But as late as 2002:* David Pitts; "The Gettysburg Address to Be Read at 9/11 Commemoration," *Department of State Washington File*, Sept. 9, 2002; http://canberra.usembassy.gov.hyper/2002/0909/epf111.htm.

197   *With World War II: "For Us the Living"—A Footnote to the Gettysburg Address.* A Linguaphone Recording, 1941, accompanied by a booklet of the same title; the quotation from the recorded text is printed on p. 11. Wolcott derided Andrews's *Perfect Tribute* as a "misleading . . . sturdy bit of sentimentalizing," but quoted Marine colonel John W. Thomason, who had claimed to have found a letter "in a trunk in an attic down in Texas" from a Confederate captain who heard Lincoln speak and wrote home to his father: "Pop, we've got to stop fighting that man!" Colonel Thomason believed, Wolcott wrote, that Lincoln spoke at Gettysburg "to the South, of course," pp. 7, 9. Recordings of the Gettysburg Address range from "Edison Gold molded" for player pianos to DVDs.

197   *Aaron Copland, perhaps the greatest:* The charge by André Kostelanetz, who commissioned the work, quoted in Howard Taubman, "Copland on Lincoln," www.nytimes.com/books/99/03/14/specials/copland-onlincoln.html; Copland's Program Notes for the Boston Symphony Orchestra, 1943. Among other composers who wrote about Lincoln, often touching on the Gettysburg Address, are Robert Russell Bennett,

Herbert Elwell, Carlisle Floyd, Morton Gould, Henry Hadley, Roy Harris, Paul Hindemith, Charles Ives, Ulysses Kay, Daniel Gregory Mason, George Mysles, Carl F. Mueller, Vincent Persichetti, Roger Sessions, Elie Siegmeister, Peter Morgan Thall with Beatrice Thronton Fisk, Peter Tinturin, and Jacob Weinberg. At least two operas have been composed, in 1938 by Morris Hutchins Ruger, *Gettysburg*, and in 1976 by Sam Raphling, *President Lincoln*—Alen Guelzo helped with this note. The Archives of Lincoln Memorial University, Harrogate, Tenn., hold a great collection of sheet music related to Lincoln.

198   *As World War II ended:* James Daugherty, *Lincoln's Gettysburg Address* (Chicago: Albert Whitman, 1947).

198   *His finest successor in the genre:* Sam Fink, *The Illustrated Gettysburg Address* (New York: Random House, 1994).

198   *President Harry S. Truman:* Copy of resolution in the author's possession.

198   *If scholars went abroad:* Roy P. Basler, ed., *Lincoln's Gettysburg Address in Translation* (Washington, DC: Library of Congress, 1972).

198   *The Lincoln Sesquicentennial: Abraham Lincoln Sesquicentennial, 1959–1960. Final Report of the Lincoln Sesquicentennial Commission* (Washington, DC: n.d. [1960]), p. 12.

198   *The centennial celebrations:* John M. Coski, *The Confederate Battle Flag: America's Most Embattled Emblem* (Cambridge, MA: Harvard University Press, 2005); see also Robert Cook, "(Un)Furl That Banner: The Response of White Southerners to the Civil War Centennial of 1961–1965," *Journal of Southern History,* 68 (November 2002): 879–912.

198   *From the time Marian Anderson:* Scott A. Sandage, "A Marble House Divided: The Lincoln Memorial, the Civil Rights Movement, and the Politics of Memory, 1939–1963," *Journal of American History,* 80 (June 1993): 135–67.

199   *If in 1963 the finest:* Lerone Bennett, Jr., "Was Abe Lincoln a White Supremacist?" *Ebony* (February 1968): 35–42; and *Forced into Glory: Abraham Lincoln's White Dream* (Chicago: Johnson, 2000).

199   *In Detroit in 1969:* Smithsonian Inventory; *Detroit Free Press,* Nov. 27, 1863.

199   *When the Lincoln Prize board:* The author was present at the 2005 event. For 1865, see "Lincoln in Richmond," *Atlantic Monthly,* 15 (June 1865): 754–65; R. J. M. Blackett, ed., *Thomas Morris Chester, Black Civil War Correspondent: His Dispatches from Virginia* (Baton Rouge: Louisiana State University Press, 1989), pp. 294–95.

199   *A. L. Van den Bergen's sculpture:* Bullard, *Lincoln in Marble and Bronze,* p. 177; Smithsonian Inventory.

199   *The Abraham Lincoln Bicentennial:* The author is a member of the commission.

200   *The Lincoln scholar and co-chair:* Harold Holzer, "Lincoln's 'Flat Failure': The Gettysburg Myth Revisited," in Holzer, *Lincoln Seen and Heard* (Lawrence: University Press of Kansas, 2000), pp. 180–90. See the bibliographical notes for the historical literature of the address; and for the most recent decades especially the numerous probings of Barry Schwartz.

200   *In 2002, Allen's Lincoln:* Benton's mural is at Lincoln College, Kansas City. The Allen painting is at Gettysburg College at the President's House.

200   *Lincoln, and with him:* Speech at Springfield, Ill., June 26, 1857, *Collected Works of Lincoln,* 2:406.

200   *At the opening of a major exhibit:* I was present at the opening and heard Dinkins's speech. An audio version, obtained from the New-York Historical Society, edited out the comments about Lincoln—author's collection.

200   *About the same time: Wall Street Creations* (2005 Fall Collection): 56.

201   *The sociologist Barry Schwartz:* See Schwartz, *Lincoln and the Forge of Memory;* "Collective Memory and Historical Truth: Abraham Lincoln's Gettysburg Address," Working Paper, p. 102. For this changing image, see also Boritt's bibliographic notes to "Did He Dream of a Lily White America?" in Boritt, ed., *The Lincoln Enigma,* pp. 304–06.

201   *The British poet and playwright:* Wills, *Lincoln at Gettysburg,* is excellent on the subject. John Drinkwater, *Lincoln the World Emancipator* (Boston: Houghton Mifflin, 1920); cf. Drinkwater, *Abraham Lincoln, A Play* (Boston: Houghton Mifflin, 1919).

202   *Tolstoy called Lincoln:* S. Stakelberg, "Tolstoi Holds Lincoln the World's Greatest Hero," *New York World,* Feb. 8, 1909.

202   *Gandhi spoke: Collected Works of Mahatma Gandhi* (New Delhi: Government of India, Publications Division, 1961), vol 5, pp. 50–51.

202   *in independent India, Jawaharlal Nehru:* "Prime Minister Nehru," *Gettysburg Times,* Nov. 19, 1959.

202   *Sun Yat-sen:* Lyon Sharman, *Sun Yat-sen: His Life and its Meaning: A Critical Biography* (New York: John Day, 1934), p. 92; cf., Peterson, *Lincoln in American Memory,* p. 206; Immanuel C. H. Hsu, *The Rise of Modern China* (New York: Oxford University Press, 2000). However, scholars do not consider Lincoln a major intellectual influence on Sun.

See, e.g., Marie-Claire Bergerè, *Sun Yat-sen*, trans. by Janet Lloyd (Stanford: Stanford University Press, 1998), pp. 352–94. The literal translation of the quotation from Mandarin Chinese: "Min-tsu, Min-ch'uan, Min-sheng" is: "The people are to have, the people are to control, the people are to enjoy." I'm indebted to Dexiang Cheng and Dena Lowy for discussing this subject at length.

202   *As Africa shook off:* Buritt collection.

202   *In Latin America:* Aaron Copland quoted in Mario Cuomo and Harold Holzer, eds., *Lincoln on Democracy* (New York: HarperCollins, 1990), p. xi.

202   *Students in Hungary in 1956:* For Hungary, see "Lincoln," Melvin J. Lasky, ed., *A White Book: The Hungarian Revolution, the Story of the October Uprising as Recorded in Documents, Dispatches, Eye-witness Accounts, and World-wide Reactions* (New York: Praeger, 1957), p. 238; for Tehran, Douglas Kiker, NBC reporter, told Gabor Boritt during the preparation for an interview for the *Today* show, 1988; for Tiananmen Square and the Pope, see *New York Times*, May 29, 1989, Oct. 9, 1995. The subject of the world's reaction to Lincoln awaits its historians.

203   *But the Gettysburg Gospel:* For Lincoln's attitude toward war, see Gabor Boritt, *Abraham Lincoln: War Opponent and War President* (Gettysburg: Gettysburg College, 1987; 1989); also Boritt, ed., *Lincoln the War President: The Gettysburg Lectures*, pp. 179–212, 235–40.

203   *In the spring of 1865:* See the Second Inaugural Address, March 4, 1865, *Collected Works of Lincoln*, 8:332–33.

Chapter Eight: Coda

Page

204   *The day will be warm:* The following account relies on numerous news reports. All the quotations come from the reports of Dan Barry in the *New York Times*, Sept. 12, 2002, and Michael Powell and Christine Haughney in *The Washington Post*, Sept. 12, 2002.

205   *Farmers in overalls:* Personal observations of the author. *Gettysburg Times*, Sept. 12, 2002. The sculpture is by Seward Johnson.

205   *Ceremonies are for "us":* Paraphrasing Robert E. Neimeyer quoted in the *New York Times*, Sept. 12, 2002.

205   *Two great historic documents:* James E. McGreevey, governor of New Jersey, read the preamble of the Declaration of Independence. The mayor: Michael R. Bloomberg; the president: George W. Bush.

206   *Four score and seven years ago:* Final Text, Collected Works of Lincoln, 7:205.

206   *Americans are saying:* Whether Governor George Pataki read this final version is uncertain. His office did not reply to inquiries. The press reaction often appeared to be critical before the event but not after. Three years earlier, the governor spoke at the Gettysburg Cemetery on the 136th anniversary of Lincoln's address and took a battlefield tour. www.gettysburg.edu/academics/cwi/Lincoln_Fellowship/99Pataki speech.htm. On the first anniversary of 9/11, former Mayor Rudolph Giuliani led the reading of the names of those who had died. Earlier, three months and sixteen days after the original attack, on Dec. 27, 2001, the mayor had ended his "Farewell Address" by reciting the Gettysburg Address.

Appendix A: The Program at the Soldier's National Cemetery, November 19, 1863

Page

207   *The official printed text (hereafter OT) begins (as Everett actually began speaking in Gettysburg):* "Standing beneath this serene sky, overlooking these broad fields now reposing from the labors of the waning year, the mighty Alleghenies dimly towering before us, the graves of our brethren beneath our feet, it is with hesitation that I raise my poor voice to break the eloquent silence of God and Nature."

211   *OT:* In order that we may comprehend, to their full extent, our obligations to the martyrs and surviving heroes of the Army of the Potomac, let us contemplate for a few moments the train of events, which culminated in the battles of the first days of July.

212   *OT:* though greatly superior in numbers

212   *OT:* on the south of the Potomac and a direct march on

214   *OT:* Not a moment had been

214   *OT:* force of the

214   *OT:* partly

215   *OT:* the corps commanders of

215   *OT:* of so large a force

215   *OT:* all in ignorance of the enemy's

215   *OT:* half-passed eleven o'clock

215   *OT:* nightfall on

216   *OT:* and often shared the perils which

216   *OT:* to which I am greatly indebted

216   *OT:* This long paragraph appears as Everett's own footnote, including footnote 19 (the text of which is only in the OT).

216   *OT:* ("anticipating the promulgation of his official report")

216   *OT:* "by the detailed reports, kindly transmitted to me in manuscript from the Adjutant-General's office,"

216   *OT:* "apparently a colonel in the"

217   *OT:* He does not appear to be aware, that, in recording these wretched expedients, resorted to in order to keep up the spirits of Lee's army, he furnishes the most complete refutation of his own account of its good condition. I much regret that General Meade's official report was not published in season to enable me to take full advantage of it, in preparing the brief sketch of the battles of the three days contained in this Address. It reached me but the morning before it was sent to the press.

217   *OT:* General Reynolds, on arriving at Gettysburg in the morning of the 1st, found Buford with his cavalry warmly engaged with the enemy, whom he held most gallantly in check. Hastening himself to the front, General Reynolds directed his men to be

217   *OT:* Ridge

217   *OT:* Without a moments hesitation, he attacked the enemy, at the same time sending orders to the Eleventh Corps (General Howard's) to advance as promptly as possible. General Reynolds found himself

217   *OT:* , and had scarcely made his dispositions for the action when he fell, mortally wounded, at the head of his advance.

217   *OT:* vigorously

217   *OT:* continued

217   *OT:* of the Confederates from the main body in the neighborhood, and by the divisions of Rodes and Early, coming down by separate lines from Heidlersberg and taking post on our extreme right, turned the fortunes of the day.

217   *OT:* General Howard deemed it prudent to withdraw the two corps

217   *OT:* The greater part of the First Corps

217   *OT:* , in the crowd and confusion of the scene,

218   *OT:* had in the course of the morning caused Cemetery Hill to be occupied by General Steinwehr, with the second division of the Eleventh Corps. Abut the time of the withdrawal of our troops to the hill, General Hancock arrived, having been sent by General Meade, on hearing of the death of Reynolds, to assume the command of the field till he himself could reach the front. In conjunction with General Howard,

General Hancock immediately proceeded to post troops and to repel an attack on our right flank. This attack was feebly made and promptly repulsed. At nightfall, our troops on the hill, who had so gallantly sustained themselves during the toil and peril of the day, were cheered by the arrival of General Slocum with the Twelfth Corps and of General Sickles of the Third.

218   *OT:* decided

218   *OT:* withdrawal

218   *OT:* considerable

218   *OT:* of which the wanton burning of the Harman House had given the signal

218   *OT:* weary

218   *OT:* painful

218   *OT:* reached the ever-memorable field of service and glory.

218   *OT:* and informed by the reports of General Hancock and Howard of the favorable character of the position, he determined to give battle to the enemy at this point. He accordingly directed the remaining corps of the army to concentrate at Gettysburg with all possible expedition, and breaking up his headquarters at Taneytown at 10 P.M., he arrived at the front at one o'clock in the morning of the 2d of July. Few were the moments given to sleep, during the rapid watches of that brief midsummer's night, by officers or men, though half of our troops were exhausted by the conflict of the day, and the residue wearied by the forced marches which had brought them to the rescue.

218   *OT:* The Second and Fifth Corps, with the rest of the Third, had reached the ground by seven o'clock, A.M.; but it was not

218   *OT:* afternoon

218   *OT:* who were posted upon the opposite and parallel ridge, distant from a mile to a mile and a half, overlapping our position on either wing, and probably exceeding by ten thousand the army of General Meade. (Footnote added by Everett) In the Address as originally prepared, judging from the best sources of information then within my reach, I assumed the equality of the two armies on the 2d and 3d of July. Subsequent inquiry has led me to think that I underrated somewhat the strength of Lee's force at Gettysburg, and I have corrected the text accordingly. General Hallock, however, in his official report accompanying the President's message, states the armies to have been equal.

218   *OT:* by it at daylight

219   *OT:* a great disaster.

219   *OT:* on the part of his corps

219   *OT:* Second

219   *OT:* our success was decisive, and

219   *OT:* in the memorable advance between Round Top and Little Round Top,

219   *OT:* force was driven back with great loss in killed and prisoners.

219   *OT:* In the course of the night,

219   *OT:* the Third Corps. He immediately engaged the enemy, and, after a sharp and decisive action, drove them out of our lines, recovering the ground which had been lost on the preceding day. A spirited contest was kept up all the morning on this part of the line; by General Geary, reinforced by Wheaton's brigade of the Sixth Corps, maintained his position, and inflicted very severe losses on the Rebels.

220   *OT:* two hundred and fifty

220   *OT:* from the opposite ridges

220   *OT:* Their attack was principally directed against the position of our Second Corps.

220   *OT:* crossing the intervening plain,

220   *OT:* charged furiously up to our batteries.

220   *OT:* of the Second Corps, supported by Doubleday's division and Stunnard's brigade of the First,

220   *OT:* , and was covered with the killed and the wounded; the tide of battle flowed and ebbed across the plain

220   *OT:* While these events were in progress at our left centre, the enemy was driven, with a considerable loss of prisoners, from a strong position on our extreme left, from which he was annoying our force on Little Round Top. In the terrific assault on our centre, Generals Hancock and Gibbon were wounded. In the Rebel army, Generals Armistead, Kemper, Pettigrew, and Trimble were wounded, the first named mortally, the latter also made prisoner, General Garnett was killed,

220   *OT:* The superiority of numbers was with the enemy, who were led by the ablest commanders in their service; and if the Union force had the advantage of a strong position, the Confederates had that of choosing time and place, the prestige of former victories over the Army of the Potomac, and the success of the first day. Victory does not always fall to the lot of those who deserve it; but that so decisive a triumph, under circumstances like these, was gained by our troops, I would ascribe, under Providence, to the spirit of exalted patriotism that animated them, and a consciousness that they were fighting a righteous cause.

221   *OT:* in front of our left, which, assuming the appearance of a new posi-

tion, were intended probably to protect the rear of his army in their retreat.

221 *OT*: By nightfall,

221 *OT*: short as the nights were,

221 *OT*: notwithstanding a heavy rain,

221 *OT*: Owing to the circumstance just named, the intentions of the enemy were not apparent on the 4th.

221 *OT*: on the Cashtown road and through the Emmitsburg and Monterey passes, and by Sedgwick's corps on the Fairfield Road.

221 *OT*: necessarily

221 *OT*: Passing trough the South Mountain

221 *OT*: expectation that the enemy

222 *OT*: which had rendered the most important services during the three days, and in harassing the enemy's retreat, was now

222 *OT*: at Falling Waters

222 *OT*: again

222 *OT*: with the probable loss of about a third part of his army

222 *OT*: Few

222 *OT*: of the killed, and the missing, the enemy has made no return. They are estimated, from the best data which the nature of the case admits, at 23,000. General Meade also captured 3 cannon, 28,178 small arms, and 41 standards, and 24,978 small arms were collected on the battle-field.

222 *OT*: adequately depict

222 *OT*: Christian benevolence

223 *OT*: exceeded by those who work for their

223 *OT*: and Christian

223 *OT*: forget not Who it is that will hereafter say to you,

223 *OT*: Which of the two parties to the war is responsible for all this suffering,

223 *OT*: seems to intimate

223 *OT*: his grandson

223 *OT*: as it seems to me,

224 *OT*: disloyal

224 *OT*: for the sake of dismembering it and establishing a new government south of the Trent

225 *OT*: against which the Supreme Majesty of heaven sent forth the armed myriads of his angels, and clothed the right arm of his Son with the three-bolted thunders of omnipotence.

225 *OT*: and geographical position

225	*OT:* whose names can hardly be repeated without a wondering smile,
225	*OT:* strives to
225	*OT:* little
225	*OT:* such, forsooth, as Peace, War, Army, Navy, Finance, Territory, and Relations with the native tribes
226	*OT:* and judicial
226	*OT:* who cannot even establish a post office on their own soil
226	*OT:* tenth
226	*OT:* that amendment
226	*OT:* in italics
226	*OT:* in italics
226	*OT:* in italics
226	*OT:* in italics
226	*OT:* though it was not
226	*OT:* in italics
227	*OT:* there was by implication
227	*OT:* declaring
227	*OT:* expressly
227	*OT:* by implication (for an express reservation is not pretended)
227	*OT:* individual
228	*OT:* the worst of criminals
228	*OT:* after a free discussion,
228	*OT:* of the revolutionary and constitutional age, to follow the agitators of the present day.
228	*OT:* the first days of
228	*OT:* a sad forboding
229	*OT:* Refusing a just exchange of prisoners, while they crowd their armies with paroled prisoners not exchanged,
229	*OT:* outbreak of the
230	*OT:* to mount the throne
230	*OT:* —a fate worse than starvation in Libby—
230	*OT:* (it is a royalist that is speaking,)
231	*OT:* New paragraph
231	*OT:* —which was the shortest of all and waged in the most civilized age,
231	*OT:* whose seat no one knew, whose power none could escape,
231	*OT:* There are controversies in that country, at the present day, but they grow mainly out of the rivalry of the two leading powers.
231	*OT:* as if to shame the degenerate sons of America, are joining
232	*OT:* causing the death of so many thousands of their fellow-men

232   *OT:* I care not with what trumpery credentials he may be furnished,

233   *OT:* when its rifled cannon shall begin to roar, the hosts of treasonable
sophistry,—the mad delusions of the day,—will fly like the Rebel army
through the passes of yonder mountain.

Appendix C, Part 3: What Lincoln Read at Gettysburg

Page

272   *Comparisons:* Fifty-four years later, after the Gettysburg Address grew
into mythology, Joseph I. Gilbert told of having been the AP reporter.
"Fascinated" by Lincoln's "intense earnestness and depth of feeling,"
Gilbert wrote, "I unconsciously stopped taking notes and looked up at
him just as he glanced from his manuscript with a far away look in his
eyes as if appealing from the few thousand before him to the invisible
audience of countless millions whom his words were to reach." Lincoln
came to the rescue and allowed the reporter to copy the speech: "the
press report was made from the copy no transcription from shorthand
notes was necessary." "Lincoln in 1861," pp. 134, 137. (John Russell
Young also recalled, not necessarily independently, that the AP had obtained the manuscript: *Men and Memories,* vol. 1, p. 70; cf. *Philadelphia
Star,* July 25, 1891.) All the same, the specifics of Gilbert's recollection
needs to be taken with a grain of salt. The AP archives that are just
being organized and have very modest nineteenth-century holdings
are not likely to provide corroboration. If Gilbert was the reporter at
Gettysburg (he did work for the AP at times), most likely he took
shorthand notes and hurriedly corrected them from Lincoln's manuscript. The AP report missed "poor" before "power," a word that was
caught by numerous other reporters and is also in the Second (Hay)
draft. That draft does not have "under God" that Lincoln appears to
have added at the moment of delivery. If the AP reporter copied the
text, where did the phrase in the AP report come from? Conceivably
Lincoln's speaking copy has been lost—but that is a lot to deduce from
a recollection, especially when it contains various errors, including
mentioning a beardless Lincoln in late February, 1861, p. 131. Gilbert's
1917 paper ended with the Gettysburg Address, but he provided the
Second Baltimore Fair (Bliss) version, with some punctuation changes,
and not what the AP had reported in 1863. Then the AP had noted repeated applause; in 1917 Gilbert wrote "I heard none," p. 135. By then
eyewitnesses had long divided into applause and no-applause camps.
His paper was read by Frederick J. Rose of Chicago, and it is unclear

whether Gilbert was present. Scholars have relied on Barton's transcription that has minor errors, *Lincoln at Gettysburg*, 189–92, and apparently misreported Gilbert's middle initial as "L." The AP version here comes from the *New York Tribune*, November 20, 1863, the newspaper with probably the widest and most copied distribution. Papers that printed the AP version some days later, in a less hurried issue, succeeded in getting some words apparently more accurately, closer to the Second Draft, but also often managed to insert new errors. For example the *Boston Journal*, November 23, 1863, used "unfinished work" in place of "refinished work," but then printed "what we may say here," instead of "what we say here." Intriguingly the same paper changed "We are met to dedicate a portion of it" into "We are met to dedicate a portion of that field" which in fact appears in Lincoln's later versions and so raises the question: Did he say that at Gettysburg, or did he adopt the expression from AP reports as he prepared new copies, or as he made new copies did he arrive at the expression on his own?

272 *But some historians believe:* Printed in *Address of his Excellency John A. Andrew, to the Two Branches of the Legislature of Massachusetts, January 18, 1864* (Boston: Wright & Potter, 1864), p. lxxii. The *Boston Daily Advertiser*, Nov. 20, 1863, where Hale worked, also published a text that may have been based on his shorthand transcription. However, the probability is that the paper used the AP. Hale complained in a report in the above volume (signed by him and two others, all three serving as the Massachusetts Commissioners at the Gettysburg ceremonies) that newspaper publications of Lincoln's speech were "generally" not done "rightly, having been marred from errors in telegraphing." Ibid, xxxv. Six words and twenty-three punctuation marks differentiate the *Advertiser* and the Andrews versions of Lincoln's speech. As other reports (and the Second Draft) indicate, Hale's careful version still missed "poor," added the word "very" before "little note," and changed "here gave" to "have given."

273 *Baltimore Sanitary Fair copy:* Nicolay, "Lincoln's Gettysburg Address," pp. 604–05. As a result of that revision, Nicolay printed the second Baltimore Sanitary Fair copy, pp. 602–03.

273 *words "under God":* Mearns and Dunlap, *Long Remembered*, n.p. [12], argue for that hypothesis even as they admit that their "evidence is not abundant." And they note that "before Lincoln made these corrections the [Second] copy differed in wording from the press reports in seven instances. After the corrections, the number increased to ten." It is not clear what specific A.P. text these scholars used in their comparison. See

also Mearns' typescript speculations in his Papers, as well as the subsequent debunking of his and Dunlap's hypothesis (in addition to a case made for the "Second Draft" being the reading copy) by the staff of the Illinois State Historical Society, Clyde C. Walton to Foster Cannon, April 20, 1964 with 12 pp. enclosure, "We have examined Cannon's evidence. . . ." LC, Box 148. Among others, Barton, *Lincoln at Gettysburg*, *passim*, argues in favor of the Second Draft. The best, but hardly good, claim for Lincoln having written the Second version after returning to Washington, was put on paper nearly eight years after Hay's death: Nelson Thomasson to Elihu Root, Feb. 21, 1913, copy enclosed with Clara S. Hay to Helen Nicolay, Feb. 28, 1913, Nicolay Papers, LC; cf. Nicholson and Lambert referred to in "We have examined Cannon's evidence," p. 7; *N.Y. Times*, June 29, 1913; "Chronology," Mearns Papers, LOC.

Appendix D: Dollar Signs

Page

287   *Lincoln's first secretary:* John G. Nicolay to Richard Watson Gilder, September 19, 1885, Nicolay Papers; cf. Nicolay, "Lincoln's Gettysburg Address," p. 601.

287   *Nicolay and Hay:* David C. Mearns, *The Lincoln Papers: The Story of the Collection with Selections to July 4, 1861*, 2 vols. (New York: Doubleday, 1948), 1:22, 45, 89, 91, et passim.

287   *In 1885, we know:* Nicolay to Gilder, Sept. 19, 1885. A little later Robert Lincoln wrote to Bell F. Keys, December 16, 1885, that he had did not know what happened to the first copies of the Address. Barton, *Lincoln at Gettysburg*, p. 107.

287   *Hay thus had assembled:* Martin P. Johnson, "Who Stole the Gettysburg Address," *Journal of the Abraham Lincoln Association* 24 (Summer 2003): 1–19.

288   *They have been there:* Mearns, *Lincoln Papers*, 1:135.

288   *"The President, in a firm free way":* Hay Diary, 113–14 (November 19, 1863). While working on their Lincoln biography with Nicolay, Hay wanted the Gettysburg Address tacked on to the end of the chapter on the battle. Hay to Nicolay, August 29, 1885, William R. Thayer, *The Life and Letters of John Hay*, 2 vols. (Boston: Houghton, 1915), 2:36. They ended up with a full chapter entitled "Lincoln's Gettysburg Address," but most of it focused on Everett. Lincoln got only the facsimile of the Baltimore Fair version of his speech and two additional pages. Nicolay and Hay, *Lincoln*, 8:189–204.

288   *The public did not know:* James Grant Wilson, "Recollections of Lin-
       coln," *Putnam's Magazine* 5 (February 1909): 526–27. Johnson, "Who
       Stole the Gettysburg Address," 5n.14, indicates that the suggestion of
       Mearns and Dunlap, *Long Remembered,* n.p. [p. 22], that collector Lam-
       bert revealed the existence of the "Hay" draft in 1906 is erroneous.

288   *Earlier when Hay had been asked:* Burrage, *Gettysburg and Lincoln,* 133;
       John P. Nicholson, ed. and compiler, *Pennsylvania at Gettysburg: Cere-
       monies at the Dedication of the Monuments Erected by the Commonwealth of
       Pennsylvania.* . . . , 2 vols. (Harrisburg: Wm. Stanley Ray, 1904), 1:iii.

288   *Along the way, various people:* George Sidney Hellman, *Lanes of Memory*
       (New York: Knopf, 1927), pp. 6, 47–48.

288   *That amount would have been:* Peterson, *Lincoln in American Memory,*
       p. 148.

288   *in today's dollars:* The figure comes from calculations based on the His-
       torical Statistics of the U.S. (to 1970) and the data of the Bureau of Eco-
       nomic Analysis (www.bea.gov) and www.inflator.com. Professor Ann
       Harper Fender of Gettysburg College assisted with the work.

288   *Helen Hay Whitney:* Helen Hay Whitney to [George Sidney] Hellman,
       1907; see also George H. Hellman to Fred B. Adams, February 3, 1957,
       Morgan Library.

288   *These, he added, "I shall try":* Hay to Robert Todd Lincoln, April 12,
       1888, Thayer, ed., *Life and Letters,* 2:44–45.

289   *Though the sale was advertised, no evidence:* Thomas F. Madigan quoted in
       the *New York Times,* February 12, 1930. See also Warren, *Lincoln's Get-
       tysburg Declaration,* pp. 165–66.

289   *"Before me as I write":* Thomas F. Madigan, *Word Shadows of the Great:
       The Lure of Autograph Collecting* (New York: Stokes, 1930), pp. 260–61;
       see also pp. 164–65.

289   *Senator Keyes's son:* Henry W. Keyes to Guy Allison, January 22, 1952,
       quoted in Guy Allison, *Man's Most Valuable Words* (Gettysburg: L. E.
       Smith, 1956), pp. 19–20. Allison attempts to reconstruct the history of
       the five copies of the Address including their financial stories. See also
       Isabella Keyes to John Hay, July 11, 1904 (copy), Mearns Papers, LC.

289   *Madigan in turn sold it:* Allison, *Man's Most Valuable Words,* 18. Unlike
       the bulk of this book, up to here the discussion of the Third Draft is
       based on recollections and secondary sources and therefore its accu-
       racy is open to question.

289   *Under the leadership: New York Times,* March 22, 1944.

289   *Bliss had hoped:* Alexander Bliss to John G. Nicolay, March 7, 1864; John
       P. Kennedy to Lincoln, March 4, 1864, LP; John F. Kennedy, ed., *Auto-*

graph Leaves of Our Country's Authors (Baltimore: Cushings & Bailey, 1864).

290   *"It is an American historical document":* Madigan to Louis A. Warren, April 18, 1935, Gettysburg Address Scrapbook, vol. 4, Lincoln Library.

290   *Indianapolis dealer, Arthur Zinkin:* David Randall to David C. Mearns, December 11, 1962; N. H. Noyes to Tom Mahoney, July 24, 1963; Felix Reichman to David C. Mearns, July 28, 1959, Mearns Papers.

290   *Along the way, or so a story goes:* Allison, *Man's Most Valuable Words*, pp. 21–22.

290   *However, even that price: Lincoln's Gettysburg Address, the Unique and Final Holograph Manuscript Known as the Bliss Copy.* . . . (New York: Parke-Bernet, 1949); *New York Times*, April 19, 24, 28, 1949. The quotation is from the *Washington Evening Star*, April 28, 1949, and the *New York Times*, April 24, 28, 1949.

291   *After his death in 1957:* Loraine W. Pierce to David C. Mearns, June 7, 1961, Mearns Papers. "The disposition of the Cintas estate is a most complicated one, and the probability is that the assets will not amount to much. The Castro regime has taken care of that." Paul Angle to David C. Mearns, May 19, 1961, Mearns Papers. See also the *New York Times*, May 12, 1957; July 14, 1959; February 23, March 7, 1961.

291   *Mearns was dubious:* David C. Mearns to Ralph G. Newman, April 4, 1963, copy, Mearns Papers, LC.

291   *Garry Wills's popular:* Wills, *Lincoln at Gettysburg*, pp. 195–98.

291   *Wills did indeed ask:* Wills to Lincoln, November 23, 1863, LP.

291   *In fact, he appears:* Wills to William H. Lambert, referred to in Barton, *Lincoln at Gettysburg*, p. 103.

291   *Edward McPherson, who knew Wills:* McPherson to Nicolay, November 28, 1893, Nicolay Papers, LC.

291   *Gary Wills had warned:* Ibid., p. 198.

291   *On February 11, 1991:* Klement, *Gettysburg*, 152–66, provides a history of this document. See also Lloyd Ostendorf, "Turning the Pages of History: A New Draft of the Gettysburg Address Located," *Gettysburg Magazine* 6 (January 1992): pp. 107–12.

291   *When the Ostendorf estate:* Seth Kaller to Gabor Boritt, May 20, 2006.

292   *Early in the twenty-first century:* Seth Kaller to Gabor Boritt, May 22, 2006. The 72-page illustrated Leonardo manuscript, created circa 1508–10 in mirror-image writing, sums up the artist's exploration of nature and brought $30.8 million at Christie's in New York on November 11, 1994, the most ever paid at auction for any manuscript or scientific work.

292 *In 2005, the earliest pamphlet: The Gettysburg Solemnities* (Washington: *Washington Chronicle*, 1863); Seth Kaller to Gabor Boritt, May 26, 2006.

292 *Compare the newly discovered:* www.loc.gov/exhibits/gadd/gadrft.html; www.papersofabrahamlincoln.org/Gettysburg%20Address.htm®c .library.cornell.edu/gettysburg/good_cause/address_pic_pl.htm; Mearns and Dunlap, eds., *Long Remembered.*

A BIBLIOGRAPHICAL NOTE:
DWARFS AND GIANTS

Antecedents and Sources

This Bibliographic Note will serve readers who wish to identify works that helped shape the book and to read further on some topics. It also discusses briefly some of the more important earlier writings on Lincoln's great speech. However, a full list of the works consulted is not provided either here or in the Notes, lest they prove overwhelming. To illustrate: fifty-four soldiers' newspapers published in Union camps during the Civil War have been tracked—the list taken from the pioneering research of Chandra Miller Manning, *What This Cruel War Was Over: Why Union and Confederate Soldiers Thought They Were Fighting the Civil War*, PhD dissertation, Harvard University, 2002. Most of these newspapers, as it turned out, have no surviving issues for the last months of 1863, when one might expect to find reactions to the dedication of the Soldiers' National Cemetery. The very few issues that survive for the period do not contain useful information. Indeed, the only soldiers' paper that reflected on the subject was found in Utah by my talented first-semester, first-year student, Skye Montgomery. The *Union Vedette* of Salt Lake City, then, is the only soldiers' paper noted in this book.

Except for chapter 7, Gloria, the Notes mostly cite contemporary primary sources. The reason for relying little, and then with great care, on the reminiscences is their most signal characteristic: constant contradiction. Thus, many remembered that Lincoln's words had been received with applause at Gettysburg; many also recalled the precise opposite. A book-length scholarly examination of the reminiscences will be a welcome contribution to Lincoln scholarship.

Notes that refer to newspapers had to be abbreviated—listing every paper that referred to John Forney as "Lincoln's dog" could take up perhaps a page.

So the Notes only provide a sample of the sources. A full collection of contemporary articles on the Gettysburg dedication, nearly all from late 1863, will be placed on the Internet. To provide as full a database as possible for future scholars, the search for newspapers continues, though no substantially new information is likely to emerge. Another ongoing project related to this book, conducted in cooperation with statisticians, will present a quantitative examination of the exact wording of Lincoln's speech that newspapers placed before the public in 1863.

Secondary sources are mentioned in the Notes only when they have played a very large role in the creation of this book. When a source pointed the way to a primary source, the Notes do not credit the former. For example, Kent Masterson Brown dug up Lafayette Guild's letter about Confederate arrangements for the wounded left behind in Gettysburg—the *Official Records*, 27:2, 328, merely noted that it was "not found." Following Brown's trail, the original was located, but the Notes at p. 297 acknowledge only this document and Brown's *Retreat from Gettysburg*, which helped in other ways, too, and is acknowledged here only in general terms. To provide another example, Roland R. Maust's fine, massive study of the Union Second Corps Hospital pointed the way to surgeon Harry McAbee's letter of resignation (p. 10), but is only acknowledged in a general way below.

The Gettysburg Address

The scholarly study of the subject begins with John G. Nicolay, "Lincoln's Gettysburg Address," *Century*, 47 (February 1894): 596–608, an article considered in chapter 7.

Henry Sweetser Burrage, *Gettysburg and Lincoln: The Battle, the Cemetery, and the National Park* (New York: Putnam, 1906), devotes the middle part, pp. 81–135, to a fine summation of the knowledge of the time and concludes that the address was well received in 1863. Burrage explains that the "fifth draft," the second Baltimore Fair (Bliss) version, should be the one "handed down to future generations" (p. 133). The story of the address is told in combination with the histories of the battle, the Gettysburg Battle-Field Memorial Association, and the National Park Commission.

Numerous other studies of more or less value followed, and a few deserve notice. Clark E. Carr, *Lincoln at Gettysburg: An Address* (Chicago: McClurg, 1906), the author an 1863 participant, took chief responsibility for the invitation to Lincoln. Long afterward, Carr would still make newspaper headlines like those in the Galesburg, Ill., *Register-Mail*, Nov. 19, 1949: "But for Clark E.

Carr, Gettysburg Address Might Not Have Been" (Gettysburg Address Scrapbook, 2:6).

Orton H. Carmichael, *Lincoln's Gettysburg Address* (New York: Abingdon, 1917), is the first valuable book-length study of the subject, even if its judicious tone at times sums up history and myth without discrimination. Insights include noting that in revising the address, Lincoln moved from "the particular to the universal" (p. 116).

Henry Eyster Jacobs, *Lincoln's World-Message* (Philadelphia: United Lutheran Publication House, 1919), also reflected ably the thinking of his time, describing the speech as a paean to the democratic form of government, but with black people written out of the story. An eyewitness as a boy, the son of the Gettysburg professor Michael Jacobs affirmed, as intellectuals have done since Sumner's day, that "Gettysburg will live in history" more because of Lincoln's address than the battle. Jacobs also explained that Lincoln was an orthodox Christian, even if the president himself did not think so.

William E. Barton, *Lincoln at Gettysburg: What He Intended to Say; What He Said; What He Was Reported to Have Said; What He Wished He Had Said* (Indianapolis: Bobbs-Merrill, 1930), a sprightly reading, served as the standard work for the next generation. It contains material that cannot be found elsewhere, but its chief virtue is the substantial collection of memoirs (though not always reproduced accurately). The moral of the collection is nicely summed up in a possibly apocryphal anecdote related by Barton. In 1913, in Gettysburg, a speech on Lincoln's address put to sleep four old men, also on the stage, all of whom had been eyewitnesses to the 1863 dedication. When the time came for them to speak, the first was woken, "tottered to his feet and said, 'Well, my friends, it was a rainy day, and I heard Mr. Lincoln speak in a loud voice, etc.' Great applause." The second old man, woken, explained that "I remember the day well indeed. The sun shone clear and there wasn't a cloud in the sky, but Mr. Lincoln couldn't be heard, he spoke so low." The audience tittered, and by the time the other two finished reminiscing, "the crowd roared" with laughter (pp. 156–57).

F. Lauriston Bullard, *"A Few Appropriate Remarks": Lincoln's Gettysburg Address* (Harrogate, TN: Lincoln Memorial University, 1944), is a brief, well-written, standard account that includes a long list of antecedents for the expression "a government of the people, by the people, for the people." The theme of Lincoln's speech was democracy, Bullard explained. Writing in the midst of World War II, he concluded, "it is for the same cause that the United States is at war today" (p. 71).

David C. Mearns and Lloyd A. Dunlap, eds., *Long Remembered: The Gettys-*

burg Address in Facsimile (Washington, DC: Library of Congress, 1963), provides the best brief look at the subject, with a substantial introduction, thorough notes, and the five facsimiles of the speech. The editors were the first to reach high professional standards. All the same, they claimed as "incontrovertible fact" that Lincoln's words came out of "careful thought and preparation." By way of concrete proof, however, Mearns and Dunlap only suggest that no surviving copy of the address was written on the train to Gettysburg, since none are in a wobbly hand, so repeating unwittingly what Nicolay had written in 1894. These fine researchers can be best understood in the context of the legend popularized by Andrews's *The Perfect Tribute*, with its story of a speech scribbled on a train. Hay, too, had combated the same legend, advocated by many long before Andrews, writing in 1891 to *Century* editor Richard Watson Gilder that Lincoln did not speak off-the-cuff but "carefully considered" his words, which were "reduced to writing before it was delivered,—and very little changed in subsequent copy." *Letters of John Hay and Extracts from Diary* (3 vols., New York: Gordian Press, 1969), vol. 2, p. 214.

Elsewhere Mearns considered the many false recollections about the speech in "Unknown at This Address," in Allan Nevins, ed., *Lincoln and the Gettysburg Address* (Urbana: University of Illinois Press, 1964), pp. 118–33. Together with Dunlap, he intended to write a full-scale study of the Gettysburg Address, but death intervened.

Louis A. Warren, *Lincoln's Gettysburg Declaration: "A New Birth of Freedom"* (Fort Wayne, IN: Lincoln National Life, 1964), took the stage right after the 100th anniversary of Gettysburg. The product of decades of careful probing, Warren's encyclopedic knowledge was not matched by equally solid judgments, though he seemed to make equality a central message of the address. The quaint footnoting is annoying. Though Warren superseded Barton, the book never captured much of the attention of either scholars or the public.

Leo Paul S. de Alvarez, ed., *Abraham Lincoln, The Gettysburg Address and American Constitutionalism* (Dallas: University of Dallas Press, 1976), was an attempt by five scholars to come to grips with Lincoln as a political thinker. Glen E. Thurow and George Anastapolo, two of the contributors, went on to write book-length works in which the Gettysburg Address and political religion played a large role: Thurow, *Abraham Lincoln and American Political Religion* (Albany: State University of New York Press, 1976); and Anastapolo, *Abraham Lincoln: A Constitutional Biography* (Latham, MD: Rowman & Littlefield, 1999).

Important to Alvarez, et al., are the opposing views of Wilmore Kendall and Harry V. Jaffa. The first argued that the Gettysburg Address falsified history by making 1776 and equality, not 1789 and liberty, the American founding: Kendall, *The Conservative Affirmation* (Chicago: Regnery, 1963), pp. 17–18, 252.

Kendall found an ally in M. E. Bradford, who took up the cause in various places, see, e.g., "The Heresy of Equality: A Reply to Harry Jaffa," in *A Better Guide to Reason: Studies in the American Revolution* (LaSalle, IL: Sugden, 1979), 29–57. Bradford was denied the chairmanship of the National Endowment for the Humanities for his trouble.

Opposing them, Jaffa analyzed the tension between liberty and equality but with deep admiration for Lincoln, in *Crisis of the House Divided: An Interpretation of the Issues in the Lincoln-Douglas Debates* (Seattle: University of Washington Press, 1959). Jaffa later published his remarkable *New Birth of Freedom: Abraham Lincoln and the Coming of the Civil War* (Latham, MD: Rowman & Littlefield, 2000), but the book did not go as far as the Gettysburg Address.

If contemporary politics appeared to live all too heavily in some of these works, it could also play a large role from the other side of the spectrum, as in the philosopher Arthur C. Danto's reaction to a visit to the Gettysburg battlefield, which led him to describe Lincoln's address as "a cry of victory as gloating as anything that issued from the coarse throat of Ajax"—"Addressing Gettysburg," *Harper's Magazine* (July 1987): 36–40.

Philip B. Kunhardt, Jr.'s *A New Birth of Freedom: Lincoln at Gettysburg* (Boston: Little, Brown, 1983), is a well-written, well-illustrated, popular account that embraces various legends and includes treasures. Kunhardt's enlarged photo of the Gettysburg Cemetery's platform party provides fascinating speculations about who is pictured. (See illustration page 9.)

Garry Wills's dazzling *Lincoln at Gettysburg: The Words That Remade America* (New York: Simon & Schuster, 1992) has been repeatedly noted already. Its "great man, great moment" view of history reflected the views of Lincoln's time, and the success of the book with the late twentieth-century reading public indicated a hunger for such greatness. Wills accepted Kendall's view that the address's interpretation of the Declaration of Independence remade America; but, unlike his predecessor, he saw this as a great good, cunningly administered. By giving the United States a new Constitution that made equality its foundation—among the races, too—Lincoln gave Americans "a new past" and therefore a new future. "Words had to complete the work of the guns" (p. 38). Lincoln came to Gettysburg "to change the world" and he "did" (p. 175).

Soon after Wills, a collection of mostly previously published articles appeared: Frank L. Klement's *The Gettysburg Soldiers' Cemetery and Lincoln's Address: Aspects and Angles* (Shippensburg, PA: White Mane, 1993). The book contains a wealth of information, but with essays unedited for the volume, they often repeat themselves and sometimes contradict each other. Klement died before he would write a definitive study. Steven K. Rogstad's introduction provides a useful outline of the literature of the address.

European scholarship of American history has been flowering since the end of the World War II. Ekkehart Krippendorff: *Abraham Lincoln: Gettysburg Address, 19 November 1863* (Hamburg: Europaische Verlagsanstalt, 1994), sees the speech as the clearest definition of democracy and Lincoln the only great politician-statesman of history.

Linda Giberson Black, *Gettysburg Remembers President Lincoln: Eyewitness Accounts of November 1863* (Gettysburg: Thomas, 2005), is a slender useful, collection of secondary sources and recollections, with no attempt to test their validity against contemporary sources.

It is a thankless task to select from among the many recent essays on the subject, but here are some choices: Ronald Reid, "Newspaper Responses to the Gettysburg Address," *Quarterly Journal of Speech*, 53 (1967): 50–60; Glenn LaFantasie, "Lincoln and the Gettysburg Awakening," *Journal of the Abraham Lincoln Association*, 16 (Winter 1995): 73–89; Harold Holzer, "Lincoln's 'Flat Failure': The Gettysburg Myth Revisited," in *Lincoln Seen and Heard* (Lawrence: University Press of Kansas, 2000), pp. 191–98; and Martin P. Johnson, "Who Stole the Gettysburg Address?" *Journal of the Abraham Lincoln Association*, 24 (Summer 2003): 1–19.

Kent Gramm, *November: Lincoln's Elegy at Gettysburg* (Bloomington: Indiana University Press, 2001), is a personal meditation in a class by itself. See also Gramm's deconstruction of Andrews's little book: "A More Perfect Tribute," *Journal of the Abraham Lincoln Association*, 25 (Summer 2005): 50–58.

Lincoln's address has attracted some remarkable artists, as chapter 7 indicates. Some of their work appeared in book form and the best deserve mention. The paintings in James Daugherty, *Lincoln's Gettysburg Address: A Pictorial Interpretation* (Chicago: Albert Whitman, 1947), connect the speech to World War II and are masterpieces of the illustrative art of the time. Michael McCurdy, *The Gettysburg Address* (Boston: Houghton Mifflin, 1995), intended for young people, has black and white drawings that resemble nineteenth-century woodcuts. Sam Fink's *The Illustrated Gettysburg Address* (New York: Random House, 1994) brims with ingenuity, wonder, and affection for Lincoln. Many exhibits touch on the address; Fink's focuses fully on it, as in a 2000 exhibition at Gettysburg College entitled "Lincoln Is Alive and Well at Gettysburg." Each of the Fink paintings includes the full text of the address and continues to be exhibited periodically.

Chapters One and Two: After Battle and Rebirth

The history of the Gettysburg area is considered in Robert L. Bloom, *A History of Adams County, Pennsylvania, 1700–1900* (Gettysburg: Adams County Historical Society, 1992). Some of the older works identified in Bloom's footnotes also can be useful. The periodical *Adams County History*, published by the Adams County Historical Society, is important. The society's archives, as well as those of the Gettysburg National Military Park, are the most important repositories of primary sources. Marilyn Brownfield Rudawsky's "After July: The Effects of the Battle of Gettysburg on the People of Adams County," Master's Thesis, Youngstown State University, 1979, deserves attention. William Frassanito's *Early Photography at Gettysburg* (Gettysburg: Thomas, 1995) is not only a treasure trove of photographs and photographers but of Gettysburg history in general.

John W. Busey and David G. Martin, *Regimental Strengths and Losses at Gettysburg* 4th ed. (Hightstown, NJ: Longstreet House, 2005), provides the most reliable figures. Details about casualties can be found in John W. Busey, *These Honored Dead: The Union Casualties at Gettysburg* (Hightstown, NJ: Longstreet House, 1988); and for the Confederates in Robert K. Krick, comp., *The Gettysburg Death Roster: The Confederate Dead at Gettysburg* (Dayton, OH: Morningside, 1981). The National Archives hold not only the Gettysburg damage claims but also much information about the prisoners, wounded or otherwise.

The aftermath of the battle can be examined in the published reports of the United States Sanitary Commission and the United States Christian Commission. New York also put out a useful report. Those interested in a fine bibliography may turn to Ronald R. Maust's encyclopedic study: *Grappling with Death*. The book pictures heroic work that saved lives. A section on the flooding after the battle, pp. 879–94, concludes that "an indefinite number of Confederates was carried away by the rapid rise of the water, and drowned" (p. 893).

Gregory A. Coco's pioneering work includes *A Strange and Blighted Land, Gettysburg: The Aftermath* (Gettysburg: Thomas, 1995) and *A Vast Sea of Misery: A History and Guide to the Union and Confederate Field Hospitals at Gettysburg, July 1–November 20, 1863* (Gettysburg: Thomas, 1988). The latter catalogues not only the sites but also the names of many of the surgeons and physicians who served after the battle. Robert D. Deadrick, "Field Medical Support of the Army of the Potomac at Gettysburg." Typed manuscript, U.S. Army War College, Carlisle Barracks, PA, 1989, is another early effort. Newspaperman Gerard A. Patterson's *Debris of Battle: The Wounded of Gettysburg* (Mechanicsburg, PA: Stackpole, 1997), its many problems with footnotes notwithstanding, tells a lively tale about how the town coped with the casualties. Margaret S. Creighton's beautifully written work *The Colors of Courage: Gettysburg's Forgotten History. Immigrants, Women, African Americans in the Civil War's Defining Battle* (New York: Basic, 2005), which received the honorable mention of the

Lincoln Prize, pays attention to neglected parts of the story. And see the pioneering work of my own student, Christina Ericson, " 'The World Will Little Note Nor Long Remember': Gender Analysis of Civilian Responses to the Battle of Gettysburg," in William Blair and William Pencak, eds., *Making and Remaking Pennsylvania's Civil War* (University Park, PA: Pennsylvania State University Press, 2001), pp. 81–102.

For African-Americans, see the pioneering work of another of my students, Peter C. Vermilyea, "The Effect of the Confederate Invasion of Pennsylvania on Gettysburg's African American Community," *Gettysburg Magazine*, 24 (2001): 112–28; Vermilyea, "John Hopkins' Civil War," *Adams County History*, 11 (2005): 4–21; Margaret Creighton, *The Colors of Courage*; and David G. Smith, "Race and Retaliation: The Capture of African Americans During the Gettysburg Campaign," in Peter Wallenstein and Bertram Wyatt-Brown, eds., *Virginia's Civil War* (Charlottesville: University of Virginia Press, pp. 2005), 137–51.

My able predecessors at Gettysburg College have approached after-battlefield Gettysburg before me: Robert Fortenbaugh, "Lincoln as Gettysburg Saw Him," *Pennsylvania History* 14 (Jan. 1947), 1–12; and Robert Bloom, " 'We Never Expected Battle:' The Civilians of Gettysburg, 1863," ibid., 55 (Oct. 1988), 161–200. Gerald R. Bennett, whose excellent efforts play a central role in placing historic markers in Gettysburg, has a broader scope in *Days of "Uncertainty and Dread": The Ordeal Endured by the Civilians of Gettysburg* (Littlestown, PA: Bennett, 1997). The same is true of newspaperman George Sheldon's account: *When the Smoke Cleared at Gettysburg: The Tragic Aftermath of the Bloodiest Battle of the Civil War* (Nashville, TN: Cumberland House, 2003). Timothy H. Smith, "A Tour of Gettysburg's Visual Battle Damage," *Adams County History*, 2 (1996): 41–71, provides a comprehensive picture. Smith discusses the *New York Times* attack on the reputation of the town in " 'These Were Days of Horror': The Story of the Gettysburg Civilians," in Barbara J. Finfrock, ed., *Unsung Heroes of Gettysburg*, Program of the Fifth Annual Gettysburg Seminar (Gettysburg: GNMP, 1996), pp. 81–89. The same subject is considered in Jim Weeks, " 'Disgrace That Can Never Be Washed Out': Gettysburg and the Lingering Stigma of 1863," in Blair and Pencak, eds., *Pennsylvania's Civil War*, pp. 189–210; and it is touched on in David L. Valuska and Christian B. Keller, *Damn Dutch: Pennsylvania Germans at Gettysburg* (Stackpole, 2004), pp. 70–71, and Creighton's *Colors of Courage*, p. 157.

A fascinating David Wills still awaits his biographer. The ACHS, the GNMP, and the LOC all hold overlapping primary sources. The best brief sketch, by Elwood W. Christ, is *David Wills House: Historic Structure Report for the Borough of Gettysburg and the National Park Service*, by ICON architecture, inc. and John Bowie Associates (2002), GNMP.

Ira M. Rutkow, *Bleeding Blue and Gray: Civil War Surgery and the Evolution of American Medicine* (New York: Random House, 2005), is the standard work on the subject. Jane E. Schultz, *Women at the Front: Hospital Workers in Civil War America* (Chapel Hill: University of North Carolina Press, 2004), is the best on its subject and received honorable mention of the Lincoln Prize. For the U.S. Sanitary Commission, see William Quentin Maxwell, *Lincoln's Fifth Wheel: The Political History of the United States Sanitary Commission* (New York: Longmans, 1956), and Judith Ann Giesberg's outstanding *Civil War Sisterhood: The U.S. Sanitary Commission and Women's Politics in Transition* (Boston: Northeastern University Press, 2000). See also Giesberg's "From Harvest Field to Battlefield: Rural Pennsylvania Women and the U.S. Civil War," *Pennsylvania History*, 72 (Spring 2005): 159–91. David A. Raney, "In the Lord's Army: The United States Christian Commission, Soldiers, and the Union War Effort," in Paul Cimbala and Randall M. Miller, eds., *Union Soldiers and the Northern Home Front: Wartime Experiences and Postwar Adjustments* (New York: Fordham University Press, 2002), pp. 263–92, provides a fine introduction. Bonnie Ellen Blustein, *Preserve Your Love of Science: Life of William A. Hammond, American Neurologist* (Cambridge: Cambridge University Press, 1991), gives credit to the Surgeon General for modernizing the Medical Department of the army. Nina Silber, *Daughters of the Union: Northern Women Fight the Civil War* (Cambridge, MA: Harvard University Press, 2005), shows that the war encouraged patriotic women to step outside the home and family, taking on new civic responsibilities and a new relationship with the nation-state, even as female submissiveness and subordination in a bureaucratic world dominated by men changed little. For a fine history of the college building that served as a hospital, see Charles H. Glatfelter, *Yonder Beautiful Stately College Edifice: A History of Pennsylvania Hall (Old Dorm), Gettysburg College, Gettysburg, Pennsylvania* (Gettysburg: Gettysburg College, 1970).

David E. Stannard, ed., *Death in America* (Philadelphia: University of Pennsylvania Press, 1975), provides a general introduction to the subject. For a broad national picture of the war period, the best work is John R. Neff's *Honoring the Civil War Dead: Commemoration and the Problem of Reconciliation* (Lawrence: University Press of Kansas, 2005). See also Drew Faust's pioneering *"A Riddle of Death": Mortality and Meaning in the American Civil War*, Fortenbaugh Lecture (Gettysburg: Gettysburg College, 1995). For Lincoln and death, see Stephen B. Oates, *With Malice Towards None: The Life of Abraham Lincoln* (New York: Harper, 1977), and Robert V. Bruce, "The Riddle of Death," in Gabor Boritt, ed., *Lincoln the War President: The Gettysburg Lectures* (New York: Oxford University Press, 2001), pp. 130–45. The cumulative effect of these works is to suggest that the Civil War redefined the relationship between the state and the individual, focused on liberty and the abolishment of slavery, and recognized the individual's right to identity and personhood. As part of the growing reach of human rights, the government assumed a duty to the dead, including the missing, as well as to the living survivors.

For the Gettysburg Cemetery, printed primary sources can be found in *Report of the Select Committee Relative to the Soldiers' National Cemetery* (Harrisburg, PA: Singerly & Myers, 1864), and John Russell Bartlett, *The Soldiers' National Cemetery at Gettysburg* (Providence, RI: Providence Press, 1874). See also Harlan D. Unrau, *Administrative History: Gettysburg National Military Park and National Cemetery* (Washington, DC: Department of Interior, 1991). Kathleen Georg credits New York's Theodore S. Dimon for suggesting the idea of the National Cemetery as well as David McConaughy for initiating the preservation of the battlegrounds; see "Gettysburg—A Happy and Patriotic Conception" and " 'This Grand National Enterprise': The Origins of Gettysburg's National Cemetery and Gettysburg Battlefield Memorial Association," GNMP. David Wills, however, did the lion's share of the work.

For the rural cemetery movement, see Stanley French, "The Cemetery as a Cultural Institution: The Establishment of Mount Auburn and the 'Rural Cemetery' Movement," in Stannard, *Death in America*, pp. 69–91; Donald E. Simon, "The Worldly Side of Paradise: Green-Wood Cemetery," in Martha V. Pike and Janice Gray Armstrong, eds., *Expressions of Grief in Nineteenth Century America* (Stony Brook, NY: Museum of Stony Brook, 1980), pp. 51–66, which contains other valuable essays; and Blanche Linden-Ward, *Landscapes of Memory and Boston's Mount Auburn Cemetery* (Columbus: Ohio State University, 1989). See also Garry Wills's excellent chapter in *Lincoln at Gettysburg*, pp. 63–89.

Chapter Three: Lincoln Comes to Gettysburg

George Rogers Taylor, *The Transportation Revolution*, is the first major work to focus on the central role of the railroads in American economic history. Classics on the subject include Robert William Fogel, *Railroads and American Economic Growth: Essays in Economic History* (Baltimore: Johns Hopkins University Press, 1964), and Albro Martin, *Railroads Triumphant: The Growth, Rejection, and Rebirth of a Vital American Force* (New York: Oxford University Press, 1992).

Many works touch on the racial dimension of travel; none focus on it. Amy G. Richter, *Home on the Rails: Women, the Railroad, and the Rise of Public Domesticity* (Chapel Hill: University of North Carolina Press, 2005), takes a pathbreaking look at the role of women. In addition, the introduction provides a wonderful summary of the literature on the cultural and social meanings of the railroads. The classic works include Leo Marx, *The Machine in the Garden: Technology and the Pastoral Ideal in America* (New York: Oxford University Press, 1964), which emphasizes the ambiguity of the railroad. Daniel Walker Howe, ed., *Victorian America* (Philadelphia: University of Pennsylvania Press, 1976), pp. 3–28, identifies hegemonic values in nineteenth-century America that fixated on the railroads. John F. Kasson, *Civilizing the Machine: Technology and Republican Values in America, 1776–1900* (New York: Viking, 1976), considers broad issues. John Stilgoe, *Metropolitan Corridor: Railroads and the American Scene* (New Haven: Yale University Press, 1983), and James A. Ward, *Railroads and the Character of America, 1820–1887* (Knoxville: University of Tennessee Press, 1986), analyze the symbiosis of national character and the rails. Wolfgang Schivelbusch, *The Railway Journey: The Industrialization of Time and Space in the 19th Century* (Berkeley: University of California, 1986), sees the embodiment of modern life in the railroad. Edwin P. Alexander, *Down at the Depot: American Railroad Stations from 1831–1920* (New York: Potter, 1970), provides a gallery of photographs. Jeffrey Richards and John M. McKenzie, *The Railway Station: A Social History* (London: Oxford University Press, 1986), puts the American railroad station in a global context. For architecture, see Carroll L. V. Meeks, *The Railroad Station: An Architectural History* (New Haven: Yale University Press, 1956). John H. White, Jr., *The American Railroad Passenger Car* (Baltimore: Johns Hopkins University Press, 1978), remains the definitive work. In 1967, Michel Foucault pronounced a memorable sentence about the railroad: "It is something through which one goes, it is also something by which one can go from one point to another, and then it is also something that goes by"—"Of Other Spaces," *Diacritics*, 16 (Spring 1986): 22–27 (for a variation, see http://foucault.info/documents/heteroTopia/foucault.heteroTopia.en.html).

Bradley R. Hoch, *The Lincoln Trail in Pennsylvania: A History and Guide* (University Park, PA: Pennsylvania State University Press, 2001), provides a fine chapter on the president's trip to Gettysburg. A brief glance at the subject appears in Gerald Bennett's pamphlet, *The Gettysburg Railroad Company & Lincoln Station* (Gettysburg: Gettysburg Lincoln Railroad Station Restoration Project, 2002). John W. Starr, Jr., *Lincoln and the Railroads: A Biographical Study* (New York: Dodd, Mead, 1927), collects relevant information. For the newspaper culture of Civil War America, see the discussion of sources in chapter 6, p. 391.

Chapter Four: Carousing Crowds

Most of the works about the Gettysburg Address touch on the night before the consecration of the cemetery; none examines it with care. Nor is there much of a literature on the broader subjects covered in this chapter. However, three books deserve mention: W. J. Rorabaugh, *The Alcoholic Republic: An American Tradition* (New York: Oxford University Press, 1979); Simon P. Newman, *Parades and the Politics of the Street: Festive Culture in the Early American Republic* (Philadelphia: University of Pennsylvania Press, 1997); and Susan G. Davis, *Parades and Power: Street Theater in Nineteenth Century Philadelphia* (Philadelphia: Temple University Press, 1986)

Chapter Five: The Gettysburg Gospel

The works cited at the beginning of this essay review the literature on Lincoln's address. Apart from the discussion in Wills, nothing appears to have reached the reading public about Everett for a long time. By the late nineteenth century, the famous orator Robert G. Ingersoll would say that Lincoln's speech "will never be forgotten. . . . The oration of Everett will never be read"— Robert G. Ingersoll, *Abraham Lincoln: A Lecture* (New York: Farrell, 1895), p. 49. By the early twentieth century, Everett could be caricatured in " 'But What is the Truth?' Asked Testing Pilate" (clipping in GA Scrapbook, 3:6) as the man who "talked for 3 hours and a ¼ and the audience had been bored to unconsciousness." Today, even the scholarly world tends to use Everett as foil to Lincoln's greatness. A recent textbook on the Civil War era notes only that "he droned on for two hours" at Gettysburg. (I will not identify my friends who wrote the book and so embarrass myself.) One can be reasonably certain that none of those who make Everett a butt of jokes have read *his* Gettysburg Address.

A modern biography is much needed for a man who could be described by an admirer this way: "Suppose you had lived in the United States of America from 1794 to 1865 and that Daniel Webster had likened his half-century of friendship with you to 'a long streak of clear, blue, cerulean sky, without cloud, or mist, or haze.' Suppose further that Ralph Waldo Emerson had paid tribute to your 'radiant beauty of person,' your 'rich tones . . . precise and perfect utterance . . . the most mellow and beautiful and correct of all the instruments of the time.' What if John Adams had written on your behalf a letter of introduction to Thomas Jefferson describing you as 'the first literary character' of your age: What if John Quincy Adams had confided to his diary that your orations were 'among the best ever delivered in this country' and would 'stand the test of time.' Imagine that Oliver Wendell Holmes had written a poem in honor of your inauguration as President of Harvard College. Assume that you had been well known to Presidents Adams, Jefferson, Madison, John Quincy Adams, Jackson, Van Buren, Tyler, Polk, Fillmore, Buchanan, and Lincoln. Then picture yourself passing the time of day with Goethe, Byron, Macaulay, and Scott. Think of yourself as Congressman, Senator, and Governor of Massachusetts, Tyler's Ambassador to England, and Fillmore's Secretary of State. Listen to such speakers as Daniel Webster and Wendell Phillips praise you as 'the golden-mouthed orator.' Yet in just ninety years suppose all these others were remembered and you forgotten. And, the final straw, what if references to you were confined chiefly to contrasting unfavorably your two hour speech at Gettysburg with Lincoln's two minute masterpiece! You might have cause to ask the Muse of History for another hearing"—Fred Stripp, "The Other Gettysburg Address," *Civil War History*, 1 (1954): 161–73; the quotation comes from p. 161. (Quoted with permission of Kent State University Press.)

The only full-length biography is by Paul Revere Frothingham: *Edward Everett: Orator and Statesman* (Boston: Houghton, 1925). See also Norval F. Pease, "The Forgotten Gettysburg Address," *Central States Speech Journal*, 15 (1964): 107–10. George Forgie, *Patricide in the House Divided: A Psychological Interpretation of Lincoln and His Age* (New York: W. W. Norton, 1979), pp. 159–74, looks at Everett's antebellum oratory. Among more recent studies, Ronald F. Reid employs the perspective of a professor of speech and enjoys arguing with historians: *Edward Everett: Unionist Orator* (Westport, CT: Greenwood, 1990), and Paul A. Varg dissects Everett's thought: *Edward Everett: Intellectual in the Turmoil of Politics* (Cranbury, NJ: Associated University Press, 1992). Everett needs the critical edition of his speech.

For Lincoln's connection with Seward, see Doris Kearns Goodwin's wonderful read, *Team of Rivals: The Political Genius of Abraham Lincoln* (New York: Simon & Schuster, 2005), which was awarded the Lincoln Prize. Seward, as well as his young secretaries Nicolay and Hay, are also considered by the master historian David Herbert Donald, *"We Are All Lincoln Men": Abraham Lincoln and His Friends* (New York: Simon & Schuster, 2003).

The importance of the Declaration of Independence to Lincoln's thought is considered in most standard works. One must start however with Charles Sumner, "Promises of the Declaration of Independence and Abraham Lincoln. Eulogy . . . ," June 1, 1865, in Charles Sumner, *His Complete Works*, 20 vols. (New York: Negro University Press, n.d. [1969 reprint of 1900 ed]), 12:271–72. See also Thurow, cited above; Merrill D. Peterson, *"This Grand Pertinacity": Abraham Lincoln and the Declaration of Independence* (Fort Wayne, IN: The Lincoln Museum, 1991); and Douglas L. Wilson's penetrating "Lincoln's

Declaration," in *Lincoln Before Washington: New Perspective on the Illinois Years* (Urbana: University of Illinois Press, 1997), pp. 166–81.

Lincoln's language and oratory have been examined in numerous studies, from Daniel Kilham Dodge, *Abraham Lincoln: The Evolution of his Literary Style, The University Studies*, 1 (University of Illinois, May 1900), through Lois Einhorn's *Abraham Lincoln the Orator: Penetrating the Legend* (Westport, CT: Greenwood, 1992), to the shining work of Ronald C. White, Jr., *The Eloquent President: A Portrait of Lincoln Through His Words* (New York: Random House, 2005), which puts the speech in the context of other Lincoln writings and focuses on the growth of his powers. Kenneth Cmiel, *Democratic Eloquence: The Fight Over Popular Speech in Nineteenth-Century America* (Berkeley: University of California Press, 1990), sets Lincoln in the larger American context.

Lincoln's participation in funeral services yet awaits its historian. Wayne C. Temple, *Abraham Lincoln: From Skeptic to Prophet* (Mahomet, IL: Mayhaven, 1995), touches upon the subject repeatedly and also considers the Gettysburg Address. For the connection between regeneration and apocalypse, see James Moorhead, *American Apocalypse: Yankee Protestants and the Civil War 1860–1869* (New Haven: Yale University Press, 1978), and Moorhead, "Between Progress and Apocalypse: A Reassessment of American Millennialism in American Religious Thought, 1800–1880," *Journal of American History*, 71 (December 1984): 524–42. For the influence of ancient Greece on Lincoln's America, a fine new contribution is Caroline Winterer's *The Culture of Classicism: Ancient Greece and Rome in American Intellectual Life, 1780–1910* (Baltimore: Johns Hopkins University Press, 2002). Much has been written about Lincoln's religion. The classic in the field is William J. Wolf, *Lincoln's Religion* (Philadelphia: Pilgrim Press, 1970), this is the same book that appeared under the titles *The Almost Chosen People* (1959) and *The Religion of Abraham Lincoln* (1963). Reinhold Niebuhr, "The Religion of Abraham Lincoln," *Christian Century (Feb. 10, 1959):* should not be forgotten. Recent, in many ways conflicting works include Lucas Morel, *Lincoln's Sacred Effort: Defining Religion's Role in American Self-Government* (Lexington Books: Lanham, MD., 2000); Joseph R. Fornieri, *Abraham Lincoln's Political Faith* (DeKalb: Northern Illinois University Press, 2003); Stuart Winger, *Lincoln's Religion and Romantic Cultural Politics* (DeKalb: Northern Illinois University Press, 2003). See also William Lee Miller, *Lincoln's Virtues: An Ethical Biography* (New York: Knopf, 2002). The two most enlightening recent works about Lincoln's religious outlook, though not focused on that subject alone, are Allen C. Guelzo, *The Redeemer President* (Grand Rapids, MI: Eardmans, 1999), and Richard J. Carwardine, *Lincoln* (London: Pearson, 2003), republished in the U.S. as *Lincoln: A Life of Purpose and Power* (New York: Knopf, 2006), both winners of the Lincoln Prize.

Chapter Six: Echoes

Lincoln and the press is best covered in Richard J. Carwardine, "Abraham Lincoln and the Fourth Estate: The White House and the Press During the Civil War," *American Nineteenth Century History*, 7 (March 2006): 1–27. Menahem Blondheim, " 'Public Sentiment is Everything': The Union Public Communications Strategy and the Bogus Proclamation of 1864," *Journal of American History*, 89 (December 2002): 869–99, develops the point about the role of telegraph control by the military after 1862. See also Blondheim's excellent *News Over the Wires* (Cambridge, MA: Harvard University Press, 1994).

Robert S. Harper, *Lincoln and the Press* (New York: McGraw-Hill, 1951), and Harry J. Maihafer, *War of Words: Abraham Lincoln and the Civil War Press* (Washington, DC: Brassey's, 2001), provide anecdotal coverage of their subject. Harry J. Carman and Reinhard H. Luthin in *Lincoln and the Patronage* (New York: Columbia University Press, 1943), pp. 118–29, explore thoroughly how the president courted "those ultra-potent forces—the newspaper men" (p. 118).

Among the more general studies, see William E. Huntzicker, *The Popular Press, 1833–1865* (Westport, CT: Greenwood, 1999); the anecdotal and sometimes inaccurate James M. Perry, *A Bohemian Brigade: The Civil War Correspondents—Mostly Rough, Sometimes Ready* (New York: John Wiley, 2000); Andrew S. Coopersmith, *Fighting Words: An Illustrated History of Newspaper Accounts of the Civil War* (New York: New Press, 2004); and Jeffrey A. Smith, *War and the Problem of Press Freedom* (New York: Oxford University Press, 1999).

Chapter Seven: Gloria

Merrill D. Peterson, *Lincoln in American Memory* (New York: Oxford University Press, 1994), is the fine standard historical work on the subject. Earlier, Benjamin Thomas, *Portrait for Posterity* (New Brunswick: Rutgers University Press, 1947), focused on writers of history. Frank Thompson, *Abraham Lincoln: Twentieth Century Portrayals* (Dallas: Taylor, 1999), looks at theater, film, television, and actors. Sociologist Barry Schwartz, in a class by himself, wrestles most persistently with Lincoln's memory. His works include *Abraham Lincoln and the Forge of National Memory* (Chicago: University of Chicago Press, 1992); "Frame Images: Towards the Semiotics of Collective Memory," *Semiotica*, 121-1/2 (1998): 1–40; "The New Gettysburg Address: A Study in Illusion," in John Y. Simon and Harold Holzer, eds., *The Lincoln Forum: Rediscovering Abraham Lincoln* (New York: Fordham University Press, 2002), pp. 160–86; "The New Gettysburg Address: Fusing History and Memory," *Poetics*, 33 (2005):

63–79; and, with Howard Schuman, "History, Commemoration, and Belief: Abraham Lincoln in American Memory, 1945–2001," *American Sociological Review*, 70 (April 2005): 183–203, with online supplement, 1–7. In addition, Professor Schwartz shared a working manuscript, "Collective Memory and Historical Truth: Abraham Lincoln's Gettysburg Address," which focuses on the twentieth century, from the Progressive period onward. His work concentrates on the distinction between memory and history, on how the past and present shape each other; he insists that historians consistently distort the past. This is debatable, though his sociological perception is accurate that "modern people's breadth of historical knowledge is unprecedented while their identification and continuity with the past steadily declines." Schwartz is particularly hard on the historians of the last thirty some years, when they "lifted the siege on myth and memory and became part of them" (p. 113). See also his "Christian Origins: Historical Truth and Social Memory," in Alan Kirk and Tom Thacher, eds., *Memory, Tradition, Text: Uses of the Past in Early Christianity* (Atlanta, GA: Society of Biblical Literature, 2005), p. 46. Schwartz's work exerted substantial influence on my book.

The same is true of David Blight, *Race and Reunion: The Civil War in American Memory* (Cambridge, MA: Harvard University Press, 2001), a remarkable Lincoln Prize–winning book that makes painfully clear that one cost of reunion after the Civil War was the "resubjugation" of African-Americans. Given its focus, the book does not consider deeply what a great achievement reunion was, after a war that made casualties of about 5 percent of the country's population. In Blight's very important book, "reconciliation" becomes a dirty word.

Some consideration of the 1913 reunion can be found in Edward Tabor Linenthal's fine work, *Sacred Ground: Americans and Their Battlefields* (Urbana: University of Illinois Press, 1991), and John S. Patterson, "Patriotic Landscape: Gettysburg, 1863–1913," *Prospects*, 7 (1982): 315–33. For a photographic record, see Stan Cohen, *Hands Across the Wall, the 50th and 75th Reunions of the Gettysburg Battle* (Charleston, WV: Pictorial Histories Publishing, 1982). One awaits eagerly the transformation of Amy J. Kinsel's PhD Dissertation, " 'From These Honored Dead': Gettysburg in American Culture, 1863–1938," Cornell University, 1992, into a book. Meanwhile, Kinsel's look at the evolving meaning of the battlefield deserves attention: "From Turning Point to Peace Memorial: A Cultural Legacy," in Gabor Boritt, ed., *The Gettysburg Nobody Knows* (New York: Oxford University Press, 1997), pp. 203–22.

Wayne Craven, *Sculpture in America* (New York: Crowell, 1968), is a classic. For Lincoln, in addition to the Smithsonian Inventory, see Donald Charles Durman, *He Belongs to the Ages: The Statues of Abraham Lincoln* (Ann Arbor, MI: Edwards, 1951), and F. Lauriston Bullard, *Lincoln in Marble and Bronze* (New

Brunswick, NJ: Rutgers University Press, 1952). They catalogue public monuments. A scholarly study is much needed.

Allen C. Guelzo's Lincoln Prize–winning book, *Lincoln's Emancipation Proclamation* (New York: Simon & Schuster, 2004), pp. 235–50, touches on the afterlife of the document. E. J. Hobsbawm, *The Invention of Tradition* (New York: Cambridge University Press, 1983), considers how people's needs create legends. Harold Holzer, Gabor Boritt, and Mark E. Neely, Jr., *The Lincoln Image: Abraham Lincoln and the Popular Print* (New York: Scribners, 1984), is a pioneering study. See also the same authors' *Changing the Lincoln Image* (Fort Wayne, IN: Louis A. Warren Lincoln Library and Museum, 1985), and "Francis Bicknell Carpenter (1830–1900): Painter of Abraham Lincoln and His Circle," *American Art Journal*, 16 (Spring 1984): 66–89, which notes that "Carpenter dated copies painted years even decades later, as '1864' " (p. 84). Wayne Craven, "Albion Harris Bicknell, 1837–1915," *Antiques* (September 1974): 443–49, provides an introduction to the painter. See also Barry Schwartz, "Picturing Lincoln," in William Ayres, ed., *Picturing History: American Painting, 1770–1930* (New York: Rizzoli, 1993), pp. 141–44.

So ends a long list of the often important scholarly work that has sustained this book. It bears repeating that it is impossible to note all the sources for a work stemming from a lifetime of study, and so my apologies to all those omitted.

Let the reader go away with a final thought from Umberto Eco's *The Name of the Rose:* "We are dwarfs . . . but dwarfs who stand on the shoulders of those giants, and small though we are, we sometime manage to see farther on the horizon than they."*

---

* Umberto Eco, *The Name of the Rose*, trans. William Weaver (San Diego: Harcourt Brace & Co., 1980), p. 86.

ACKNOWLEDGMENTS

I have lived and taught for a quarter of a century at what my middle son, Jake's fine film, *Adams County USA*, calls "America's most famous small town." Teaching about Gettysburg in Gettysburg is a matchless learning experience. Holding the last class of a year on Little Round Top, or at the National Cemetery where Lincoln spoke, is unforgettable. The first thanks then go to my students who listened to me all these many years, challenged me, and taught me. They sometimes found bits and pieces in their researches that fit into my work, and I borrowed them with thanks—though never without finding the original sources.

Acknowledging my students must be quickly followed by acknowledging my student assistants—those who received modest pay, and those who helped for the pleasure of the work. Some gave four years or whole summers free of charge. Over twenty-five years all too many dear names accumulated and with a few exceptions, I have mentioned here only those who have directly worked on this book during the writing stage, since the fall of 2003, though research has never ended. I trust the student assistants have learned as much as they gave. Some worked harder than others but friends all, I salute you. Jill Abrahamson, Bethany Bromwell, Cora Chandler, Joseph Cook, Charley Dittrich, Andrew Douglas, Joshua Easterson, Stephen Fetzer, Sarah Hammell, Nancy Moll Hillman, Emily Hummel, Deborah Huso, Brian Jordan, William Lippincott, Amber Moulton-Wiseman, Chris Myers, Susan Fiedler Newman, Timothy Nichol, Timothy Parry, Isabel Patterson, Jason Patton, Jared Peatman, Katie Porch, Craig Schneider, Heidi Shuster, Ashley Towle, and Leo Vaccaro. The last two fine students proofread the book (as did I and Bradley Hoch) and rechecked quotations.

I must also thank the high school teachers for whom I conduct week-long summer seminars. I had the privilege of being there at the founding of the Gilder Lehrman Institute of American History and have led a seminar on Lincoln and Gettysburg for eleven years. The GLI selects its teachers from a highly competitive national pool of applicants, some with Ph.D.s or LLd.s, and discussing history with them has been an unfailing source of inspiration.

The same is true of the annual Civil War Institute sessions that bring more than three hundred people each summer to Gettysburg. I thank you and salute you. We are a band of brothers and sisters.

Though this book stems from the work of many years, much remains to be done on the subject. Indeed almost every chapter could be turned into a lengthy study—and perhaps, spurred by this and other work, will be. Because I have studied Lincoln for much of my adult life, my obligations to my teachers, students, and colleagues are too numerous to enumerate. So focusing on contributions to this book alone, however ungrateful, appears to be the only reasonable approach to acknowledgments.

And so after my students I would like to thank colleagues and friends from coast to coast who helped. For the sake of brevity this honor roll of names is put forth without institutional affiliations, and with apologies to those whom I may have inadvertently but inexcusably left out. Many helped, though my requests often seemed far removed from their duties: John Adler, Jim Basker, Kent Masterson Brown, Gianna Celli, John M. Delaney, Doris Dysinger, Jason Emerson, Joe Glatthaar, Tim Goeglein, Leslie Herrmann, Earl Hess, Randall Jimerson, Martin Johnson, Seth Kaller, Elizabeth Kaplan, Maja Keech, Valerie Komor, Philip Kunhardt Jr., Glenn LaFantasie, Lew Lehrman, Jerry Linderman, Larry Logue, Jim Madison, Pete Maslowski, James McPherson, Carolyn Murphy, John Neff, Susette Newberry, Jim Paradis, Katherine Reagan, Bud Robertson, Charles Scribner III, John Sellers, Kevin Sheets, Richard Sloan, Albert Small, Louise Taper, Mark Thistlewaite, Sharon Van Meter, Pete Vermilyea, Laura Washington, Dan Weinberg, Fred Weiser, and Jeff Wert.

Thanks next go to people who either provided continuous help over the years or went far beyond the call of duty. At the Library of Congress I called upon many members of the staff, especially at the Manuscript Division. Jeff Flannery, how does one thank a learned archivist who finds precious items a researcher cannot locate and who, after a long exhaustive day of work, stays well beyond closing time to help? How?

At the National Archives Mike Musick was not only ever helpful, even after retirement, but also an inspiration. John Deeben, my former student, helped, too, as did Richard Peuser, Trevor Plante, and D'Ann Blanton. But it was my youngest son, Dan Boritt, who helped there the most. I had gone through the pension and other files relating to Company K, 30th Pennsylvania (1st Reserves) Infantry, who hailed from the Gettysburg area. I often felt that I was looking at documents that had not been touched since they were originally deposited back in the nineteenth century. I took a number of my classes there to research and write about the company's soldiers and their loved ones. But finally it was Dan who went through every file one more time, copying all items that mattered.

Also in Washington, Christine Hennessey, Chief, Art Information Resources, Smithsonian American Art Museum, provided invaluable aid as I studied "Lincoln art."

At the Smithsonian's National Museum of American History, Brent Glass, the director, and Harry Rubenstein, chair, Division of Politics and Reform, came to the aid of this project.

In Baltimore Elizabeth Schaaf, Archivist and Curator of the Archives of the Peabody Institute of the Johns Hopkins University, helped on a moment's notice.

In Philadelphia, at Union League Club, Jim Mundy helped, as did my old friend Ed Johnson.

In New York the staff of the Morgan Library proved ever helpful over the years, but especially Leslie Fields, Associate Curator, Literary and Historical Manuscripts. At the New-York Historical Society, Sandra Trenholm, another former student, Curator of the Gilder Lehrman Collection, kept me informed about new acquisitions and performed many special favors year after year.

In Massachusetts Dina Malger of the Malden Public Library, and at the Massachusetts State House, Susan Greendyke Lachevre, Art Collections Manager, provided help with the work of Albion Bicknell. At the Boston Public Library I am indebted to Diane Parks and Dawn Riley; at the Massachusetts Historical Society to Dennis Fiori.

At the Kroch Library, Cornell University, Patrick J. Stevens came to my aid; at the Western Reserve Historical Society, in Cleveland, Connie Hammond did. At the Clements Library of the University of Michigan, Ann Arbor, where I taught as a young professor, Janet Bloom provided valuable help with the letters of Cornelia Hancock. Also at Ann Arbor, Van and Anita Parunak, two old friends from our days at Harvard, where we worked with the outstanding mathematical statistician Fred Mosteller, created the heart of the Parunak Report that forms a part of Appendix C.

At the Lincoln Museum in Fort Wayne, Carolyn Texley, Director of Collections/Archivist, shared her valuable time and knowledge unstintingly. So did her colleague Cindy VanHorn, Registrar and Library Assistant, who came in on a weekend, obviously ill with a cold, to extend the time available to me for research. The Director of the Museum, Joan Flinspach, my colleague on the Lincoln Bicentennial Commission, made everything pleasant.

Libby Mahoney of the Chicago Historical Society responded cheerfully to my various SOS messages; at the University of Chicago Library Julia Gardner did.

In Springfield, at the Abraham Lincoln Presidential Library, and before that magnificent facility was built at the Illinois Historic Preservation Agency, thanks for generous hospitality and expert help more times than I dare recall go to the incomparable Tom Schwartz, Illinois State Historian. Kim Bauer, former Curator of the Henry Horner Lincoln Collection, also helped in various ways, including calling to my attention James Conkling's July 4th oration that begins:" "Four score years ago. . . ." The Library's Curator of Manuscripts, Cheryl Schnirring, Glenna Schroeder Lein, also of the manuscript department, and many others aided my searches during my various trips to Springfield. Gene Fink, an alumnus of my GLI seminar, made special arrangements and expertly guided Jake and me through the Lincoln Home. Richard E. Hart kindly shared his knowledge of Springfield's African-American history.

The generous Wayne Temple, Deputy Director of the Illinois State Archives, came to my aid all too often.

The same was true at Galesburg, where Doug Wilson, the Director of the Lincoln Studies Center, replied to queries rapidly and generously.

Help also came in expeditious and trustworthy ways from Leanne Garland, Archivist-Librarian at Lincoln Memorial University, Harrogate, Tennessee, and from Olga Tsapina, Curator of American Historical Manuscripts, the Huntington Library, San Marino, California, a place I fondly recall from my days as a Fellow there.

Now to head back toward my home grounds. Thanks to my friend, Dick Sommers, of the U.S. Army War College, also Louise Arnold, and their colleagues, who shared knowledge and friendship not only with me but my numerous students.

In nearby Hershey, Professor Gregory M. Caputo, Robert E. Dye, M.D. Professor of Medicine of the Pennsylvania State University Medical School, not only nursed me back to health after work on this book in fourteen-hour days, months after months, took its terrible toll, but also discussed with me Lincoln's variola infection.

At the Pennsylvania State Archives, Civil War Institute alum Richard C. Saylor provided help.

In Gettysburg, Jerry Bennett shared his knowledge of local history. Both Joan E. Bryce and John B. Horner spoke about their ancestors who guarded Lincoln during his visit. Elwood Christ shared his knowledge of the Wills House. Bill Frassanito shared priceless photographs. John Longenecker made available his father's collection.

At the Gettysburg National Military Park, encouragement and help came from its strong and visionary superintendent, John Latcher; ever helpful historian Scott Hartwig; also his colleagues John Heiser and Barb Sanders; fine archivist Greg Goodell, and his colleague, Elizabeth R. Trescott.

At the Adams County Historical Society, director Wayne Motts, and his predecessor, Russell Swody, and their staffs provided unstinting help to my students and me.

Gettysburg College has been my home for twenty-five years, and the friendship of colleagues proved indispensable. Bill Parker, of the Chemistry Department, explained the mysteries of the snowlike disinfectant of old. Ann Fender of Economics helped with converting early twentieth-century dollars to early twenty-first century ones. Historians Michael Birkner, Bill Bowman, Dina Lowy, and Tim Shannon gave encouragement or solved problems.

At Mussleman Library, Director Robin Wagner and her staff provided crucial assistance. Kim Breighner and Sharon Birch helped with computer tabulations. James Rutkowski did gallant work to help create useable scans of illustrations for this book. The Director of Special Collections, Karen Drickamer, and her staff, especially Christine Ameduri, made the College treasures accessible. The enormous number of interlibrary loan requests that sent staff looking at databases that list the holdings of about fifty thousand depositors worldwide, especially the relentless demands from me and my students for hundreds and hundreds of newspapers on microfilm, pushed the staff beyond all reasonable limits. Yet John Barnett, Mary Holland, and Susan Roach persevered heroically. I also wish to thank those nameless but often wonderful librarians who helped at the other end.

Don Speelman served as my peerless computer guru, though others, too, helped solve problems.

Dave Crowner, retired colleague from the German Department, is largely responsible for the translations from German newspapers. Others helped, too, with translation or finding papers, including a former Gettysburg colleague, Christian Keller; my student assistant John Capasso; my student Jay Hagerman; Carolyn Schafer of St. Louis; and Columbia University graduate student Alice Peterson. We searched far and wide for German-language American newspapers of the Civil War era. My student Skye Montgomery searched for other non–English language American newspapers from Gettysburg, from her home in Utah, and from Berkeley, California. Another colleague, Larry Gregorio, assisted with French translation.

Dexter Weikel, retired colleague from the Music Department, discussed with me nineteenth century hymns.

I worked with Robert Natter, Conductor of *Camarata*, and Lewes Peddell, Conductor of the *Wind Ensemble*, both of the College, to research the music performed at the consecration of the National Cemetery on November 19, 1863. They in turn assembled a group of scholars and students, and Diane Brennan of the Civil War Institute's staff, who searched extensively for the elusive *Homage d'un Heros* by Adolph Birgfeld—and when failure stared us in the face, turned up, with the help from the library of the U.S. Marine Band, a funeral march that may have been played as the parade marched to the Cemetery. From this work was born on November 19, 2005, the Camarata's and the Wind Ensemble's performance of the 1863 program—for the first time since Lincoln came to Gettysburg. (Though it was not possible to include a recording with this book, I'm persevering and hoping to make a recording available to the public.)

Thanks must be offered for help from abroad, too, to the fine classical musicians Dou Ghirbizzo, Paola Minussi and Joachim Geissler of Como, Italy, in whose home chapter 7 of this book, "Gloria," was written—as I listened to the recording of their elegant music. At the Sorbonne, my counterpart and old friend Jacques Portes hunted down for me Ernest Duvergnier de Hauranne. Jorg Nagler of the University of Jena brought Ekkehart Krippendorff to my attention. In Hungary, András Csillag of the University of Szeged identified the Ohio speech of Lajos Kossuth that includes a precursor to Lincoln's words, "a government of the people, by the people, for the people." During a trip to Budapest, historian Lászlo Ritter sprung upon me, in conspiracy with my son, Jake, the record I had searched for long and that turned out to be from a radio station in Dunaujváros (formerly Sztalinváros), which appealed to the world for help during the Revolution of 1956 with the words of the Gettysburg Address, broadcasting from a moving bus so that it could not be readily tracked and silenced.

Though mistakes surely remain in the book, many colleagues have contributed to reducing their number. Chapters 1 and 2 have been read by my sister, Judith Boritt, M.D., and by Judy Ann Giesberg of Villanova University and by independent historians Roland Maust of Millersburg, Ohio, and Tim Smith of Gettysburg. Part of chapter 3, as well as chapters 5, 6, and 7, received the searching and encouraging scrutiny of Menahem Blondheim of the Hebrew University, Jerusalem. Chapter 8 benefited from the comments of David Blight of Yale, Eric Foner of Columbia, Harold Holzer of the Metropolitan Museum of Art, and Nina Silber of Boston University. John Emerson of Middlebury College served as an outside reviewer of the Parunak Report.

The entire manuscript has been scrutinized by Allen Guelzo, my two-time Lincoln Prize–winning colleague and Luce Professor at Gettysburg; Bradley Hoch, neighbor, author, and long-time friend; Daniel Walker Howe, Rhodes Professor emeritus at Oxford and my partner at Bellagio; my erstwhile coauthor, Mark E. Neely Jr., McCabe Greer Professor at Pennsylvania State University, who won the Pulitzer Prize as soon as he stopped coauthoring with me; Matthew Pinsker, Pohanka Professor of Dickinson College, the most promising Lincoln scholar of the coming generation; Michael Burlingame, Sandowski Professor emeritus at Connecticut College, indefatigable researcher and generous colleague; and sociologist Barry Schwartz, professor emeritus at the University of Georgia, who knows more than anyone else about Lincoln in American memory. Finally, my son Jake provided valuable criticism. Had I followed all his advice, this would be a better book. I am grateful to all these readers for their challenging ideas and for helping to eliminate embarrassing errors such as my turning "public attention" into "pubic attention," and Lincoln's "immortal speech" into his "immoral speech."

Financial support, which in a society that so prizes money also means moral support, came from the Rockefeller Foundation, the Lehrman Institute, the Gilder Lehrman Institute of American History, and Gettysburg College. To the College I'm indebted not only for research funds but also for a generous sabbatical policy.

Just as important as financial support has been the opportunity to talk about my findings. Even when a lecture on Lincoln did not specifically focus on the Gettysburg Address, I was honing thoughts for this book. Thanks will go to institutions, not to individuals, grateful though I am to many, because often whole departments served as hosts and names could grow into mountains and lose meaning. I have limited my thanks to the last five years, when my ideas were taking firm shape. Thanks then for speaking invitations from the National Security Seminar of Johns Hopkins University; Hanover College's Center for Free Inquiry; the McMurtry Lecture of the Lincoln Museum, Fort Wayne, Indiana; the White House Fellows (twice); the Nieman Fellows, Harvard University, who came to Gettysburg; the Gettysburg Battlefield Museum Foundation; the White House; the Herbert S. Schell Lecture of the University of South Dakota, my alma mater; the Ewing Lecture of Lycoming College, Pennsylvania; the Keynote Lecture for the Inaugural Conference on the Civil War at the University of Mississippi, Oxford; and the Center for Public Policy and Leadership, University of Illinois, Springfield.

Abroad I must thank the Nobel Institute in Oslo; the Atlantic World Seminar at Oxford University; the President of Colombia, Alvaro Uribe, who recited Lincoln's Address at my farm in Gettysburg and facilitated the invitation to speak at the Universidad des los Andes, Bogota; the University of Veszprém in Hungary; and most important, the Rockefeller Foundation's Villa Serbeloni Seminar in Bellagio, Italy.

Up on the hills above Bellagio I chose the title of this book in the fall of 2003.

The subtitle was more difficult. I looked for something modest; my publisher wanted something that would catch the eye. An author puts decades of work into a book; a publisher puts up not only funds but much talent to bring a book before the public. Both have a stake. I came up with a compromise with a distinguished ancestry: *The Lincoln Speech That Nobody Knows*. The inspiration came from my friend and mentor Richard N. Current's 1958 classic, *The Lincoln Nobody Knows*. Current, in turn, had adopted his title from the bestselling book by advertising executive Bruce Barton: *The Man Nobody Knows* (1925), who wrote about Jesus as a great salesman. In the 1990s I had invited outstanding scholars, with a bow to Professor Current, to write essays on important controversial aspects of the Battle of Gettysburg under the title *The Gettysburg Nobody Knows* (1997). None of these books considered the Gettysburg Address. Since long years of research on the subject made clear that a great deal about Lincoln's speech was unknown not only to the literate public but also to scholars, the subtitle offered itself.

Under President Bill Clinton and First Lady, now Senator, Hillary Rodham Clinton, my wife, Elizabeth Lincoln Norseen Boritt, and I had the privilege of visiting the house where Lincoln had lived for four difficult years. But President George W. Bush and First Lady Laura Bush made it possible for Liz, Jake, and me to go upstairs to the "Lincoln bedroom," as part of the Abraham Lincoln Bicentennial Commission and gaze with shameless adoration at the White House copy of the Gettysburg Address.

The staff of the Civil War Institute wholeheartedly supported their ever-demanding boss and the work on this book, led by the exceptional Tina Grim, and backed up by three fine people, Susan Oyler, Diane Brennan, and Pam Dalrymple, as well as a host of lively students. My former assistant Marti Shaw returned to work and not only turned footnotes into endnotes per the publisher's instructions, but also fixed many mistakes.

My editor, Bob Bender, showed excellent skill and judgment and is a fine human being. His assistant, Johanna Li, was ever competent. Copy editor Ann Adelman is due thanks. I also wish to express thanks for the encouragement of Victoria Meyer, Executive Director of Publicity, Tracey Guest, and Senior Publicist Rebecca Davis.

I finish every class in every semester by wishing that my students find what I found in my life: love and work that one loves. The work is here for readers to see. The love of my life, my wife, Liz, and the love of our sons, Norse, Jake, and Dan, and our daughter-in-law, Mimi, has been all important. Norse also read one of the chapters, liked it, and created the dedication design while keeping mum about it. Jake read it all and talked with me repeatedly about the subject. Dan never got to read much but spread his blessed sunshine around.

And so to a final note of appreciation. In the early 1990s I received a telephone call from Connecticut. An older man told me that since he was a child his family had had on its wall a copy of the Gettysburg Address. It looks old, he explained, it feels genuine. The family decided to drive down to Gettysburg to ask me to pass judgment on the document's authenticity.

Many a reproduction has been brought to me with high hopes and always the same result. This family happened to be black and, I suspected, far from wealthy. I went to great length to explain that almost certainly they had a reproduction in their possession. I was very sure, I told them. I offered to take a look at a photocopy and assured them that I could provide a useful opinion on such a basis.

But the family of three insisted on driving to Gettysburg, bringing their document. On the day we set for their visit they called from New Jersey. Their car had broken down and they had to rent another. By the time they arrived, dressed in Sunday best, I had a class waiting for me. I welcomed the sojourners into my office but explained that students had to be taught. I apologized; we had to be quick. They unwrapped their treasure. As I expected, it was the same parchmentlike paper reproduction that any of the tourist shops in town offered for sale.

I no longer recall the name of these beautiful people who made the trip to Gettysburg. But they understood. Even if they were disappointed on that day, they held a treasure in their hands, the treasure of a great nation that they are an important part of.

This book is dedicated to the American people, and so it is dedicated to this family from Connecticut—and to my own family, too.

INDEX

ABOUT THE AUTHOR

Gabor Boritt lives with his wife, Elizabeth Lincoln Norseen, on their farm located about a mile from the site of Pickett's Charge. Together they restored an abandoned pre–Civil War home with their own hands and raised three sons here. Boritt was born and raised in Hungary and educated in South Dakota and Massachusetts. He is the author of numerous books, and his work has been translated into five languages. He has held visiting appointments at the universities of Cambridge, London, Michigan, Harvard University, and Washington University in St. Louis. He has lectured at the universities of Budapest, Belfast, Cambridge, Harvard, Oxford, and the Sorbonne, as well as at the Carter Library, the National Geographic Society, the Library of Congress, the Smithsonian Institution, the Nobel Institute, and the White House.

The Boritt farm outside of Gettysburg with Big and Little Round Top and Cemetery Ridge in the background